War, Hunger, and Displacement

VOLUME 1

QUEEN ELIZABETH HOUSE, INTERNATIONAL DEVELOPMENT CENTRE, UNIVERSITY OF OXFORD (QEH)

is the Centre for Development Studies in Oxford University, encompassing anthropology, economics, history, law, politics, and sociology. It is also the focus of a world-wide network of scholars and practitioners in developing countries, many of whom come to QEH as academic visitors. QEH comprises a core of established academic staff, junior researchers, and about a hundred graduate students.

Development Studies is an interdisciplinary and multidisciplinary enquiry into change and transformation. We seek to challenge narrow theoretical and policy approaches derived from a single model of development. Our aim is to encourage innovative and critical approaches to research and development, always maintaining rigorous standards.

UNU WORLD INSTITUTE FOR DEVELOPMENT ECONOMICS RESEARCH (UNU/WIDER)

was established by the United Nations University as its first research and training centre and started work in Helsinki, Finland in 1985. The purpose of the Institute is to undertake applied research and policy analysis on structural changes affecting the developing and transitional economies, to provide a forum for the advocacy of policies leading to robust, equitable, and environmentally sustainable growth, and to promote capacity strengthening and training in the field of economic and social policy-making. Its work is carried out by staff researchers and visiting scholars in Helsinki and through networks of collaborating scholars and institutions around the world.

War, Hunger, and Displacement

The Origins of Humanitarian Emergencies

VOLUME 1: *Analysis*

Edited by

E. WAYNE NAFZIGER, FRANCES STEWART,
AND RAIMO VÄYRYNEN

A study prepared for Queen Elizabeth House, International Development Centre, University of Oxford (QEH) and the World Institute for Development Economics Research of the United Nations University (UNU/WIDER)

OXFORD
UNIVERSITY PRESS

FOREWORD

Between the mid-1980s and the late 1990s, the number of humanitarian crises escalated sharply. The International Red Cross estimates that the number of persons involved is increasing by about ten million annually. As a result, millions of people have been left dead, starving, displaced, and homeless, while many others could be affected in the not too distant future unless preventive corrective measures are introduced. This surge in emergencies—the most important source of human suffering in the world today—is attributable not to an increase in natural disasters but rather to factors that are man-made.

Traditional responses to this new scourge have mostly focused on *ex post* interventions; that is, interventions carried out after the conflicts have arisen. In addition, most analyses of the causes of such emergencies have focused on factors like ethnicity, the collapse of the Soviet Bloc, the vanishing of aid, and so on. While not irrelevant, these explanations are partial and overlook the *ex ante* impact of failed development policies and institutional collapse. This two-volume work aims at filling this analytical gap by focusing on a comprehensive analysis of the long-term economic, social, and political roots of humanitarian emergencies and on early measures to help prevent such disasters.

The first volume provides a general overview of the nature and causes of the emergencies, including economic, political, and environmental factors. The second volume presents detailed case studies of thirteen conflicts, including, among others, Rwanda, Burundi, and Afghanistan. The volumes emphasize the importance of protracted economic stagnation and decline, high and rising inequality, especially horizontal inequalities (i.e. inequalities among distinct social groups, including those associated with government exclusion), and state failure and predatory rule in causing emergencies. They debunk some common beliefs which recur in the literature, for example that the prime causes of emergencies are deteriorating environmental conditions or structural adjustment. Moreover, they find that deep-seated ethnic animosity is not a primal cause but is rather created and enforced by political manipulation, facilitated by economic and social inequalities among groups.

This work provides the intellectual underpinning for focusing on policies emphasizing the prevention of wars, through a better understanding of their fundamental causes, and not only on conflict mediation and reconstruction during and after war. Indeed, the volumes argue in favour of shifting the policy focus to the *ex ante* prevention of humanitarian crises by means of appropriate economic and social development policies, meaningful forms of foreign aid, a strengthening of essential state and civil society institutions, and political institutional reforms. Future researchers will look to these volumes as pathbreaking efforts in identifying the determinants of humanitarian emergencies. I strongly recommend this study to researchers and policy makers with an interest in understanding the origins of war and displacement in developing countries.

UNU/WIDER gratefully acknowledges the financial contributions to the project by the Ministry for Foreign Affairs of Finland and the Government of Sweden (Swedish International Development Cooperation Agency-Sida), and the active co-sponsorship of the project by the Queen Elizabeth House, Oxford University.

Giovanni Andrea Cornia
Director, UNU/WIDER

CONTENTS

Contents

VOLUME 2

ACKNOWLEDGEMENTS

We owe a great debt to Giovanni Andrea Cornia, Director of UNU/WIDER, for his vision in initiating this research, and for his support and guidance throughout. We thank the UNU/WIDER and QEH staffs for their tireless efforts. In particular we thank Janis Vehmaan-Kreula and Denise Watt, who spent many hours word processing, editing, and arranging travel and housing for meetings in Helsinki, Oxford, and Stockholm, Liisa Roponen for her word processing and copyediting, Barbara Fagerman for helping to plan the policy conference in Stockholm, Tuula Haarla for organizing reporting and publishing, and UNU/WIDER post-graduate interns Helinä Melkas and Henry Owusu, and QEH graduate students Meghan O'Sullivan and Tillman Bruck for invaluable research assistance.

We wish to express our indebtedness to the United Nations and its agencies for their support and encouragement. The UN University, including Jacques Fomerand at the New York office and Rector Hans J. A. van Ginkel, provided support for the research project and its dissemination. We hope that our work here will influence the UN and the world community to provide resources for preventing wars through tackling the roots of conflict, while continuing to fund reconstruction and humanitarian aid after wars.

While we are grateful to all who have contributed to this work, we remain solely responsible for its errors.

NOTES ON THE CONTRIBUTORS

JOCELYN ALEXANDER is a lecturer at the Department of Historical Studies, University of Bristol, UK. Her doctoral work at Oxford University was on African politics and agrarian policies in Zimbabwe. She has conducted extensive research in Zimbabwe and Mozambique, and is co-author of *Violence and Memory: 100 Years in the 'Dark Forests' of Matabeleland North* with Terence Ranger and JoAnn McGregor.

JUHA AUVINEN is a docent of international politics at the University of Helsinki. His research interests are third world conflicts and conflict transformation, quantitative international politics, and international political economy. He has worked as consultant to the Finnish Ministry for Foreign Affairs on early warning and conflict prevention in South Africa and Somalia, and for the European Union on South Asian development and conflict in the African Great Lakes region.

JAMES FAIRHEAD is a reader in social anthropology at the School of Oriental and African Studies, London University. He was global environmental change fellow at the School of Oriental and African Studies and lecturer in anthropology and development, Queen Elizabeth House, University of Oxford. Dr Fairhead is the author of *Misreading the African Landscape: Society and Ecology in a Forest-Savannah Mosaic*, and *Reframing Forest History: Statistics, Policy and Power in West Africa*.

KALEVI J. HOLSTI is University Killam Professor of Political Science at the University of British Columbia, Vancouver, Canada. Recent books include *The State, War, and the State of War*; *Peace and War: Armed Conflict and International Order*; *The Dividing Discipline*, and *International Politics: A Framework for Analysis*. He was president of both the Canadian Political Science Association and the International Studies Association, and has served as editor of the *International Studies Quarterly* and co-editor of the *Canadian Journal of Political Science*.

DAVID KEEN is lecturer in development studies at the London School of Economics and Political Science. Dr Keen is author of *The Benefits of Famine: A Political Economy of Famine and Relief in Southwestern Sudan, 1983–89*; *The Economic Functions of Violence in Civil Wars*; *The Kurds in Iraq: How Safe is their Haven Now?*, and *Refugees—Rationing the Right to Life*. He has also worked as a journalist and consultant.

JOANN MCGREGOR is lecturer in geography at the University of Reading. She received Economic and Social Research Council funding for a research project titled 'Forced Migration in Southern Africa: The Local Politics of Incorporation and Exclusion', and her doctoral work was on environmental history in Zimbabwe. She is co-author of *Violence and Memory: 100 years in the 'Dark Forests' of Matabeleland North* with Jocelyn Alexander and Terence Ranger.

CHRISTIAN MORRISSON is a professor of economics at the University of Panthéon-Sorbonne (Paris). He has been a chief of division at the OECD Development Centre and a consultant to the World Bank and ILO. Professor Morrisson is the author of four books on adjustment and equity, and on the political feasibility of adjustment and was the general editor of 13 books published in two series (*Adjustment and Equity in Developing Countries* and *The Political Feasibility of Adjustment in Developing Countries*) by the OECD Development Centre.

E. WAYNE NAFZIGER is University Distinguished Professor of Economics at Kansas State University. He is author of *Inequality in Africa: Political Élites, Proletariat, Peasants and the Poor*; *The Debt Crisis in Africa*; *The Economics of Developing Countries*; *The Economics of Political Instability*, and numerous other books and articles on developing nations. Dr Nafziger has been research fellow at the University of Nigeria; visiting Fulbright Professor at Andhra University, India; fellow at the East-West Center; visiting professor at the International University of Japan; visiting scholar at Cambridge University and the Nigerian Institute for Social and Economic Research; Hewlett Visiting Fellow at the Carter Center; and senior research fellow at UNU/WIDER.

TERENCE RANGER is Rhodes Professor of Race Relations and African Studies at Oxford University and visiting professor at the Institute of Development Studies at the University of Zimbabwe. He has taught in Zimbabwe, Tanzania, and California. His monographs include *Revolt in Southern Rhodesia, 1896–7*; *The African Voice in Southern Rhodesia, 1898–1930*; *Peasant Consciousness and Guerrilla Warfare in Zimbabwe*; *Are We Not Also Men? The Samkange Family and African Politics in Zimbabwe*, and the forthcoming *Voices from the Rocks: The Modern History of the Matopos*. He is co-author of *Violence and Memory: 100 years in the 'Dark Forests' of Matabeleland North* with Jocelyn Alexander and JoAnn McGregor.

FRANCES STEWART is director of the International Development Centre, Queen Elizabeth House, at the University of Oxford and professor of development economics and fellow of Somerville College. Her numerous books include *Technology and Underdevelopment*; *Planning to Meet Basic Needs*; *Adjustment with a Human Face* with G. A. Cornia and R. Jolly, and *Adjustment and Poverty Options and Choices*. She has been president of the Development Studies Association of UK and Ireland, senior consultant to the UN Development Programme on the Human Development Report, and member of the UN Committee for Development Planning.

ASHOK SWAIN is associate professor of peace and conflict research and director of the Programme of International Studies at Uppsala University, Sweden. His research interests include environmental conflicts and cooperation, regional water management, and democracy and development. His recent publications include *The Environmental Trap* and *International Fresh Water Resources: Conflict or Cooperation* with Peter Wallensteen.

RAIMO VÄYRYNEN is a professor of government and international studies and served in 1993–98 as Regan Director of the Joan B. Kroc Institute for International Peace Studies, University of Notre Dame, Indiana. In addition to several books in Finnish on globalization and other topics, he has recently authored or edited *Globalization and Global Governance, Breaking the Cycles of Violence; Global Transformation: Economics, Politics, and Culture; Military Industrialization and Economic Development*, and *New Directions in Conflict Theory*. Dr Väyrynen has been visiting fellow and project coordinator at UNU/WIDER, visiting professor at Princeton University and the University of Minnesota, visiting scholar at Harvard University and MIT, dean of social sciences and professor of international relations at the University of Helsinki, director of the Tampere Peace Research Institute, and secretary-general of the International Peace Research Association.

LIST OF TABLES

LIST OF FIGURES

1

The Root Causes of Humanitarian Emergencies

FRANCES STEWART

1. Introduction

Complex humanitarian emergencies (CHEs) have caused widespread death and suffering over the last two decades.[1] Over the twentieth century an estimated 169 million people were killed in large-scale collective violence, including seventeen individual episodes where more than one million people were killed (Rummel 1997). While the number of deaths in contemporary armed conflicts may not be as large as those instigated by Hitler and Stalin, protracted warfare subjects civilian populations to continuing suffering. Not only do complex emergencies cause an immediate tragic toll in greatly increased deaths and forced displacement, but they are also one of the most important causes of prolonged underdevelopment and impoverishment. While recent tragedies in Kosovo, Bosnia, Rwanda, and Angola have made the world more aware of the terrible human toll involved, the international community has yet to develop effective policy responses to prevent such crises erupting.

The formulation of strategies for tackling the underlying causes of complex emergencies is one of the most important challenges facing policymakers, nationally, regionally and internationally. For this reason, UNU/WIDER (Helsinki) and Queen Elizabeth House (Oxford) initiated a research programme devoted to understanding the root causes of CHEs and identifying appropriate policies. The research programme comprised 40 papers, including a dozen country studies. This two volume study presents the main results of this project. The present volume contains general analysis of the characteristics and fundamental economic, political and environmental causes of CHEs, while the second volume, *Weak States and Vulnerable Economies: Humanitarian Emergencies in Developing Countries*, includes thirteen case studies and two summary articles.[2]

---

[1] I am grateful for very helpful comments on a previous draft from E. Wayne Nafziger, Meghan O'Sullivan and Raimo Väyrynen.

[2] A third volume focused on preventative policies is also to be published, edited by E. Wayne Nafziger and Raimo Väyrynen, *War and Destitution: The Prevention of Humanitarian Emergencies*, London: Macmillan (forthcoming).

The aim of the project as a whole was to identify the 'root causes' of complex humanitarian emergencies. To attempt to answer this difficult question, we have adopted a multidimensional approach encompassing theoretical considerations backed up by empirical evidence from political scientists, anthropologists, historians, and economists, together with a number of case studies of particular conflicts. This chapter presents an overview of the study, drawing conclusions from the analysis presented and the evidence contained in the case studies, and identifying some policies that appear relevant to the prevention of conflict derived from these conclusions.[3]

It is apparent from the case studies (presented in Volume 2), and also from evidence published elsewhere, that no simple generalizations are plausible. Cases include state instigated violence combined with international economic sanctions (Iraq and Haiti); those where power-seeking interacting with ethnicity has played a key role (for example, Burundi and Rwanda); those where power-seeking cliques (even gangs) with broadly homogeneous ethnicity have initiated and perpetuated conflict leading to situations of near anarchy (for example, Liberia, Somalia, Sierra Leone); to those where deep class inequalities have constituted the underlying cause (Central America, Cambodia). Moreover, there are countries which, until the conflict broke out, were middle-income countries (Iraq, El Salvador, Bosnia), and others among the poorest in the world (Somalia). In some countries, the conflict was preceded by a period of economic growth (Rwanda, Iraq) while elsewhere conflict followed prolonged economic stagnation.

The econometric evidence appears to point to some more definitive conclusions. Using a dataset from 1980 to 1995, in Chapter 3 Nafziger and Auvinen identify some conditions that are likely to increase country vulnerability to humanitarian emergencies—notably low incomes and low growth in incomes and food output, high inequality, inflation, military expenditure, and a tradition of conflict. Yet while these do appear to be predisposing conditions, the small amount of the variance explained by all these factors put together—from 15–19 per cent—indicates that we have by no means captured the whole story. Moreover, the data cover just 1980–95. The data cannot capture the causal processes leading to those emergencies which broke out in 1980 (nine out of the twenty four—see Nafziger and Auvinen 1999: 274 [Table 1]). Some reverse causality is also present, as they indicate.[4] It is well established that large-scale conflict

---

[3] This chapter uses the thirteen case studies investigated in the project as the sample from which evidence is drawn. The sample was selected so as to obtain a broad range of examples of different types of CHE. The set of case studies overlaps with, but is not identical to, the CHEs identified by Väyrynen (Chapter 2), nor the 18 cases identified by Holsti (Chapter 7).

[4] Nafziger and Auvinen test for causality and find that 'the relationship is stronger from GDP growth to emergencies than vice-versa'.

leads to decline in incomes and growth, and especially food production per capita (see, for example, Stewart, Humphrey and Lee 1997).

The combination of the case studies and econometric analysis thus help to identify some predisposing conditions, but do not allow simple generalizations. This itself is an important conclusion, also emphasized by Holsti in his analysis of the political causes of complex emergencies in Chapter 7 of this volume. After this study it should not be possible to state—as many do—that conflict is inevitable because of primordial ethnic divisions, nor that it is the outcome of underdevelopment and that policies to combat low incomes and poverty will also automatically reduce the risk of conflict. The lessons from this study are more complex: the causes are to be found in the interactions of power-seeking with group identity and inequalities. There are important policy implications, but not of the rather simple variety which typically form part of international discourse. To elucidate these conclusions, this chapter is organized as follows: Section 2 will briefly consider the definition of the topic, that is, 'complex humanitarian emergencies' and its interpretation in the rest of the chapter. Section 3 presents a simple framework for understanding and analysing motives for conflict among and between groups, with a particular focus on economic motivation. A major conclusion from this analysis is that horizontal inequality forms a key element in understanding motives for group violence. Section 4 elucidates the distinction between this type of inequality (defined as horizontal) and vertical inequality, which is the measure normally used to identify inequality in society. Section 5 draws on the evidence in the case studies following the framework presented in Section 3 to assess the importance of the various elements in the major CHEs explored in the country studies. Section 6 puts forward policy conclusions.

2. Definitions of the Topic

The topic appears not to need much attention to definitions. We are discussing situations in which physical fighting between people, typically inhabitants of the same country, leads to a huge amount of human suffering, associated with large numbers of deaths arising both from the fighting and from the indirect effects of the conflict on food supplies and health. Hence in looking for root causes we should investigate the fundamental causes of such fighting. There are two ways to proceed from this starting point. One is to adopt a simple definition of conflict and investigate the causes of any war which leads to significant numbers of deaths, with a rather arbitrary cut-off point, for example, more than 1,000 in a year (Wallensteen's definition of a civil war).[5] But this could be argued to be

---

[5] See, for example, Wallensteen and Sollenberg (1997).

unsatisfactory from two perspectives: first, there may be a major difference in causality according to the size of the conflict which could be missed if all are grouped together in this way. Secondly, there does not seem to be anything very 'complex' about this definition, though, of course, any situation leading to deaths of 1,000 or more would be likely to have both complex causes and complex effects.

One approach to the definition of complex humanitarian emergencies is that of Voutira, who follows Foucault's strategy towards language and discourse and searches for a definition by analysing the language and norms of the international community, while seeking for hidden political agendas (Voutira 1998). With this approach, complexity is seen to arise not so much from the situation *per se*, but from the 'changing nature of international responses, including the proliferation and multiplicity of actors, interests, and political agendas which contribute to the perception of crises as increasingly more "complex"' (Voutira, summary). As Voutira shows, different agencies have adopted different definitions: probably the nearest to a standard definition is that of the United Nations Department of Humanitarian Affairs (DHA) which defines a complex humanitarian emergency as:

A humanitarian crisis in a country, region, or society where there is a total or considerable breakdown of authority resulting from internal or external conflict *which requires an international response that goes beyond the mandate or capacity of any single agency and/or ongoing UN country programme* (in 47th Session of the General Assembly 1994; see IASC 1994) [emphasis by author].

Others have included a checklist of 'events' associated with CHEs. For example, a United Nations Inter-Agency Task Force included the following elements: domestic or interstate armed conflict; long-lasting duration; forced migration; political or military constraints on logistics; security risks for relief workers; requirements for high degrees of political will and negotiation; necessity for peace-making or peace-keeping; and difficult ethical dilemmas (Mohonk Criteria developed by an Inter-Agency Task Force on Ethical and Legal Issues in Humanitarian Assistance, see Mohonk 1994).

If CHEs are defined, as they evidently are by the international community, at least partly in terms of the response of the international community, then analysis of root causes has to investigate why some crises lead to a strong international response while others are ignored. This would take us into the geopolitical significance of the country, the activities of the media etc. Such causal analysis would be a valid and important activity. But it is not the prime intention of this study, which fundamentally aims to understand the causes of conflict-related human suffering. Hence we need a definition which includes all such conflicts, and not only those defined as CHEs by the international community.

Väyrynen presents a comprehensive definition of conflict-related suffering in Chapter 2. He defines a complex humanitarian emergency as 'a profound social crisis in which a large number of people unequally die and suffer from war, disease, hunger, and displacement owing to human-made and natural disasters'. Such a definition appropriately describes a *humanitarian* emergency, given the human suffering arising from all four aspects, while the *complexity* of the emergency emanates from the multi-dimensionality of the concept as well as 'the politicized nature and persistence of the crisis'. Relatively 'objective' indicators of the four elements—that is, numbers killed and/or wounded for war, numbers affected by diseases and/or high or rising mortality for the incidence of disease, food availability and/or malnutrition for hunger, and numbers of refugees or internally displaced persons for displacement—may then be used to signify the presence of a CHE. This leaves three key issues: whether a combination of all four factors must be present to constitute a CHE, and if so whether there is any particular weight each element must take; the 'cut-off' point for a situation to 'count' as a CHE; and how the elements are to be measured.

Väyrynen answers the first question by arguing that all four elements must be present for 'strong' emergencies, but 'limited' emergencies include cases where either war deaths and refugees are present but not hunger and disease, or hunger and disease but not war deaths or refugees. The latter type of 'partial' emergency basically characterizes underdevelopment; although it is obviously of central interest to those exploring how underdevelopment can lead to human suffering, it is not the subject of this volume which has civil war as a central feature. Consequently, it is not explored further by him or others in the study, except as a possible precondition or cause of a strong CHE. Väyrynen's 'cut-off' points in the data pertaining the mid-1990s are as follows: for wars, deaths of 2,000 or more; for displacement, that the total of refugees and displaced people exceeded 385,000; for disease, countries are included when the child mortality rate was 145 or over; hunger is defined as occurring where the proportion of underweight children exceeded 30 per cent. The rationale for these cut-off points is that they single out roughly the 25 worst cases on each of the four dimensions covered.

None of the indicators is straightforward to assess in practice in conflict-ridden societies. Estimates of numbers killed or wounded vary hugely, as shown, for example, even in the case of the high-tech and well-monitored case of the Gulf War (see Alnasrawi in Volume 2) and internal displacement, in particular, can rarely be more than guessed at; data on child mortality and nutrition are also notoriously weak, especially in war zones, and are themselves strongly correlated.[6]

---

[6] Nafziger and Auvinen (Chapter 3), however, find almost no correlation between average changes in calorie supply and infant mortality, which is probably indicative of the fact

Child malnutrition is typically indicative of the presence of disease and lack of preventative health measures as much or more than food availability. However, it is often proposed as an indicator of hunger in the absence of alternative indicators such as measures of adult body mass index (see, for example, Dasgupta 1993).

Nonetheless, Väyrynen's approach undoubtedly identifies the cases which would come up in most people's lists of the civil conflicts which cause major human suffering.[7] Major CHEs, as defined by Väyrynen, usually develop from relatively small conflicts characterized by war deaths alone, often without the presence of the other three elements in significant quantities. Hence, for the analysis of root causes and preventative measures, it is important to include such cases as well. For this reason, the analysis below will adopt a simple definition of conflict, with deaths from deliberate and organized physical violence as being the defining characteristic. Usually, the remaining trio of Väyrynen's characteristics will also be present, sometimes as cause, sometimes as effect, and often both.[8] But in searching for root causes, the analysis will focus on the causes of *significant organized violence*.

3. Motivation, Mobilization and Conflict: A Framework

The human motivation of the actors involved is clearly at the centre of any conflict situation. If a conflict is to be avoided or stopped, this motivation must be understood, and the conditions leading to a predisposition to conflict reduced or eliminated. This section of this chapter sketches the elements that determine such motivation. While the focus is on economic motivation, other factors (political, cultural) are also obviously of importance. They are incorporated in the analysis that follows in a fundamental way since it is such factors (themselves influenced and sometimes determined by economic factors) which decide the way people view themselves, and are viewed (that is, the groups they form), as well as playing a large role in the distribution of resources. In fact, it is rarely possible to disentangle political, cultural, and economic elements, as each is embedded in the other.

The type of conflicts with which we are concerned are *organized group conflicts*: that is to say, they are not exclusively a matter of individuals randomly committing violence against others. What is involved is, therefore,

that child malnutrition has less to do with aggregate food supplies and more with its distribution and infant health.

[7] As he shows comparing his list with a list of countries identified by the CIA as 'simmering emergencies'.

[8] Nafziger and Auvinen (Chapter 3) find a strong correlation of 0.57 between battle deaths and displacement, but weaker correlations with their indicators of hunger and disease.

group mobilization, and we need to understand the underlying motivation for such mobilization. Groups are here defined as collections of people who identify with each other, for certain purposes, as against those outside the group; such groups often also identify with characteristics of some other group(s) with whom they are in conflict. Group organization may be quite informal, but it exists, implying that there is some agreement (frequently implicit) on purposes and activities within the group. This means that normally there are those within any group instigating conflict who lead or orchestrate the conflict, including constructing or enhancing the perception of group identity in order to achieve group mobilization; and those who actively carry out the fighting, or give it some support (active or passive)—for shorthand, we shall describe these two categories as leaders and followers, though there can be considerable overlap between the two. The violence is not, at least purportedly, the objective, rather it is *instrumental*, used in order to achieve other ends. Usually, the declared objective is political—to secure or sustain power—while power is wanted for the advantages it offers, especially the possibilities of economic gains. However, as Keen points out in Chapter 8, sometimes, especially as wars persist, political motivation may disappear or become less important, and the wars are then pursued for the economic advantage conferred directly on those involved, the possibilities of looting, etc. But even then conflicts remain predominantly group activities.[9] The group element, and the fact that the conflicts are instrumental usually with political objectives, differentiate them from crime, though in the extreme case where fighting parties have disintegrated into gangs whose efforts are devoted to maximizing their short-run economic gains (see Keen, Chapter 8 and 1998), the distinction between crime and conflict becomes blurred.

Accepting that groups are central to violent organized conflict, the question is why and how groups are mobilized. For group mobilization, there must be some way that group members perceive themselves as differentiated from others. The case studies show a number of different ways groups have been differentiated and mobilized in contemporary emergencies. In central Africa, ethnic identity is the major source of group definition and mobilization; in Central America, group identification and organization is along class lines; the case of the Iraq/Iran War, the Gulf War and subsequent sanctions, is largely of one nation against the world, though, of course, the Kurds present an ethnically defined opposition within Iraq; in Northern Ireland, religion forms the differentiating principle; in Somalia, it is clans (different lineages within broadly the same ethnic group). Another source of differentiation may be regional location,

---

[9] The central role of 'groups' in ethnic has been emphasised by a number of political scientists in recent analysis such as Posen (1993); Lake and Rothschild (eds.) (1998). These scholars see the fear and insecurity of groups leading to stronger intragroup cohesion and the escalation of inter-group hostilities.

which can, but does not always, coincide with ethnic or language divisions—for example in Biafra, Eritrea and East Pakistan (Bangladesh).

The question of how groups are formed and when they become salient is complex and contested, and cannot be treated adequately here. This issue, considered in relation to groups defined by ethnicity, forms the central theme of the chapter by Alexander, McGregor and Ranger. The view adopted in the present chapter is that group identity is constructed by political leaders, who find group cohesion and mobilization a powerful mechanism in their competition for power and resources, adopting a strategy of 'reworking of historical memories' to engender group identity. Numerous examples presented in Chapter 9, as well as by Cohen, Turton, and others have shown how 'ethnicity was used by political and intellectual élites prior to, or in the course of, wars' (Alexander, McGregor and Ranger). Yet, as Turton points out, 'neither the constructedness nor the instrumentality of ethnicity [or other similar sources of identity which are used to make groups cohere such as religion or class] can be explained unless we are prepared to see it as an independent as well as a dependent variable in human affairs' (Turton 1997: 84; and see Smith 1988). Some shared circumstances are needed for group construction—for example, speaking the same language, sharing cultural traditions, living in the same place, or facing similar sources of hardship or exploitation. Past group formation, although possibly constructed for political purposes at the time, also contributes to present differences. Hence what was a dependent variable at one point in history can act as an independent variable in contributing to current perceptions.[10]

For the emergence of group conflict, a degree of similarity of circumstance among potential members of a group is not by itself enough to bring about group mobilization. Several other conditions must be present. Leaders must see the creation or enhancement of group identity as helpful to the realization of their political ambitions and work actively to achieve this, using a variety of strategies, including education, propaganda, etc. In many cases, it has been shown that political leaders set out to create group consciousness in order to achieve a basis for power. Lonsdale points out that in Kenya 'conflict between political élites for state (and hence economic) power led to the emergence of "political tribalism"' (quote from Alexander, McGregor and Ranger). Government policies, particularly towards education, frequently play a role by discriminating in favour of some category and against others. The story of how differences between the Hutu and Tutsi were possibly created and certainly strongly enhanced by colonial and post-colonial governments is powerfully illustrated by the Burundi and Rwanda studies (Gaffney on Burundi, and Uvin on Rwanda in Volume 2). In the Rwanda case, the *interhammwe*—the extremist leaders

---

[10] Smith has argued that 'the [past] acts as a constraint on invention. Though the past can be "read" in different ways, it is not any past' (Smith 1991: 357–8, quoted in Turton 1997).

of the Hutu massacre of the Tutsi—deliberately and efficiently cultivated Hutu consciousness and fear of Tutsi for several years before the disaster. Some group mobilization occurs as a defensive reaction, in response to discrimination against them and attacks by others. Often people do not recognize themselves as members of a group until this is 'pointed out' by outsiders. Differences in actual underlying conditions with respect to political control and economic conditions, facilitate the development of group identity and mobilization. Without any differences in these factors, group identification is likely to be weak and remain a cultural rather than political or conflict-creating phenomenon.

The hypothesis is that in any society there are some differences in individuals' circumstances—including cultural, geographic, economic—which provide the potential for the construction of group identity as a source of political mobilization. Political leaders, in government or outside, may use this potential in their competition for power and resources, in the course of which they enhance group identification by reworking history, introducing new symbols, etc. However, cultural differences alone are not sufficient to bring about violent group mobilization. As Cohen points out, 'Men may and do certainly joke about or ridicule the strange and bizarre customs of men from other ethnic groups, because these customs are different from their own. But they do not fight over such differences alone. When men *do*, on the other hand, fight across ethnic lines it is nearly always the case that they fight over some fundamental issues concerning the distribution and exercise of power, whether economic, political, or both' (Cohen 1974: 94).

Economic and political differentiation among groups is then of fundamental importance to group mobilization. This is the reason that *relative* position rather than absolute is more often observed to be the underlying determinant of conflict (see Gurr 1993; Nafziger and Auvinen, Chapter 3 of this volume). If a whole society is uniformly impoverished, there may be despair, but there is no motivation for group organization. Even if political leaders hoped to use group mobilization as a source of power, they would find it difficult to secure sufficient response among followers without some underlying economic differences among the people they wished to mobilize. Hence in general if there is group conflict, *we should expect sharp economic differences between conflicting groups associated (or believed to be associated) with differences in political control.* Relevant economic differences vary according to the nature of the economy (for example, land may be irrelevant in modern urban societies and employment relevant, but the converse could be true in rural-based economies). Nonetheless, the absolute situation may also be relevant, since an absolute deterioration in conditions may force attention onto the relative situation (for example, when water becomes a scarce resource people may fight over it, but not when it is plentiful), while, conversely, when incomes/resources are generally increasing people may mind less about their relative position. The latter situation occurred in Kenya in the 1960s and 1970s, and was argued to be one reason why despite persistent relative inequality among tribal groups, large-scale conflict did not result (see Klugman, Volume 2). But in some contexts, improving conditions, if regarded as being unfairly shared, can give rise to conflict, as in Nigeria in the late 1960s (Nafziger and Auvinen, Chapter 3).

Political power is an important instrument of economic power, setting the rules and determining allocation of employment, of government economic and social investments, and incentives for private investment. In general one would expect that political power would be a more compelling means of securing (or conversely being deprived of) economic resources, the greater the role of government in the economy, and especially the more its discretionary power. It is plausible to argue that the role of the state relative to the market, and the discretionary decisions of government, may initially increase and are then likely to fall as development proceeds. That is, in very underdeveloped societies, government expenditure and employment are low; this increases as does governments' discretionary economic power as countries industrialize; but in the later stages of industrialization, the market tends to take a larger role and government decisions are less discretionary and more rule-based. This would suggest that struggles to control state power might be greatest in the middle stages of development.

It should be noted that it is not necessarily the relatively deprived who instigate violence. The privileged may do so, fearing loss of position. For example, the prospect of possible loss of political power can act as a powerful motive for state-sponsored violence which occurs with the aim of suppressing opposition and maintaining power. Since the government has access to an organized force (police/army) and to finance, state terrorism is sometimes an important source of humanitarian emergencies. This was the case, for example, in most of the major episodes of violence in Uganda, in Haiti, and in Iraq's suppression of the Kurds. Holsti (Chapter 7) points out that in recent conflicts, state violence was more often than not the initiating cause.

In many societies organized violence persists at some level over very long periods. Given underlying conditions that are conducive to conflict, there may be low-level conflict for certain periods, and then periods of violence on a greater scale (civil war), sometimes culminating in major catastrophes. The past history of violence then contributes to group identification, animosities and mobilization increasing the likelihood of future conflict. This is shown statistically by Nafziger and Auvinen in Chapter 3. Such a long history of violence of fluctuating strength appears to have occurred in many of the cases studied here—for example, Somalia, Sudan, Rwanda, Burundi. Hence a full understanding of causes must include an explanation both of the underlying vulnerability to conflict and the particular triggers that led to a sharp escalation. Preventative policies should address both the underlying causes and the 'trigger'. The trigger necessarily involves some change—which may include a sudden change in relative deprivation, or a political event such as a coup.

3.1. Dimensions of differentiation in the political, economic, and social position of groups

Leaders often seize on, change, and exaggerate some cultural or religious differences—or symbolic systems[11]—as a mechanism of group mobilization. But it is suggested here that to make these symbolic systems 'work' effectively, it is necessary that there are parallel differences in political and/or economic dimensions. For simplification, we can categorize the latter into four areas: political participation; economic assets; incomes and employment; and social aspects. Each of these categories contains a number of elements. For example, political participation can occur at the level of the cabinet, the bureaucracy, the army, and so on; economic assets comprise land, livestock, machinery, etc.

The four categories and the main elements are presented in the table below, with a column for each category. Each of the four categories is important in itself, but most are also instrumental for achieving others. For example, political power is both an ends and a means; control over economic assets is primarily a means to secure income but it is also an end. Clearly as noted earlier, the relevance of a particular element varies according to whether it forms an important source of incomes or well-being in a particular society. The allocation of housing, for example, is generally more relevant in industrialized countries, while land is of huge importance where agriculture accounts for most output and employment, but becomes less important as development proceeds. Water, as a productive resource, can be very important in parts of the world where rain-water is inadequate, as Swain (Chapter 5) points out. Access to minerals can be a source of great wealth, and gaining such access an important source of conflict in countries with mineral resources, as powerfully shown in the chapters by Fairhead (Chapter 4) and Reno (Volume 2).

A trigger-event causing the initiation of conflict, or its escalation, may arise from a *change* in relative access to any important resource in the table or from some political development which gives rise to expectations about such a change. Such changes may be associated with some political event (as in Afghanistan with the Russian invasion), or because of endogenous or policy changes. Holsti (Chapter 7) defines a 'tipping event' as some

---

[11] 'Symbolic systems' are the values, myths, rituals and ceremonials which are used to organize and unite groups (see Cohen 1974).

Table 1.1. Sources of differentiation among groups

Dimensions of differentiation	Political participation	Economic assets	Employment and incomes	Social access and situation
	Political parties	Land	Government	Education
	Government ministers, senior	Human capital	Private	Health services
Elements of categories	Government ministers, junior	Communal resources, inc. water	'Élite' employment	Safe water
	Army	Minerals	'Rents'	Housing
	Parliament	Privately owned capital/credit	Skilled	Unemployment
	Local government	Government infrastructure	Unskilled	Poverty
	Respect for human rights	Security against theft	Informal sector opportunities	Personal and household security

discrete political development, as do Gurr and Harff (1995). Such events clearly often do act as triggers, and would be included here too, but other structural and policy changes may also act as triggers in vulnerable societies. For example, trigger-events may include:

Endogenous (or semi-endogenous) developments include growing population/land pressures; environmental changes (for example, desertification); or changes brought about by success or failure of the development model resulting in changing absolute and relative access to employment and incomes.

Policy changes including *institutional changes*: property rights; water regulations; commons access; a*djustment/stabilization* policies involving changes in the terms of trade (devaluation; price deregulation); employment and incomes; changes in state benefits; and *politically* inspired changes in the distribution of state benefits.

External developments can also trigger changes in the relative access of different groups. Such changes include market access; the international terms of trade; debt and interest payments; and capital flows (including aid). Our studies give examples—the Iraq emergency was caused by a combination of an aggressive state and a near complete cutoff from external markets, capital flows, and aid. In contrast, the Rwanda study suggests that the failure of the development model, heavily aid-financed, contributed to the crisis.

3.2. *Main elements to be considered in an analysis of the causes of conflict*

In exploring the causes of conflict we need to differentiate the following:

(i) The *reality* or actual conditions of the situation of the various conflicting groups, *absolutely* and *relatively* to others in the dimensions shown in Table 1.1.

(ii) The *private* benefits and costs of conflict to members of a group. Individual action is taken partly (the extreme neoclassical position would argue entirely) as a result of a calculus of individual or private costs and benefits of action. Of course, especially at times of high tension, group gains or losses also become a consideration. In some situations, people have been observed to take action which is completely counter to their private interests—for example, rioters have burned down factories in Sri Lanka where they themselves work, thereby destroying their own employment.[12] The role of leaders (see below) is to see that group considerations override private ones, for which they may use propaganda, incentives, and force.

Individuals and groups may *gain* from conflict—for example, by looting, use of forced labour, changes in the terms of trade in their favour, the creation of new economic opportunities, controlling emergency aid. Both de Waal (1989) and Keen (1994, 1998 and in this volume) have analysed such gains in Sudan and elsewhere; Väyrynen's analysis of the conflicts in Angola, Colombia, Serbia, Tajikistan, and Northern Iraq in Volume 2 shows how the search for material gains drives both group politics and violence.

However, many people lose from the physical violence, disrupted markets, reduced state benefits, theft, and looting. The private calculus of costs and benefits also depends on the gains from avoiding conflict in terms of potential state benefits and economic rewards from development in a peaceful environment. Hence the general prospects for economic development and the extent to which the individual and the group to which (s)he belongs is likely to share in development gains is an important consideration. If these are low, the calculation is more likely to come out in favour of conflict. The costs and benefits may be differentiated by gender (and by group).

The cost/benefit calculation may be different for leaders and followers and also between those actively involved and the rest of the population.

(iii) *Leadership* and *organization* of groups. The conflicts considered in this volume are organized. There are typically 'leaders' (those who organize/employ armies, etc.) and 'followers' (who make up the armies; provide food, finance, etc.) For conflict, both leaders and followers (whose

---

[12] M. O'Sullivan, personal communication.

interests can diverge) must be convinced of the advantage of fighting. But their calculus can be rather different. Leaders are generally seeking to form a government, control resources, secure high office, and so on. But leaders can do little without followers. However, if the followers—i.e., those providing the manpower and other resources—are strongly supportive of conflict, against the views of their existing leaders, new leaders may emerge.

Any long-run 'solution' must try and change the calculus of both leaders and followers with respect to individual and group calculations. Individuals (leaders and followers) can be offered 'bribes' to stop fighting—for example, power and status for leaders, finance and jobs for followers. But unless the group differences that formed the underlying causes are also addressed, new leaders and followers are likely to emerge, if not immediately in the medium term.

(iv) The *perceptions* of reality and of the private costs/benefits of conflict are decisive rather than the actual situation. The actual situation is filtered by education, the media, political argument, and propaganda. All are more effective in influencing perceptions if there is consonance between the picture of reality people are presented with by the various channels and actual conditions.

(v) *Constraints*: even with strong motives for conflict on the basis of individual and group calculations, a strong state (or other authority) can prevent, eliminate or reduce conflict, while a weak authority may not be able to constrain violence. Some of the conflicts in the former Soviet Union can be seen as primarily due to the weakening of state authority and its ability to suppress conflicts so that old conflicts may again be openly expressed, rather than to new motives for conflict. In some of the African conflicts, too, the weakening of the state—for example in Somalia and Sierra Leone—has permitted conflicts to erupt and enlarge, which might have been suppressed with a stronger state. In Kenya, in contrast, a relatively strong state has kept violent conflict to a fairly small level (Klugman). But, as noted earlier, the state can also deliberately foster violence to undermine opposition groups, often provoking violent reactions by its actions. State violence was a key instigating cause in Uganda under both Obote and Amin (see Stewart, Humphrey and Lee 1997). In the studies here, the state has instigated violence by attacking opposition groups in a number of cases, including Haiti, Rwanda, and Burundi.

(vi) *Opportunities*: conflicts need resources, including arms, soldiers, and food. Some can be seized from the local territory—more easily if the conflict is popular locally, which again depends on whether the group involved regards itself as being seriously disadvantaged. Fighting groups can survive without outside resources, but the availability of support from outside—credit, food, technical advice, and arms—clearly helps the resource situation and thus feeds the conflict. The cold war conflicts were largely financed from outside: since the cold war, external support has continued to be important—from governments (outside and within the region), from NGOs and from the private sector. External resources played a role in Central America (still a cold war event), in Afghanistan (from the US, Pakistan and Russia during the cold war era, and subsequently from Pakistan and NGOs); in Sierra Leone and the Congo (mainly private sector). The genocide in Rwanda, however, was mostly self-financed, as has been the persistent conflict in Somalia and the conflicts in Burundi, showing that external resources are not essential.

The same *reality*—(i) above—that is, the relative and absolute position of groups in political and economic terms, may have different effects in terms of conflict-occurrence according to the other dimensions, (ii) to (vi), just discussed. A poor situation in terms of group inequality may not translate itself into conflict if there is a strong state which suppresses it, or if ideological elements are such that the inequalities are not widely perceived. A new conflict may emerge either if objective conditions change or if some of the other elements change—for example, the state weakens, new sources of external support for conflict develop, or leaders emerge who powerfully and effectively communicate the actual inequalities to the members of the group.

According to this view, the underlying reality about the absolute and, especially, the relative position of the group is of paramount importance. This is because the other factors are all permissive, but would be extremely unlikely to result in a conflict in the absence of these inequalities

Section 5 will draw on the case studies to provide support for this conclusion. The conclusion has important lessons for conflict prevention policies, which will be considered in the last section.

4. Horizontal versus Vertical Inequality

The analysis of the causes of conflict presented above places overriding emphasis on inequality among groups, along a number of dimensions. Yet high levels of inequality, as normally assessed, are not invariably associated with conflict; for example, high inequality has been present in Kenya, Thailand, and Brazil without leading to large-scale conflict. This is partly because other factors mentioned above may prevent the high inequality causing conflict, for example, because absolute conditions improve, or a strong state is able to suppress potential conflict. But it is also because of the way inequality is normally assessed and measured. Most measures of inequality relate to the distribution of *income* only and measure it as *vertical* rather than *horizontal* inequality. This is not the relevant way to assess inequality for understanding conflict.

In the analysis above, a matrix of 28 potentially relevant aspects of inequality were presented, made up of four broad categories, consisting of P (political), A (assets), Y (incomes/employment) and S (social) dimensions. Each category consists of a vector of different elements, that is, P = Pi, Pii, Piii, . . .; A = Ai, Aii, . . . etc. where Pi, Pii, . . . Ai, Aii are different kinds of political participation and economic assets. Table 1.1 picked out seven in each category, but is it possible to extend them and indeed to imagine additional categories that might be relevant in some societies.

Inequality in income distribution—economists' normal space for measuring inequality—is a summary measure of the incomes/employment dimension but fails to capture, or gives only a partial indicator of, the others. Moreover, income distribution is generally defined as a *vertical* measure, that is, it takes every individual or household in society from 'top' to 'bottom' and measures their incomes and the consequent inequality. What is needed for our analysis is a *horizontal* measure of inequality which measures inequality between groups, where groups are defined by region/ethnicity/class/religion, according to the most appropriate source of group identification in the particular society.

It is possible to have sharp vertical inequality in any dimension without any horizontal inequality—for example if the average income of all groups were the same and distribution within each group was highly unequal. Conversely, it is possible to have considerable inter-group inequality, while overall societal vertical inequality is small because intragroup inequality is small. However, there is necessarily some connection between vertical and horizontal inequality since any overall measure of societal inequality of income distribution (like the Gini or the Theil coefficients) (that is, vertical measures) can be decomposed into the weighted sum of two elements—inter-group inequality and intragroup inequality.[13] Moreover, where group differentiation is according to economic class—for example, peasants and landlords, as in Central America—then horizontal inequality (that is, between these groups or classes) also involves vertical inequality as between individuals. Even then there remains an important distinction between the two types of inequality: it is the inequality between the groups (landlords versus peasants) which is potentially politically explosive because it may give rise to group struggle, rather than the vertical inequality among individuals.

Like vertical inequality, there can be a number of alternative measures of horizontal inequality. It is possible to use the same measures as for vertical inequality, where the population consists of groups rather than individuals, for example, the Gini coefficient or Theil index. Generally, these are more complex measures (especially where there are only a few salient

---

[13] For a decomposition of the Gini of this kind, see Fei, Ranis and Kuo (1978); and for a decomposition of the Theil, see Anand (1983).

groups) than seems necessary. A simpler summary measure is the coefficient of variation. The ratio of the worst performing group to the average and to the best performance are other useful measures. From the perspective of causing resentment and ultimately conflict, it is possible that *consistent relative deprivation* over a number of dimensions may be as significant as the actual coefficient of variation with respect to any one dimension. Consistent deprivation over a number of dimensions may be measured by looking at rankings in performance on different dimensions and averaging them. *Persistence* in the horizontal inequalities between groups over time is another relevant factor. If gaps between groups narrow or reverse, this reduces their potential to cause conflict. Conversely, widening gaps are more likely to provoke conflict. Whether high levels of horizontal inequality are likely to cause serious conflict also depends on the numerical importance of the various groups. Where groups are very small, even if discriminated against consistently, their potential to cause conflict on a substantial scale, that is, enough to constitute a CHE, is limited.

In practice, data may not be available to measure horizontal inequality, since most concern to date has been with vertical inequality (and even measures of this are often lacking). Moreover, in politically tense societies, governments are not likely to want to publicize horizontal inequalities. Nonetheless, it is important to collect such data, since it is essential for identification of potential problems and possible solutions. Measurement may be relatively easy for some elements (for example, some aspects of political participation); while for others rough estimates may be made, or proxies used, such as taking regional data to represent differences among ethnicities, or distribution of land as a proxy for distribution of agricultural incomes.

Identifying the appropriate groups for measuring horizontal inequality presents some rather fundamental difficulties. In conflicts, group differentiation is not based on some obvious objective differences between people (for example, all people over 6 foot tall versus all those below 6 foot in height), but, as pointed out above, is constructed or created in order to mobilize people for political purposes, as discussed earlier. Group construction is dynamic and fluid, changing with circumstances. In some situations, group identification may nonetheless be obvious (for example, where a conflict has been ongoing for many years and the lines of differentiation are clearly drawn) but in others, groups may split or new groups may emerge in response to the developing situation. Then identification of groups for the purpose of measuring horizontal inequality may not only be difficult but may actually change the on-the-ground situation, either by re-enforcing distinctions, or by creating some perceived political advantages in new alliances and groupings. Moreover, the announcement of the existence of a large degree of horizontal inequality may actually provoke conflict. It is clearly of the greatest importance that the act of measurement, and the subsequent policies, avoid worsening a conflict situation. But to avoid any assessment of horizontal inequality altogether for these reasons, would be to lose an important tool for analysis of causes and prevention of conflict. My conclusion is that measurement of horizontal inequality and the uses to which it is put should be conducted sensitively.

5. Some Evidence from the Case Studies

The development of the general approach to analysing causes of conflict laid out in Section 3 was influenced by the case studies, from which some examples were drawn. This section uses the case studies, presented in schematic form in Appendix Table A1.1, to provide some more systematic evidence on the role of the factors picked out in Section 3 as being likely to lead to conflict.

Some of the major findings are given below.

5.1. Group categorization: the categorization of relevant groups differed across cases

Cambodia and the two American cases, El Salvador and Haiti, came closest to classic class conflicts. In Cambodia, the Khmer Rouge represented the impoverished peasants and attacked the urban élite. In the case of El Salvador, it was mainly a case of landed interests versus peasants; this was also true of Nicaragua and Guatemala. In Haiti, the division was between the élite (largely dependent on the President and state) and the masses (mainly peasants).

Ethnicity was important as a differentiating element in Burundi, Rwanda, as the conflict proceeded in Matabeleland (Zimbabwe), and potentially in Kenya. Elements were present in Afghanistan and also Cambodia, but not as the most important factor.

Clans were the source of group differentiation in Somalia and Afghanistan and in South Caucasus where kinship relations and clans are an important part of social fabric (although they were modified in the Soviet era).

Warlords created groups (by force and financial incentives) in Sierra Leone and Liberia. In Liberia, the distinction between the American-Liberian élite and local origin Africans also played a small role. This also appears to be an element of the situation in Somalia.

This sample suggests that the popular image of modern civil wars as being ethnically motivated is only true in a minority of cases.

5.2. *Dimensions of inequality between groups: this too differed among the cases*

Differential political access and control were virtually universal, but to a lesser extent in the one case studied which had not developed into a complex humanitarian emergency—Kenya. Congo under Mobutu also distributed his patronage fairly broadly, for the most part. In both these cases, political patronage was widely though unevenly shared, albeit some important groups were left out. In all the other cases, political power and the benefits it confers were monopolized by one group. In some countries this was the majority (the Hutu in Rwanda; the Shona in Zimbabwe; the peasant class in Cambodia). In others, minorities, such as the Tutsi in Burundi, the dictatorships in Central America, the various strongmen in Liberia and Sierra Leone.

An invariable consequence of unequal access to political power was unequal benefits from state resources. In some countries, the president and a small coterie took a massive share for their own private accumulation, for example, the Duvaliers in Haiti; Mobutu in the Congo. In others, a broader élite benefited—the élite Hutu in Rwanda, the Tutsi in Burundi, and in Kenya the Kikuyu—disproportionately under Kenyatta and the Kalenjin and allied tribes under Moi. Half of government investment in Burundi went to Bujumbura and its vicinity, from where the élite Tutsi came.

Unequal access to land was important in El Salvador and for some clans in Somalia but does not seem to have been so relevant elsewhere. However, land pressure leading to rising land-related conflicts is believed to have been an important factor in Rwanda, while competition for use of land between cattle-herding and pastoralists has occurred elsewhere (for example, Kenya).

Education was an important element differentiating groups in Rwanda, Burundi, Cambodia, Kenya, El Salvador and Haiti. In Burundi and Rwanda, privileged access to education goes back to colonial times. In Burundi it has continued with deliberate attempts to limit access to Hutu. Differential access to education both reflects differences in incomes and causes it, an important instrument in the perpetuation of inequalities, as recognized in Burundi, where educated Hutu were targeted for killing in the 1970s.

Where minerals resources were in evidence, access to the revenues tended to be dominated by whoever was in control, denying others access—for example, Sierra Leone and Iraq. This greatly increased the economic advantages to be secured by political control.

The matrix in Table 1.1 provides a categorization of potential elements that might differentiate groups. Although there is not enough detailed evidence in many of the studies to permit a full analysis of all the elements in the matrix, some broad conclusions emerge. There was differentiation in almost all cases along the vector of *political participation*. In the vector of *economic assets*, land was the most important source of differentiation in Central America but less so elsewhere, minerals in some African countries, and the reduction of communal resources appears to have been a factor in Somalia. But this sample gives support to Fairhead's view that environmental *riches* rather than impoverishment often causes conflict, although many people, often the majority, may be impoverished in the context of environmental riches at a country level; the gross inequalities then become a source of conflict. For example, environmental riches were at issue in Liberia, Sierra Leone, Iraq, and South Caucasus (oil in Azerbaijan, cultivable land in Georgia). However, the worsening economic situation of the rural masses in Rwanda, Cambodia, Afghanistan, Burundi, Haiti, Somalia, Central America, and Armenia—which in each case was partly due to a worsening environmental situation—undoubtedly contributed to the support they gave to the violence. Biased regional distribution of government infrastructure was observed in Kenya (and also in Uganda) and featured in the Congo and Zimbabwe. Water did not turn out to be an important element in these cases. Swain's review shows that this is a near-universal finding. Water access has often been a cause of serious disputes, even violent disputes on a relatively minor scale, but ultimately the disputes have generally been solved by negotiation and not full-scale war. However, Swain anticipates that water disputes may increasingly cause violent conflicts as shortages become more acute. The main humanitarian effect of various water policies (dams, diversion of rivers, etc.) is displacement, not violent conflict.

In the dimension of *employment and incomes*, government employment, élite jobs and the ability to earn rents were heavily biased in favour of the group in power. The desire to preserve these privileges was a clear motive for the frequent occurrence of state-sponsored violence directed at suppressing opposition. Where the state was not strong enough to suppress opposition but attempted to do so, violence from opposition groups was aimed at securing state control so as to generate these privileges for themselves. However, although it is evident that groups in power were able to enrich themselves, relatively and absolutely, considerable within-group inequality remained so that not all members of the ruling group gained. This was notable among the Hutu in Rwanda where there was substantial impoverishment, and one reason why the Hutu élite resorted to provoking ethnic animosities was probably to prevent political expression of this economic impoverishment which, in turn, partly explained the massive response of the Hutu peasantry. Sharp within-group inequalities also occurred in Kenya, especially among the Kikuyu, making the élite among them less prone to violent opposition since they had much to lose economically. The Kikuyu élite were able to maintain much of their economic privileges because they depended in part not on state but on private activities so that control over the state was less essential to sustain high incomes. In countries where the private sector is very small—which is true of many of the countries studied—control over the state may present almost the only source of enrichment. In the absence of an effective state, private control over natural resources (Liberia and Sierra Leone) or of the drug trade (Afghanistan) essentially duplicates state control and battling for control can become a source of violent conflict.

Systematic evidence on the social access vector was rather thin in many of these studies. Biases in the provision of education and government infrastructure (noted above) are indicative of unequal provision. Evidence for Kenya and Uganda shows severe inequalities in social access and social indicators. Strong inequities are also shown, dating from the colonial era, in Rwanda, Burundi and Cambodia. These were carried forward in the post-colonial era in Burundi and until the Khmer revolution in Cambodia, while efforts were made to reverse them with Hutu control in Rwanda and under the Khmer Rouge—in the latter case by providing only minimal education for all. In Haiti and El Salvador the peasants suffered from relatively (and absolutely) poor access to health and education, with high unemployment rates in Haiti. High rates of poverty outside the élite governing group were to be seen in almost all cases.

5.3. Perceptions

As noted in Section 3, it is not enough that groups actually have unequal opportunities. Group identity, sufficient to bring about violence, also requires strong perceptions of group identity and of injustice in the group's position. These perceptions are created historically and may be enhanced by deliberate actions by potential leaders who want to use group mobilization to attain or retain power. Thus in Somalia, 'Militia leaders manipulated and used clan identities and lineage alliances as an important resource which could be mobilized' (Auvinen and Kivimäki, Volume 2). In most cases, except in the most 'privatized' and commercial conflicts, leaders took similar actions.

In both Burundi and Rwanda, the colonial powers had strongly differentiated between Tutsi and Hutu, despite the fact that the people share language, religion, dress, diet, housing and territory, treating Tutsi as superior. (The Tutsi were regarded as 'natural aristocrats and the Hutu as servile peasant folk' [Gaffney, Volume 2]). Thus historical perceptions of differences were entrenched. They were enhanced by new histories and propaganda. For Burundi, the Hutu in exile developed a history of their country in which the Hutu claimed 'rightful moral and historical precedence over the Tutsi' (Malkki 1995: 59, quoted in Gaffney). In Rwanda, 'For decades, anti-Tutsi racism had served as a deliberately-maintained strategy of legitimization of the powers-that-be, and was kept alive through a systematic public structure of differentiation and discrimination, in which the "Tutsi problem" was never allowed to be forgotten' (Uvin, Volume 2). The Belgians also introduced ethnic distinctions in the Congo, 'inventing' the Ngala and issuing ethnic identity cards; but ethnic divisions were not enhanced under Mobutu who was able to retain power through extensive use of patronage (Emizet, Chapter 9, Volume 2). In Zimbabwe, the conflict started as a political one, but gained an ethnic dimension as the killings occurred. In Somalia, a similar type of discourse was used to promote clan solidarity, emphasizing the superiority of particular clans. 'We are Darod—we are wealthy, religious and educated . . . whereas the mental capacity of the Hawiye is limited' (quoted in Auvinen and Kivimäki, Volume 2).

In contrast, ideology was used to promote group consciousness in El Salvador, Haiti and Cambodia. In both El Salvador and Haiti, populist ideology was used by opposition leaders to raise group consciousness and cement support. In Cambodia, revolutionary rhetoric about the need for total revolution to end injustice and oppression was combined with strict party discipline.

In other conflicts, alliances were short-lived and changing (Sierra Leone and Liberia) and deep seated perceptions of group solidarity or superiority were absent. Groups were cemented together by short-term interests— money, force and fear. Afghanistan is an intermediate case in which religion and ideology (communism versus Islam), ethnicity and clan solidarity played some role, but financial self-interest and force also developed as the conflict proceeded.

5.4. Private costs and benefits

For leaders the potential benefits from gaining power were huge in states where there were few checks and balances, and rulers and their immediate allies could accumulate massive fortunes. In Cambodia, the situation was summarized by Prud'homme, 'Power provided access to wealth rather than wealth provided access to power' (quoted in Le Billon and Bakker, Volume 2). These gains were more attractive where there were few alternative opportunities—when without political power, exclusion from state benefits was near total and the private sector was small and undynamic.

The lesson that conflict was intended as a means of private accumulation by leaders, with ethnicity—or other cementing ideology—an instrument to gain support, is repeated in many of the chapters. Reno summarizes this conclusion in his chapter on Sierra Leone and Liberia— the most venal of the conflicts: 'War is an intensification of competition for the resources of the patronage system' (Reno, Volume 2). But the extent to which this applied varied across the cases. In the class-based populist movements—El Salvador, Haiti, Cambodia—private accumulation was undoubtedly a major motive of the pre-revolutionary governments seeking to retain power, but not among the populist leaders. In many other cases, the retention (or attaining) of political power was the prime objective, the possibilities of personal enrichment this power permitted providing strong motivation. In this type of dispute, ethnicity was used as an instrument (most notably Rwanda and Burundi). In conflicts where the state had disintegrated, there was a more direct connection between force and enrichment as control of particular areas permitted warlords to gain access to the resources of the region without acquiring formal political power.

Absence of attractive alternative sources of income increased the strength of the accumulation motive. To the extent that there are other 'legitimate' sources of wealth which would be threatened by war, as in the private sector in Kenya, violence appears less appealing from a private cost benefit perspective. In Cambodia, the lack of opportunities for the newly educated provided potential leadership for the revolutionary movement.

The followers also benefited from some trickle down if their group achieved power. More immediately, their role as soldiers offered an alternative to unemployment or very low income earning opportunities, less for the pay (often non-existent) and more for the possibilities of theft, looting, etc. At a quite petty level, the economic gains that conflict can offer to young men with few alternatives may be enough to make them wish to perpetuate the conflict as a profitable way of life (see Keen in this volume). In such a situation, a political 'solution' may not end the violence. Force and fear are another motive for followers to carry out a war—undoubtedly present in some cases, for example, Cambodia.

5.5. Constraints, resources and external action

A strong state can suppress potential violent opposition. However, in several of the cases, the state was undermined by a combination of corruption and private profiteering, a deteriorating economic situation, economic policy reforms which diminished the size of the state, and the success of opposing groups: a radical weakening of the state occurred most notably in Sierra Leone, Liberia and Somalia. In such contexts, quite small factions were unconstrained in their military activities, whereas a strong state could prevent such violence erupting on any scale. On the other hand, in many cases it was the state itself which was responsible for much of the violence, a common situation as noted by Holsti. In such cases—like Cambodia, Zimbabwe, and Haiti—the presence of a relatively strong state does not prevent violence but actually causes it.

Resourcing these conflicts was not a problem: frequently, governments were receiving generous aid and military assistance which sustained them and directly or indirectly financed the conflict. The US financed the El Salvador conflict and supported Duvalier in Haiti for many years. Substantial international aid supported Rwanda shortly before the genocide, Liberia during the cold war, and Somalia in the 1980s, and the Congo, intermittently, as well as the more peaceful case of Kenya. Foreign resources of various kinds flowed into Afghanistan (from the USSR, from the West, from Islamic states, from NGOs and from drug money) much of which went to finance the war. Similarly, Cambodia has received substantial external support from the West (which supported the Sihanouk regime and then Khmer Rouge in the 1980s), China, and Vietnam.

International support for peace has been less in total, and also less effective, than the war-financing. UN intervention was on balance probably effective in peace-making in Cambodia and in El Salvador, but notably unsuccessful in Somalia. The international community stood by, without intervention, in the worst cases—Cambodia and Rwanda. Indeed, there were some UN troops in Rwanda prior to the massacres, but they were withdrawn just before the massacre. Moreover, the massive aid flows to many of the countries in the pre-conflict years did nothing to prevent a conflict situation and may have contributed to it.

The contribution of aid to international conflict arose in two ways: first, aid resources were a major source of enrichment for rulers, and consequently high aid flows became a motive to retain or secure political power; secondly, the aid projects themselves did not contribute to reducing horizontal inequality but often had the opposite effect, with the benefits being strongly biased in favour of particular groups (as in Rwanda). If the large aid flows had succeeded in promoting broadly based development—as perhaps occurred in Kenya in the 1970s—they would have had a peace-promoting effect to counterbalance these conflict-prone effects. But the aid failed to do so for this group of countries—which by its nature is a biased sample with a disproportionate representation of weak and corrupt governments leading to aid diversion, poor projects, and generally weak economic performance.

IMF and World Bank conditionality is another source of international influence which is sometimes thought likely to promote conflict because of its harsh effects on vulnerable groups. For this set of cases, such conditionality was largely irrelevant as programmes were rarely properly carried out since political events intervened. From an *a priori* perspective one would expect IFI (international financial institutions) conditionality to have both positive and negative effects on conditions liable to make countries vulnerable to conflict. On the positive side, removing discretionary power from governments should reduce the strong private incentive to acquire power, since it should reduce the opportunities for private enrichment. In addition, if the programmes succeed in promoting a strong private sector, they would improve the economic opportunities outside the government. On the negative side, reducing the size of the state reduces the benefits conferred by the state and therefore the gains from peace and adherence to law and order. As access to social services, food subsidies, etc. is reduced, the social compact has less to offer. In addition, the short term changes resulting from economic policy reform can hurt particular groups in ways that may act as triggers to violence if the underlying situation predisposes to it. Auvinen and Nafziger, however, find that IMF programmes are *negatively* associated with CHEs (that is, more likely in the absence of IMF programmes), though this could be, as the authors note, because few countries that are in a violent situation are able to reach agreements with the IMF. In his careful review of these issues, Morrisson (Chapter 6) finds that while IMF programmes often lead to civil protests even involving some deaths, they cannot be blamed for the massive conflict of CHEs.

6. Policy Conclusions

The analysis of the sources of conflict contained above has some strong implications for policy formulation aimed at preventing, or ending, conflict. Policy needs to address the underlying causes systematically—other permissive elements (resources for conflict, for example) are relevant too, but action on these aspects would not have lasting effects unless the root causes are tackled. As a first priority, policy formulation needs to consider both the issues of horizontal inequality among groups and that of the private incentives to leaders and followers. The two sets of issues, the conditions of groups and the private incentives, overlap but are not the same.

Policy change is particularly difficult to achieve in the context of a country prone to violence, perhaps currently experiencing it, and having a recent and longer history of violence. In this context there are inherited memories and grievances, entrenched group identity and inter-group animosities. The government is rarely broad based, normally representing only a subset of the groups potentially involved in conflict. It would often be naive to think that the government even *wants* to promote peace, given the prevalence of state-instigated violence. Hence the policies to be suggested below may fall on hostile ears as far as the government is concerned. The same may be true of the international community which has its own reasons for pursuing the actions it has taken, which, too, have often been conflict-provoking. Hence the context for introducing policy change must be recognized as structurally unfavourable. Nonetheless, it is worth elucidating policies liable to reduce vulnerability to conflict since some governments may wish to pursue them, as would some international donors, at least judged by their rhetoric; and for others, these policies can act as a standard against which actual policies may be judged.

6.1. Group (or horizontal) inequality

The general direction of policy change must be to reduce group inequalities. To achieve this it is essential to have *inclusive government, politically, economically and socially*. Inclusive government politically means that all major groups in a society participate in political power, the administration, the army and the police. Inclusive government economically implies that horizontal inequality in economic aspects (assets, employment, and incomes) is moderate; and inclusive government socially implies that horizontal inequality in social participation and achieved well-being is also moderate. It is necessary to determine what will count as a moderate degree of group inequality. If one group is more than twice as well off as another one, horizontal inequality might be taken to be quite severe. But the significance of any degree of inequality is increased if it occurs systematically over a number of dimensions and grows over time. Hence the extent of consistency over different dimensions, and developments over time, should be considerations in determining what is an acceptable degree of horizontal inequality. *Horizontal equity* is used to describe an acceptable degree of horizontal inequality.

The general objective of inclusivity and moderate horizontal inequality will translate differently into specific policy recommendations in particular cases depending on the relevant groups in the society, the dimensions of importance in the particular society and those in which there is substantial horizontal inequality.

The most universal requirement is for political inclusivity because it is monopolization of political power by one group or other that is normally responsible for many of the other inequalities. Yet achieving political inclusivity is among the most difficult changes to bring about. It is not just a matter of democracy defined as rule with the support of the majority, as majority rule can be consistent with abuse of minorities, as was seen in the cases of Rwanda, Cambodia, and Zimbabwe. In a politically inclusive democratic system, particular types of proportional representation are needed to ensure participation by *all* major groups in the elected bodies. For inclusive government, representation of all such groups is also essential at the level of the cabinet and other organs of government. For political inclusivity members of major groups also need to be included at all levels of the civil service, the army, and the police.

Since every case of conflict we have observed lacks such political inclusivity, this requirement can be regarded as a universal prescription for conflict-prone societies. Such politically inclusive policies have been adopted by well-known peace-making regimes, for example, the post-

Pinochet Chilean government, Museveni in Uganda, South Africa under Mandela.

These political requirements for conflict-prone countries do not currently form part of the dialogue of political conditionality adopted by some bilateral donors—as noted above, at times the requirement of political inclusivity may even be inconsistent with the normal political conditionality. At other times, it may be a matter of adding requirements to the usual set of political conditions. This set includes rule with the consent of the majority, multiparty democracy, and respect for human rights. Political conditions for avoiding conflict would certainly include the requirement of respect for human rights. But the requirement for majority rule is not a sufficient condition for conflict-avoidance, as noted above, while multiparty democracy may not be consistent with conflict prevention since political parties are often formed on ethnic (or other group) lines and can encourage group animosity (see Stewart and O'Sullivan 1999).

Some of the specific economic and social recommendations are likely to differ among countries. Those concerning government expenditure and jobs, however, are universal:

(i) To ensure balance in group benefits from government expenditure and aid (including the distribution of investment, and jobs).

(ii) To ensure balance in group access to education at all levels; health services; water and sanitation; housing and consumer subsidies (if relevant). Equality of access in education is particularly important since this contributes to equity in income-earning potential.

The private sector can be an important source of group differentiation. It is a less explosive source politically than an inequitable state sector as it is less directly under political control. Nonetheless, in societies where the private sector forms a major source of group inequality in jobs, incomes and assets, this could be conducive to conflict and in such a situation it would be necessary to follow policies to reduce the horizontal inequality present in the private sector. The situation in South Africa represents an example where a huge amount of horizontal inequality stems from private sector activity. The particular policies to be followed to deal with private sector sources of horizontal inequality differ across countries, but may include:

(iii) Land reform so as to ensure fair access to land by different groups. This policy would only be relevant where differential access to land is an important aspect of horizontal inequality. In our cases, El Salvador was a clear example.

(iv) Policies to ensure balanced participation in education and the acquisition of skills at all levels. This has been an important and effective policy measure in Malaysia.

(v) Policies to promote balanced access to industrial assets and employ-
    ment. This is more difficult to achieve than reform of public sector
    policies and need only be attempted where the private sector is a
    major source of group inequality—which was not the case in most
    of the countries studied here. Private sector firms may be required
    to have an equal opportunities policy; they should be monitored
    and where horizontal inequality is high may be required to provide
    a certain proportion of jobs at every level to members of the main
    groups. Similarly, banks may be required to spread their lending
    across groups. Asset redistribution across groups can be achieved
    by government purchase of assets and redistribution to disadvan-
    taged groups. These sorts of policies were introduced by the
    Malaysian government in its New Economic Policy (NEP) which
    effectively narrowed the gap in incomes, employment, and assets
    among the major groups.

While the detailed policy requirements would differ according to the situation in a particular country, the important recommendation is the general
requirement to follow inclusive policies, offsetting major elements of horizontal inequality.

Since, as noted, many governments are pursuing precisely the opposite
policies, it is critically important that such policies are built into the
requirements of the international community in its dealings with conflict-
prone countries. In fact at present they are not—certainly not explicitly.
Aid allocation within a country depends on efficiency considerations and
sometimes vertical equity but not horizontal equity. Pursuing horizontal
equity may sometimes conflict with efficiency or even with vertical equity.
These are trade-offs that may have to be accepted. In the long term, both
growth and poverty would benefit more from the avoidance of conflict
than is lost from any short-term output reduction that the new policy
might involve. Mostly, there would not be a significant trade-off with
poverty reduction as balanced policies are also likely to be poverty-reduc-
ing, while extending education to the deprived would be likely to contribute to economic growth. Malaysia, for example, has been remarkably
successful in achieving economic growth and poverty reduction as well as
horizontal equity through the NEP.

IMF and World Bank policy conditionality is 'blind' to these issues, that
is, they take no account of horizontal equity in their policy prescriptions
(and also pay little attention to vertical inequality), nor do they allow for
the possible undermining of the state resulting from excessive cutbacks
following their recommendations. As lead institutions, it is essential that
they incorporate these considerations into their conditionality, not only
with respect to project allocation but also in the policy conditionality
applied to government economic interventions and expenditures. This

would require a quite marked change in their programmes for conflict-prone countries.

6.2. Private incentives to violence

The policies just sketched were all addressed to the need for inclusivity and group equity. When applied to a situation not yet affected by conflict, these policies, if effective, might be sufficient to eliminate the underlying causes of conflict, although an additional requirement is that there is a sufficiently strong state to avoid violence erupting for private benefit in a near-anarchical situation. If these conditions are met, then it may not be necessary to introduce policies to tackle the private incentives to violence of leaders or followers. But when conflict is ongoing, policies to tackle the root causes may need to be accompanied by policies to encourage particular individuals involved to stop fighting and enter more peaceful occupations, i.e. to change the private incentives.

The private incentives of leaders of major groups may best be turned round by offering them positions in government. Lower level leaders may be offered jobs in the state army or civil service, or money. This proposal may often fall on deaf ears, for political reasons—as with other policy proposals suggested here—only governments seriously intending to end violence and enhance national unity will follow the recommendation. Yet post-conflict governments have done so—for example, Museveni's government (and army) incorporated many of those who had been fighting against him; the first post-apartheid government in South Africa likewise. Those who had previously been active soldiers (the 'followers') need income-earning employment—finance or jobs in works schemes, or, where appropriate land or agricultural credit, can be offered in exchange for arms. In some contexts the offer of a lump sum on demobilization appears to have been quite effective (for example, after the Ugandan and Mozambique wars—see Collier 1994; Dolan and Schafer 1997). Such policies can be expensive and need international support. Moreover, they are difficult to apply in less organized conflicts where large numbers move in and out of a conflict, and there is no clear demarcation between those who fought in the conflict and those who did not. Improving the income-earning opportunities for the young generally, especially for males, is then needed. To some extent this would happen by itself if peace were restored, as farms can again be worked on, and other private sector activities may resume (though some other war-related activities would cease). But in most cases there is likely to be an interval when special employment schemes or financial handouts may be needed.

As with the earlier policies, what is appropriate inevitably differs among countries. The general requirement is that these issues are explicitly considered when conflict is ending.

6.3. General development policies

Both general analysis and some of the econometric evidence suggest a connection between predisposition to conflict and levels and growth of per capita incomes, although the correlation is not strong (see Nafziger and Auvinen, Chapter 3; FitzGerald, forthcoming; Stewart, Humphrey and Lee 1997). Economic growth would be likely to reduce the propensity to conflict, if it is equitably distributed. Equitable and poverty reducing growth would normally be likely to reduce horizontal inequality, and might make persisting inequalities more tolerable. Hence policies that succeed in promoting such growth should form part of any pro-peace policy package. But it should be stressed that the growth must be widely shared. Inequitably distributed growth can re-enforce horizontal inequality and thus be conflict-promoting, as occurred, for example, in Rwanda.

A great deal of policy analysis has been devoted to delineating the conditions for widely shared growth. Policies include measures to promote human development especially through the spread of education; measures to increase savings and investment; price and technology policies to encourage labour-intensive technologies; new credit institutions to extend credit to the low-income; measures to encourage the informal sector; land reform and support for small farmers; international policies to improve market access and terms of trade and reduce debt burdens. Many of these policies can be designed specifically to reduce horizontal inequality as well as to promote growth and reduce poverty. There is no question that a successful development strategy of this kind would reduce conflict-propensity. However, it is difficult to envisage the success of such policies in countries with the major structural divisions which bring about a CHE. Hence, while successful development would undoubtedly contribute to our objective, it seems likely that the more specific policies discussed above concerning group differentials and individual incentives will be needed not only for themselves but also as preconditions for general development success.

Preventative policies are obviously especially needed in 'conflict-prone' countries. It is therefore necessary to determine which countries are 'conflict-prone'. Conflict proneness may be identified by the following characteristics: (i) serious past conflict at some time over the previous twenty years; (ii) evidence of a considerable degree of horizontal inequality; (iii) low incomes; (iv) economic stagnation, and (v) political conditions, including exclusionary political systems and arbitrary rule.

Condition (i) by itself is a serious sign, especially when one of the other four conditions is present. The analysis above suggests that the presence of (ii) together with either (iii), (iv) or (v) should be taken as indicating conflict-proneness even if there is no history of conflict. This is also broadly the conclusion of Stavenhagen.[14] The delineation of conflict-proneness is important because it would be more effective to focus conflict-prevention policies on the subset of most vulnerable countries, and also to channel aid and/or debt relief to these countries. Special care should also be taken in conflict-prone countries to avoid providing resources (in the form of aid or military assistance) which is likely to help finance conflict. This might seem an obvious point, yet the case studies show that international resources have poured into countries on the brink, or in the process, of conflict.

The subject of this volume is a large and evolving one, covering a huge range of countries and situations. Obviously, one research programme cannot achieve definitive conclusions. The findings of this chapter must in one sense be regarded as tentative. Yet because of the ongoing nature of these crises, it is important that action is taken on the basis of current knowledge, without waiting for further confirmation. It is in this spirit that the policy conclusions have been presented above as a set of definitive recommendations.

One conclusion stands out: in every complex humanitarian emergency there is an interaction between factors, with group perceptions and identity (normally historically formed), being enhanced by sharp group differentiation in political participation, economic assets and income and social access and well-being. Action on any one front alone is not likely to work—for example, addressing economic inequalities without political, or conversely; or attempting to 'educate' people to change their views of their identity and their imaginary communities without changing the underlying inequalities among groups.

---

[14] Writing of ethnic conflict, he concluded: 'When regional and social disparities in the distribution of economic resources also reflect differences between identified ethnic groups, then conflicts over social and economic issues readily turns into ethnic conflict' (Stavenhagen 1996: 294). But I believe this holds more widely to any form of differentiation among groups—religious, class, clan—not merely ethnic.

Table A1.1. The case studies summarized

Case	Relevant groups	Source of horizontal inequality	Perceptions	Economic development prior to conflict	State role	Resources	Comment
Afghanistan	Ideological (Communism v. Islam); ethnic (Pashtun v. non-Pashtun); factional	Control over external resources	Initially some ideological element—Islam v. communism; but increasingly became ethnic/ factional; 'the actors formed new alliances based on ethnic and regional considerations and purely opportunistical tactical criteria' (Rubin). Alliances shifting	Poor economy, but stable, pre-conflict	Weak state pre-1979. Destabilization through Soviet invasion. Post 1986 (Soviet withdrawal) state disintegrated	Resources supplied by USSR (up to 1986); US, Pakistan. Later unofficial flows from drug money; Islamic support; MNCs for pipelines. Heavy role of NGO on humanitarian side	War not caused by ethnic divisions, but they were one consequence. Main divisions 'local solidarity groups'. War acquired own logic. What kept it going not same as initial impetus. Society transformed from largely self-supporting peasant one to dependency on international donors and drug dealers
Bosnia and Herzegovina	Ethnic differences: Serbian, Croatian and Moslems	Political power and jobs	Extreme nationalist leaders promoted ethnic identity and mobilization	Economic stagnation; de-industrialization; IMF sponsored austerity programme; liberal reforms and economic decentralization	Weak state after rest of Yugoslavia disintegrated; reduced powers of state with economic reforms	Criminal networks and neighbouring states	Socialist years had held country together ideologically and through strong state. Post-socialism, the politically ambitious used identity politics as a source of power

Burundi	Hutu; Tutsi; (and Twa—small and irrelevant) [Tutsi minority]	Political; distinction between farming (Hutu) and cattle rearing (Tutsi); severe imbalances favouring Tutsi in land; education; govt. jobs; army; govt. investment; privatization	Hutu in exile developed new history claiming Hutu 'rightful moral and historical precedence'	Moderate growth 1960s–80s; stagnation 1990s in context of worsening international environment	Tutsi dominate govt. State sponsored selective killing of Hutu, 1972; and 1990s	Human rights violations by state ignored by international community—aid to govt.	Complex interactions between Burundi and Rwanda, on perceptions and fears
Cambodia	Peasants; élite (some overlapping ethnic dimension—peasants Khmer and some newly educated; élite Sino-Khmer and Vietnamese; also Muslim Cham targeted by Khmer Rouge)	Location—urban/rural; Occupation—élite and salaried versus peasants; education. All associated with large differences in incomes	Communist ideology of Khmer Rouge: "total revolution" … To redress injustice and remove the causes of oppression' (Le Billion and Bakker), including radical egalitarian collectivism	Economic stagnation from mid-1960s; high inequality and unemployment; even many of urban élite suffered	Weak state, 1970–75, state (and US) violence against opposition (large casualties); 1975–79 Khmer Rouge massive killings of élite and urban population	Resources for Khmer Rep. (1970–75) provided largely by US; aid and direct military support; Chinese support for Khmer Rouge; Soviet and Vietnam support for overthrow of Khmer Rouge and subsequent regime; West, China supported Khmer Rouge in civil war that followed	Political mismanagement (corruption/factionalism) combined with extreme impoverishment of peasants led to take-over by murderous left wing regime

Table A1.1. *cont.*

Case	Relevant groups	Source of horizontal inequality	Perceptions	Economic development prior to conflict	State role	Resources	Comment
Congo	Power-holder versus others in Mobutu era; also some ethnic divisions; post-Mobutu more distinctions and conflicts according to ethnicity	Ethnic divisions created by Colonial state, but became less important in early post-colonial era. Ethnic conflict and regional polarization did not emerge in the 1970s and 1980s on a major scale because of the patronage system Mobutu institutionalized. Ethnicity more salient in post-Mobutu era	Little ideology	Stagnation as rents used to enrich ruling class	Highly repressive state, end 1989 security apparatus employed 45,000. Mobutu state instigated violence to keep power	International support for Mobutu. Post-cold war withdrawn. Kabila received support from Uganda, resource hungry MNCs, and subsequently aid donors. Subsequently, Uganda supported Tutsi rebels against Kabila; Zimbabwe supported Kabila	Sporadic state terrorism throughout Mobutu era. Major CHE avoided by Mobutu state repression and patronage which operated with regional bias rather than ethnic
El Salvador	Landlords peasants [landlords minority]	Political; land distribution highly unequal between classes; communal property abolished 1882	FMLN (leading violent opposition), communist inspired. US characterized conflict as 'textbook case of armed aggression by communist powers'	Healthy growth prior to conflict, slowed down as tensions mounted	Violent repression	US supported state with finance; equipment	As importance of business class increased and that of landed élite reduced, pressure for peace increased

Haiti	Élite surrounding President versus others (mainly peasants; also black middle class)	Control over state resources among 19th century cliques. Cliques; education; language; land; econ. opportunities	Latin American liberation theology. Populist movement, anti-dictatorial and corrupt regime	Downward trend, worsened by international sanctions, 1991–4	Duvalier strong repressed all opposition. Aristide attacked corruption and privilege, provoking military coup	International community supported Duvalier dictatorship; sanctions v. 1991 military, and eventually UN invasion to restore democracy	Similar to Central America; privileged and corrupt elite versus masses
Iraq	Chiefly Iraq nation versus world; plus Kurds	Within Iraq strong discrimination in all resources against Kurds; and élite domination of govt. jobs and contracts	Nationalistic rhetoric of Hussein	High growth until the launch of attack against Iran, 1980. Negative subsequently	State initiated violence against Iran, Kuwait and Kurds	Enormous human suffering caused by international sanctions	Internal opposition suppressed by strong state
Kenya	Ethnic groups	Political; and economic, social differentiation. Economically and socially favoured group (Kikuyu), not in Moi alliance; not favoured for investment or patronage etc.	Ethnic dimension not explicit in govt. statements or opposition but voting largely on ethnic lines	Economic growth, fairly widely shared across ethnicities, 1960s–1980s. Stagnation in 1990s	Some state sponsored violence, not large-scale. Fairly strong state repression of opposition	International support for regime strong for most of period. Some wavering in 1990s with attacks on corruption and democratic conditionality	Broad ethnic alliance of Moi, with exceptions of Kikuyu. But Kikuyu benefited from market economy. Danger with economic stagnation

Table A1.1. *cont.*

Case	Relevant groups	Source of horizontal inequality	Perceptions	Economic development prior to conflict	State role	Resources	Comment
Liberia	Strongmen and factions; Americo-Liberians; locals	Political; control over state resources; natural resources	War essentially commercial operation; little ideology on any side	Economic decline	State drastically undermined as aid fell and NGO share rose; patronage reduced; could no longer maintain control		
Rwanda	Hutu; Tutsi; Twa - very small [Tutsi minority]	Political; colonial era: sharp inequalities favouring Tutsi—in education, employment, political participation. Post-colonial Hutu gained power. Privileged class of Tutsi remained. But all policies—employment, aid projects etc., army, diplomatic service, parliament reserved for Hutu. Access of Tutsi to higher education and	Ideology of Hutu power: 'Rwanda belongs to the Hutu, who were its true inhabitants, but had been subjugated brutally for centuries by . . . the Tutsi (Uvin). Ethnic images supported by proverbs, stories and myths from colonial times	Sustained growth in per capita incomes, 1965–88	State sponsored violence against Tutsi, culminating in genocidal attack, 1995	Generous aid, (among highest in world) used in highly discriminating way. Govt. praised for development orientation and appropriate objectives by World Bank Report 1989	High levels of poverty and illiteracy among Hutu. Majority did not benefit from aid. Govt. used violence against Hutu as way of maintaining support

Sierra Leone	Strongmen; factions.	Political; control over state resources; natural resources; state jobs limited by quota. Ethnic IDs	As Liberia	Economic decline	State undermined by loss of control over diamond revenue as taken by illicit consortia; aid increasingly directed to projects, not available for patronage; IMF reforms reducing size of state	Diminished state revenue; turned to private sources of finance and private security firm (Executive Outcomes); rebels controlled some natural resources	Neither ethnic, class, region or ideology—war as a means of private accumulative, action supported by foreign firms as they saw their interests threatened
Somalia	Clans (key); Classes (state dependent modern petite bourgeoisie / bureaucrats and ordinary Somali); agriculturalists / pastoralists	Control over state resources; agriculturalists favoured relative to pastoralists; land reform favoured modern élites against traditional agriculturalists	Clan distinctions emphasized for political ends. (For example, 'We are Darod—we are wealthy, religious and educated whereas the mental capacity of the Hawiye is limited: they come from the bush' (Kivimäki from interview)	Economic stagnation and decline 1980s and 1990s	State sponsored violence under Barre (1969–91); Barre followed divide and rule policy among clans. Post-Barre state power almost non-existent	1980s ODA very high. Important source of state resources. Source of élite rivalry. US military support to Barre up to 1989. 1992 Operation Restore Hope achieved little	Clan divisions used by élites in fight to control resources in context of weak state. Situation made worse by generous aid resources. Use of traditional dispute resolution mechanisms beginning to work

Table A1.1. *cont.*

Case	Relevant groups	Source of horizontal inequality	Perceptions	Economic development prior to conflict	State role	Resources	Comment
Transcaucasia	Religious, ethnic and among clans	Soviet supported 'nominated' nationalist élite, and discriminated against minorities, politically and economically	Nationalist ideology, used as mobilizing force, against Soviet domination and in favour of particular nationalities	Severe economic decline in the 1990s. Vertical inequality low, but rising. Inflation reached very high levels mid-1990s	Strong State in Soviet era suppressed uprisings. Post-Soviet era, state severely weakened both in economic and military ways	Paramilitary groups got resources from drugs and criminal activities. Weapons taken from Soviet depots	Many divisions across religions and nationalities erupted as Russia and the communist party lost power
Zimbabwe (Matabeleland)	Political, geographic and ethnic	Political power	Political overtly: state argued that violent rebellion threatened. Labelled as ethnic by foreign observers. Ethnic perceptions enhanced by conflict	Moderate economic progress	Majority democratic govt. led violence in order to suppress opposition	Govt. resources abundantly funded by taxation etc.	Conflict aimed at political opposition but became ethnic in practice. No strong economic basis apparent

Source: country studies, Volume 2.

References

Alnasrawi, A. (forthcoming). 'Iraq: Economic Embargo and Predatory Rule', in E. Wayne Nafziger, Frances Stewart and Raimo Väyrynen (eds.), *Weak States and Vulnerable Economies: Humanitarian Emergencies in Developing Countries*, Volume 2 of *War, Hunger and Displacement: The Origins of Humanitarian Emergencies*. Oxford: Oxford University Press.

Anand, S. (1983). *Inequality and Poverty in Malaysia*. Oxford: Oxford University Press.

Auvinen, J., and T. Kivimäki (forthcoming). 'Somalia: The Struggle for Resources', in E. Wayne Nafziger, Frances Stewart and Raimo Väyrynen (eds.), *Weak States and Vulnerable Economies: Humanitarian Emergencies in Developing Countries*, Volume 2 of *War, Hunger and Displacement: The Origins of Humanitarian Emergencies*. Oxford: Oxford University Press.

Auvinen, J., and E. W. Nafziger (1999). 'The Sources of Humanitarian Emergencies'. *Journal of Conflict Resolution*, 43 (3) June: 267–90.

Cohen, A. (1974). *Two-Dimensional Man, An Essay on the Anthropology of Power and Symbolism in Complex Society*. Berkeley, CA: University of California Press.

Collier, P. (1994). 'Demobilisation and Insecurity: A Study in the Economics of the Transition from War to Peace'. *Journal of International Development*, 6: 343–52.

Dasgupta, Partha (1993). *An Inquiry into Well-Being and Destitution*. Oxford: Clarendon Press.

De Waal, A. (1989). *Famine that Kills: Darfur, Sudan 1984–5*. Oxford: Clarendon Press.

Dolan, C., and J. Schafer (1997). 'The Reintegration of Ex-combatants in Mozambique: Manica and Zambezia Provinces'. Final Report to USAID. Oxford: Refugee Studies Programme, Queen Elizabeth House.

Emizet, K. (forthcoming). 'Congo (Zaire): Corruption, Disintegration, and State Failure', in E. Wayne Nafziger, Frances Stewart and Raimo Väyrynen (eds.), *Weak States and Vulnerable Economies: Humanitarian Emergencies in Developing Countries*, Volume 2 of *War, Hunger and Displacement: The Origins of Humanitarian Emergencies*. Oxford: Oxford University Press.

Fei, J., G. Ranis, and S. Kuo (1978). 'Growth and Family Distribution of Income by Factor Components'. *Quarterly Journal of Economics*, XCII: 17–53.

FitzGerald, E. K. V. (forthcoming). 'Global Linkages, Vulnerable Economies and the Outbreak of Conflict', in E. Wayne Nafziger and Raimo Väyrynen (eds.), *War and Destitution: The Prevention of Humanitarian Emergencies*. London: Macmillan.

Gaffney, P. (forthcoming). 'Burundi: The Long Sombre Shadow of Ethnic Instability', in E. Wayne Nafziger, Frances Stewart and Raimo Väyrynen (eds.), *Weak States and Vulnerable Economies: Humanitarian Emergencies in Developing Countries*, Volume 2 of *War, Hunger and Displacement: The Origins of Humanitarian Emergencies*. Oxford: Oxford University Press.

Gurr, T. (1993). *Minorities at Risk: a Global View of Ethnopolitical Conflict*. Washington, DC: United States Institute for Peace Press.

Gurr, T. R., and B. Harff (1995). *Early Warning of Communal Conflicts and Genocide. Linking Empirical Research to International Responses*. Tokyo. The United Nations University Press.

IASC (International Assembly of Security Council) (1994). 'Working Paper on the Definition of Complex Emergencies' (including comments made by participants) prepared in connection with the Xth meeting of IASC. 9 December. New York: UN.

Keen, D. (1994). *The Political Economy of Famine and Relief in Southwestern Sudan, 1983–1989*. Princeton, NJ: Princeton University Press.

Keen, D. (1998). 'The Economic Functions of Civil Wars'. *Adelphi Paper* 320: 1–88. London: International Institute of Strategic Studies.

Klugman, J. (forthcoming). 'Kenya: Economic Decline and Ethnic Politics', in E. Wayne Nafziger, Frances Stewart and Raimo Väyrynen (eds.), *Weak States and Vulnerable Economies: Humanitarian Emergencies in Developing Countries*, Volume 2 of *War, Hunger and Displacement: The Origins of Humanitarian Emergencies*. Oxford: Oxford University Press.

Lake, D., and D. Rothschild (eds.) (1998). *The International Spread of Ethnic Conflict. Fear, Diffusion, and Escalation*. Princeton: Princeton University Press.

Le Billon, Philippe and K. Bakker (forthcoming). 'Cambodia: Genocide, Autocracy, and the Overpoliticized State', in E. Wayne Nafziger, Frances Stewart and Raimo Väyrynen (eds.), *Weak States and Vulnerable Economies: Humanitarian Emergencies in Developing Countries*, Volume 2 of *War, Hunger and Displacement: The Origins of Humanitarian Emergencies*. Oxford: Oxford University Press.

Malkki, L. (1995). *Purity and Exile: Violence, Memory and National Cosmology among Hutu Refugees in Tanzania*. Chicago: Chicago University Press.

Mohonk Criteria for Humanitarian Assistance in Complex Emergencies (1994). New York: World Conference on Peace and Religion.

Nafziger, E. W., and R. Väyrynen (eds.) (forthcoming). *War and Destitution: The Prevention of Humanitarian Emergencies*, London: Macmillan.

Posen, B. (1993). 'The Security Dilemma and Ethnic Conflict', in M. E. Brown (ed.) *Ethnic Conflict and International Security*. Princeton: Princeton University Press.

Reno, W. (forthcoming). 'Liberia and Sierra Leone: The Competition for Patronage in Resource-Rich Economies', in E. Wayne Nafziger, Frances Stewart and Raimo Väyrynen (eds.), *Weak States and Vulnerable Economies: Humanitarian Emergencies in Developing Countries*, Volume 2 of *War, Hunger and Displacement: The Origins of Humanitarian Emergencies*. Oxford: Oxford University Press.

Rubin, Barnett R. (forthcoming). 'Afghanistan: The Last Cold War Conflict, The First Post-Cold War Conflict, in E. Wayne Nafziger, Frances Stewart and Raimo Väyrynen (eds.), *Weak States and Vulnerable Economies: Humanitarian Emergencies in Developing Countries*, Volume 2 of *War, Hunger and Displacement: The Origins of Humanitarian Emergencies*. Oxford: Oxford University Press.

Rummel, R. J. (1997). *Power Kills. Democracy as a Method of Nonviolence*. New Brunswick, NJ: Transaction Publishers.

Smith, A. D. (1988). 'The Myth of the "Modern Nation" and the Myths of Nations'. *Ethnic and Racial Studies*, 11: 1–25.

Smith, A. D. (1991). 'The Nation: Invented, Imagined, Reconstructed?' *Millenium: Journal of International Studies*, 20: 353–68.

Stavenhagen, R. (ed.) (1996). *Ethnic Conflict and the Nation State*. New York, St. Martin's Press.

Stewart, F., F. Humphrey, and Nick Lee (1997). 'Civil Conflict in Developing

Countries over the Last Quarter of a Century: An Empirical Overview of Economic and Social Consequences. *Oxford Development Studies*, 25 (1).

Stewart, F., and M. O'Sullivan (1999). 'Democracy, Conflict and Development—Three Cases', in G. Ranis *et al.* (eds.), *The Political Economy of Comparative Developments into the 21st Century, Essays in Memory of John Fei*. Hants: Edward Elgar.

Turton, D. (1997). 'War and Ethnicity: Global Connections and Local Violence in North East Africa and Former Yugoslavia'. *Oxford Development Studies*, 25: 77–94.

Uvin, P. (forthcoming). 'Rwanda: The Social Roots of Genocide', in E. Wayne Nafziger, Frances Stewart and Raimo Väyrynen (eds.), *Weak States and Vulnerable Economies: Humanitarian Emergencies in Developing Countries*, Volume 2 of *War, Hunger and Displacement: The Origins of Humanitarian Emergencies*. Oxford: Oxford University Press.

Voutira, E. (1998). 'The Language of Complex Humanitarian Emergencies'. Paper prepared for UNU/WIDER/Queen Elizabeth House (Oxford) Programme on The Political Economy of Humanitarian Emergencies. Helsinki, 6–8 October 1996.

Wallensteen, P., and M. Sollenberg (1997). 'Armed Conflicts, Conflict Termination and Peace Agreements, 1989–96'. *Journal of Peace Research*, 34 (3): 353–70.

2

Complex Humanitarian Emergencies: Concepts and Issues

RAIMO VÄYRYNEN

1. The Age of Dualism

Complex humanitarian emergencies (CHE) are the ultimate manifestation of the economic fragmentation, political turmoil, and human suffering that are spreading in the less developed part of the world. These emergencies can result both from deliberate and predatory governmental policies and the general anarchy and lawlessness prevailing in the society. In both cases, the key aspect of humanitarian crises is usually large-scale domestic violence which, in addition to killing people, exacerbates the existing problems of external and internal displacement of people, their food provision, and health care. The use of military force has, of course, a rationale, often the lust for power and wealth by warring parties, but it may have been also propelled by a missionary ideology or hardened and competitive nationalist identities. Complex humanitarian emergencies manifest infrapolitical violence which is embedded in social structures and thus lead to everyday suffering of the people. They have personal and social identities, but in the global media they are often treated as nameless masses almost as if they were not a part of the same humankind. Media reports on humanitarian disasters often deteriorate into stereotyping of the victims and their plight (Moeller 1998).

1.1. The declining state

The twentieth century has been called the 'age of extremes', 'century of total wars', and 'century of genocides'. These characterizations are based on the unprecedented human and physical damage of warfare, caused by the use of nuclear, chemical, and conventional weapons on the battlefields. The carnage of the twentieth century has not been limited to the world wars and major regional conflicts, but violence has also pervaded every-day life. In the 1990s, the certainty of bipolarity and nuclear deterrence has yielded to uncertainty and unpredictability or, as Eric Hobsbawm (1994:

562) has remarked, 'The century ended in a global disorder whose nature
was unclear, and without an obvious mechanism for either ending it or
keeping it under control'. The ongoing transition to a new international
system is unstable, including recurrent resort to military force, deepening
socio-economic gaps, and the mobility of people within and across borders. The risk of nuclear holocaust has receded, but the danger of civil
wars, refugee crises, and famines is as least as real as during the cold war.

These crises are often linked with the dissolution of state structures
which manifests itself in two different ways: the local power centres and
the central state have antagonistic mutual relations and/or they both have
their own transnational connections undermining the coherence of the
state. In fact, the world may be entering a new era of non-state civil conflict and infrapolitical violence. Fueled by differences in political ambitions, economic interests, and ethnic identities, civil conflicts reflect
tensions between state sovereignty and self-determination and manifest in
entirely new types of security threats (Rondos 1994).

The state is globally in decline; in the industrial world, the state's power
is delegated and evaporating, while especially in developing and transitional countries its monopoly over coercive power is weakening. The loss
of the state's power monopoly has resulted in 'the democratization and
privatization of the means of destruction, which transformed the prospect
of violence and wreckage *anywhere* on the globe' (Hobsbawm 1994: 560;
emphasis in the original). Indeed, most wars occur in disintegrating polities; either states or multinational empires. The traditional assumption
that domestic systems are based on a hierarchical and enforceable public
order, while interstate relations are anarchical and insecure, has been seriously challenged by recent experiences. In particular, peripheral states are
becoming internally anarchical, failing to perform the basic political and
economic tasks expected from sovereign states (Holsti 1995).

The fragmentation of state structures has fostered the emergence of non-
state actors as parties to civil wars; they include armed political clans, ethnic military bands, and mercenaries. Such non-state actors have seldom a
strategic, long-term political rationale for using force. Instead, their goals
are usually rather concrete and short term, i.e., the acquisition of wealth
and power for the group and its leaders. Thus, in a larger sense, they are
'rebels without a cause'. The crumbling of the state structures, together
with the deterioration of economic and ecological conditions, has given
rise to fears that the world is sliding into a medieval anarchy.

The future prospect is not entirely bleak, however. Instead, the world
seems to be entering a new phase of development under the influence of
novel and contradictory trends. During the cold war, the proneness of a
country to external intervention depended, in the first place, on its capabilities and position in the spheres-of-influence arrangement. No wars
were waged across the bloc divide, but they occurred, instead, within an

established sphere of influence, especially in the Soviet zone and Western hemisphere, or in regions where the sphere was contested. In the latter case, civil wars were waged, with the help of the great powers, in the contested zones, including Afghanistan, Angola, Ethiopia, Mozambique, Nicaragua, and Somalia.

During the cold war, adequate defense capabilities and internal stability helped countries, as a rule, to remain outside violent conflicts. On the other hand, many industrialized countries have frequently intervened, often for imperial reasons, in weak peripheral states. French war-fighting in Algeria and Indochina, Portuguese colonial wars in Africa, US interventions in Vietnam and the Caribbean, and the Soviet occupation of Afghanistan are examples of such involvements.

In the wake of the twentieth century, with the exception of the crisis over Kosovo and the border war between Eritrea and Ethiopia, warfare in interstate relations is a rare event; these relations have been mostly pacified and the risk of a major interstate war seems to be increasingly remote. This is the case both between the core and peripheral countries and within these groups. The real possibility of a major interstate war seems to exist only in the Korean Peninsula, South Asia, the Middle East, and the Persian Gulf, while, on the other hand, the probability of civil wars seems to be very limited in these areas. This obviously raises the question whether there is a trade-off between interstate and civil wars, the former possibly repressing the latter.

Robert O'Connell (1995) traces the origins of war to the rise of agricultural societies and their struggles for territory and natural resources. In the second phase, war became increasingly associated with the growth of the bureaucratic-industrial state which accumulated capabilities for large-scale physical and human destruction (Porter 1994). With the decline of agriculture and subsequently of mass industrialization, and the rise of information societies, war seems to be waning as a social institution, especially among the industrialized countries. This trend means that violence may continue to devastate low-income, agricultural regions where the control of scarce productive land and other resources still matters. On the other hand, the spread of digital capitalism has created an economy where the prosperity of society depends on intellectual and social capital rather than on material resources. These forms of capital cannot be conquered by military means, but only destroyed by them.

As the emergence of information society portends economic renewal, social pluralism, and peace, people in the industrialized countries should be reasonably optimistic about the future. In the last couple of decades, famines and disease, with some African exceptions, have been under better control than perhaps ever before in the human history. Life expectancy has been increasing in most parts of the world and most contagious diseases have been tamed by more effective and fairer health care systems.

Improvements in food production and distribution systems have made mass starvation an unlikely event in most countries. On the other hand, new diseases or more resistant variants of the old ones have become more common again. Famines continue to plague some regions (they were again in 1999 a real risk in Somalia and Sudan, for instance) and in some others, ominous signs exist about the food production increasingly lagging behind the population increase. The dualism of our age is manifested in the fact that progress in providing food security has been accompanied by no decline in the absolute number of undernourished people in the world (Parikh 1990).

Although most people are still firmly attached to their home territories, there is an unmistakable global trend towards the growing mobility of people both within and between societies. Much of that mobility is voluntary and motivated by hopes for a better life. In the mid-1990s, the global stock of immigrants was about 125 million. Net gains in immigration have been the biggest in North America and Western Europe, while Asia and Latin America have been the main providers of immigrants. Intra-regional differences are significant; for instance, South, Central, and North Africa have been net recipients of migrants, while East and West Africa have been net providers (Martin and Widgren 1996). While Russians are firmly attached to their home ground, more than 9 million people in the former Soviet Union left their homes in the 1990s because of economic decline, ethnic tensions, and ecological disasters.

Even the non-political movements of people can be unsettling. Mass migrations can lead in their destinations to cultural and ethnic tensions and distributional conflicts between the local people and the immigrants who may be perceived both as an economic burden and a security threat (Weiner 1995). In addition to non-political mobility across borders, the number of refugees has significantly grown in the 1990s, due to the political and military instabilities and the collapse of social order within states, though their number has very recently turned to some decline.

The existence of dualist patterns in warfare, famines, disease, and displacement reflects the bifurcated nature of the present era. This dualism is largely due to the rapid and uneven accumulation of economic assets in some regions and deprivation in others. The distribution of world income among states is increasingly bimodal as both wealth and misery have concentrated (Jones 1997). The world is becoming more polarized not only along the north-south cleavage, but also within regions and societies. This trend is, in turn, accompanied by increasing social and economic vulnerabilities to disasters.

Major humanitarian emergencies have been absent in the industrial core of the world and in the group of countries catching up. The world has experienced a lot of savagery after World War II, but little of it has occurred in developed countries. Neither has violence been organized in the world primarily along ethnic or civilizational lines. Solid economic growth and democracy at home, and integration with the world market, seem to be effective antidotes to human-made disasters as they cushion the population against potential natural disasters and enhance the society's capacity to cope with emergencies (Sadowski 1998).

On the other hand, humanitarian crises have been amply present in the world's peripheries. While democracy and interdependence prevail in the north, chaos and fragmentation reign in many parts of the south. Benign economic and political conditions in the north, as a rule, prevent the outbreak of major interstate wars or internal crises, but the periphery remains vulnerable in both respects; contrasts between the core and periphery are stark indeed (Goldgeier and Vescera 1992). From a global perspective, most of the core is a 'zone of peace', while much of the periphery is located in a 'zone of turmoil' (Singer and Wildavsky 1993). Thus, humanitarian welfare is vested with a top position in the world system, while humanitarian emergencies grow out of poverty and marginalization.

The world economic change interacts with the transformation of the international political order from a territorial, state-based system to a more multilayered and fragmented one. In the north, advances in communication technology, financial interpenetration, and cultural integration have all eroded the territorial political control. Yet, the states in the north seem to control more effectively their national territories and societies than those in the south where the failure to perform their basic functions is common. Especially in Africa, external economic discipline shrinks public spending, economic development fails to take off, ethnic differences lead to hostilities, and new centres of power arise to contest the government monopoly of force. Instead of operating as a coherent unit, economy becomes a network of connections between the mercantile cities and the hinterland locations controlling some saleable assets (Ayoob 1995; Ellis 1996).

Humanitarian emergencies manifest the dualist pattern of the current international development. Concurrent with the progress in peace, interdependence, and development, the world has experienced in recent years some of its worst economic, social, and human catastrophes. These crises have not been individual aberrations, but signs of a deeper, unsettling trend which portends continuing death and suffering of people, especially in developing countries. Neither can these cataclysms be traced to any single cause, but they can be due to 'rurality' (poor conditions of peasants), 'landslide crises' of socio-economic character, 'one-party state' (totalitarianism), 'missionary ideology' (nationalism or other life-or-death convictions), or other comparable factors (Nairn 1997).

1.2. New vulnerabilities

Emergencies can be due to nature (for example, hurricanes and earth-quakes), technology (for example, nuclear and mining accidents), mis-managed economy (for example, crop failure and deforestation), or politics (for example, war and human rights violations). Over a short term, man cannot much influence natural calamities, while technological, eco-nomic, and political disasters are caused by human interventions or their failures (Richmond 1994). Often, though, the natural sources of dangers and human interventions interact with each other.

As pointed out above, disasters happen in many guises.[1] The number of human emergencies has roughly doubled in every decade since the 1960s when an annual average of 53 disasters was reported while in the 1970s and the 1980s, 113 and 223 disasters took place, respectively. In the 1980s, the most common natural disasters were floods, earthquakes, and wind-storms victimizing people by killing, injuring, and making them homeless. In 1971–95 natural calamities claimed three million deaths; two-thirds of them in Africa. Measured by the number of victims, the most devastating disasters have been droughts and famines, earthquakes, cyclones, and floods. If measured by the number of people killed in and affected by dis-asters, the picture is less consistent. In the period 1972–96, the number of people affected or made homeless is increasing rather steadily, but mea-sured by the number of people killed, the periods of 1977–81 and 1992–96 have witnessed only minor emergencies (Albala-Bertrand 1993; Blaikie *et al.* 1994; *World Disasters Report* 1995, 1997, and 1998).

These trends suggest the increasing vulnerability of societies to disas-ters, due, among other things, to deforestation, land erosion, and increas-ing social polarization and marginalization, especially among the poor in developing countries. Marginalization means that poor people are pushed to live in conditions which are either physically dangerous (for example hillside slums) or unable to provide adequate living (for example, South Africa's bantustans and impoverished grazing lands). Social exclusion is itself a potential source of humanitarian crisis, but it also indirectly increases the vulnerability of people to extreme physical events. Vulnerability is, in fact, the key to understanding the exposure of social groups to humanitarian disasters (Susman, O'Keefe and Wisner 1983; Albala-Bertrand 1993; Alexander 1997).

Increasing vulnerability of societies to physical disasters can be traced to a chain of factors. A comprehensive study argues that the progression of vulnerability starts from root causes, such as limited access to power and resources which, in turn, permit dynamic pressures to operate. These pressures can be both global (for example, rapid population growth,

---

[1] On the various types, phases, and effects of natural disasters, see Cuny (1983: 21–61).

urbanization, economic and environmental crises) and local (for example, the lack of institutions, resources, and skills). Finally, should natural disasters occur, their adverse effects multiply as growing dynamic pressures translate stronger root causes into unsafe conditions of the people. These unsafe conditions are manifested in increasingly fragile environmental and economic conditions and the lack of local institutional and resource capabilities to respond to physical hazards (Blaikie *et al.* 1994; see also Alexander 1997).

An important lesson of this model is that while global factors may catalyse the progression of vulnerability, the root causes of crises are ultimately located in the domestic political and economic systems. Thus, the causes of the recent humanitarian crises can hardly be traced directly to increasing global dynamic pressures, although they can affect societies in which the root causes of emergencies are brewing. Moreover, global economic pressures and their local consequences may also increase the possibility of some hazards, especially flooding and landslides, resulting from the overuse and erosion of soil.

In summary, the propensity of societies to humanitarian crises is affected primarily by two sets of factors: dissolution of the political order and increasing vulnerability of the people in exposed groups and societies. The decline of the state permits the resort to subnational violence, weakens the capacity to meet the basic needs of citizens, and gives a greater role to fear and revenge. Vulnerability increases both as a result of poverty and social inequality, which marginalize increasing numbers of people, and the deterioration of economic and environmental living conditions. Usually, the decline of the state and increasing socio-economic vulnerability interact with each other in bringing about a humanitarian crisis.

This chapter aims to define and operationalize the concept of a humanitarian emergency, describe its characteristics, and assess its consequences. A thorough analysis of the root causes of humanitarian emergencies is possible only if we define and specify the class of such events. The focus of this definitional effort is on the pivotal role of violence in human suffering, but also in bringing about other negative consequences, such as hunger, disease, and displacement. Keeping in mind the multidimensionality of a humanitarian emergency, we will define it as a *profound social crisis in which large numbers of people unequally die and suffer from war, displacement, hunger, and disease owing to human-made and natural disasters.*

2. Genocide and War

2.1. *Genocide and politicide*

In the effort to define a humanitarian emergency, a major issue concerns
the choice between absolute and relative measures of suffering as they
assess the loss of human life differently. Both measures are justified, but
by different arguments. If the life of each and every individual is valued
equally, then the absolute death toll should be the yardstick of the seriousness of an emergency. On the other hand, if group rights are emphasized, then seriousness depends on the share of community members
perishing in war, famine, or disease.

To explore whether genocide is a prototypical humanitarian emergency,
one may refer to the absolute measures of human losses by Rummel who
has listed 17 mass murders in the twentieth century in which a minimum
of one million people have been killed. Rummel's list of 'democides' is
topped by the 'Soviet Gulag State' (62 million victims), followed by the
'Communist Chinese Anthill' (35 million), and the 'Nazi Genocide State'
(21 million). In all, 169 million people have been killed during this century
in large-scale collective violence (Rummel 1994).

People can be mass-murdered, either at home or abroad, only by an
effective and repressive state machinery. In 'internal' mass-murders, the
aim is to spread terror and eliminate the 'enemy of the people' to prevent
with this action the emergence of anti-government opposition. This
requires that the victimized group is singled out and segregated by
racial, ethnic, religious, or class criteria and then destroyed. While mass
murder may also be motivated by economic gain, it is more likely perpetrated in the name of an undemocratic ideology and state power. Thus,
'power kills', but 'democracies don't murder their citizens' (Rummel
1997: 91–8).

A genocidal state can be said to possess despotic power which refers to
the 'distributive power of state elites over civil society'. To be able to exercise despotic power, the state needs also infrastructural power, i.e. institutional capacity to penetrate the society. Together, these two forms of
power provide the basis for an 'authoritarian' state. The state can obtain
effective despotic power only if it uproots the civil society and its capacity
to resist (Mann 1993: 59–60).

The cruel exercise of despotic power requires the dehumanization of
opponents whose badness must be proved by historical and social reconstruction. The rise of despotism is made more likely if the power élite
holds vengeful memories of the past wrongs inflicted by its opponents.
The sense of revenge, motivated by fear and the lust for power, may lead
to forceful efforts to eliminate 'alien' values and purify the society of the
elements representing them (Indonesian massacres in 1965 provide an

example). The death toll increases if the military supports the political élite and its mission to destroy its enemies by massive violence (Chirot 1994).

Theories stressing the genocidal nature of the authoritarian state ideology can be contrasted with structural theories focusing either on deep social divisions, systemic repression, or empire-building (Fein 1990). Historically, colonial expansion involved genocides that annihilated entire peoples. Mass killings of Hereros in South West Africa (Namibia) by the Germans, native Americans by the European settlers, and Siberian tribes by Russians provide further examples of genocidal policies pursued by the expanding powers. States have also killed tribal people to clear the way for government and companies to exploit natural resources on tribal lands. This has happened, for instance, in Bangladesh, Brazil, and Burma (Bodley 1992).

The Convention on the Prevention and Punishment of the Crime of Genocide, passed by the UN General Assembly in 1948, defines genocide in its Art. II as:

... the intent to destroy, in whole or in part, a national, ethnic, racial, or religious group as such: (i) killing members of the group; (ii) causing serious bodily or mental harm to members of the group; (iii) deliberately inflicting on the group conditions of life calculated to bring about its physical destruction in whole or in part; (iv) imposing measures intended to prevent births within the group; (v) forcibly transferring children of the group to another group.

This legal definition has two major implications; to qualify as genocide, murderous policy does not need to be total if it is directed at a 'national, ethnic, racial, or religious group'. Therefore, 'genocide could take place even when it was employed partially, as a method of weakening rather than murdering all the members of a people' (Rieff 1996: 33). According to another definition,

... genocide is sustained purposeful action by a perpetrator to physically destroy a collectivity directly or indirectly, through interdiction of the biological and social reproduction of group members, sustained regardless of the surrender or lack of threat offered by the victim (Fein 1990: 23–25; also Fein 1993: 818).

A common feature in these definitions is that the distinctiveness of genocide is attributed to the intentional and persistent nature of murders by its perpetrators (Chalk 1994). The ways of the legal UN definition and political approaches are, however, parted in one important respect; the former excludes the destruction of political and social classes from the definition, while the latter tend to include them. Social classes are explicitly included in the definition by Chalk (1994: 49–53) who argues that, 'genocide is a form of one-sided mass killing in which a state or other authority intends to destroy a group, as that group and membership in it are defined by the perpetrator'. The reason for excluding political murders from the legal definition of genocide is, not surprisingly, political. In the aftermath of World War II, especially the USSR was unwilling to accept political criteria in the definition as that would have criminalized Stalin's purges of ideological 'enemies'.

Strict adherence to the UN definition of genocide leads to both empirically and ethically untenable conclusions as exemplified by the Cambodian case. In 1975–77, Pol Pot's regime killed close to one-fifth of Cambodia's population of eight million people. Inhabitants of Phnom Penh and other urban centres were evacuated to the countryside where most killings took place. Victims of the Khmer Rouge government included ethnic minorities, such as the Chinese, Vietnamese and various religious groups, especially Buddhist monks, but most of them were fellow Khmers. To conclude that the Cambodian tragedy was not a genocide because of its primarily ideological nature, would be either the worst kind of academic hairsplitting or political whitewash to justify Khmer Rouge's particular brand of communism and the support of Western powers to it (Kiernan 1996).

There is a growing consensus that the systematic elimination of political opponents ('politicides' as opposed to 'ethnicides') must be included in the definition of genocide. The literature on genocides contains extensive efforts to define and categorize them (Harff and Gurr 1987; Charny 1994). This is not the place to discuss these categories in any detail, but only to pay attention to two crucial interrelated issues: (i) have genocidal policies to rely on the use of physical violence; and (ii) what is the relationship of internal war to genocide? Genocides do not necessarily require the use of physical force, but people may also perish because of ecological destruction (Charny 1994) or their identities may be shattered by cultural genocide.

To qualify as genocide, the policies of perpetrators must be intentional. In 1958–61 perhaps 30 million rural Chinese perished in the Great Leap Famine which resulted from the introduction of agricultural production brigades as the basis of the rural economy. The failure of this ideological experiment was obvious from its early stages, but the communist leadership continued it in spite of the tragic consequences. Does the Great Leap qualify as genocide? It appears that contrary to Stalin's policy, the primary intention of Mao Zedong was not to kill rural people because of their social class, but to try an ideological solution to the problem of agricultural productivity despite its huge costs. Thus, the Great Leap was not genocide, but a massive humanitarian disaster caused by misdirected, unresponsive, and authoritarian policies of the Chinese Communists in general and Mao Zedong in particular (Becker 1996; Yang 1996).

Similarly, one can argue that the famine in North Korea, which has killed about 1.5 million people since 1995, is not genocide, but a humanitarian crisis due to Kim Il Jong's autocratic policies. On the other hand, the deaths in China and North Korea are produced by a political system that

has been intentionally constructed to serve specific ideological and material purposes. In that sense, large-scale death is caused by a human
agency which should be held accountable for the suffering. A common
feature of genocides and humanitarian emergencies is that they are both
intentionally produced. While it is true that most humanitarian disasters
are linked with civil wars and politicides, one cannot entirely exclude the
cases in which death and suffering are produced by governments by
means other than direct violence.

After World War II, genocides have claimed up to 2.6 times the number
of lives lost in natural disasters and as many victims as in all organized
warfare in the world (Harff and Gurr 1987; Fein 1993). Fein identifies 19
cases of genocide from the end of World War II to the late 1980s. These lists
contain cases which continued to plague the world in the 1990s, especially
Afghanistan, El Salvador, Ethiopia, and Sri Lanka (Harff and Gurr 1987;
Fein 1990). Genocides/politicides are often associated with civil wars,
partly because such wars open up new opportunities to murderous policies (Krain 1997). Genocides are, however, more intentional and systematic in nature than civil wars; they aim to annihilate systematically an
ethnic, religious, linguistic, and/or political group perceived as an obstacle to the policies of the perpetrator. For this purpose, the perpetrator not
only kills people, but may also destroy the living environment, communal
structure, and cultural identity of the target group. Thus, while the
absolute number of victims matters, the intensity of genocide depends on
the effort to eliminate political, ethnic, and cultural diversity in society.

According to a narrow definition, the twentieth century has witnessed
three genocides; the Ottoman massacre of the Armenians in 1915, the
Holocaust during World War II, and the extermination of Tutsis in
Rwanda in 1994. On the other hand, this definition of genocide has been
criticized as too formalistic and restrictive (Rieff 1996). Especially in the
case of the Holocaust, the debate has persisted on whether it was a unique
occurrence or just one of the several genocides (Fein 1990). If absolute and
relative criteria are combined, the Holocaust is unique as it killed six million people and two-thirds of the European Jewry in the 'industry' of gas
chambers. In comparison, Stalin's politics of starvation killed 'only' 20 per
cent of the Ukrainians. It may also be suggested that the intentional and
systematic character of the Holocaust makes it different from other genocides. On the other hand, the mass murder of Khmers by Pol Pot's government and the Hutu killings by the Tutsi were also intentional and well
organized.

A less restrictive definition of genocide has been adopted by Harff and
Gurr who add 'politicides' and 'group repression' to their list. They have
listed seven genocides and 45 politicides for the post-World War II period.
The genocides include two episodes from the Soviet Union and Uganda
each, and one from Cambodia, China, and Rwanda. In addition, recent

politicides have occurred in Afghanistan, Bosnia, Burundi, Iraq, Iran, El Salvador, Ethiopia, Mozambique, Myanmar, Somalia, Sudan, Syria, and Zaïre (Harff and Gurr 1995).

The conclusion from above is that an intentional genocide, driven by totalitarian ideology and state interests, is necessarily also a humanitarian disaster because of its huge death toll. A humanitarian emergency is, however, a broader concept as it also covers death caused by famines and epidemics (in which intentions and structural causes interact). In fact, the list of politicides by Harff and Gurr seems to cover most cases which are conventionally considered humanitarian emergencies.

2.2. Civil wars

The nature and extent of warfare in recent international relations have been mapped by a number of scholars. In Peter Wallensteen's definition, to qualify as a 'war', the conflict must produce a minimum of a thousand battle-related deaths in a given year. 'Minor conflicts' result in less than a thousand battle-related deaths during the course of the conflict, while 'intermediate conflicts' produce more than a thousand such casualties during the conflict, but less than a thousand in a particular year. According to Wallensteen, there were altogether nineteen full-fledged wars in both 1989 and 1990, twenty wars both in 1991 and 1992, fourteen wars in 1993, but seven wars in 1994, six in 1995 and 1996 each, and again seven in 1997. In 1988–97 the following military conflicts qualified as wars in at least two of the years: Afghanistan, Algeria, Azerbaijan, Angola, Bosnia, Chechnya, Colombia, El Salvador, Ethiopia (Eritrea and Tigray), India (Kashmir and Punjab), Lebanon, Liberia, Mozambique, Peru, the Philippines, Rwanda, Somalia, South Africa, Sudan, Sri Lanka, Tajikistan, Turkey (Kurdistan), and Uganda. Armed conflicts were most frequent in Africa and Asia, totalling, respectively, nine and thirteen in 1995, fourteen in each in 1996 and 1997 (Wallensteen and Sollenberg 1996, 1997, and 1998).

In Wallensteen's statistics, the total annual number of conflicts, including also intermediate and minor wars, varied between 42 and 51 in 1989–94 and decreased to 36 in 1996, and 33 in 1997. Another dataset, using rather liberal criteria of war, estimated that in 1996 there were altogether 28 wars and 21 armed conflicts underway (Rabehl and Trines 1997). Wallensteen and Sollenberg (1998) observe that in 1989–97 only nine wars have been interstate and foreign intervention has been made in only nine armed conflicts out of the total of 103. While civil wars usually have domestic and historical roots (Howard 1996), one should not underestimate their interstate elements. India and Pakistan are clashing over Kashmir, India has played a role in the Sri Lankan conflict, Armenia and Azerbaijan are at war over Nagorno Karabakh, Iraq has been divided by external powers, Israel and Syria are heavily involved in Lebanon, and Nigerian peacekeepers have been a party to the civil wars in Liberia and Sierra Leone. Moreover, and perhaps most importantly, wars in the former Yugoslavia have been waged between internationally recognized states.

Wars may tell more about humanitarian emergencies than genocides as they cover a broader spectrum of cases. It should be kept in mind, though, that in many armed conflicts the number of deaths is relatively small and dispersed over time; present wars involve protracted low-level violence rather than a quick and decisive use of military force. Despite its low profile, protracted warfare may, however, subject civilian populations to continuing human suffering and thus increase the risks of malnutrition, disease, and displacement.

2.3. Limits of the CHE concept

The concept of a complex humanitarian emergency (CHE) faces several definitional problems. One of them asks whether the rate of its destruction must accelerate and pass a certain threshold before it qualifies as a crisis or should drawn-out disasters, whose costs accumulate only over a period of time, also be included in the definition? One solution to this dilemma is to distinguish between accelerated and protracted humanitarian crises. Emergencies seldom come as a bolt out of the blue; especially economic and other structural factors require a long gestation period and escalate only after trigger events transform a latent conflict into an emergency. The different rates of acceleration also mean that emergencies can move from one category of intensity to another as, for instance, Zaïre did in 1996 and Kosovo in 1998–99.

Another critical question is whether the number of deaths is an adequate measure of a humanitarian emergency. Especially protracted, accumulating crises may result, in a given period, in relatively few deaths. Various coping strategies can keep the manifest costs of a crisis in check, even though its risk keeps growing (Blaikie *et al.* 1994). This calls for efforts to develop rather broad sets of indicators to gauge a humanitarian crisis. Very seldom can the number of battle-related deaths alone measure the intensity of such a crisis as it often overlooks civilian casualties whose number can be many times higher than those dying in the battles. In the 1990s, the share of civilian casualties in wars has never been below one-half and has often approached 100 per cent (Sadowski 1998).

The state is not always the best unit of analysis; instead, a minority group or a regional unit may be a more valid entity in gauging the extent and intensity of the crisis. The focus on the state too easily overlooks, for instance, endemic urban violence which is not organized as war, but can still be very devastating. One needs only to refer to several US cities, and

Johannesburg, Karachi, Lagos, Moscow, and São Paulo. For example, in 1995 'the Battle of Karachi' claimed 2,100 lives lost to widespread crime and political clashes between various ethnic groups. In Pakistan, rural poverty, the concentration of landownership, and the rapid population growth all push rural masses to cities where they confront, often violently, other ethnic and social groups (*The Economist* 1996; Gizewski and Homer-Dixon 1996).

The focus on deaths neglects some significant dimensions of crises. Not every victim of an emergency dies of physical violence, disease, or starvation. There are also less drastic, but often prolonged forms of suffering as people experience displacement, hunger, poverty, and environmental degradation. Thus, a humanitarian disaster cannot be operationalized by any single criterion; rather the criteria should consider the totality of suffering by vulnerable people.

Warfare can be seen both as an aspect and a cause of a humanitarian emergency. Wars produce massive economic and social dislocations disrupting the living conditions of people and increasing their suffering. Using a comparative, counter-factual analysis of recent wars in East Timor, Iraq, Kashmir, Mozambique, Peru, Sudan, and the former Yugoslavia, a detailed study found, not surprisingly, that their successful prevention would have saved huge social and economic costs and permitted a quicker and more balanced development of the countries concerned (Cranna 1994; see also Brown and Rosecrance 1999).

However, causality can also work the other way around as non-military crises can propel violence. A deepening economic crisis may create a volatile social situation which permits the acquisition of political power by coercion and manipulation which permits, in turn, aggressive internal and external policies and deprives people of constructive means to defend their interests. Moreover, the economic slump contributes to unemployment and creates, as happened in the former Yugoslavia and the South Caucasus, a pool of idle men who can be recruited as soldiers.

These simple models can be refined by considering a third set of factors, power struggles between groups, which can cause both socio-economic and military deterioration. The struggle for political and economic power can foster discrimination in distributing food supplies and the use of weapons to enforce and resist inequities. Frequently, rivals have promoted their political interests by omitting to deliver food to those in need, destroying storages and fields, or provided food only to politically obedient groups. Thus, humanitarian aid has been integrated into conflicts and may have even exacerbated them (Macrae and Zvi 1994; Keen 1994; Prendergast 1996). This line of argument has important implications for the study of humanitarian disasters. They may not be caused by the spread of disease or the lack of food as such, but by more fundamental struggles for the control of power and resources in society. The escalation of a social and political crisis into open violence erodes health services and food security, but also exacerbates struggles for increasingly scarce resources, resulting in privileges for the few and discrimination against the many.

A simple model of humanitarian crises would suggest that the absolute or relative scarcity of resources defines both the intensity of competition and the extent of suffering. Amartya Sen's theory of entitlements provides for a more complex approach to grasp the causes of humanitarian emergencies. It suggests that members of society have material assets and social claims defining their access to food and other basic needs (Sen 1981). If the entitlement fails, people will suffer from hunger, disease, and displacement. Sen's theory has been criticized for its under-appreciation of the political nature of crises. It does not expect the state to be repressive and deliberately discriminate against people, but attributes famines to institutional and policy failures.

In reality, humanitarian emergencies hit marginal groups hardest either because they are inherently more vulnerable or specifically targeted to suffer. Marginalized groups are usually minorities, including indigenous people and immigrant labour, but they may also be the numerical majority (for example, Hutus in Burundi and Rwanda). Marginalization often means that the exposed groups are not only discriminated against and oppressed, but that the distinctiveness and inferiority of their identity is emphasized by the power holders (Nolutshungu 1996).

3. Complex Humanitarian Emergencies

3.1. *Human security and politics*

In the study of humanitarian crises, one must make a clear distinction between their root causes, triggers, and manifestations. This section deals with the manifestations (which may trigger each other, though). Physical violence, expressed in war and repression, is the most important aspect of emergencies, but it has to be complemented by other defining features. The complexity of the humanitarian crisis is due to its multidimensionality and, on the other hand, to its politicized and persistent nature.

Some authors argue that humanitarian crises are not accidental, but intentionally created to permit the transfer of assets from the weak to the strong. Different forms of low-level violence are used to strengthen one's own power base and to undermine that of the other side. The supply of and access to food, health services, and humanitarian assistance become an instrument of local power politics rather than an entitlement. Crises become highly politicized and protracted, and develop their own structures of power. That is why complex emergencies tend to occur in areas suffering from a drawn-out economic crisis, social vulnerability, non-conventional warfare, and contested governance (Macrae and Zwi 1994; Duffield 1994). On the other hand, the intentionality behind humanitarian crises should be not be seen too narrowly. The primary goal is not to capture a relief convoy or steal cattle, but to produce a system of political and economic power that yields power and plenty to the élite through its very existence.

Complex emergencies reflect the multiplicity of threats to human security which provides both a conceptual and normative point of departure for the present analysis. Human security considers death and suffering produced also by means other than weapons, such as hunger, epidemics, environmental disasters, and threats to personal and community identity (UNDP 1994). The expansion of the scope of the security concept beyond survival and physical threats is inspired by the liberal tradition in which the freedom of an individual from fear and want has been regarded as a collective good serving the best interests of the community (Rothschild 1995). However, the liberal tradition may overlook some important aspects of human security, such as social equity and cultural identity. In reality, security threats can also be due to economic, ecological, and cultural risks against which people also want to protect themselves (Chen 1995).

Humanitarian crises are characterized by the interaction of accumulation and marginalization. Wealth and power accumulates to the élites, while vulnerability and social marginalization characterize the life of the underprivileged groups which are, however, usually 'fully integrated into society as the reserve army of the unemployed and rural producers of cheap food. The condition of marginality results not from the action of the marginal group itself but from the interdependent relationship that the group has with other classes and interest groups in society' (Susman, O'Keefe and Wisner 1983: 277–8). In other words, the poor and the rich are interdependent, although they are socially kept apart from each other. Poverty in society may threaten the privileged, but it is also functional as poor people perform menial and itinerant jobs, purchase low-quality goods and services which the rich would not use, and inhabit degraded areas (Øyen 1996).

Vulnerability as social marginalization results both from the uneven progress of global capitalism and the local inequities and differences. The Great Potato Famine in Ireland in 1845–48 provides telling evidence on how the interaction of global and local forces can produce a massive emergency. Ireland, as a peripheral plantation colony, had a one-sided economy serving British interests which, in turn, lacked responsiveness to Irish needs. The development of Irish capitalism created a subsistence sector to provide a cheap labour force for which potato was the staple. Matters were made worse by overpopulation and unfair landownership by which

British landlords pushed Irish peasants to small plots and marginal lands. When the potato blight hit, the socio-economic conditions were ripe for a major humanitarian disaster (Regan 1983). The crisis was not primarily caused by violence, but by socio-economic structures that were, however, deliberately created.

Thus, in a humanitarian crisis one has to study the organization of relations between those suffering and those prospering. This emphasis shifts the focus of research; the root causes of emergencies are not seen only in the internal and external material conditions, but also in the internal and external social relations of the crisis-ridden community. The humanitarian crisis, its nature and seriousness, is structured by economic and political actions and interactions in a context in which various vital assets become scarce or unavailable. Often scarcity is a relative thing and touches only upon those who do not have means to buy the goods that may be amply available to those with purchasing power.

The above discussion suggests that there is a need to broaden the concept of humanitarian emergency. In addition to the casualties of direct physical violence, i.e. people killed in wars and other collective acts of violence, one has to consider the victims of famines and disease, and displaced people (especially if the human agency causing their misery can be identified). This line of thinking leads, in effect, to a revised four horsemen theory of humanitarian emergencies (this imagery has been also used by Green 1994). Originally, the Apocalypse was said to result from the riding of death, war, pestilence, and famine (Rev 6: 2–8). In the revised concept, War, Pestilence (i.e. disease), and Famine are complemented by displacement as a source of death and suffering.[2]

The violation of political and socio-economic human rights can be considered an important aspect of humanitarian emergencies. Human rights criteria may even be used to operationalize an emergency by setting country-specific minimum standards for the realization of social and economic rights (Eide 1989). If these standards are not met, a humanitarian crisis can be said to exist. This approach may not work in practice, however. Economic and social rights and obligations are often vaguely defined and do not necessarily yield any clear criteria. Moreover, human rights are almost inevitably violated in an emergency in which people lose their homes, income, and even lives. Therefore, it is more appropriate to think that human rights, instead of constituting an independent dimension of suffering, are embedded in each of the four specific aspects of humanitarian emergencies which interact with each other.

As argued above, deaths provide only a partial measure of the seriousness of the humanitarian crises. At a minimum, one has to consider also

---

[2] This operationalization of the complex humanitarian emergencies as the combination of war, displacement, hunger, and disease was first suggested in Väyrynen (1996). Since, its use has spread; see, for example, *World Disasters Report* (1998: 165).

those physically and psychically wounded by violence, paralysed by disease, undernourished by inadequate food supply, and uprooted by displacement, i.e. those suffering without dying. As stated above, a complex humanitarian emergency can be defined as a profound social crisis in which large numbers of people unequally die or suffer from war, displacement, hunger, and disease owing to human-made and natural disasters. The reference to inequality of suffering points to the importance of ascertaining the distributional effects of an emergency in addition to its absolute and relative intensity. Natural disasters, though excluded as such from the definition, are mentioned for the reason that they often interact with and amplify the intensity of human-made crises.

The multi-dimensionality of humanitarian crises leads to specify indicators to operationalize them. The measures of war, disease, hunger, and displacement tap mainly the consequences of emergencies, not their causes, although an effect may trigger others and thus deteriorate the crisis further. As a catalytic event, violence in particular can worsen the situation further as it fosters social and political disruption, blocks economic activities, spreads hunger and disease, and kindles refugee flows. Used as a means to acquire political and material benefits, violence weakens the opportunities to cope with the adverse consequences of emergencies, thus making the road from poverty to destitution shorter (de Waal 1990).

Large-scale physical violence can be regarded as a necessary, but not a sufficient condition for the existence of a complex humanitarian emergency; i.e. not all wars produce such an emergency. Of course, there are people living in dismal conditions even if they do not face the risk of physical violence; in fact, only a minority of the 1.3 billion poor people of the world are directly threatened by violence (UNDP 1997). These people suffer from a silent, continuing emergency which is particularly bad in South Asia and Sub-Saharan Africa (Dasgupta 1993b). However, we are primarily interested in the death and suffering produced directly or indirectly by physical violence rather than poverty as a general problem. In other words, we consider complex humanitarian emergencies essentially political and politicized crises.

3.2. War casualties

To tally the number of casualties in civil wars is a difficult task. In addition to differences in criteria, casualty figures are inflated, and deflated, by the propaganda machines of the warring parties and their supporters. Thus, for instance, the estimates of the lives lost in Bosnia vary anywhere between 25,000 and 250,000. George Kenney, who estimates 25,000 to 60,000 deaths for military and civilians on all sides, argues that the high figure came directly from the Bosnian government and was uncritically accepted by the international media (1996). Another example can be fetched from the casualty estimates in the Chechnyan war. According to standard Russian estimates, 30–40,000 people died in the war. On the other hand, Alexander Lebed has suggested that as many as 80,000 people have been killed and 240,000 wounded—an estimate which various independent agencies have confirmed, but also disputed (Gordon 1996).

The construction of any precise statistics is further complicated by the problem of the timeframe. Some humanitarian emergencies have been sudden, brief eruptions of violence and hunger. More often the crises are, however, protracted and phases of different intensity have followed each other. The figures of the war casualties given in this section indicate the total number of people dying in the peak year (given in the parentheses) during the period 1992–94 and in 1997. Table 2.1 contains twenty-two most murderous countries in that period and, at the same time, establishes the minimum threshold of 2,000 deaths (if there is an estimated range of deaths, the average has been calculated). The figures for Peru in 1997 and for India in 1992–94 (including only Kashmir and Punjab) cover only battle deaths. In 1997, the inadequate data reflect either the fact that the war has ended for all practical purpose (Croatia, Guatemala, and Mozambique) or that the number of deaths has not been available. In most cases, the number of casualties has declined significantly since 1992–94,

Table 2.1. Number of war casualties in 1992–94 and 1997

	1992–94		1997
Rwanda	500,000	(1994)	10,000
Angola	100,000	(1994)	n.a.
Burundi	100,000	(1993)	1,000
Mozambique	100,000	(1992)	—
Liberia	35,000	(1993)	n.a.
Bosnia	20,000	(1992)	n.a.
Tajikistan	17,000	(1992)	1,000
Croatia	10,000	(1992)	—
Afghanistan	6,000	(1992)	10,000
Sudan	6,000	(1993)	10,000
Somalia	6,000	(1993)	n.a.
India	5,500	(1992)	3,500
Azerbaijan/Armenia	4,500	(1993)	n.a.
Sri Lanka	4,000	(1993)	4,000
Turkey	4,000	(1993)	4,000
South Africa	3,750	(1993)	n.a.
Columbia	3,500	(1992)	2,000
Peru	3,100	(1992)	200
Algeria	2,500	(1993)	10,000
Georgia	2,000	(1993)	100
Iraq	2,000	(1993)	1,000
Guatemala	2,000	(1993)	—

Source: World Disasters Report (1995, Table 16) for 1992–94 and *State of World Conflict Report 1997–98* for 1997.

but obviously has not reached zero yet (for example, Bosnia, Liberia, and Somalia).

Some of the wars have accelerated quickly and resulted in mass killings in relatively short periods of time. If the tripling of the casualties from the previous year is used as the benchmark of accelerated wars, the following countries fall in this category in 1992–94: Angola (1994), Azerbaijan/Armenia (1993), Bosnia (1992), Burundi (1993), Croatia (1992), Liberia (1993), Mozambique (1992), Rwanda (1994), and Tajikistan (1992). Other wars have been protracted military crises either at a higher (Afghanistan, Algeria, Somalia, Sudan, and Turkey) or lower level of casualties (Colombia, Georgia, Guatemala, India, Iraq, Peru, South Africa, and Sri Lanka).

3.3. Disease

Communicable diseases continue to afflict people of the world much more than wars. In 1993 altogether 16.5 million people died of such diseases, officially accounting for 32 per cent of the global mortality. The most deadly diseases are respiratory infections (4.1 million deaths), diarrhoea (3 million), tuberculosis (2.7 million), malaria (2.5 million), and measles (1.2 million). Respiratory infections and diarrhoea kill especially young children, usually those under five. Aids killed 0.7 million people in 1993 and its annual death toll is expected to rise to 1.8 million by the end of the 1990s. Some 60 per cent of about 24 million HIV-infected people live in Africa (especially Zimbabwe and Botswana) and many of the rest in Asia (especially Thailand and Burma). In 1995, 4.7 million new HIV infections occurred globally, of which 2.5 million in Southeast Asia and 1.9 million in sub-Saharan Africa.

Some of the diseases which were thought to have been eradicated or significantly decreased have either returned (tuberculosis), spread to new areas (cholera and yellow fever), or developed drug-resistant varieties (pneumonia, malaria, and gonorrhoea). Entirely new diseases have emerged (hepatitis C and D, and ebola and other haemorrhagic fevers). In addition to deaths from disease each year, many people are sick, having either the chance to recover (for example, malaria) or being terminally ill (for example, tuberculosis and Aids). Infectious diseases are caused and disseminated by degrading environment (for example, lack of clean water), the growing density of population, increased contacts between the people across distances, and civil wars (Platt 1996a and 1996b; WHO 1996). Disease saps economic productivity, pose new challenges of societal governance, and erode the social fabric (Price-Smith 1997).

The World Health Organization makes available detailed statistics on the number of cases for various infectious diseases; Aids, tuberculosis, malaria, polio, measles, and neonatal tetanus (WHO 1995 and 1996). These figures are, however, difficult to use to operationalize a humanitarian emergency. For instance, one cannot know whether and when a disease leads to death. Obviously, one can argue that the number of disease cases is a better measure of the intensity of an emergency than that of deaths. In both cases, however, problems of measurement remain (for example, the numbers of people suffering and dying from various diseases cannot be meaningfully added up to provide a combined indicator). One solution is to use disability-adjusted life years (DALYs), which weighs disabilities by their severity as the indicator (World Bank 1993). Another solution is to find surrogate indicators that measure the deadliness of humanitarian emergencies and use, for instance, life expectancy at birth or infant mortality (either at birth or under five years of age) as such indicators (Dasgupta 1993a). A more comprehensive measure is the annual death rate standardized by age and sex, as it provides a more simple and direct measure of death than life expectancy. In the end, the choice between these indicators may not matter much as they tend to correlate strongly with each other.

An important feature of a humanitarian emergency is that the level and intensity of suffering departs suddenly and significantly from the prevailing standard (although if the crisis takes place in a society where diseases are rare, it is usually able to cope with the epidemic). Therefore, the disease and hunger components of the emergency must consider both the level of destitution and the rate of deterioration. Humanitarian emergencies hit most strongly the youngest and the eldest. For example, of 52 million deaths in 1995, 21 per cent were children under five and in all of Africa their share of deaths was 40 per cent. Globally, child mortality has been declining (from 134 per 1000 live births in 1970 to 80 in 1995), but the differences between developed and developing countries remain big. In the north, child mortality rate was 8.5 in 1995, but in the south 90.6 (WHO 1996).

In the following, child mortality under the age of five is used to indicate the health component of humanitarian crises. Table A2.1 in the Appendix lists for 1992 and 1995 those countries with the highest under-five mortality rates in the world. Child mortality has decreased in many of the countries most severely plagued by it. The biggest improvements in 1992–95 were recorded for Niger, Mozambique, Angola, Liberia, and Eritrea, most of which started a transition from war to peace during this time. A general improvemement in the global health situation is indicated by the fact that in 1980–96 infant mortality rates increased only in the Republic of Congo, Rwanda, and Zambia (World Bank 1998/99). However, the situation continues to be particularly bad in Afghanistan, Sierra Leone, Malawi, Guinea-Bissau, Burkina Faso, and Mali. In these countries child mortality is among the highest in the world and shows no real signs of improvement. Despite some improvement, the situation is also bad in Niger, Angola, Mozambique, Chad, and Ethiopia.

If a sudden deterioration in the health situation is considered a sign of an humanitarian emergency, Afghanistan and Sierra Leone, together with some other African countries, deserve special attention. If attention is also paid to somewhat less serious, but deteriorating cases of child mortality, a crisis has been been worsening so quickly in Kenya and Zimbabwe that a humanitarian early warning should be issued (even though neither of these two countries are experiencing civil war, yet) In general, among the countries listed in the appendix, seven are included in the war statistics of Table 2.1, while four others have recently and three others in a more distant past waged a civil war. This leaves twelve countries in which child mortality is high even though they have not suffered from major outbreaks of violence. Clearly, warfare is not the only and perhaps not even the main cause of the health crisis in developing countries.

3.4. Hunger

Hunger afflicts most parts of the world today and undernutrition is an everyday phenomenon, but it is seldom due to the absolute scarcity of food. To the contrary, in the postwar years food production has been growing in most developing countries more rapidly than their population and even more quickly than production in developed countries (Uvin 1994). In other words, the dualist pattern of development is again in evidence. To operationalize hunger, it can be misleading to use countries as units of analysis because starvation is a distributional conflict and anchored in the internal structures of societies. On the other hand, in comparative analyses there is often no other alternative than to utilize national averages, say, of calorie or protein intake, while keeping in mind that hunger is a 'societal crisis induced by the dissolution of accustomed availability of, and access to, staple foods on a scale sufficient to cause starvation among a significant number of individuals' (Watts 1983: 13).

In the first place, famines are not caused by natural conditions, such as drought, but they are rather a phase in a sequence of events leading to a subsistence crisis. In other words, 'the drought only hastens . . . the crisis of social reproduction . . . and renders visible what had been, up to a certain point, largely latent process' (Solway 1994: 492). In the sequence, growing vulnerability of the people is the most critical element. When the food crisis comes, it critically tests the ability of the affected communities to cope with its consequences. The importance of social and political factors in the process and outcomes of famines has been stressed in case studies on Nigeria and Sudan (Watts 1983; Keen 1994). Famines are not only due to economic and institutional failures, but they may also be deliberately imposed by the power holders on an opposed group of people. David Keen's analysis of the Sudanese famine in 1988 shows how various exploitative strategies, such as the raiding of food and denial of coping activities, converged to produce a crisis which was further exacerbated by inadequate relief. He points out that the use of food as a weapon was 'a cheap counterinsurgency tactic' which economically benefitted Sudan's political élites and their supporters, such as merchants and other middlemen (Keen 1994).

Serious starvation may lead to death, but it does not have a one-to-one relationship with mortality. It has been even noted that famine is often not the principal perpetrator of poverty, although it will probably accentuate endemic poverty by having deleterious influence on the long-term living standards. Even if starvation leads to death, it does not need to do so directly. Thus, there is no linear relationship between mortality and the amount and price of food consumed (Osmani 1996; Ravallion 1997). In fact, famine mortality can also be due more to the 'disease environment'.[3] Thus, the disease environment defines the standard rate of mortality which can be enhanced by disruptions in the health care systems and the spread of epidemics among the physically weakening population (de Waal 1990).

Redefining the link between famine and mortality raises the question of whether deaths due to starvation are a proper measure of the intensity of a hunger crisis in a humanitarian emergency. Amrita Rangasami in particular has argued that mortality is only a biological culmination of the starvation process and, therefore, an inadequate measure of the crisis intensity. He even concludes that 'mortality is not a necessary condition of famine' (1985: 1748). He distinguishes between three phases of a famine process; 'dearth', 'famishment', and 'morbidity' which tap the movement of the crisis from the scarcity of food to starvation and, ultimately, to death. In his view, 'famishment' rather than 'morbidity' reflects the real face of starvation in which the distribution of benefits and losses is skewed (Rangasami 1985: 1749–50).

The definition of a hunger crisis as a phased process in which intermediary stages may be more important than the final death of a victim is consistent with my earlier discussion on the role of violence in humanitarian emergencies. Thus, the disposal of productive assets, such as livestock and land, is an important indicator of a humanitarian crisis along with the distress and death of the people affected (Watts 1991a). This leads us back to stress the command of power and resources as the ultimate determinant of a social crisis, reflected in the occurrence of hunger, disease, displacement, and other humanitarian problems. Criticizing Sen's theory of entitlement, such a view draws attention to extra-legal means to deny and obtain food (de Waal 1990; Edkins 1996; Ravaillon 1997; Keen in this volume).

---

[3] On the links between hunger and mortality, see WHO (1995: 6–8); UNDP (1993: 75–82).

If the centrality of politics in famines is accepted, then 'we need to re-define famine and identify the various factors—political, social, psychological and economic—that operate to keep large classes in the population under a continuous pressure' (Rangasami 1985). It also becomes relevant to assess the rules and institutions that regulate the access to and use of productive resources in a society (Curtis, Hubbard and Shepherd 1988). Famine is nothing less than an ultimate test, especially in rural areas, on how the society operates and who benefits from it. Thus, it makes sense to consider 'disaster as an extension of everyday life' (Susman, O'Keefe and Wisner 1983).

Since 1970 the amount of hunger has significantly decreased in the Asia-Pacific region and the Middle East, but it continues to plague Sub-Saharan Africa and South Asia. In the early 1990s, 23 million Southern and Eastern Africans depend on emergency food for their survival and 37 per cent of the continent's population is undernourished. In South Asia, especially children suffer from chronic undernutrition (the growth of more than one-half of them is stunted). In Latin America, hunger and malnutrition have been on the decline, but the positive trend stopped in the 1980s as a result of the austerity policies (for a detailed analysis, see Uvin *et al.* 1995).

Hunger is almost always linked with poverty and inequality, and exacerbated by other adverse conditions such as warfare and ethnic discrimination. The occurrence of wars and famines correlated at least in the 1980s with each other (Watts 1991b). Hunger has been severe in many war zones, such as Angola, Mozambique, Rwanda, and especially Somalia where the 1992 famine was a direct result of fighting. The Somalian famine was made worse both by men (warlords) and nature (poor rainfall). The clan leaders and their militia, controlling the famine zone, benefited handsomely from their position of power. In effect, one reason why Mohammed Farah Aideed in 1993 turned against the international intervention was its stated goal to foster national reconciliation, break warlordism, and thus reduce his political and military clout. Today, Somalia continues to be politically divided, but the territorial spheres of influence and the balance of power between the clans have created conditions for a 'wild-frontier economy'. According to one observer, 'Somalia has made a remarkable, if uneven, economic comeback since those desperate days. Harvests have been plentiful, hunger has been banished, and trade is brisk in the towns and cities' (Finnegan 1995: 64). Somali politics has become 'radically localized' which is linked with the informal, and illegal internationalization of the country's economy (Prendergast 1997).

The need to supply food to starving people has prompted extensive international relief operations, though they have relied too much on food handouts and overlooked the importance of interventions for public health (Ravallion 1997). Aid deliveries have often needed military protection and may have even become an integral part of the conflict pattern.

Humanitarian operations have no doubt helped suffering people, but they have also benefited state treasuries, food speculators, and armed groups controlling the distribution of food. Humanitarian relief is geared to benefit the weak, but in reality it has often ended up serving the interests of the strong (Duffield 1994; Prendergast 1996). Humanitarian support to the Khmer Rouge in Cambodia and the Rwandan Hutu refugees in Zaïre helped to prolong rather than solve the local political and military crises. Then it may become a part of the problem rather than a part of the solution leading to a 'relief failure' (Keen 1991; Rangasami 1985; Väyrynen 1999). Lasting solutions to food crises, and humanitarian emergencies in general, can only be achieved by providing relief early on, empowering the likely victims, and ensuring their right to food by practical reforms (Watts 1991b).

There are major difficulties in measuring the prevalence of hunger among the people, and there is no single measure to indicate its human and economic costs. One possible indicator is the percentage of children under five suffering from underweight. Especially if related to the person's height, it measures in a direct way her/his nutritional status (Dasgupta 1993b). Underweight and stunted growth of children, in turn, impact on well-being and physical productivity in the adult age, partly because deficient nutrition limits maximal oxygen intake. Moreover, malnutrition and infections are closely linked with each other (Dasgupta 1993a; Scrimshaw 1997). Table A2.2 in the Appendix contains information on the percentage of children under five who were underweight in 1975 and 1990. Data show how serious a problem hunger is in the developing world, especially in Africa and South Asia. A silent emergency reigns in these regions, keeping more than a hundred million children undernourished. Hunger is also a long-lasting phenomenon as only two countries out of the twenty-five listed for 1975 were replaced by others in 1990. Those dropped from the list are the Republic of Congo (43 to 28 per cent) and Botswana (37 to 27 per cent).

The situation continues to be disastrous, especially in Bangladesh, India, Nepal, Mozambique, Niger, Vietnam, Sri Lanka, Pakistan, and Ethiopia. In some other cases, the prevalence of hunger may not be as bad as in the countries mentioned above, but the situation is worsening. These countries include Afghanistan, Angola, Madagascar, Nigeria, and Zaïre/Congo. In all of them, and many other countries, hunger is a major sign of underdevelopment, although there is no one-to-one relationship between them. There are countries where per capita income is among the lowest in the world, but still hunger is not pervasive; for example, Benin, Gambia, Kenya, Senegal, Tanzania, and Togo. On the other hand, in economically better-off countries, such as Iran, Sri Lanka, and the Philippines, children suffer from serious hunger problems. The large number of people in South and South East Asia, suffering from the combination of poverty and hunger, makes the problem particularly salient.

While there is a positive correlation between child mortality (disease) and underweight (hunger), these indicators tap somewhat different aspects of underdevelopment. Eleven countries appear in the 1990s on both disease and hunger lists and have thus experienced a major humanitarian crisis: Afghanistan, Angola, Bangladesh, Ethiopia, Central African Republic, Laos, Mozambique, Niger, Nigeria, Rwanda, and Somalia. Six of them have experienced a recent major civil war, while the rest have been also plagued by turmoil and instability.

3.5. External and internal displacement

Since the 1970s, the absolute number of external and internal refugees has been almost constantly on the increase suggesting the deterioration of the global human conditions, although the numbers have started to decline since the middle of the 1990s. Refugee populations in excess of 10,000 people can be found in more than 70 countries, mostly in Africa and Asia, but increasingly also in Europe. The total number of refugees and asylum seekers stayed between 16–17 million in 1991 and 1993 to decline to 15 million in 1995 and 14 million in 1997. The total number of internally displaced people (IDPs) increased from 22 million in 1991 to over 24 million, but has declined since then to 20 million in 1995 and close to 17 million in 1997 (*World Disasters Report* 1998; *World Refugee Survey* 1998).[4] It is often asserted that refugee flows are due to local wars uprooting people who cannot return before stability has been restored in their home country (Kane 1995; Akokpari 1998). On the other hand, various indicators of warfare and refugeeism correlate, at least in the Horn of Africa, only imperfectly; i.e. refugeeism has also other causes than war (Bariagaber 1995).

The regionalization of crises in the south has a less often noted effect; the leading countries of asylum are not industrialized countries, but neighbouring developing countries. At the end of 1996, the biggest refugee populations were in Iran (2.02 million), Jordan (1.36 million), Pakistan (1.22 million), Gaza (0.72 million), Guinea (0.65 million), Russia (0.48 million), and Zaïre (0.46 million). Only after them came Germany with 0.44 million refugees and asylum seekers. All in all, in 1996 Middle East had 5.84 million, Africa 3.68 million, Europe 2.48 million, and South and Central Asia 1.80 million refugees. Europe, including South Caucasus, has had only 15–20 per cent of the total refugee population in the world (*World Refugee Survey* 1997). Large refugee populations, even if they receive international

---

[4] International statistics on the number of refugees and IDPs are plagued by surprising paucity and unreliability. In particular, the number of refugees in key receiving developing countries is never known exactly. The UNHCR estimates that in 1995 there were a total of 320,000 IDPs in Liberia, 200,000 in Sri Lanka, and 185,000 in Afghanistan (UNHRC 1996: 21). On the other hand, the *World Refugee Survey* (1996: 6) gives the following figures: 1,000,000 IDPs in Liberia, 850,000 in Sri Lanka, and 500,000 in Afghanistan.

assistance, are straining the resources of developing countries, some of which are themselves suffering from a humanitarian crisis (for case studies, see Cohen and Deng 1998).

The large number of refugees and IDPs is a part of the increasing human mobility in the world. Due to the population explosion in the south and the economic attractiveness of the industrial centres, immigration flows to North America, the European Union, and Japan have been rising, thus exposing them to new tensions and pushing to close their borders. In addition, there are pockets in the world economy, such as the oil producers in the Persian Gulf and Singapore, which are dependent on imported labour. Both the growing flows of refugees and migrant labour reflect the restructuring and globalization of the world economy; the push-and-pull of immigration derives, in part, from the changing global dynamics (Castles and Miller 1993; Pellerin 1993). Economic motivations to emigrate often intermingle with the political desire to leave war and repression behind. In many countries there is a mass movement of people from the rural areas to cities. The ensuing rapid rate of urbanization may become, because of overcrowding and tensions between different social and ethnic groups and identities, a source of future instability.

Although the number of refugees and IDPs is declining, frequent civil wars continue to push people away from their homes (in June 1999, out of the total of 1.8 million Kosovo's Albanians, 800,000 had left the country and 600,000 were internally displaced). The problem of internal war is compounded by the increasing number of state failures which lead to the collapse of the public order, pushing people to more stable and orderly areas. The weak and lopsided nature of peripheral states is an important reason for the refugee and IDP flows (Akokpari 1998). Also specific forms of displacement, such as ethnic 'cleansing', the killing and displacement of unfavoured ethnic or religious communities, have become a strategic objective of parties waging war. People are pushed out from their homes to make the region more homogenous and to consolidate the political and economic rule of the wartime leaders. In addition to the former Yugoslavia, ethnic 'cleansing' has been deliberately practised in the South Caucasus (*The State of the World's Refugees* 1995).

Table 2.2 uses the figures of the *World Refugee Survey* which covers the situation better than any other source (though in a few cases I have supplemented its data from other sources). The table gives an idea which countries have sent out most refugees and accommodated IDPs.[5] In the table, the absolute number of refugees and IDPs is related also to the size of the population in the countries of origin.

---

[5] The table does not contain figures on the Palestinian refugees, even though they are by far the biggest refugee group in the world (3.3 million in 1995). The reason is technical; there are no data available for the Palestinians on other aspects of their humanitarian crisis.

The table shows clearly how big a problem external and internal displacement is both for the countries suffering from the crisis and those located in their neighbourhood. The spill-over potential of internal conflicts and refugee displacement creates several problems. The neighbouring countries may start taking stronger measures to keep unwanted refugees out unless there are strong ties of identity or politics to justify a more liberal policy. One reason for the increasing political caution, especially in divided societies, is that a significant number of refugees can tilt the internal balance of the country or come otherwise a 'fifth column'.

The absolute size and the relative impact of external and internal displacement are two quite different matters. Using the figures in Table 2.2, one can develop a typology based on the absolute number of displaced people on the one hand and their relative share of the population on the other (the terms 'high' and 'low' are used in reference to other cases in the sample in which all countries have high absolute figures in comparison to

Table 2.2. Refugees and internally displaced people in 1995

	Refugees	IDPs	Total	Share
Afghanistan	2,328,000	500,000	2,828,000	14.1
Bosnia	906,000	1,300,000	2,206,000	63.0
Sudan	448,000	1,700,000	2,148,000	7.6
Rwanda	1,545,000	500,000	2,045,000	25.7
Turkey	15,000	2,000,000	2,015,000	3.3
Angola	313,000	1,500,000	1,813,000	16.4
Liberia	725,000	1,000,000	1,725,000	56.7
Iraq	623,000	1,000,000	1,623,000	8.0
Sierra Leone	363,000	1,000,000	1,363,000	30.2
Sri Lanka	96,000	1,000,000	1,096,000	6.0
Azerbaijan	390,000	670,000	1,060,000	14.0
Burma	160,000	750,000	910,000	2.0
Somalia	480,000	300,000	780,000	8.4
Ethiopia	500,000	111,000	611,000	1.1
Colombia	—	600,000	600,000	1.7
Mozambique	97,000	500,000	597,000	3.7
Eritrea	325,000	200,000	525,000	14.9
South Africa	10,000	500,000	510,000	1.2
Burundi	290,000	216,000	506,000	7.9
Peru	—	480,000	480,000	2.0
Tajikistan	174,000	300,000	474,000	7.8
Croatia	200,000	225,000	425,000	9.6
Lebanon	—	400,000	400,000	13.2
Armenia	200,000	185,000	385,000	10.7
Georgia	105,000	280,000	385,000	7.1

Sources: *World Refugee Survey* (1996, Tables 3 and 4). Its data have been supplemented by information from *World Disaster Report* (1995, Tables 12 and 14) and UNHCR (1996). The population figures for 1995 have been obtained from WHO (1996: Table A1).

Note: 'Share' refers to the proportion of refugees and IDPs of the total population.

Table 2.3. Dimensions of the displacement problem

Relative burden		Total displacement	
		High	Low
High	External	Afghanistan, Bosnia, Rwanda, Liberia, Azerbaijan	Somalia, Eritrea, Croatia, Armenia
	Internal	Angola, Sierra Leone	Lebanon
Low	External	—	Ethiopia, Burundi, Tajikistan
	Internal	Sudan, Turkey, Iraq, Sri Lanka, Burma	Colombia, Mozambique, South Africa, Peru, Georgia

the rest of the world). The third dimension in the typology is the balance between internal and external displacement.

A rather clear-cut statistical pattern emerges from the table. Countries which are burdened by a serious crisis of overall displacement tend to push their people abroad, while those with a relatively lower burden displace them internally. Only six countries out of the total 25 deviate from this pattern. One possible explanation is the total population and its density; the smaller the population, the heavier the relative burden imposed by the displacement problem on the society, and the higher the pressure to push people out. On the other hand, the relative impact of displacement tends to be more limited in large countries which can handle the problem internally.

Moreover, in more intense crises the fighting has been more sustained (Afghanistan, Ethiopia, Eritrea, and Somalia) or sudden and ferocious (Bosnia, Croatia, and Rwanda). In such intense crises, of which Kosovo was an example in 1999, a relatively larger share of the population is either pushed out or tries to escape to safety abroad. Of the deviant cases, Burundi and Tajikistan are close to this pattern as the relative burden of their displacement was near to the statistical average. On the other hand, crises in populous countries seem to be more connected with internal repression and guerilla wars against the government (Colombia, Iraq, Burma, Peru, Sudan, Turkey, and South Africa), leading more likely to internal than external displacement. The deviant case of Georgia can be explained by the fact that as most of the affected people were displaced from Abkhazia and South Ossetia to Georgia proper, the movement happened technically within the country. In Mozambique, the end of the civil war has resulted in the return of a significant number of external refugees, adding to internal displacement in a country in which domestic reconstruction had not yet made adequate progress. Recently, significant number of refugees have returned also to Liberia and Rwanda.

In many countries, the number of refugees has been relatively constant or decreasing in the 1990s. The following countries have, however, experienced major upsurges in outward refugee flows, i.e. the number has at least tripled in comparison to the previous two years; Burundi (1993), Eritrea (1993), Iraq (1992), Burma (1992), Rwanda (1994), and Sierra Leone (1991). On the other hand, Azerbaijan (1992–93), Bosnia (1992), Croatia (1991), Burma (1991), Somalia (1991–92), and Tajikistan (1992) have suffered from major sudden problems of internal displacement (*World Disaster Report* 1995).

4. The Operationalization of Humanitarian Crises

4.1. The selection of cases

One of the basic choices in selecting the cases of humanitarian emergencies concerns the unit of analysis. Most statistical data are available only for states, while often a subnational community or a regional crisis complex could be a more appropriate unit of analysis. For instance, Gurr (1993) has used a minority rather than a state as the main unit (see also *State of the Peoples* 1993). The choice of unit has implications for the priority accorded to absolute and relative measures of suffering. To opt for the state as the primary unit tends to favour absolute measures, while relative measures would better tap the intensity of a humanitarian crisis in various subnational units. This study uses the state as the main unit of statistical units of analysis, though it recognizes the importance of intranational factors in the analysis of the causes, dynamics, and outcomes of humanitarian emergencies; in effect, most crises covered here are primarily internal in nature. The key variables describe various aspects of humanitarian disasters (war, disease, hunger, and displacement) and tap their economic and political root causes. The data mostly originate from the first half and the middle of the 1990s as the number of humanitarian emergencies seems to have peaked then.[6]

---

[6] If the dataset would have been extended to the late 1990s, a few more cases of humanitarian emergencies would have appeared. At least the Democratic Republic of Congo seems to meet all the criteria of a complex emergency as does Kosovo (which is a subnational unit, though). In Kosovo in May 1999, there were a total of 700,000 refugees, 600,000 IDPs, among whom hunger was widespread. According to the NATO estimates, 4,600 people were killed in March–May 1999, while tens of thousands of men remained unaccounted for. In North Korea, there was practically no violence, but a large number of people (estimates vary between 0.8 and 3.0 million) had died of hunger and refugee flows, especially to China, had started increasing.

Depending on the criteria of inclusion, the number of recent emergencies can vary from a couple of dozen to a couple of hundred. In the depiction of the extent and intensity of humanitarian crises, I will continue to rely on a modernized 'four horsemen' theory which defines the crises by four scourges of humankind: war, disease, hunger, and refugees. They are operationalized, respectively, by the number of war casualties, the mortality of children under five, the share of underweight children under five, and the total number of external and internal refugees. The emphasis on the condition of children can be justified by the fact that the depth of a crisis in society is best revealed by looking at its weakest members. The condition of children also has a long-term impact on the social and economic development of society.

It is prudent to recognize that the four variables used in the operationalization are not statistically independent of each other. Especially war and displacement on the one hand and hunger and disease on the other are linked with each other through a variety of mechanisms. As the aim is to find patterns and categories of humanitarian crises that provide bases for case studies, these correlations are not, however, an insurmountable problem. There are reasons to believe that while violence and poverty are interlinked, their correlation is not necessarily high; poverty neither needs to lead to violence, nor is poverty primarily caused by it.

From these vantage points, one can expect that there are three main types of humanitarian crises:

(i) *violent humanitarian crises* in which suffering is due to the large numbers of casualties in wars and the external and internal displacement of people;

(ii) *poverty crises* in which large-scale human suffering is due to hunger and disease; and

iii) *complex humanitarian crises* in which violence, displacement, and poverty are combined to produce an entrenched social crisis.

In this effort at operationalization, I am most interested in complex and violent humanitarian emergencies. The most serious, non-violent poverty crises are also listed to report the results of the empirical exercise, but they are not analysed further in this report. Due to the limitations of data, a reliable rank ordering of emergencies on the basis of their severity is not possible. Instead, I will distinguish strong and limited cases of complex emergencies. The strong cases include those countries whose people have experienced deep suffering on all four dimensions of humanitarian crises. Limited complex emergencies include those cases in which people have severely suffered from war and refugeeism, and either from hunger or disease. This effort resulted in the following typology of complex humanitarian emergencies (they are ranked in the approximate order of seriousness):

Table 2.4. A typology of complex humanitarian emergencies in the 1990s

	War	Disease	Hunger	Displacement	Type
Afghanistan	X	X	X	X	Strong
Mozambique	X	X	X	X	Strong
Angola	X	X	X	X	Strong
Somalia	X	X	X	X	Strong
Rwanda	X	X	X	X	Strong
Liberia	X	X		X	Limited
Burundi	X	X		X	Limited
Sri Lanka	X	X		X	Limited
Sierra Leone	X	X		X	Limited
Sudan	X		X	X	Limited
Ethiopia		X	X	X	Limited
Eritrea		X	X	X	Limited
Burma		X	X	X	Limited

All these humanitarian crises have been serious as they have witnessed at least three of the four syndromes. The most common combinations of 'limited' cases involve either war, disease, and displacement or disease, hunger, and displacement. The experience of famine is the main differentiating factor between the 'strong' and 'limited' cases of complex humanitarian emergencies. Had they have experienced a large-scale hunger problem, Liberia, Burundi, Sri Lanka, and Sierra Leone would have been placed in the category of 'strong' emergencies. By applying somewhat different criteria, Ethiopia could also have been labelled a 'strong' case of an emergency as extensive human suffering continues there (*World Disasters Report* 1995). Had the time period extended to the 1980s, other cases, especially Cambodia, should have been added.

Complex humanitarian emergencies are characterized by the simultaneous occurrence of war, displacement, and disease, and in the most serious cases also of hunger. *In partial humanitarian emergencies* only two of these syndromes appear, as detailed in the following table (p. 75).

As pointed out above, hunger and disease have given rise to a silent humanitarian crisis in many developing countries. By relaxing the criteria somewhat, several African countries, such as Burkina Faso, Guinea-Bissau, Malawi, and Niger could have been added to the list of poverty crises. Although impoverishment has devastating human costs, they should not be discussed primarily in terms of humanitarian emergencies which refer to the acute, deep, multidimensional, and politicized crises in society. Therefore, I have excluded poverty crises from the definition of humanitarian emergencies.

The statistical exercise and qualitative judgement carried out above led to an operational definition of humanitarian crises which include five

Table 2.5. Partial humanitarian emergencies

	War	Disease	Hunger	Displacement	Type
Bosnia	X			X	Violence
Croatia	X			X	Violence
Tajikistan	X			X	Violence
Colombia	X			X	Violence
Azerbaijan	X			X	Violence
Armenia	X			X	Violence
Georgia	X			X	Violence
Iraq	X			X	Violence
Niger		X	X		Poverty
Nigeria		X	X		Poverty
Bangladesh		X	X		Poverty
Laos		X	X		Poverty
Central African Republic		X	X		Poverty
India	X		X		Mixed

'strong' cases of complex emergencies (Afghanistan, Mozambique, Angola, Somalia, and Rwanda), eight 'limited' cases (Liberia, Sudan, Burundi, Sri Lanka, Sierra Leone, Ethiopia, Eritrea, and Burma), and seven cases of 'partial' violent crises (Bosnia, Croatia, Tajikistan, Azerbaijan, Armenia, Georgia, and Iraq). In the 1990s, Afghanistan, Angola, Ethiopia, Eritrea, Mozambique, Sierra Leone, Somalia, and Sri Lanka have experienced a permanent crisis, while in others there was an upsurge in violence and suffering in 1991–95.

As has been repeated above, any statistical effort to identify the most serious humanitarian crises is plagued with measurement problems and conceptual ambiguities. Therefore, one should try to validate the list developed above. For this purpose, I compared my operationalization with the countries identified by the US Central Intelligence Agency as the most serious humanitarian emergencies requiring urgent international attention (*Global Humanitarian Emergencies* 1996). This list can be summarized by focusing on two factors: the total number of persons and the share of the total population at risk.

The CIA considers Afghanistan, Burundi, and Sierra Leone to be the most intense emergency conflicts. Chechnya, Rwanda, Somalia, Sri Lanka, Sudan, and Tajikistan are classified as simmering emergencies. Other cases include Angola, Armenia, Azerbaijan, Bosnia, Cambodia, Croatia, Georgia, Ethiopia, Eritrea, Haiti, Iraq, Liberia, Mozambique, North Korea. The two lists correlate strongly with each other. In fact, every case, except Burma, in my typology is also listed by the CIA. In addition, it regards Haiti, Cambodia, Chechnya, and North Korea as complex humanitarian emergencies. In all of them, there is certainly a major humanitarian crisis, but they are not included for various empirical reasons in the above typologies. In real life, one should be more flexible, however, and therefore Haiti, Cambodia, and Chechnya are included as case studies in the companion volume of this publication. If a longer time perspective is adopted, then one can on good grounds add—as Kalevi Holsti does (this volume)—at least Nigeria, Lebanon, and Uganda.

4.2. Regional emergencies

Both international cooperation and conflicts become regionalized when intraregional linkages are stronger than connections with the external world. Thus, regionalism can be founded on both common interests and common aversions. States are bound together both by gains derived from mutual exchange and threats due to the potential escalation of hostilities within the region or through a spillover from outside it. Barry Buzan suggests that a regional security complex exists 'where a set of security relationships stands out from the general background by virtue of its relatively strong, inward-looking character, and the relative weakness of its outward security interactions with its neighbours' (1991: 193). Civil wars also have a strong regional component; 69 per cent of all wars in 1989–97 were linked with a war in one or more neighbouring countries (Wallensteen and Sollenberg 1998). In a similar vein, one may talk of regional humanitarian crises, i.e. a given crisis cannot be analysed solely in a national context, but one must consider its linkages with the humanitarian conditions in neighbouring countries.

In fact, practically every humanitarian emergency has a strong regional outlook without which they are difficult to comprehend. Therefore, emergencies have to be contextualized in space and time and can seldom be seen merely as national or bilateral problems. Rather they are shaped by the regional context which can influence the actors' propensity to a crisis in two principal ways; a specific region is exposed either to the same adverse ecological or economic conditions or destabilizing economic and political influences spill over the borders. Obviously, a major economic crisis can engender cross-border movements of people and political influences are fuelled, in turn, either by vertical or horizontal dynamics.

Natural conditions, such as droughts and floods, have often a strong regional dimension. The Great Plains in the United States in the 1930s, the Sahel in the 1970s and Southern Africa in the early 1990s are all examples of the zones of disaster due to drought. The effects of floods and coastal storms are seldom restricted to one country, but tend to wreak havoc in a larger area. The looming crisis over water cannot be limited to individual countries, but conflicts over its supply and quality concern aquifers and rivers stretching across national boundaries. Finally, worldwide environmental problems, such as the depletion of the ozone layer and global warming, affect individual regions quite differently (Myers 1993; Akokpari 1998).

Regional ecological risks can be studied systematically by identifying environmentally risky regions. Roger E. Kasperson and others have stated that 'criticality denotes a state of both environmental degradation and associated socio-economic deterioration . . . Critical region denotes an area that has reached such a state of interactive deterioration'. The criticality of a region is anchored in nature-society relationships which can be defined on the basis of how the natural and social systems exposed to ecological pressures and their resilience to withstand these changes. Depending on the criticality of this relationship, the result may be either environmental endangerment (short-term crisis), impoverishment (long-term crisis), or, in the positive case, sustainability. Amazonia, the Basin of Mexico, and the Aral Sea provide examples of environmentally critical cross-border regions (Kasperson *et al.* 1995). Obviously, the more critical a given environmental region, the higher the risk of a humanitarian crisis there.

Another mechanism by which humanitarian emergencies become regionalized is the dissemination of influences and the construction of policy linkages across the borders. David Lake's suggestion that a regional system can be best defined by the existence of positive or negative externalities across the borders is particularly useful here. Externalities can be created both by material cross-transborder links and intangible policy influences (Lake 1997). In a humanitarian crisis, regional externalities are created by the cross-border impact of warfare, refugee flows, and the transmission of disease. Externalities can be also economical. If there is a dominant economic power in the region, its negative or slow growth will have repercussions in neighbouring countries. The demand of their products may decline, the instability of currencies can be contagious, and unemployment may create pressures to emigrate. While the development in the centres of the world economy is crucial for the periphery, as the recent Asian economic crisis shows, one should not underestimate the adverse effects of a regional economic crisis. For instance, economic problems in Nigeria, South Africa, India, or Indonesia have immediate negative consequences for the ECOWAS, the SADC, the SARC, and the ASEAN region, respectively. The regional transmission of economic woes will, in turn, deepen political and social crises.

Ethnic, religious, and political ties create transborder identities and coalitions which defy the formal borders of states. These transnational coalitions can challenge governments in one or more countries. On the other hand, governments can, in turn, coalesce against the sub- and transnational communities demanding secession or autonomy. Kurdistan, the nation of 24 million Kurds, though afflicted by internal political conflicts, forms a cross-border coalition which is integrated in a complex way with the politics of the region. Similarly, East Timor is an example of a sub-national crisis with regional repercussions.

The complex relations between the Hutu and Tutsi communities in Burundi and Rwanda, and in exile in Tanzania and Congo, could be used to illustrate the regional complexities of humanitarian crises. In the province of North Kivu, eastern Zaïre, the relations between the local Hutus and Tutsis were relatively peaceful until 1993. Since then the tensions in neighbouring Rwanda spilled over and were further aggravated by the exodus of 1.5 million Hutus to Goma and other refugee camps in Zaïre. In North Kivu, 50,000 people, mostly *Banyamulenge* Tutsis, were killed and 300,000 made homeless in 1994–96. This prompted them to join Laurent Kabila who, supported by Rwanda and Uganda, started a successful military campaign to oust Mobute from power in Zaïre. Most of the Hutus in refugee camps returned as a long, marching line to Rwanda, while others fled Kabila's army to the interior of the country (according to estimates, 200,000 of them remain unaccounted for). The Hutu militias in Congo have continued to attack the Rwandan border areas and to help their ethnic brethren in Burundi in their fight against the local Tutsis. In response, Burundi's army has started expelling Hutu refugees from Northern Burundi back to Rwanda. The regionalization of warfare and expulsion of refugees have deteriorated the humanitarian crisis in the Great Lakes region and undermined efforts at reconstruction. In fact, the region has developed into an interwoven fabric of political and ethnic alliances which are financed by smuggling and other informal economic operations. The old interstate borders have only limited influence in defining and dividing the Great Lakes region (Griggs 1997; Väyrynen 1999).

Refugee flows, created by wars and famines, have a direct impact on neighbouring countries. These flows are increasingly due to internal wars and the socio-economic crises associated with them. A major part of these refugee flows concentrate on particular regions, 'bad neighbourhoods' such as the South Caucasus, the Horn of Africa, the Great Lakes region, West Africa, and the area around Afghanistan. Refugees have also been fleeing from Haiti to the Dominican Republic and the United States (Weiner 1995 and 1996). In West Africa, there is a dense web of refugee movements. In 1995, there were 125,000 Sierra Leonean refugees in Liberia and 190,000 in Guinea. On the other hand, there were close to 400,000 Liberian refugees in Guinea and Ivory Coast each, and 16,000 in Sierra Leone (*The State of the World's Refugees* 1995 and 1997). Together with the widespread poverty, rising crime rate, and social fragmentation, criss-crossing refugee flows create a volatile situation leading to warnings that West Africa, and especially Sierra Leone, will be one of the main hotspots of the 'coming anarchy' (Kaplan 1996).

The crossborder movement of refugees has a direct impact on regional conflicts. Algeria has supported Sahrawi struggle for its independence,

Pakistan has been a springboard for military operations in Afghanistan, Kenya has offered a haven for southern Somalis, while Sudan has been hospitable to both Tigrayan and Eritrean resistance forces (Rondos 1994). Sudan is, in fact, a prime example of an internally unstable country which has become a regional hub of both interstate conflicts, especially with Egypt and Ethiopia, and crossborder alliances between different political forces in Uganda and Eritrea (Waller 1996).

Power can be accumulated and used in an emergency both by regional core actors, such as Sudan and Nigeria, and external powers. In most regional conflicts, there is a heart of crisis in which the emergency is deepest. In the Great Lakes region this heart has been in Rwanda and Burundi while in West Africa, the Liberian civil war has spilled over to Sierra Leone and Guinea. In Central Asia, the crisis in Tajikistan radiates to the entire region, in Central America conflicts in Nicaragua and El Salvador were interlinked in the 1980s, and wars in the former Yugoslavia were centred in the rivalry between Croatia and Serbia. In many humanitarian crises the role of external powers has been significant; the conflict dynamics in Central Asia and the South Caucasus are shaped and shoved by Russia, while the United States has been a key force in Central America, and France in Central Africa.

Central Asia provides a pertinent example of the regionality of humanitarian crises. Its landlocked countries are tied together by the legacy of the planned Soviet economy in which they were assigned to agriculture based on large-scale irrigation. This monoculture has created a series of environmental crises of which the gradual drying of the Aral Sea and the salinization of land are the most devastating ones. The cotton monoculture has also resulted in major health risks due to the irresponsible use of herbicides and defoliants. In the most critical regions of the Aral Sea basin, the mortality rates have increased 15 times since the middle of the 1970s and infant mortality can be as high as 110 per 1,000 newborn (Glazovsky 1995; Pomfret 1995). Central Asian countries are tied together by negative environmental and economic externalities, but their political, ethnic, and economic ties, on the other hand, cut across them in a multitude of ways. Governments in the region have tried to promote mutual cooperation, but it has been complicated by the national and religious divisions and the divisive impact of external powers, especially Russia, Turkey, Iran, and Pakistan, whose interests conflict with each other (Lounev and Shirokov 1995).

Central Asia also shows how political instability can cut across the borders. The hotbed of its crisis is the Fergana valley which Stalin divided in 1921 between Uzbekistan, Tajikistan, and Kyrgystan. The valley has become a flashpoint of political tensions between groups having conflicting ethnic, religious, and political identities. The situation in Fergana reflects also the Uzbek-Tajik divide which may be fundamental to Central

Asia's political future. Iran's alleged promotion of Greater Tajikistan creates frictions both with Afghanistan and Uzbekistan, the leading power in Central Asia (Kaplan 1996). Problems are further compounded by the multiple internal divisions and lack of stateness in Tajikistan. Obstacles to economic exchange and conflicts over water and other resources, together with the economic stagnation, have also exacerbated tensions in the region.

To sum up, most humanitarian emergencies of the 1990s are clustered in critical regions in which they fuel each other: Central Asia, South Caucasus, the former Yugoslavia, the Horn of Africa, the Great Lakes region, and West Africa. Although other countries suffering from humanitarian crises have regional links, their problems seem to be more idiosyncratic: Colombia, Iraq, Burma, and Sri Lanka, to mention some examples.

5. Conclusion

A main theme running through this exploratory chapter on the definition and meaning of humanitarian emergencies has been the emphasis on the inherently dualistic nature of the present era. This dualism rejects the notion that the humankind is inexorably and continuously progressing towards a more perfect society. Instead, the development of national and international societies are characterized by discontinuities, shifts, and turning points. A humanitarian emergency is perhaps the most serious form of discontinuity as the established social, political, and economic structures collapse, and people die and suffer massively.

Humanitarian emergencies can be seen as a downside of modernity; a development, supposedly benign, that has gone awry. They are a sign that either modernity has not yet won, or that we have moved to a postmodern era in which beauty and ugliness, promise and disappointment, coexist. Against this backdrop, it is important to reflect upon the nature and functions of the recent wave of humanitarian emergencies which spread like prairie fire, especially in the early 1990s. A fundamental question is whether this wave of emergencies is a temporary aberration or a permanent feature of international relations. I am inclined to vote for the long-lasting nature of these crises, for several reasons. Most importantly, the forces that foster different aspects of humanitarian crises are not disappearing. Hunger and disease, spread by poverty, continue to afflict a sizable part of the population in developing countries. Economic dislocations, and the ensuing social vulnerability, continue to be essential traits of their development, creating in turn fertile breeding ground for political instabilities and humanitarian disasters.

Problems are compounded by the growing domestic inequities; the distribution of benefits in society becomes more and more unequal. This is especially so in countries ridden by deep humanitarian emergencies which can be divided into acute and protracted crises. In protracted crises, new power structures and parallel economies are established. Those possessing power and resources are often opposed to the settlement of the crisis as it would erode their power basis.

It has been stressed above that large-scale violence is a pivotal element in humanitarian crises as it triggers other adverse developments. In fact, such violence seems to be a necessary and almost a sufficient condition for the emergence of a humanitarian crisis. Serious political violence has contributed almost in all cases also to increasing humanitarian costs measured by hunger, disease, and displacement. From this perspective, the recent decline in the number of serious civil wars is a welcome trend. If it continues, the present wave of humanitarian emergencies may subside, although not entirely.

Parts of Africa and Asia continue to be the main candidates for future emergencies. True, there has been some improvement, but major wars in Africa and South Asia in particular cannot be ruled out. Moreover, the obstacles to economic growth in Africa are formidable due to the failure of macroeconomic policies, but also the tendency of the outside world to assign higher risk to investments on the continent than warranted by the circumstances (Collier and Gunning 1999).

It may well be that the present 'time-out' in humanitarian emergencies is, in part, due to the dramatic lessons learned by the international community in Bosnian, Rwandan, and Somalian disasters. When their memories fade in the public consciousness, the cycle of emergencies may start again. It may be, though, that the humankind has become more conscious of the most extreme humanitarian emergency, genocide, and may be able to detect its signs and act upon them earlier than what has been the case in the past. For this to be possible, more active and effective policies of conflict prevention are needed (though the crisis in Kosovo may not lend much credibility to this suggestion).

In identifying potential humanitarian emergencies of the future, one should pay special attention to economic, political, and cultural faultlines and breaking points in society. One should be able to develop indicators to tap such lines and points (this is emphasized in Leatherman *et al.* 1999). For instance, thinking about the Rwandan case in hindsight, it can be recalled that the country's economy deteriorated sharply in the early 1990s, the hierarchical Hutu social organization was mobilized into action, its ideology was defined in increasingly exclusive terms, and the ethnic hate propaganda was disseminated without much constraint. Thus, several breaking points have been visible in the Rwandan society as they have been also in Burundi (Prunier 1995).

In an early-warning mode, it has been also suggested that the environmental degradation, overtilling of the soil, overgrazing, and overpopulation in the Senegal River basin are leading to major economic and social crises which are exacerbated by ethnic strife in Mauritania and Senegal (both countries are high up on poverty indicators). In addition to these, several other African countries, such as Malawi, Central African Republic, and Niger, need continuing analysis and attention. While information gathering is necessary for a functioning early-warning system, only focusing attention and engaging the international community can provide a sufficient condition for effective crisis prevention (Taylor 1995).

Future humanitarian crises are not necessarily new ones. Many of today's unresolved crises, such as Angola, Iraq, and Sudan, may continue as protracted confrontations because their solution would require so profound internal compromises and external engagement that they cannot be realistically anticipated. It may also be that some of the emergencies which are now somehow under control may be only temporarily so, and that they erupt in the future into new cycles of violence and displacement (for example, Afghanistan, Bosnia, Burma, Cambodia, Rwanda, and Somalia).

New humanitarian crises may also erupt. Egypt and Indonesia are examples of countries in which economic, environmental and demographic pressures are growing quickly, the civil society is becoming more restless, and the structures of political governance are too weak and compromised to be able to maintain stability. Pakistan may be heading to the slippery political and social slope and the future coherence of India cannot be guaranteed, either. In Nigeria, it is interesting to follow up whether the crisis has the point of no return or whether the return to civilian administration can ameliorate the situation. Kenya's economic progress and political stability seem to be deteriorating into a deeper social and political crisis. The future is unpredictable, but one things is sure: humanitarian emergencies will not wither away in any foreseeable future.

Table A2.1. Mortality rate under five years of age per 1000, 1992 and 1995

	1995	1992	Change (%)
Afghanistan	251	257	−2.3
Sierra Leone	246	249	−1.2
Malawi	215	226	−4.8
Guinea-Bissau	207	239	−13.4
Guinea	200	230	−13.0
Gambia	193	n.a.	
Burkina Faso	189	150	+26.0
Mali	188	220	−14.5
Niger	186	320	−41.2
Angola	184	292	−37.0
Somalia	180	211	−14.7
Mozambique	179	281	−37.6
Chad	175	209	−16.3
Ethiopia	174	208	−16.3

	1995	1992	Change (%)
Uganda	174	185	−5.9
Gabon	171	158	+8.2
Equatorial Guinea	171	n.a.	
Djibouti	166	n.a.	
Rwanda	162	222	−27.0
Benin	161	147	+9.5
Senegal	160	145	+10.3
Yemen	159	177	−10.2
Liberia	155	217	−28.5
Central African Republic	152	179	−15.1
Eritrea	150	208	−27.9
Bhutan	149	201	−25.7
Nigeria	149	191	−22.0
Lao DPR	148	145	+2.1
Bangladesh	148	127	+16.5
Burundi	146	179	−18.4
Mauritania	145	206	−29.6

Sources: WHO (1995: 101–4) and (1996: 123–6).

Table A2.2. Underweight children under the age of five, in 1975 and 1990, % of all children under five

	1992	1990	1975	Change, %
Bangladesh	11,480	66	84	−21.4
India	69,345	63	71	−11.3
Nepal	1,665	51	63	−19.0
Mozambique	1,195	47	44	+6.8
Niger	676	44	50	−12.0
Vietnam	3,860	42	55	−23.6
Sri Lanka	762	42	55	−23.6
Pakistan	3,725	42	47	−10.6
Ethiopia	3,810	40	45	−11.1
Afghanistan	1,995	40	19	+110.5
Somalia	656	39	47	−17.2
Iran	4,145	39	43	−9.3
Indonesia	8,660	38	57	−33.3
Madagascar	834	38	30	+26.6
Cambodia	522	38	43	−11.6
Papua New Guinea	210	36	39	−7.7
Nigeria	7,480	35	30	+16.7
Angola	641	35	24	+45.8
Sudan	1,525	34	36	−5.5
Lao DPR	255	34	41	−17.1
Philippines	3,045	34	39	−12.8
Burma	1,985	33	41	−19.5
Zaïre	2,425	33	28	+15.2
Central African Republic	n.a.	32	53	−39.6
Rwanda	457	32	37	−13.5

Source: UNDP (1994: 134–5) and (1995: 162–3).

References

Akokpari, John K. (1998). 'The State, Refugees and Migration in Sub-Saharan Africa'. *International Migration*, 36 (2): 211–31.

Albala-Bertrand, J. M. (1993). *Political Economy of Large Natural Disasters*. Oxford: Clarendon Press.

Alexander, David (1997). 'The Study of National Disasters, 1977–1997: Some Reflections on a Changing Field of Knowledge'. *Disasters*, 21 (4): 284–304.

Ayoob, Mohammed (1995). *The Third World Security Predicament. State Making, Regional Conflict, and the International System*. Boulder, CO: Lynne Rienner.

Bariagaber, Assefaw (1995). 'Linking Political Violence and Refugee Situations in the Horn of Africa: An Empirical Approach'. *International Migration*, 33 (2): 209–34.

Becker, Jasper (1996). *Hungry Ghosts. Mao's Secret Famine*. New York: The Free Press.

Blaikie, Piers, Terry Cannon, Ian Davis, and Ben Wisner (1994). *At Risk. Natural Hazards, People's Vulnerability, and Disasters*. London: Routledge.

Bodley, John H. (1992). 'Anthropology and the Politics of Genocide', in Carolyn Nordstrom and JoAnn Martin (eds.), *The Paths to Domination, Resistance, and Terror*. Berkeley: University of California Press, 37–51.

Brown, Michael E., and Richard N. Rosecrance (1999). *The Costs of Conflict. Prevention and Cure in the Global Arena*. Lanham, MD: Rowman and Littlefield.

Buzan, Barry (1991). *People, States, and Fear. An Agenda for International Security Studies in The Post-Cold War Era*. London: Harvester Wheatsheaf.

Castles, Stephen, and Mark J. Miller (1993). *The Age of Migration. International Population Movements in the Modern World*. London: Macmillan.

Chadda, Maya (1997). *Ethnicity, Security and Separatism in India*. Calcutta: Oxford University Press.

Chalk, Frank (1994). 'Redefining Genocide', in George J. Andreapoulos (ed.), *Genocide: Conceptual and Historical Dimensions*. Philadelphia: University of Pennsylvania Press, 47–63.

Charny, Israel W. (1994). 'Toward a Generic Definition of Genocide', in George J. Andreapoulos (ed.), *Genocide: Conceptual and Historical Dimensions*. Philadelphia: University of Pennsylvania Press, 64–94.

Chen, Lincoln (1995). 'Human Security: Concepts and Approaches', in Tatsuro Matsumae and Lincoln Chen (eds.), *Common Security in Asia. New Concepts in Human Security*. Tokyo: Tokai University Press, 137–46.

Chirot, Daniel (1994). *Modern Tyrants. The Power and Prevalence of Evil in Our Age*. New York: The Free Press.

Cohen, Roberta, and Francis M. Deng (eds.) (1998). *The Forsaken People. Case Studies of the Internally Displaced*. Washington, DC: The Brookings Institution Press.

Collier, Paul, and Jan Willem Gunning (1999). 'Explaining African Economic Performance'. *Journal of Economic Literature*, 37 (1): 64–111.

Cranna, Michael (ed.) (1994). *The True Costs of Conflict. Seven Recent Wars and their Effects on Society*. New York: The New Press.

Cuny, Frederick C. (1983). *Disasters and Development*. New York: Oxford University Press.

Curtis, Donald, Michael Hubbard, and Andrew Shepherd (1988). *Preventing Famine. Policies and Prospects for Africa*. New York: Routledge.

Dasgupta, Partha (1993a). 'The Economics of Neglect', in Kevin M. Cahill (ed.), *A Framework for Survival. Health, Human Rights, and Humanitarian Assistance in Conflicts and Disasters*. New York: Basic Books, 82–100.

Dasgupta, Partha (1993b). *An Inquiry into Well-Being and Destitution*. Oxford: Oxford University Press.

de Waal, Alex (1990). 'A Re-assessment of Entitlement Theory in the Light of Recent Famines in Africa'. *Development and Change*, 21 (4): 469–90.

Duffield, Mark (1994). 'The Political Economy of Internal War: Assett Transfer, Complex Emergencies and International Aid', in Joanna Macrae and Anthony Zwi (eds.), *War and Hunger. Rethinking International Responses to Complex Emergencies*. London: Zed Books, 50–69.

Edkins, Jenny (1996). 'Legality with a Vengeance: Famines and Humanitarian Relief in 'Complex Emergencies'. *Millennium*, 25 (3): 547–75.

Eide, Asbjørn (1989). 'Realization of Social and Economic Rights and the Minimum Threshold Analysis'. *Human Rights Law Journal*, 10 (1–2): 35–51.

Ellis, Stephen (1996). 'Africa after the Cold War: New Patterns of Government and Politics'. *Development and Change*, 27 (1): 1–28.

Fein, Helen (1990). 'Genocide: A Sociological Perspective'. *Current Sociology*, 38 (1): 1–126.

Fein, Helen (1993). 'Revolutionary and Antirevolutionary Genocides: A Comparison of State Murders in Democratic Kampuchea, 1975 to 1979, and in Indonesia, 1965 to 1966'. *Comparative Studies in Society and History*, 35 (4): 796–823.

Finnegan, William (1995). 'Letter from Mogadishu: A World of Dust'. *The New Yorker*, 20 March 20: 64–77.

George, Alexander (1979). 'Case Studies and Theory Development: The Method of Structured, Focused Comparisons', in Paul G. Lauren (ed.), *Diplomacy: New Approaches in History, Theory and Policy*. New York://publisher//43–68.

Glazovsky, Nikita F. (1995). 'The Aral Sea Basin', in Jeanne X. Kasperson *et al.* (eds.), *Regions at Risk. Comparisons of Threatened Environments*. Tokyo: The United Nations University Press, 92–139.

Global Humanitarian Emergencies (1996). New York: United States Mission to the United Nations.

Goldgeier, James M., and Lawrence Vescera (1992). 'A Tale of Two Worlds: Core and Periphery in the Post-Cold War Era'. *International Organization*, 46 (2): 467–91.

Gordon, Michael R. (1996). 'Chechnya Toll Is Far Higher, 80,000 Dead, Lebed Says. *New York Times*. 4 September: A3.

Green, Reginald Herbold (1994). 'The Course of Four Horsemen: Costs of War and its Aftermath in Sub-Saharan Africa', in Joanna Macrae and Anthony Zwi (eds.), *War and Hunger. Rethinking International Responses to Complex Emergencies*. London: Zed Books, 37–49.

Griggs, Richard (1997). 'Designs for Peace. Redrafting Regional Boundaries and Other Proposals'. *Track Two* (Rondebosch), 6 (1): 18–25.

Gurr, Ted Robert (1993). *Minorities at Risk. A Global View of Ethnopolitical Conflicts*. Washington, DC: The United States Institute of Peace.

Harff, Barbara, and Ted Robert Gurr (1987). 'Toward Empirical Theory of Genocides and Politicides: Identification and Measurement of Cases since 1945'. *International Studies Quarterly*, 31 (3): 359–71.

Harff, Barbara, and Ted Robert Gurr (1995). 'Victims of the State. Genocides, Politicides and Group Repression from 1945 to 1995'. *PIOOM Report*, 7 (1): 25–39.

Hobsbawm, Eric (1994). *The Age of Extremes. A History of the World, 1914–1991*. New York: Pantheon Books.

Holsti, K. J. (1995). 'War, Peace, and the State of the State'. *International Political Science Review*, 16 (4): 319–40.

Howard, Rhoda E. (1996). 'Civil Conflict in Sub-Saharan Africa: Internally Generated Causes'. *International Journal*, 51 (1): 29–53.

Hunger 1995. (1994). Causes of Hunger. Fifth Annual Report on the State of the World Hunger. Silver Spring: Bread for the World Institute.

Jones, Charles I. (1997). 'On the Evolution of the World Income Distribution'. *Journal of Economic Perspectives*, 11 (3): 19–36.

Kane, Hal (1995). 'The hour of Departure: Forces that Create Refugees and Migrants'. *Worldwatch Paper* 125. Washington, DC: Worldwatch Institute.

Kaplan, Robert D. (1996). *The Ends of the Earth. Journey at the Dawn of the 21st Century*. New York: Random House.

Kasperson, Roger *et al.* (1995). 'Critical Environmental Regions: Concepts, distinctions and issues', in Jeanne X. Kasperson, Roger E. Kasperson and B. L. Turner (eds.), *Regions at Risk. Comparisons of Threatened Environments*. Tokyo: The United Nations University Press, 1–41.

Keen, David (1991). 'A Disaster for Whom? Local Interests and International Donors during Famine among the Dinka of Sudan'. *Disasters*, 15 (2): 150–64.

Keen, David (1994). *The Benefits of Famine. A Political Economy if Famine and Relief in Southwestern Sudan, 1983–1989*. Princeton, NJ: Princeton University Press.

Kenney, George (1996). 'Steering Clear of Balkan shoals'. *The Nation*, 8–15 January: 21–4.

Kiernan, Ben (1996). *The Pol Pot Regime. Race, Power, and Genocide under the Khmer Rouge, 1975–79*. New Haven: Yale University Press.

Krain, Matthew (1997). 'State-sponsored Mass Murder. The Onset and Severity of Genocides and Politicides. *Journal of Conflict Resolution*, 41 (3): 331–60.

Lake, David A. (1997). 'Regional Security Complexes: A Systems Approach', in David A. Lake and Patrick M. Morgan (eds.), *Regional Orders. Building Security in a New World*. University Park: The Pennsylvania University Press, 45–67.

Leatherman, Janie, Patrick D. Gaffney, William DeMars, and Raimo Väyrynen (1999). *Breaking Cycles of Violence. Conflict Prevention in Intrastate Crises*. West Hartford, CT: Kumarian Press.

Lounev, Sergei, and Glerii Shirokov (1995). 'Central Asia as a New Region in World Politics', in Roald Z. Sagdeev and Susan Eisenhower (eds.), *Central Asia. Conflict, Resolution, and Change*. Chevy Chase, MD: CPSS Press, 293–310.

Macrae, Joanna, and Anthony Zwi (1994). 'Famine, Complex Emergencies and International Policy in Africa: An Overview', in Joanna Macrae and Anthony Zwi (eds.), *War and Hunger. Rethinking International Responses to Complex Emergencies*. London: Zed Books, 6–36.

Mann, Michael (1993). *The Sources of Social Power, Volume 2: The Rise of Classes and Nation-States, 1760–1914*. Cambridge: Cambridge University Press.

Martin, Philip, and Jonas Widgren (1996). 'International Migration: A Global Challenge'. *Population Bulletin*, 51 (1).

Moeller, Susan D. (1998). *Compassion Fatigue: How Media Sell Disease, Famine, War and Death*. London: Routledge.

Myers, Norman (1993). *Ultimate Security. The Environmental Basis of Politics*. New York: W. W. Norton.

Nairn, Tom (1997). 'Reflections on Nationalist Disasters'. *New Left Review*, 230: 145–52.

Nolutshungu, Sam C. (1996). 'International Security and Marginality', in Sam C. Nolutshungu (ed.), *Margins of Insecurity. Minorities and International Security*. Rochester, NY: University of Rochester Press, 1–35.

O'Connell, Robert L. (1995). *Ride of the Second Horseman. The Birth and Death of War*. New York: Oxford University Press.

Oliver-Smith, Anthony (1991). 'Successes and Failures in Post-disaster Settlement'. *Disasters*, 15 (1): 12–23.

Osmani, S. R. (1996). 'Famine, Demography, and Endemic Poverty'. *Journal of International Development*, 8 (5): 597–623.

Øyen, Else (1996). 'Poverty Research Rethought', in Else Oyen, S. M. Miller and Syed Abdus Samad (eds.), *Poverty. A Global Review*. Oslo: Scandinavian University Press, 3–17.

Parikh, Kirit S. (1990). 'Chronic Hunger in the World: Impact of International Policies', in Jean Drèze and Amartya Sen (eds.), *The Political Economy of Hunger*. Volume 1: *Entitlement and Well-Being*. Oxford: Clarendon Press/WIDER, 114–45.

Pellerin, Helene (1993). 'Global Restructuring in the World Economy and Migration: The Globalization of Migration Dynamics'. *International Journal*, 43 (2): 240–54.

Platt, Anne (1996a). 'Confronting Infectious Diseases', in Lester R. Brown *et al.*, *The State of the World 1996*. New York: W.W. Norton, 114–32.

Platt, Anne (1996b). 'Infecting Ourselves: How Environmental and Social Disruptions Trigger Diseases'. *Worldwatch Paper* 129. Washington, DC: Worldwatch Institute.

Pomfret, Richard (1995). *The Economies of Central Asia*. Princeton, N.J.: Princeton University Press.

Porter, Bruce D. (1994). *War and the Rise of the State. The Military Foundations of Modern Politics*. New York: The Free Press.

Prendergast, John (1996). *Frontline Diplomacy. Humanitarian Aid and Conflict in Africa*. Boulder, CO: Lynne Rienner.

Prendergast, John (1997). *Crisis Response. Humanitarian Band-Aids in Sudan and Somalia*. London: Pluto Press.

Price-Smith, Andrew T. (1997). 'Infectious Diseases and State Failures. Developing a New Security Paradigm'. Paper prepared for the 38th Annual Convention of the International Studies Association, Toronto, 18–22 March.

Prunier, Gerard (1995). *The Rwandan Crisis. History of Genocide*. New York: Columbia University Press.

Rabehl, Thomas, and Stefan Trines (1997). 'Das Kriegsgeschehen 1996. Register der Kriege und bewaffneten Konflikte'. Universität Hamburg. Foschugstelle Kriege, Rüstung und Entwicklung. Arbeitspapier No. 6.

Rangasami, Amrita (1985). 'Failure of Exchange Entitlements' Theory of Famine'. *Economic and Political Weekly*, 20 (41) and (42): 1747–52, 1797–1801.

Ravallion, Martin (1997). 'Famines and Economics'. *Journal of Economic Literature*, 35 (3): 1205–42.

Regan, Colm (1983). 'Underdevelopment and Hazards in Historical Perspective: An Irish Case Study', K. Hewitt (ed.), *Interpretations of Calamity from the Viewpoint of Human Ecology*. Boston: Allen and Unwin, 98–120.

Richmond, Anthony H. (1994). *Global Apartheid. Refugees, Racism, and the New World Order*. Toronto: Oxford University Press.

Rieff, David (1996). 'An Age of Genocide'. *The New Republic*, 29 January, 33–5.

Rondos, Alex (1994). 'The Collapsing State and International Security', in Janne E. Nolan (ed.), *Global Engagement. Cooperation and Security in the 21st Century*. Washington, DC: The Brookings Institution, 481–503.

Rothschild, Emma (1995). 'What is Security?' *Daedalus*, 124 (3): 53–98.

Rummel, R. J. (1994). *Death by Government. Genocide and Mass Murder since 1900*. New Brunswick, NJ: Transaction Publishers.

Rummel, R. J. (1997). *Power Kills. Democracy as a Method of Nonviolence*. New Brunswick, NJ: Transaction Publishers.

Sadowski, Yahya (1998). *The Myth of Global Chaos*. Washington, DC: The Brookings Institution Press.

Scrimshaw, Nevin S. (1997). 'Nutrition and Health from Womb to Tomb'. *Food and Nutrition Bulletin*, 18 (1): 1–19.

Sen, Amartya K. (1981). *Poverty and Famines*. Oxford: Oxford University Press.

Singer, Max, and Aaron Wildavsky (1993). *The Real World Order. Zones of Peace/Zones of Turmoil*. Chatham, NJ: Chatham House Publishers.

Solway, Jacqueline S. (1994). 'Drought as a "Revelatory Crisis": An Exploration of Shifting Entitlement and Hierarchies in the Kalahari, Botswana'. *Development and Change*, 25 (3): 471–95.

State of the Peoples. A Global Human Rights Report on Societies in Danger (1993). Boston: Beacon Press/Cultural Survival.

State of World Conflict Report 1997–98 (1998). Atlanta, GA: The Carter Center.

The State of the World's Refugees (1995)

Susman, Paul, Phil O'Keefe, and Ben Wisner (1983). 'Global Disasters. A Radical Interpretation', in K. Hewitt (ed.), *Interpretations of Calamity from the Viewpoint of Human Ecology*. Boston: Allen and Unwin, 263–83.

Taylor, Paul (1995). 'Options for the Reform of the International System for Humanitarian Assistance', in John Harriss (ed.), *The Politics of Humanitarian Intervention*. London: Pinter, 91–143.

The Economist (1996). 'Pakistan: The Belfast of Asia'. 1 June: 34–5.

UNDP (various years). *Human Development Report* 1994, 1995 and 1997. New York: Oxford University Press/UNDP.

UNHRC (1996). *Populations of Concern to the UNHRC: A Statistical Overview, 31 December 1995* (July 1996). Geneva: UNHCR.

Uvin, Peter (1994). *The International Organization of Hunger*. London: Kegan Paul International.

Uvin, Peter *et al.* (1995). 'Overview of World Hunger', in *Hunger 1995. Causes of Hunger*. Silver Spring, MD: Bread for the World Institute, 9–20.

Väyrynen, Raimo (1996). 'The Age of Humanitarian Emergencies'. Research for

Action No. 25. Helsinki: The World Institute of Development Economics Research.

Väyrynen, Raimo (1999). 'More Questions than Answers: Dilemmas of Humanitarian Action'. *Peace and Change*, 24 (2): 172–96.

Wallensteen, Peter, and Margareta Sollenberg (1996). 'The End of International War? Armed Conflict 1989–95'. *Journal of Peace Research*, 33 (2): 353–70.

Wallensteen, Peter, and Margareta Sollenberg (1997). 'Armed Conflicts, Conflict Termination and Peace Agreements, 1989–96'. *Journal of Peace Research*, 34 (3): 339–58.

Wallensteen, Peter, and Margareta Sollenberg (1998). 'Armed Conflict and Regional Conflict Complexes, 1989–97'. *Journal of Peace Research*, 35 (5): 621–34.

Waller, Robert (1996). 'Sudanese Security. Rogue State in Crisis'. *Jane's Intelligence Review*, 8 (7): 311–15.

Watts, Michael (1991a). 'Entitlements and Empowerment? Famine and Starvation in Africa'. *Review of African Political Economy*, 51: 9–26.

Watts, Michael (1991b). 'Heart of Darkness: Reflections on Famine and Starvation in Africa', in R. E. Downs, Donna O. Kerner and Stephen L. Reyna (eds.), *The Political Economy of African Famine*. Amsterdam: Gordon and Breach, 23–68.

Watts, Michael (1983). *Silent Violence. Food, Famine and Peasantry in Northern Nigeria*. Berkeley: University of California Press.

Weiner, Myron (1995). *The Global Migration Crisis. Challenge to States and Human Rights*. New York: HarperCollins.

Weiner, Myron (1996). 'Bad Neighbors, Bad Neighborhoods: An Inquiry into the Causes of Refugee Flows'. *International Security*, 21 (1): 5–42.

WHO (World Health Organization) (1995). *The World Health Report 1995. Bridging the Gaps*. Geneva: WHO.

WHO (World Health Organization) (1996). *The World Health Report 1996. Fighting the Disease, Fostering Development*. Geneva: WHO.

World Bank (1993). *World Development Report 1993: Investing in Health*. New York: Oxford University Press

World Bank (1999). *World Development Report 1998/99: Knowledge for Development*. New York: Oxford University Press for the World Bank.

World Disasters Report (various years). London: International Federation of Red Cross and Red Crescent Societies/Oxford University Press.

World Refugee Survey (various years). Washington, DC: Immigration and Refugee Services of America.

Yang, Dali L. (1996). *Calamity and Reform in China. State, Rural Society, and Institutional Change since the Great Leap Famine*. Stanford, CA: Stanford University Press.

3

The Economic Causes of Humanitarian Emergencies

E. WAYNE NAFZIGER AND JUHA AUVINEN

1. Introduction

A complex humanitarian emergency is a man-made crisis, in which large numbers of people die and suffer from war, physical violence (often by the state), or displacement, and is usually accompanied by widespread disease and hunger (see Väyrynen, Chapter 2).[1] In Auvinen and Nafziger (1999), we conducted, to our knowledge, the first econometric analysis of the relationship between humanitarian emergencies and their hypothesized sources, based on data from developing countries. We constructed four indicators of humanitarian emergencies and examined their origins with pooled cross-national time-series regression techniques.

Our analysis showed that stagnation and decline in real (inflation-adjusted) gross domestic product (GDP), slow growth in average food production, high income inequality, a high ratio of military expenditures to national income, and a tradition of violent conflict are sources of emergencies. Also inflation and low levels of International Monetary Fund (IMF) funding are associated with emergencies, although causality may run from emergencies to high inflation and low Fund assistance, rather than, or as well as, the other way round (Auvinen and Nafziger 1999).

In the next section, we sketch the methods and findings of that econometric study as a prelude to the main body of the chapter, which concentrates on the politico-economic explanations for the findings.

2. A Sketch of the Econometric Methods and Findings

The database for emergencies includes annual data on 124 countries from 1980 to 1995. To ensure broad representation, we include all low- and

[1] We thank Tony Addison, G. A. Cornia, Kisangani Emizet, Valpy FitzGerald, Helinä Melkas, Manuel Montes, Germano Mwabu, Henry Owusu, Renato Paniccià, Manuel Pastor, Barnett Rubin, Frances Stewart, Cecilia Ugaz, Peter Uvin and Raimo Väyrynen for helpful comments, but we are solely responsible for errors.

middle-income countries with more than one million people,[2] as indicated by the World Bank's *World Development Report 1996*,[3] except upper middle-income oil-exporting countries Libya, Saudi Arabia, Oman, and Bahrain (with a relative abundance of resources but a lack of conflict data); European Union member Greece; and Eritrea, independent in 1993 and lacking data before then. All Eritrean battle deaths and refugee data are classified as a part of Ethiopia's civil war.

We use four indicators to measure our concept of humanitarian emergencies. Battle deaths,[4] a proxy for deaths resulting from direct violence, measures the intensity of armed conflict in the country. However, because of the limitations of our dataset, our proxy for war deaths excludes the large number of civilian deaths, including those that result from genocides.[5] The number of refugees indicates the extent of displacement across national boundaries. The daily calorie supply per capita is used as a proxy for malnutrition, and infant mortality rate is used as a proxy for disease. We elaborate on these measures in Appendix I.[6]

Are the four indicators—deaths, refugees, malnutrition, and disease—a part of a single phenomenon, complex humanitarian emergencies? The simple correlations between deaths and refugees is strong ($r = 0.57$), with the coefficient significant at the 1 per cent level (2-tailed), suggesting the two indicators are part of a single phenomenon, complex humanitarian emergencies. However, except for the correlation of refugees with calorie growth ($r = 0.27$), the other intercorrelations are not very strong. We con-

---

[2] Despite a population of less than one million, six more significant continental microstates are included in the dataset: Belize (population in 1995, 211,000), Djibouti (615,000), Equatorial Guinea (415,000), Guyana (821,000), Suriname (423,000), and Swaziland (841,000). Their common borders with other nations and/or natural conditions make them much more susceptible to complex humanitarian emergencies than the small island states excluded from the analysis.

[3] The World Bank (1996c: 188–9) divides countries into four groups on the basis of per capita GNP. In 1994, these categories were low-income countries (less than US$ 750), lower-middle-income countries (US$ 750–2,900), upper-middle-income countries (US$ 2,900–8,500), and high-income countries (more than US$ 8,500). While the margin of error is substantial and the boundary between category rises each year with inflation, few countries shifted categories between 1974 and 1994 (Nafziger 1997: 9–37).When we use the World Bank concept, all transitional countries are also developing countries.

[4] Battle deaths is correct, and not, as Collier and Hoeffler (1998) indicate, battle-related deaths (implying, in addition, civilian deaths associated with battles). Http://biscu.its.yale. edu/cgi-bin/s-despires/925.spires, which describes the Singer-Small Correlates of War Project: International and Civil War Data used by Collier-Hoeffler and us, indicates that while 'Part I, the International Wars file . . . [includes] battle and total deaths, . . . Part 2, the Civil War file describes . . . number of battle deaths'.

[5] Most genocides take place during wars, so our dataset, by identifying wars, identifies most occurrences of genocides but understates civilian deaths during the period.

[6] In interpreting our results, we have considered (i) problems in the measurement and validity of different components of emergencies (discussed in the Appendix, Chapter 1, and Melkas 1996) and (ii) missing observations systematically related to low levels of economic development (one of our explanatory variables) or wars (a component of complex humanitarian emergencies by our definition).

sidered this information when constructing composite indicators for the dependent variable, humanitarian emergencies (Appendix I).

For the first part of the analysis, we decided not to construct a dichotomous dependent variable, patterned after Väyrynen's Chapter 2, which would have recorded 1 if a country experienced a humanitarian emergency during 1992–94 and 0 if it did not. First, this procedure would have involved establishing an arbitrary threshold for complex humanitarian emergencies: how can we determine the moment when deaths and disability have reached an emergency in one country while in another one they had not? Second, in numerous instances, such as Ethiopia and Uganda, countries moved in and out of humanitarian emergencies, and sometimes as in Burundi, Somalia, and Liberia, back again, during the 1980 to 1995 period.

According to our measure of humanitarian emergencies, HUMEMERG (Appendix I), 22 countries experienced both battle deaths and refugees during a given year in 1980–1994, a picture remarkably similar to Väyrynen (Chapter 2, Tables 2.1 and 2.2), despite the fact that he concentrates on the 1990s. Compared to his tables, we also identify humanitarian emergencies in Cambodia in 1980–91, Chad 1980–88, El Salvador 1980–92, Guatemala 1982–84, Lebanon 1980, Nicaragua 1982–90, the Philippines 1980–88, and Uganda 1980–88, primarily countries where wars occurred before 1990 or less populated countries, since Väyrynen's threshold of 2,000 war casualties, based on numbers of casualties rather than deaths as a percentage of the population, is biased toward countries with larger populations. Since HUMEMERG does not include genocides and requires *both* war deaths and external refugees, we do not identify humanitarian emergencies in Algeria, Colombia, Georgia, India, Peru, Sierra Leone, South Africa, and Turkey (Auvinen and Nafziger 1999, Table 1).

Figure 3.1 shows an increase for our first measure of emergencies, DEATHREF (Appendix I), from 1980 to 1994.[7] An increasing, albeit less pronounced, trend also characterizes HUMEMERG. After 1988, the increases seem to be from the rising number of refugees in the world, in contrast to the number of battle deaths (Nafziger and Auvinen 1997: 18–20), which, according to our dataset, decline (although perhaps as a result of the limitations of the Correlates of War dataset, see Appendix I). Moreover, the decline in deaths would be more gradual and the increase in DEATHREF steeper, if we had measures for democides and politicides, which are often part of humanitarian emergencies but are not included in our battle death figures. Complicating the picture, our third measure, COHE, has declined since 1990, because of factors already mentioned, in addition to the general improvement in infant survival and calorie supply.

---

[7] Note that the logarithmic scale used in calculating the averages eliminates the impact of extremely high values.

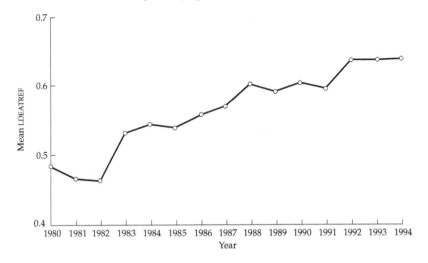

Fig. 3.1. Deaths and refugee flows, 1980–94 (annual means of values)

In Auvinen and Nafziger (1999), we applied pooled cross-country time-series regression techniques to a sample of 124 countries in 1980 to 1995, for a total of 1984 (16 x 124) cases. We discussed the justification of using pooled data, and applied several econometric methods—ordinary least squares (OLS), generalized least squares (GLS or Prais-Winsten), tobit, two-stage least squares, 'fixed effects', 'random effects', and probit models—to test the robustness of our findings. See OLS, GLS, and probit results in Appendix Tables A3.1 to A3.3.

The regression analyses on the continuous dependent variables demonstrate that humanitarian emergencies are directly associated with the Gini index of income concentration, inflation, military centrality as defined by military expenditures as a percentage of GNP, and conflict tradition,[8] and

---

[8] We also experimented with variables from Gurr's *Minorities at Risk* database (1993). Political rights' demands (POLRI) turned out to be significant in the model for DEATHREF. The variable includes ethnic minority groups' diffuse political grievances (excluding demands for political autonomy) and the groups' 'seek[ing] of greater political rights, central participation, equal civil rights and change in officials/policies'. It is notable that POLRI is the strongest correlate of humanitarian emergencies out of many candidates in the database, including economic discrimination, economic, cultural and political differentials, economic and social grievances. Our economic variables are likely to pick up some of the variation between the 'minorities variables' and emergencies but even when we restrict our variables' coefficients to zero, POLRI is more strongly associated than the economic status and demands of ethnic minorities with humanitarian emergencies. We have not included POLRI in appendix table A3.1 due to its large number of missing observations which substantially reduces the degrees of freedom in the model.

Gurr's study is an example of the ethnic model, in that the units of observation are ethnic minority groups. For criticisms of the ethnic model, including how it neglects the reshaping of ethnicity during conflict and modernization, see critiques by Peters (1999) and Widner (1999) of Collier (1999); Alexander *et al.* chapter 9; and Nafziger (1983).

inversely with GDP growth, GNP per capita, food output growth, and IMF funding as a percentage of GNP. The findings are by and large consistent through three measures of the dependent variable and whether we use ordinary least squares, generalized least squares (Prais-Winsten), fixed and random effects, tobit, or probit models. Humanitarian emergencies are most robustly associated with slow or negative economic growth, a low level of economic development, military centrality, and a tradition of violent conflict.

The probit probability model, which constituted the second part of our analysis, had the advantage of being able to express the effect of the explanatory variables on the probability of humanitarian emergencies.[9] In interpreting the coefficients we note, among other things, that in our sample: (i) a 10 per cent increase in GDP growth reduces the probability of a humanitarian emergency (LDEATHREF)[10] by 13 per cent; (ii) a 100 per cent increase (doubling) in GNP[11] per capita reduces the probability of an emergency by 13 per cent; (iii) a 10 per cent increase in the Gini index increases the probability of an emergency by 2.5 per cent; (iv) a 100 per cent increase (doubling) in military expenditures/GNP increases the probability of an emergency by 5 per cent; and (v) a 100 per cent increase (doubling) in deaths from political violence in 1963–77 would have increased the probability of an emergency by 4 per cent.

3. Stagnation and Decline in Incomes

3.1. Relative and absolute deprivation

Despite political conflicts in Quebec, Northern Ireland, and the Basque provinces, contemporary humanitarian disasters are rarely found among high-income countries, unless you include the roughly 20,000 people killed yearly, mostly by guns, in the United States' cities. Moreover, complex humanitarian emergencies are only found in low- and middle-income (that

[9] For the probit probability analysis, we constructed a dichotomous dependent variable. Rather than establishing arbitrary thresholds for our variables between complex humanitarian emergency and non-emergency countries, we set HUMEMERG and DEATHREF equal to 1 for every non-zero observation and zero otherwise, meaning that HUMEMERG was coded 1 in a year when a country experienced both battle deaths and refugees and that DEATHREF was coded 1 with either deaths or refugees.

The usual probit coefficients give us the effect on the odds and are thus difficult to interpret. However, we follow a standard procedure of evaluating the coefficients at the mean of the dependent variable which allows us to assess the change in the probability of humanitarian emergencies resulting from one unit increase in an explanatory variable.

[10] As the distributions of the variables are badly skewed, we made natural logarithmic transformations to reduce the probability of heteroskedasticity as well as the non-normality of the disturbance term. The transformed variables are listed with a prefix 'L'.

[11] GNP (gross national product) is the total output of goods and services in terms of income earned by a country's residents, and GDP (gross domestic product) the total output of goods and services in terms of income within a country's boundaries.

is, developing) countries, suggesting a threshold above which emergencies do not occur (SIPRI 1996; Holsti 1991).

Auvinen and Nafziger (1999) indicated that, holding other variables constant, slow real GDP growth helps explain complex humanitarian emergencies.[12] We use concepts of deprivation to show the effects of economic growth and stagnation on humanitarian emergencies; relative deprivation helps explain political conflict and absolute deprivation non-conflict components of emergencies. Relative deprivation is the actors' perception of social injustice arising from deprivation relative to other groups in society or a discrepancy between goods and conditions they expect and those they can get or keep. This deprivation often results from vertical or horizontal inequality (Stewart, Chapter 1), where the actors' income or conditions are related to those of others within society. Relative deprivation spurs social discontent, and sometimes anger, which provides motivation for potential collective violence (Gurr 1970). Among the various components of emergencies, war and violence have major catalytic roles, adding to social disruption and political instability, undermining economic activities, spreading hunger and disease, and fuelling refugee flows (Väyrynen, Chapter 2).

Relative deprivation is essentially a diachronic concept: people feel deprived of something they had, but subsequently lost, or when others have gained relative to them. Consequently a short-term income reduction is more important than protracted income decline or stagnation in analysing war and conflict dimensions of complex humanitarian emergencies. Indeed one who grows accustomed to being destitute may not feel frustrated at all. Deterioration of living conditions over a prolonged period thus entails absolute rather than relative deprivation. Although low or declining average incomes can become a source of relative deprivation in comparison to neighbouring countries or to incomes from an earlier period, aggression is unlikely to result from such an abstract and remote source. Tangible and salient factors such as a marked deterioration of living conditions, especially during a period of high expectations, are more likely to produce sociopolitical discontent that may be mobilized into political violence (cf. Davies 1962).

Only a portion of violence, however, results from insurgent action. In fact, Holsti (Chapter 7) demonstrates that the policies of governing élites are at the root of most humanitarian emergencies. Slow or negative growth puts more pressure on ruling élites, reducing the number of allies and clients they can support, undermining the legitimacy of the regime,

---

[12] In Auvinen and Nafziger (1999), we also found that a factor common to 12 of the 15 countries that according to Rummel (1994) have had more than one million democides (murders by the state) in the 20th century is stagnation or protracted decline in real GDP preceded. Three cases, the exceptions, had positive per capita growth but high income inequalities (below we discuss the role of income inequality).

and increasing the probability of regime turnover. To forestall threats to the regime, political élites may use repression to suppress discontent or capture a greater share of the majority's shrinking surplus. These repressive policies may entail acts of direct violence against or withholding food and other supplies from politically disobedient groups, as in Sudan in the 1980s (Keen, Chapter 8). Moreover, repression and economic discrimination may generate relative deprivation and trigger sociopolitical mobilization on the part of the groups affected, leading to further violence, worsening the humanitarian crisis.

Absolute deprivation can also contribute to a complex humanitarian emergency. Protracted economic stagnation is likely to increase the probability of non-conflict components of a complex emergency, that is, population displacement, hunger, and disease. As the literature on economic behaviour under situations of extreme distress shows, economic Darwinism tends to become dominant when food, resource, and employment scarcity becomes chronic. Under such circumstances, Darwinist behaviour tends to prevail over the behaviour dictated by the legal rules and social conventions regulating access to resources, and over the moral and judicial condemnation of theft, robbery, and expropriation. Protracted stagnation is also likely to weaken community sentiments of solidarity *vis-à-vis* weaker groups and hence redistribution in their favour. Protracted stagnation may also spur élites to expropriate the assets and resources of weaker social communities violently, particularly if political, ethnic, or class tensions already exist.

The relationship between stagnation, economic Darwinism, and the breakdown of social cohesion needs to be qualified on several counts. Obviously, countries with higher initial incomes per capita can withstand longer periods of stagnation without experiencing major social tensions and may be able to introduce the necessary political or economic reforms to address the sources of the stagnation. Also, as the situation of Tanzania suggests, economic stagnation within a context of 'shared poverty' may not be inherently destabilizing at the local level. In addition, of major relevance is the effect of stagnation on the provision of basic needs and infrastructure, and the impact of these factors on social and political integration. And finally, repression and political control may, at least temporarily, avoid the violent manifestations that could otherwise emerge if economic destitution continues unabated.

To summarize, stagnation and decline in incomes exacerbate the feeling of relative deprivation. Slow or negative growth puts ruling coalitions on the horns of a dilemma. They can expand rent-seeking opportunities for existing political élites, contributing to further economic stagnation that can threaten the legitimacy of the regime and future stability. Or they can reduce the number of allies and clients they support, risking opposition by those no longer sharing in the benefit of rule. Either strategy to manage power, in the midst of economic crises, can exacerbate the potential for repression and insurgency and, ultimately, humanitarian emergencies.

3.2. Regional cases

Since economic deceleration or collapse can disrupt ruling coalitions and exacerbate mass discontent, we should not be surprised that since 1980 the globe, particularly Africa, has been more vulnerable to political violence and humanitarian emergencies. From 1960–73 to 1973–96 (and especially after 1980), growth decelerated in both less-developed countries (LDCs) and developed countries (DCs) (Nafziger 1997)[13] based on World Bank data). Africa especially experienced a great descent in real GDP per capita after 1973. In Sub-Saharan Africa, growth fell from 2.0 per cent yearly, 1966 to 1973, to –0.7 per cent yearly from both 1974 to 1984 and 1985 to 90, and –0.9 per cent from 1991 to 1994 (World Bank 1996a; World Bank 1996b).

The majority of countries with humanitarian emergencies have experienced several years (or even decades) of negative or stagnant growth, where growth refers to real growth in GNP or GDP per capita. Virtually all emergencies listed in Chapter 2 (Tables 2.1 and 2.2) from 1992 to 1995 were preceded by slow or negative economic growth. Indeed, twelve of the sixteen Afro-Asian countries listed in these tables, for which data exist, had negative growth in the preceding period. Rwanda, Angola, Mozambique, Liberia, Sudan, Somalia, Ethiopia-Eritrea, Sierra Leone (from Sub-Saharan Africa), Lebanon, Algeria (from the Middle East), Afghanistan, and Iraq (from Asia) had negative growths in real GNP per capita in the years 1980 to 1991, while Burundi, South Africa (the Sub-Sahara), Sri Lanka, and Turkey (Asia) had positive growths (World Bank 1993).

Widespread negative growth among populations where a majority is close to levels of subsistence increases the vulnerability to humanitarian disasters. Consider low- and middle-income (developing) countries. From 1980 to 1991, 25 of 35 (71 per cent of) Sub-Saharan African countries and 40 of 58 (69 per cent of) Afro-Asian countries experienced negative growth, according to the World Bank (1993). In contrast, from 1960 to 1980, only eight of 29 (28 per cent of) Sub-Saharan countries and nine of 53 (17 per cent of) Afro-Asian countries (which includes three, Israel, Hong Kong, and Singapore, which have since graduated to high-income-country status) had negative economic growth, according to the earlier World Bank annual (1982). In addition, the positive growth of Latin America and the Caribbean during the 1960s and 1970s also reversed to a negative rate in the 1980s, according to the same World Bank sources. The following discussion, which briefly summarizes the interrelationships between growth

---

[13] Based on World Bank data.

and emergencies of the countries listed in Chapter 2 (Tables 2.1 and 2.2), suggests that the increase in political conflict and humanitarian emergencies in the 1990s is linked to the developing world's disastrous growth record of the 1980s.

3.2.1. African countries Angola and Mozambique, which fought wars of independence until 1975 and for years after that against forces supported by the United States and South Africa,[14] both suffered massive economic disruption during much of the last two decades. Sudan and Ethiopia, fighting civil wars in the 1980s, also suffered from economic collapse during the 1980s. Somalia's negative per capita growth during the period of General Siad Barre's authoritarian regime from 1969 to 1991 turned to more rapid economic decline during the fighting between factions during 1991–92, and was not reversed during the United Nations humanitarian intervention of 1992–94. The economies of Liberia and Sierra Leone, which experienced economic decline during the 1980s, virtually collapsed during their conflicts during the 1990s. Liberia's GNP fell an estimated 77 per cent from 1989 to 1993, while Sierra Leone's GNP declined by about one-half between the start of the civil war in 1991 and 1995 (Reno 1996).[15]

Rwanda's economic growth was positive until the mid-1980s, when it turned negative due to an agricultural crisis (Uvin, Volume 2, Chapter 6). Burundi grew moderately during the 1980s, not suffering from negative growth until its crisis from 1993 on.

3.2.2. Asian countries Afghanistan's growth, which was slow before the Soviet coup of 1978, was highly negative during the subsequent wars with guerrilla forces. While data are scarce, economists believe that Myanmar's internal conflicts prevented positive economic growth during the 1980s and early 1990s.

On the other hand, the civil war by the government of Sri Lanka with militant Tamil separatists from 1983 until the present devastated only a small portion of the country. As a result, Sri Lanka's moderate growth in gross domestic product per capita and high levels of social indicators (literacy and life expectancy) among Asian countries in the 1970s remained during these years, although because of wartime capital destruction, the

[14] Angola and Mozambique, together with the other seven Southern African Development Coordination Conference (SADCC now SADC) states—Botswana, Lesotho, Malawi, Tanzania, Swaziland, Zambia, and Zimbabwe—lost substantially from South African military and economic destabilization, including the disruption of transport links. The ECA (Economic Commission for Africa: 1989) estimates that the nine SADCC states lost US$ 60 billion GDP (or one-fourth), 1980–88, from South Africa's impairment. South Africa was supported in its policies in the 1980s by the 'constructive engagement' of the United States and Britain.

[15] Stewart (1993) shows that daily calories as a per cent of requirements fell in five of seven African countries at war during the 1980s: Angola, Ethiopia, Liberia, Somalia, and Sudan; remained the same in Mozambique; and increased in Uganda.

growth of *net* domestic product per capita would have been slower. In a similar fashion, Turkey's conflict with its minority Kurds had little effect in slowing down overall growth.

During the Iran–Iraq war, 1980–88, Iraq's GDP per capita (in constant 1980 prices) fell by 58 per cent. The United Nations' comprehensive embargo on Iraq beginning in August 1990, followed by the United States-led bombing and war with the US and United Nations of January–February 1991, contributed to a further 64 per cent decline in GDP per head (cumulative impact since 1980 was an 85 per cent fall) by 1991. From 1991 to 1994, average GDP declined an additional 33 per cent, for an accumulative fall of 90 per cent (Alnasrawi, Chapter 4, Volume II)!

3.2.3. Latin American countries   Urban and rural violence in Colombia, which includes clashes between the army and guerrillas that displaced hundreds of thousands of Colombians in the 1990s, has not prevented the country from a moderate rate of economic growth in recent years. Nicaragua had a negative growth in GNP per capita of 4.4 per cent yearly, 1980 to 1991 (World Bank 1993), which included a decade-long war with the United States and its Contra supporters. Guatemala has suffered economic decline from its decades-long civil war and conflict with rebels, while Peru experienced an economic setback from attacks beginning in the late 1970s from the *Sendero Luminoso* (Shining Path), based in the poverty-stricken Andean region, who were skilled in rural guerrilla warfare.

3.2.4. Central and Eastern Europe and Central Asia   In Yugoslavia, from 1980 to 1990, real GDP per capita declined and annual inflation averaged more than 35 per cent. Since the breakup of Yugoslavia and the war of the early 1990s, Bosnia-Herzegovina's economy has been massively disrupted, leading to its further collapse (Woodward 1995), while Croatia, although it resumed growth in 1994, had in 1996 a real GDP 36 per cent below its 1989 level (Bartholdy 1996).

Bartholdy (1996) indicates that after the breakdown of the Soviet Union, all of its republics experienced an income collapse, even if we assume that as much as one-fifth of income, from the black market or informal sector, is unreported. Among these were several republics facing humanitarian crises in the 1990s: Russia (with a secessionist conflict in Chechnya), Armenia, Azerbaijan, Georgia, and Tajikistan (Table 3.1).

3.3. The effect of emergencies on growth

Stewart, Humphreys and Lea (1997) show that complex humanitarian emergencies contribute to falls in GNP per capita.[16] The GLS Prais-Winsten

---

[16] Also Barro (1991) finds a direct association between economic growth and political stability but shies away from positing causation to either direction.

Table 3.1. Growth in selected former soviet republics

	Real GDP[a] (% change)							Est. level of real GDP in 1995 (1989 = 100)	Proj. level of real GDP in 1996 (1989 = 100)
	1990	1991	1992	1993	1994	1995 (est.)	1996 (proj.)		
Armenia	-7	-11	-52	-15	5	7	7	38	40
Azerbaijan	-12	-1	-23	-23	-21	-17	-7	34	32
Georgia	-12	-14	-40	-39	-35	-5	5	17	18
Russia	-4	-13	-15	-9	-13	-4	3	55	56
Tajikistan	-2	-7	-29	-11	-21	-12	-8	40	37
The former Soviet Union[b]	-4	-12	-15	-10	-14	-5	2	53	54

Source: Bartholdy (1996: 282, 291).

[a] Data for 1989–93 represent the most recent official estimates of outturns as reflected in publications from the national authorities, the International Monetary Fund, the World Bank, the Organization for Economic Cooperation and Development, the UN Economic Commission for Africa, PlanEcon and the Institute of International Finance. Data for 1995 are preliminary actuals, mostly official government estimates. Data for 1996 represent European Bank projections.

[b] Here taken to include all countries of the former Soviet Union, except Estonia, Latvia and Lithuania. Estimates for real GDP represent weighted averages. The weights used were European Bank estimates of nominal dollar-GDP for 1995.

model in Auvinen and Nafziger (1999) (Appendix Table A3.2) indicated that some of the impact of economic growth on LDEATHREF is carried over from past interactions between war, refugees and economic growth.

We estimated two-stage least squares models, with humanitarian emergencies and economic growth as the endogenous variables, to correct for the possible simultaneous equations bias caused by the two-way causality. After the elimination of the simultaneous-equations bias, the coefficient of GDP growth increases three-fold in all three models. There seems to be a two-way causal relationship between GDP growth and humanitarian emergencies but the relationship is stronger from GDP growth to emergencies than vice versa. This finding is supported when we apply different lag structures on the OLS and GLS models (Appendix Table A3.4). A poor economic performance, as indicated by sluggish real GDP growth, seems to be an important variable in explaining the rise of humanitarian emergencies, but emergencies also feed back to reduce growth.

3.4. Conclusion

Econometric and case-study evidence indicates that, holding other variables constant, slow real GDP growth helps explain complex humanitarian emergencies. Humanitarian emergencies also contribute to reduced (often negative) growth, although, according to our econometric tests, the direction of causation is weaker than from growth to emergencies. Contemporary humanitarian disaster is rarely episodic but is usually the culmination of longer-term politico-economic decay over a period of a decade or more. Negative growth interacts with political predation in a downward spiral, a spiral seen in African countries such as Angola, Ethiopia, Sudan, Somalia, Liberia, Sierra Leone, Zaire (Congo), and (post-1980) Nigeria. The metaphor appears to be not that of steadily climbing a mountain to the summit of high material welfare and ethnic harmony, but of Sisyphus pushing a huge rock uphill, where every slip means backsliding or even plunging to the abyss below.

4. Income Inequality

4.1. Inequality and emergencies

Alesina and Perotti's (1996) cross-sectional study of 71 developing countries, 1960–85, finds that income inequality, by fuelling social discontent, increases socio-political instability, as measured by deaths in domestic disturbances and assassinations (per million population) and coups (both successful and unsuccessful). Moreover, populations suffering deprivation are increasingly vulnerable to humanitarian emergencies if income concentration is high. Also, our regressions indicate that high income inequality (measured by a Gini coefficient)[17] contributes to complex humanitarian emergencies.

Severe social tensions leading to complex humanitarian emergencies may even arise under conditions of positive (even rapid) growth and expanding resource availability. High inequality can contribute to the immiseration or absolute deprivation of portions of the population, even with growth. Absolute deprivation during substantial growth was experienced, for instance, by Igbo political élites, dominant in Nigeria's Eastern Region, in 1964–65. The East lost oil tax revenues from a change in its regional allocation by the federal government, which ceased distributing mineral export revenues to regional governments.

Moreover, through the demonstration effect of consumption levels of the relatively well-off, high income concentration increases the perception of relative deprivation by substantial sections of the population, even when these do not experience absolute deprivation. The risk of political disintegration increases with a surge of income disparities by class, region, and community, especially when these disparities lack legitimacy among the population. Class and communal (regional, ethnic, and religious) economic differences often overlap, exacerbating perceived grievances and potential strife.

The trends and policies leading to this type of high income inequality may be summarized as follows:

- *Historical legacies* of discrimination (from colonialism,[18] apartheid, failed past policies, and so forth), which have remained unresolved, are often source of such inequality. Affluent classes and dominant ethnic communities use the advantages accumulated in the past—for example, access to capital, information, mobility, superior education and training, and privileged access to licences and concessions from government—to start enterprises, buy farms, and obtain government jobs in disproportionate numbers. Less affluent and influential groups are underrepresented in entrepreneurial activity, investment, and employment (Nafziger 1986). Moreover, even if current policies no longer discriminate against a particular social group, large differentials in the initial distribution of assets and opportunities lead, through market forces, to growth patterns characterized by large and rising inequalities.

[17] For Gini, we used an expanded and qualitatively improved dataset from Deininger and Squire (1996: 56–91), although we still decided not to use data from studies they relied on which used incomparable research methodologies. We were able to find relationships between Gini and war, which other researchers (such as Collier and Hoeffler 1998), without this dataset, could not find. Collier-Hoeffler indicate 'there is insufficient data to introduce distributional considerations into the empirical analysis'.

[18] Nafziger (1988); Nafziger (1983); and Nafziger (1995) discuss how colonialism and imperialism in Africa and Asia contributed to their underdevelopment and political instability.

The failure to rectify initial inequalities may, therefore, over time contribute to increasing conflicts.

- *Government policies* in distributing land and other assets, taxation, and the benefits of public expenditure, affect political and social cohesion. Included are policies that contribute to differential regional, communal, and generational opportunities in employment (especially in government), education, and the armed forces; the effects of these opportunities on regional, ethnic, and generational grievances; and the influence of these grievances on social mobilization and political protest. Another policy instrument is the access to financing by classes and communities during periods of major expansion of asset acquisition, such as indigenization, privatization, or outright expropriation.
- *Regional and ethnic economic competition* is associated with income disparities. Growing regional inequality and limited regional economic integration, associated with economic enclaves, can exacerbate ethnic and regional competition and conflict.

Regional factors contributing to conflict include educational and employment differentials, revenue allocation, and language discrimination which disadvantages minority language communities. Examples include the struggle for petroleum tax revenues and employment in the civil service and modern sector in Nigeria in the early to mid-1960s, the distribution of resources from East to West and employment discrimination against Bengalis in Pakistan in the 1950s and 1960s; the conflict between Hutu and Tutsi for control of the state and access to employment in Burundi and Rwanda; the contention over the distribution of falling economic resources and rising debt obligations in Yugoslavia in the 1980s and early 1990s, and the language, employment, and educational discrimination by the state against Tamils in post-independent Sri Lanka.

While high inequality is associated with emergencies, insurgency is more likely if the less advantaged can identify the perpetuators of their poverty and suffering. Sometimes, as in Nicaragua in the late 1970s and El Salvador, and Guatemala in the 1980s, high and increasing inequality, long-term economic decline, and political repression spur guerrilla warfare against a ruling oligarchy. Pastor and Boyce (Chapter 12, Volume 2) argue, 'Beneath the explosion into violence [in El Salvador, Guatemala, and Nicaragua] lay a long-simmering set of tensions due to inequity in the distribution of a key physical asset, land'. They indicate that longstanding tensions arising from deep economic inequalities, particularly in the distribution of land, provided the tinder for political violence, macroeconomic crises added a spark, external intervention fuelled the wars, and armed conflict propelled a downward economic spiral. Indeed Pastor and Boyce trace the roots of El Salvador's protracted emergency, a civil war from 1980 to 1992, to the late 19th century, when state decree abolished communal land and forcibly evicted indigenous communities, converting their land into *latifundia,* large (primarily coffee) estates owned by about sixty families who formed the ruling oligarchy and created nearly the most unequal land distribution in the world. El Salvador's agrarian structure is indicative of the tensions that contribute to political violence: a highly unequal land distribution combined with a proletarianized labour force, maintained in the face of popular resistant by 'intimidation, bloodshed, and other forms of organized violence' perpetuated by the ruling oligarchy that controlled the state (ibid.).

The following examples of Nigeria, South Africa, and Mexico, together with Central America, illustrate the diverse patterns of how discriminatory government policies cause economic inequality, fuel social discontent, and lead to political conflict and humanitarian emergencies. These dynamics may even occur when either the nation's real per capita GDP is growing, as in Nigeria, or when the disadvantaged group's economic position is improving, as for nonwhite South Africans from the 1970s through the early 1990s.

4.2. Nigeria: increased élite inequality during rapid growth

As indicated before, humanitarian disasters rarely occur in high-income countries. However, shouldn't we expect some instances where developing countries are split asunder into a humanitarian crisis from conflict over the potential for abundant resources and rapid economic growth? Yes, this can happen, as illustrated by the Nigerian–Biafran war, 1967–70, in which perhaps four million people died from hunger and other war-related causes and several million people were displaced. The war was fought for control of Nigeria's rich resources, especially in oil, but in the mid-1960s, political élites from the Eastern Region (subsequently Biafra) expected economic loss in the midst of rapid Nigerian economic growth. Election fraud and manipulation during Nigeria's 1964–65 elections undermined the previously critical position of Igbos, the dominant ethnic group in the Eastern Region, in the federal coalition. The East, which had produced two-thirds of Nigeria's petroleum, lost profits and other tax revenues from oil under a change in formula for revenue allocation. Moreover, Igbo and other Eastern ethnic groups were losing in the contention for key positions in the federal civil service and modern sector of Lagos, and had fled from business and high-level employment in the politically dominant North. Thus, Igbo political élites, government employees, and emigré business people experienced not only relative, but also absolute, economic decline.

The Nigerian civil war followed a period of 3 per cent real annual growth in GDP per capita from fiscal years 1958/9 to 1965/6 (at constant 1962/3 prices); petroleum expansion led the way, but industrial and agricultural growths were also steady. Moreover, in the mid- to late 1960s, Nigeria's regional élites foresaw some of the growth potential of the subsequent decade. Thus, despite the massive resource diversion and destruction, GDP per capita only fell 4 per cent yearly during the war. In addition, Nigeria's oil-fuelled real economic growth per person accelerated after the war to 8 per cent yearly from fiscal years 1969/70 to 1978/9 (at 1974/5 prices, a year of high oil prices, thus moderately overstating growth for the period) (Nafziger 1983).

But Nigeria's case is an exception. In few cases, a current humanitarian disaster is a conflict over the potential for rapid economic growth; most instead are struggles to maintain slices of shrinking economic pies.

4.3. South Africa: inequality under apartheid

The South African case, identified as having war deaths and refugees in Chapter 2 (Tables 2.1 and 2.2) demonstrates that if the perceived inequality is sufficiently grave, even improved material welfare for the disadvantaged group will not guarantee the absence of conflict. South Africa's real GDP per capita stagnated or declined from the early 1970s through the early 1990s.[19] However, per capita incomes of the white population fell, while the per capita incomes of the African population apparently increased slightly, at least during the period between 1985 and 1990 (Schlemmer 1994). Still, a survey conducted in 1988 demonstrated that only a very small proportion of a nation-wide sample of the black population was satisfied with various dimensions of their lives. More importantly, the results showed a deterioration of over 40 per cent in the blacks' perceived life satisfaction as compared with a survey in 1983 (Möller, Schlemmer and du Toit 1989). Why did grievances and dissatisfaction among the African population rise as its average income increased?

The political exclusion of the African population by the apartheid regime doubtless accounts for a great deal of the general dissatisfaction, but the role of income differentials should not be discounted either. To Africans, the increase in incomes during the previous two decades may have been insufficient, considering the substantial discrepancies in favour of the white population. In 1992, at the peak of the *de facto* civil war which led to the toppling of apartheid two years later, the GDP per capita of black, Asian, and mixed-race South Africa was I\$ 1,710,[20] about the same as Senegal's I\$ 1,680, and in excess of the I\$ 1,116 for Africa as a whole. Yet this low income for 36.1 million nonwhite South Africans stood in stark contrast to that of 7.3 million whites, I\$ 14,920 income per capita, a figure higher than New Zealand's I\$ 13,970 (Nafziger 1997).

---

[19] In 1990, real GDP per capita was about 90 per cent of its level in 1975 (Esterhuyse 1992). See also Nafziger (1997), citing annual World Bank data.

[20] I\$ stands for international dollars, or US dollars adjusted for purchasing power.

South Africa's Gini coefficient of income concentration was 0.65, with the top 10 per cent of the population receiving more than 50 per cent of the national income, while the bottom 40 per cent received less than one-tenth. This made South Africa, alongside Mexico and Brazil, one of the countries with the most unequal distribution of income in the world (Schlemmer and Giliomee 1994). Esterhuyse (1992) notes that even during the country's rapid growth in the 1960s, wealth failed to trickle down 'in any significant manner' to the black population, creating mistrust in the benefit of growth to the poor. Moreover, life expectancy was 52 years for blacks, 62 for Asians and mixed races, 74 for whites, and 54 for Africa generally, while the adult literacy rate was 67 per cent for nonwhites and 85 per cent for whites (Nafziger 1997).

It was not difficult for the African National Congress (ANC) to mobilize the masses against the apartheid regime as the perceived source of inequality. Both inequality and the emergency resulted from the actions of the regime, which dug its own grave by a conscious policy of discrimination against the majority of the population. There is mounting evidence that even the destructive political conflict of 1990–94 between the ANC and the Inkatha Freedom Party was directly manipulated and fuelled by the regime in its effort to maintain power (Auvinen and Kivimäki 1997).[21] The South African case illustrates how economic inequality, combined with authoritarian structures and rules of governance, contributes to humanitarian emergencies.

4.4. Chiapas: regional inequality

In Chiapas state, as in Mexico generally, economic and political power remained for decades in the hands of the landowning oligarchy, which had been supported by Mexico's ruling Institutional Revolutionary Party (*Partido Revolucionario Institucional* (PRI)). Moreover, in Chiapas, GDP per capita, measured in purchasing-power parity dollars, was 43 per cent below, and adult literacy 24 per cent below the national average in the early 1990s (UNDP 1994).

On New Year's Day 1994, the Zapatista army (*Ejército Zapatista de Liberación Nacional*, EZLN), representing Indian smallholders and landless workers or *campesinos*, launched a rebellion against the PRI and the oligarchy, which the EZLN held responsible for their poverty and distress. During two weeks of fierce fighting, perhaps 150–200 died before a ceasefire between the EZLN and the Mexican army. About 15,000 to 30,000 people fled the battles to more untroubled areas in Chiapas or in the

---

[21] The regime provided direct support to the Inkatha Freedom Party by arming, training, financing, and supporting the Inkatha cadres and hit squads. Inkatha supporters in the Rand were easy to mobilize for street violence from huge immigrant hostels, where they had arrived from Natal in search of work.

neighbouring Guatemala. A cholera epidemic, which had spread to the region earlier, intensified during the conflict. The Chiapas conflict can be characterized as a local humanitarian emergency that can develop in regions most neglected and discriminated against by a central government.

The Zapatistas demanded the elimination of income and land disparities between landowners and *campesinos*, as well as for greater political rights and democracy. For the Zapatistas, the government had betrayed the ideal of Emiliano Zapata, the national hero of Mexico's liberation, by implementing a constitutional reform that resulted in the commercialization of *ejidos*, the common lands, which had enjoyed special protection in the past. The rebels viewed both domestic and foreign forces as the people's enemies. Symbolically, the Zapatistas launched their rebellion on the day when the North American Free Trade Area (NAFTA) came into force. NAFTA was a threat to Chiapas' smallholder and cooperative primary producers, placing them at a disadvantage relative to high-technology and capital-intensive agricultural production in the US (Pirttijärvi 1995).

Despite the Zapatistas' nationalistic rhetoric, they were also considered Maoists, anarchists, or Trotskyists, depending on the observer. Because of their extensive use of the Internet in their information campaigns, they were labelled the first postmodern rebels. The mysterious *subcomandante* Marcos, the media hero of the Zapatistas, characterized his movement as follows:

We have always spoken about the basic rights of the human: [rights to] education, housing, health, food, land, good pay for our work, democracy, [and] liberty . . . If you want to call it Mexican socialism or the Mexican way to liberty, that's a good name for it (Weinberg 1995).

4.5. Conclusion

High income inequality can be a source of humanitarian emergencies in both rapidly- and slow-growing countries. However, once a population is dissatisfied with income discrepancies and social discrimination, as the majority of nonwhites were in white-ruled South Africa, the rising expectations associated with incremental reductions in poverty and inequality may actually spur the revolt, conflict, and state hostile action that exacerbates the probability of a humanitarian emergency (Davies 1962).

5. Inflation

Auvinen and Nafziger (1999) indicated that inflation, associated with humanitarian emergencies, may capture some income-distributional changes left unaccounted for by the relatively invariable Gini coefficient. Inflation is indicative of an unresolved conflict over incomes claims which the government has not been able to accommodate. Relative deprivation theory suggests that the more rapid the inflation, the more discontented the population, and the greater the likelihood of political conflict. Inflation reduces purchasing power and breeds uncertainty within different social groups, both rich and poor. Acute inflation can erode (and hyperinflation confiscate) the wealth of those rich and middle-class people who have failed to invest in foreign exchange, real estate, and other speculative assets whose short-term capital gains protect against rapid price increases. Among wage earners and pensioners, governments may seek to maintain legitimacy and power by indexing wages and prices to compensate their major constituencies—the military, government employees, and organized labour in the politically mobilized urban areas, penalizing those who are left outside the system. This frequently includes poor people in the informal sector, who are rarely crucial for the government's support.

To avoid social unrest, the government may even compensate informal-sector poor by some means such as subsidies for food and fuel. In the absence of any indexation, the 'inflation tax' contributes to a growing sense of social and economic injustice among those who are not compensated. This is the basic mechanism through which inflation may serve as a source of discontent and incite conflict behaviour, particularly in the cities.

The thesis of inflation's politically destabilizing effects is backed by other empirical evidence. According to Franzosi, political strikes can be expected to vary directly with high levels of inflation, although the relationship may be correlational rather than causal (Franzosi 1989). In Latin America in 1976–82, inflation was associated with 'austerity protest' (Walton and Seddon 1994). Furthermore, in Sub-Saharan Africa, inflation was found to be particularly destabilizing, whereas purchasing-power growth decreased the number of disturbances (Morrisson, Lafay and Dessus 1994). In general, social unrest from inflation may invite repressive responses from authoritarian regimes, which tend to fuel violence and spur humanitarian crises.

6. IMF Adjustment Funds

Adjustment and stabilization programmes, almost universal among developing countries during the 1980s and early 1990s, were mostly introduced in response to chronic macroeconomic imbalances and external deficits, often associated with negative or slow growth. These programmes are shaped by financing from and conditions set by the International Monetary Fund (IMF) and World Bank. The programmes change the benefits and costs among economic actors, and also their timing. Most expenditure-reducing policies (including government employment cuts, removal of subsidies, increases in real interest rates, and the control of money supply) and of some expenditure-switching policies (such as real domestic-currency devaluation) tend to impose large welfare costs immediately, while their benefits emerge only after one to two years. Stabilization and adjustment programmes affect real wages and staple commodity prices, and may thus elicit protests from the population groups especially affected (the poor and the organized middle class) (Auvinen 1996b).

Stabilization and adjustment programmes affect the distribution of power within a country. Thus, in the first place, social conflicts may erupt during the early period of stabilization and adjustment, especially if there are few funds to support the income and social services of those hurt by the programmes. Second, adjustment programmes may become a source of potential instability if the public perceives that structural measures, such as privatization, price decontrol, and public employment policies, favour specific interest groups, such as military and political leaders, leading families, dominant ethnic communities, or high-level civil servants. This can spur regional, communal, and class conflicts. Third, national leaders of developing countries, who frequently only borrow from the Bank or Fund as a last resort, complain about the secrecy of the recipient country's letter of intent, which reduces internal political dialogue and increases the difficulty of implementing the adjustment programme (Mills 1989). These problems can undermine the legitimacy of political élites, spurring a challenge to the regime.

Auvinen and Nafziger (1999) found that there was an inverse relationship between IMF credits as a percentage of GNP and emergencies.[22] Some of the explanation may stem from the IMF's refraining from funding 'basket cases' devastated by war and displacement. In that case, the negative coefficient would be picking up a reverse causal relationship. We applied a two-stage least squares model and different lag structures to inspect the relationship between LIMFGNP and humanitarian emergencies. The two-stage least squares results, with LIMFGNP as the other endogenous variable, do not dramatically differ from those of the OLS model. However, when LIMFGNP was used as a predictor for *lagged* values of dependent variables, its coefficients are generally larger than those presented in Appendix Table A3.1, indicating that perhaps emergencies keep away the IMF rather than vice versa (see Appendix Table A3.6). Thus, an emergency is likely to reduce the likelihood of receiving IMF and other international support for an adjustment programmes.

---

[22] In the empirical analysis, the expected centrality of the IMF was supported by the fact that a dummy variable for the World Bank's structural or sectoral adjustment programme had no explanatory power.

7. Stagnation, Inequality, Adjustment, and Élite Interests

How élites and masses react to these four major economic phenomena and their changes—stagnation and economic decline, high and increasing inequality, inflation, and adjustment programmes—influences the probability of political conflict and humanitarian disasters. Élites may be threatened by adverse economic changes and the reaction of non-élites to these changes. The strategies of political élites to maintain power and affluence in the midst of economic crises and shifts, may exacerbate conflict and the potential for humanitarian emergencies.

The struggle over economic benefits helps shape, consolidate, and modify the composition of ruling élites. Economic growth usually expands the perquisites and benefits that political élites can distribute to allies and subordinates, while economic decline or cuts in expenditures from liberalization shrink the clientele base, often requiring greater coercion and corruption to maintain power. Or in reaction to economic decline and liberalization, ruling élites need new ways of exercising power, and sometimes use foreign firms and private operators to regularize revenues and expenditures. Whether or not élites are successful in creating new patron-client patterns, economic and state expenditure declines increase the potential for destabilizing the polity and threatening a humanitarian crisis.

Africa's political stability has been especially threatened by the widespread negative per capita growth of the late 1970s, 1980s, and early 1990s. When growth becomes negative, as in parts of Africa, it becomes more difficult to support so large a ruling élite. Contradictions and disunity can grow among the previously dominant élite. Negative real economic growth narrows the communal and class support of ruling coalitions, and threatens political cohesion.

Slow (or negative) growth, frequently accompanied by chronic external deficits and debt, intensifies the need for economic adjustment and stabilization. Under current rules of the international economic system, countries requiring adjustment must, as a last resort, either acquire IMF credits or IMF approval for loans, aid, or debt reduction from the World Bank, other international agencies, bilateral contributors, or commercial banks. Those countries that could meet IMF conditions were less likely to be vulnerable to a humanitarian crisis than countries that failed to adjust, thus lacking access to IMF and other funds or concessions.

Let us illustrate by discussing Sub-Saharan Africa (henceforth Africa), which is disproportionately represented both among countries with slow growth and external disequilibria, and major humanitarian emergencies. In *Inequality in Africa* (1988), Nafziger shows how shrinking economic pie slices and growing political consciousness added pressures to national leaders, whose response was usually not only anti-egalitarian but also anti-growth, hurting small farmers' incentives, appropriating peasant surplus for parastatal industry, building parastatal enterprises beyond management capacity, and using these inefficient firms to dispense benefits to clients. Regime survival in a politically fragile system required marshalling élite support at the expense of economic growth.[23] Spurring peasant production through market prices and exchange rates interfered with state leaders' ability to build political support, especially in urban areas.

7.1. Liberalization and adjustment after 1980

More than a decade of slow or negative per capita growth, rising borrowing costs, reduced concessional aid, and a mounting debt crisis[24] forced African élites to change their strategies during the 1980s. In 1987, International Monetary Fund (IMF) Managing Director Jacques de Larosiere asserted, 'Adjustment is now virtually universal [among LDCs]. Never before has there been such an extensive yet convergent adjustment effort'.[25] After 1979, when most African countries were facing external debt crises and chronic international balance of goods and services deficits, economic progress depended on the success or failure of programmes of structural adjustment, macroeconomic stabilization, and reform, mostly under conditions set by IMF/World Bank lending.

African and other developing countries that were more successful in receiving IMF (and other international financial and bilateral) credits and aid experienced less conflict and humanitarian emergencies. As Bienen and Gersovitz (1985) argue, cuts in government spending are less likely to contribute to political conflict than the alternative of debt repudiation and exclusion from credit. Countries must adjust to balance-of-payments imbalances and their adjustment strategies are constrained by both international and domestic factors. Despite some violent reactions in the short run, the acceptance and implementation of IMF policies rarely lead to large-scale and persistent instability (Bienen and Gersovitz 1985). Those that lacked access to the international financial system still had to play by the same rules of adjustment and liberalization, but were nevertheless highly vulnerable economically and politically.

With liberalization and adjustment, similar to the controls of the 1960s and 1970s, contemporary African élites used their dependency on the global economy as a way to consolidate power, but they used different

---

[23] Ake (1996: 1, 18) reinforces this contention when he states that for Africa, 'the problem is not so much that development has failed as that it was never really on the agenda in the first place . . . [W]ith independence African leaders were in no position to pursue development; they were too engrossed in the struggle for survival'.

[24] Nafziger (1993) discusses Africa's slow growth and external disequilibrium, and subsequent efforts to adjust in more detail.

[25] *IMF Survey*, 23 February 1987: 50.

approaches. Indeed the distribution of benefits and costs from stabilization and restructuring have influenced the shifts of power and money within African countries. Of course, many African élites saw the handwriting on the wall, with some African political leaders, finance ministers, and government economists (similar to many of their counterparts in Central Europe in the 1990s) experiencing an overnight conversion from Marxism to the liberalism and monetarism of Milton Friedman. Most African élites supported liberalization, maintaining or expanding, with their accomplices and clients, their wealth. For privatization (which required access to credit), price decontrol, and restructuring offered these élites new opportunities for expanded clientage. Moreover, controlling restructuring also enabled these élites to protect their interests from reform and competition. Still the opportunities also came with the risk of a shrinking power base, increased conflict with newly rising classes, and displacement by new economic and political groups.

7.2. *Adjustment, clientelism, and predatory rule in Africa*

After 1979, with the increased necessity for structural adjustment and stabilization, African political élites needed to form new patterns of clientage in order to maintain legitimacy. Slow growth and chronic external deficits, together with the failure to stabilize and adjust, were conducive to patrimonialism and predation, especially in Africa.

Authoritarian regimes, which are less dependent on popular pressures and can use repression, may be better equipped to implement adjustment policies than democratic regimes (Lafay and Lecaillon 1992; Kaufman 1985; Nelson 1990; Sheahan 1980). Many authoritarian governments have also been committed to implementing adjustment policies since their legitimacy is dependent on good economic performance. Thus these governments have been more prone to choose orthodox macroeconomic stabilization policies than their democratic counterparts, especially in Latin America (Kaufman and Stallings 1989; Nelson 1990). If we identify political authoritarianism with a lack of political rights and civil liberties, and abuse of human rights, several different types of governance fall under the definition. One type is the 'efficient authoritarianism' of Pinochet's Chile (1973–89) or Alberto Fujimori's Peru (1990–). A very different type is the 'weak authoritarianism' often found in African soft states, in which the authorities who decide policies rarely enforce them (if enacted into law) and only reluctantly place obligations on people (Myrdal, volume 2, 1968). These states are dependent on buying political support through concessions to powerful interest groups. During the 1960s and 1970s, most African ruling élites eschewed policies promoting competition, decentralized decision-making, and reliance on market prices and exchange rates, as these policies reduced their ability to use subsidies, rebates, and inducements to strengthen alliances and patron-client relationships. For these élites, the introduction of stabilization and adjustment in the 1980s and 1990s was often a threat to the regime.

Clientelism, the dominant pattern in Africa, is a personalized relationship between patrons and clients, commanding unequal wealth, status, or influence, based on conditional loyalties and involving mutual benefits. Clientelism overlaps with, but reaches beyond, ethnicity. The ethnic identity of the client may be amalgamated with, widened, or subordinated to the identity of the patron, who exchanges patronage, economic security, and protection for the client's personal loyalty and obedience. Clientelism often operates within a political party, as in the case of the *Parti Démocratique de la Côte d'Ivoire* (PDCI), or the Northern People's Congress, 1960–66, an instrument of Northern Nigeria's traditional aristocracy (Lemarchand 1972).

In several African countries that experienced negative growth and political decay in the 1980s and early 1990s, such as Nigeria, Sierra Leone, Zaire, and Liberia, ethnic and regional competition for the bounties of the state gave way to a predatory state. Predatory rule is that by a personalistic regime ruling through coercion, material inducement, and personality politics, a regime that tends to degrade the institutional foundations of the economy and state (Lewis 1996; Holsti 1996). In some predatory states, the ruling élite and their clients 'use their positions and access to resources to plunder the national economy through graft, corruption, and extortion, and to participate in private business activities' (Holsti, Chapter 7). Ake (1996: 42) contends that, 'Instead of being a public force, the state in Africa tends to be privatized, that is, appropriated to the service of private interests by the dominant faction of the élite'. People use funds at the disposal of the state for systematized corruption, from petty survival venality at the lower echelons of government to kleptocracy at the top.

7.3 African case studies

Sierra Leone was caught in a bind between the end of the cold war and the pressure of adjustment and reform. In 1991, Freetown used private operators to run state services for a profit. Privatization did not eliminate the pressures of clients demanding payoffs, but merely shifted the arena of clientage to the private sector. Sierra Leone's ruling élites, needing new ways of exercising power, used foreign firms to consolidate power and stave off threats from political rivals. In the 1990s, Sierra Leonean heads of state have relied on exclusive contracts with foreign firms for diamond mining to 'regularize' sources of revenue in lieu of a government agency to collect taxes, foreign mercenaries and advisors as a replacement for the national army to provide security, and foreign contractors (sometimes the same as the mining or security firms) to provide other state services. In the process, rulers may have found it advantageous to 'destroy state agencies, to "cleanse" them of politically threatening patrimonial hangers-on and use violence to extract resources from people under their control'. To stay in power, hard-pressed rulers in weak African states often had 'to mimic the "warlord" logic characteristic of many of their non-state rivals' (Reno 1996).

In 1994, Zaire received creditor leniency in return for austerity plans reducing public employment from 600,000 to 50,000. But with the shrinking patronage base, to prevent a coup from newly marginalized groups in the army or bureaucracy, Mobutu—similar to rulers in other retrenching African states—needed to reconfigure political authority; in this situation, foreign firms and contractors served as a new source of patronage networks (Reno 1996). However, the indigenous commercial interests that profit from the new rules are not independent capitalists whose interests are distinct from the state. Indeed as Reno (1996: 16) points out, 'Those who do not take part in accumulation on the ruler's terms are punished'.

In Liberia, Charles Taylor used external commercial networks (foreign firms), some a legacy of the Samuel Doe regime of the late 1980s, to control internal power, including a large proportion of old Liberia, and at times, the eastern periphery of Sierra Leone. Taylor's territory has had its own currency and banking system, telecommunications network, airfields, export trade (in diamonds, timber, gold, and farm products) to support arms imports, and (until 1993) a deepwater port (Reno 1995; Reno, Chapter 8, Volume 2).

7.4. Adjustment in the former Yugoslavia

Another example of how failed adjustment policies contributed to a humanitarian emergency is the former Yugoslavia. Woodward (1995) blames the Yugoslav conflict not on historical ethnic hostilities but on the disintegration of government authority, and breakdown of political and civil order from transforming a socialist society to a market economy and democracy. Yugoslavia's rapid growth during the 1960s and 1970s, fuelled by foreign borrowing, was reversed by more than a decade of an external debt crisis in the midst of declining terms of trade and global credit tightening during the 1980s, and early 1990s, forcing austerity and declining living standards. Moreover, with the winding down of the cold war and the decline of the importance of Yugoslavia as an independent communist state, the country received less debt relief and concessional aid from the West. In an economy declining largely from reduced external resources and returning guest workers, the political conflicts over the distribution of falling economic resources and rising debt obligations between central and regional governments and the nature of economic and political reform became constitutional crises, and ultimately a crisis of state among politicians unwilling to compromise. For example, economic decline fuelled rising Serbian nationalist agitation, contributing to the 1987 'putsch' within the League of Communists of Serbia by Slobodan Milosevic, whose faction broke with the pattern of ethnic compromise; recentralized power within Serbia; overthrew the political leadership in Montenegro and in Serbia's autonomous provinces, Kosovo and Vojvodina; tried to subvert Croatia and Slovenia, the two republics that most vociferously opposed him; and tried to enlarge Serbia at the expense of Bosnia and Herzegovina (Lukic and Lynch 1996).

For Woodward (1995: 383):

> The primary problem, however, lay in the lack of recognition and accommodation for the socially polarizing and politically disintegrating consequences of [the 1980s' adjustment and stabilization] program . . . The austerities of policies of demand-repression led to conditions that could not easily foster a political culture of tolerance and compromise. Instead, the social bases for stable government and democratization were being radically narrowed by economic polarization between rich and poor, fiscal crises for most government budgets, deindustrialization without prospects of new investment in poorer regions, growing uncertainty and individuals' resort to nonmonetary means of obtaining necessities because of rising inflation, and serious unemployment among young people and unskilled workers that began to affect even the secure jobs and incomes of public-sector professionals, skilled workers, administrators, and their children. The architects of the programs of macroeconomic stabilization and economic austerity ignored the necessity of creating not only social safety nets but even more important a political capacity to recognize and manage these conflicts.

Amid Yugoslavia's austerity and economic collapse, Bosnia-Herzegovina, an agricultural, forestry, and mineral exporter at the periphery of the economy, was among the most vulnerable, hurt substantially by declining terms of trade and by the loss of export markets to the Middle East, Central and Eastern Europe, and the former Soviet Union. Additionally, Bosnia-Herzegovina suffered substantial deaths, dislocation, and devastation after the outbreak of war in March 1992 (Woodward 1995).

7.5. Conclusion

In Africa in the 1960s and 1970s, the state was the major focus for struggle among ruling élites and between them and the masses. Ruling élites used taxes, government spending, public programmes, market intervention, and indigenization policies to maintain their size and stabilize their rule. But Africa's slow economic growth, particularly since 1979, compelled these élites to reduce the size of the coalition they supported or use repression to extract a greater share of the majority's tiny surplus, increasing the probability of coups or other regime turnovers, and eventual humanitarian disaster. Ironically, heightened insecurity put pressure on the state class to rely even more on short-run palliatives that benefited the military, civil service, and other privileged groups but increased economic disparities and further alienated the masses.

During the 1980s and 1990s, élites in LDCs faced increasing pressure from slow growth and international debt crises, as well as external pressure by donors and international financial institutions to reform. Pressures to cut the size of the state in the midst of shrinking resources put substantial constraints on the ability of élites, particularly in Africa, to reward and sanction political actors, contributing to greater instability and the potential for humanitarian emergencies.

8. The Failure of Agricultural Development

Agriculture is a major component of GDP in low-income countries and a major influence on the rest of the economy through its contribution to food supplies, foreign exchange, labour supply, capital transfer, and markets. Frequently the failure of food and agricultural development is a key element of protracted stagnation or decline, and rising social tensions. As in several Sub-Saharan countries, agricultural stagnation may be associated with delayed technological modernization, unfavourable government policies and factor market distortions, obsolete agrarian structures, and slow institutional modernization. Declining rural productivity may not only contribute to increased economic Darwinism among severely impoverished rural populations, but may also spur rural-urban migration, increasing urban unemployment and underemployment, and political discontent, which may contribute to humanitarian emergencies.

Failure of agricultural development and international economic deterioration affect income and its distribution domestically by region, ethnic group, and class. This distribution affects social mobilization, which can set the stage for potential crises.

8.1. The food crisis

Auvinen and Nafziger (1999) suggest that slow food production per capita growth was a source of humanitarian emergencies. A test of lags and leads (Appendix Table A3.5) indicated that slow food production growth is conducive to humanitarian emergencies (when these are defined to exclude its nutritional component) rather than vice versa.

We can illustrate the relationship between food availability and humanitarian emergencies in Sub-Saharan Africa. Africa's food crisis since the 1960s has made it especially vulnerable to humanitarian emergencies. Cornia, Jolly and Stewart (1987) explain how declining real household income (through falling income or rising food prices among the low-income households) reduces household food availability, decreasing nutrient intake and increasing malnutrition, and increasing disease and mortality (especially among infants and children).

From 1962 to 1989, food output per capita grew at an annual rate of 0.5 per cent in developing countries, 0.3 per cent in developed countries, and 0.4 per cent overall, but declined 0.8 per cent in Sub-Saharan Africa, meaning that food production there grew more slowly than the population. (The data are calculated using a five-year moving average to smooth out annual weather fluctuations.) Food production per person increased from 1962 to 1989 in all world regions except the Sub-Sahara (Figure 3.2).

Africa's daily calorie consumption per capita, 2,116 (the same as in the early 1960s and less than the 2,197 of the mid-1970s), was 92 per cent of the requirement set by the FAO, 1988–90; calorie consumption in all other regions exceeded FAO requirements (UNDP 1994). Africa's food security index is low (and falling since the 1960s) (Jazairy, Alamgir and Panuccio 1992), not only because of large food deficits but also because of domestic output and foreign-exchange reserve fluctuations, as well as foreign food-aid reductions. In 1989, Adedeji (1989: 2) spoke of 'the humiliation it has brought to Africa in having to go round with the begging bowl for food aid'.

Illustrative of the enormity of the Sub-Sahara's difference from other LDCs is that while the Sub-Sahara and India both produced 50 million tons of foodgrains in 1960, in 1988 India produced 150 million tons (after the green revolution and other farm technological improvements) and

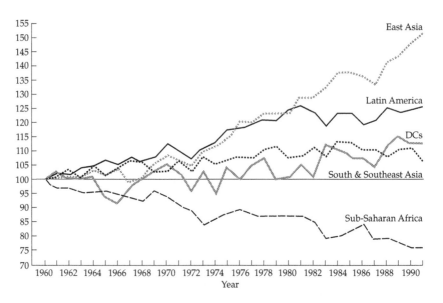

Fig. 3.2. Growth in food production per capita, 1960–91 (1960 = 100)

Sub-Saharan Africa (with faster population growth) was still stuck at little more than 50 million tons. India's yield per hectare increased by 2.4 per cent yearly, while the Sub-Sahara's grew at a negligible annual rate of 0.1 per cent. Thus, the Sub-Sahara, which was on parity with India in 1960, produced only about one-third of Indian output in 1988 (Singer 1990).

Additionally, the increasing population density on agricultural land has already exacerbated conflict and humanitarian disaster in low-income Africa and Haiti. Population pressure on limited land contributed to the diaspora from the Eastern Region to the rest of Nigeria in the one to two decades before the 1967–70 civil war. The East had a 1963 population density of 1,088 per square kilometre compared to Nigeria's density of 404. Contemporary Rwanda, with only 5 per cent of its population, and Burundi, with only 6 per cent of its population living in urban areas and low labour productivity, have a population density of 1,295 persons per square kilometre (Gaffney 1996). This density is about the same as that of Italy (1,298) which is 67 per cent urban, and exceeds that of France (717) which is 74 per cent urban. While parts of Asia have also faced high agrarian population densities, more rapid economic growth with its accompanying expansion of employment in industry and services, has generally reduced the political salience of these pressures.[26]

8.2. *Agricultural policies before liberalization*

Africa's deteriorating food position began before the droughts in the Sahel (including Sudan and Ethiopia) in 1968 to 1974 and in 1984 to 1985. While the roots of Africa's food crisis go back to colonialism (Eicher and Baker 1982; Ghai and Radwan 1983), the continuing crisis is largely due to African governments' neglect of agriculture. Here we concentrate on the policies of African political élites and government decision-makers in the decade or two before 1979, the period of liberalization.

After independence, African political élites required the support of urban élites and working classes to maintain power. Élites increased their political benefits, not through market prices for smallholders, research and extension on traditional food crops, or recognizing traditional communal property, but by expanding patronage through commercial and estate agriculture, easing land purchase by the urban affluent, and selective projects and subsidies. Furthermore, African governments preferred project-based to price-based policies to increase agricultural supplies because projects help to build and reinforce a political patron-client system.

Despite development plans proclaiming agriculture's priority and rhetoric stressing the poor rural masses, governments used pricing and exchange-rate policies, spending on investment and social services,

---

[26] Northern India, Bangladesh, and Sri Lanka are examples of exceptions within Asia.

and subsidies and protection to allocate most resources to cities, a policy of urban bias. African politicians responded to the more powerful and articulate urban dwellers. Thus, during the last quarter of the 20th century, the policies of ruling élites diverted farmland from growing food crops such as sorghum, millet, and local brands of maize, roots, and tubers for hungry villagers, to produce cash crops, including rice, wheat, hybrid maize, and export crops, like tobacco and natural rubber; this production shift and the greater concentration of wealth and income distribution and its effect on food demand meant that food crops declined more rapidly (or grew more slowly) than cash and export crops (Cornia 1994). Political leaders spent scarce capital on highways and steel mills, instead of on water pumps, tube wells, and other equipment essential for growing food. Moreover, governments used high-cost administrative and management talent to design office buildings and sports stadiums rather than village wells and agricultural extension services.

In Sub-Saharan Africa, there is generally an inverse relationship between farm size and land yields because of the low imputed costs to own labour and the low costs of monitoring and supervising labour on small farms (Cornia 1994). Yet, there is a policy bias toward large farms since government leaders and ministry officials increase clientage more by expanding production in the estate and commercial sector than by the growth of smallholder agriculture. And they profit more by subsidizing farm implement, fertilizer, and seed costs than by spurring prices to produce farm goods. Political élites can manipulate farmers better through market intervention than with a free market.

Most African states have tried to keep food prices low to satisfy urban workers and their employers (multinational corporations, indigenous capital, and government). Urban unrest from increasing living costs sometimes has contributed to governments losing power or even being overthrown. To insure political survival, insecure African ruling élites forewent policies promoting rural innovation and reducing urban-rural income gaps.

8.3. Agricultural policies during liberalization

During the liberalization of the 1980s and early 1990s, the World Bank, IMF, and external donors, in setting conditions for agricultural policy in Africa for adjustment loans, emphasized eliminating price distortions. However, empirical studies indicate that farm price distortions comprised only a fraction of the explanation for Africa's falling average agricultural output (Cleaver 1985; Cornia 1994). The rest of the explanation is from infrastructural and other institutional factors such as the insecure tenancy of cultivators, the highly inefficient new private commercial agricultural production, the limited emphasis on traditional food crops in agricultural research and extension, the increased transaction and litigation costs, and the land, credit, and insurance market imperfections, such as small farmers' lack of access to credit, that contribute to greater dualism. But in Africa, the stress of externally funded adjustment programmes on commercialization means a decline in the production of traditional food crops, increased farm shares to medium and large farmers, and an increase in the purchase of farmland by urban élites as a hedge against inflation (Cornia 1994).

The emphasis on individual property-rights systems by international financial institutions and African élites has reduced agricultural efficiency. Under most traditional community or village systems, farm families not only have tenure security but land rights are highly transferable. Greater agricultural intensification from population growth gives rise to pressure for increasingly formal private property rights. Ironically, however, registering individualized land titles reduces tenure security in the short run, as the number of land disputes surge. Clever, well-informed, and powerful individuals jockey to have parcels not previously theirs registered in their own name, while rural masses may be unaware of the implications of registration. Women especially face difficulties in having their customary rights recognized by political authorities. And in the longer run, the high costs of land registration and lack of familiarity with the government bureaucracy displace weak or politically marginalized groups, and redistribute land to the commercial and estate sectors, increasing the concentration of land holdings. As an example, Kenya's systematic compulsory individualized titling of all farmlands since the 1950s contributed to a substantial gap between the control of rights reflected in the land register and recognized by most local communities, providing opportunities for affluent town dwellers to establish property rights though land registration. In Nigeria, under cover of national development projects, state officials granted extensive land tracts to friends, dispossessing many villagers from their customary lands. But reallocation through individualized titling not only increased inequality but also reduced labour intensity, capital formation, and innovation, contributing to the inverse relationship between farm size and yields noted above (Platteau 1996; Cornia 1994).

8.4. Food entitlements, élite violence, and famines

Case-study evidence suggests that humanitarian emergencies increase nutritional vulnerability. Relief agencies indicate 20 million deaths from severe malnutrition in 1991 in six African countries—Ethiopia, Liberia, Sudan, Somalia, Angola, and Mozambique—where food trade was disrupted by domestic political conflict. Moreover, while, on the one hand food deficits contribute to refugee problems, on the other hand, the five million or so refugees annually fleeing civil wars, natural disasters, and political repression (including before 1990, South Africa's destabilization) added to Africa's food shortages (Daley 1992; Goliber 1989).

Since we are interested in famine as a component of the dependent variable, we integrate politics and economics to explain famine. The conventional economic approach examines food (or total) output and its distribution, focusing on agricultural production, poverty rates, and Gini indices of concentration. According to this explanation, famine arises from a decline in food availability (Ravallion 1997). Sen (1981, 1983b, 1995) criticizes this explanation, emphasizing that nutrition depends on society's system of entitlement. Entitlement refers to the set of alternative commodity bundles that a person can command in a society using the totality of rights and opportunities that he or she possesses. An entitlement helps people acquire capabilities (like being well nourished). In a market economy, the entitlement limit is based on ownership of factors of production and exchange possibilities (through trade or a shift in production possibilities). For most people, entitlement depends on the ability to find a job, the wage rate, and the prices of commodities bought. In a welfare or socialist economy, entitlement also depends on what families can obtain from the state through the established system of command. A hungry, destitute person will be entitled to something to eat, not by society's low Gini inequality and a high food output per capita, but by a relief system offering free food. Thus, in 1974, thousands of people died in Bangladesh despite its low inequality, because floods reduced rural employment along with output, and inflation cut rural labourers' purchasing power.

Sen argues that food is 'purchased' with political pressure as well as income. Accordingly, one-third of the Indian population goes to bed hungry every night and leads a life ravaged by regular deprivation. India's social system takes nonacute endemic hunger in its stride; there are no headlines or riots. But while India's politicians do not provide entitlements for chronic or endemic malnutrition, they do so for potential severe famine through food imports, redistribution, and relief. In Maoist China, the situation was almost the opposite. Its political commitment ensured lower regular malnutrition through more equal access to means of livelihood and state-provided entitlement to basic needs of food, clothing, and shelter. In a normal year, China's poor were much better fed than India's. Yet if there was a political and economic crisis that confused the regime so that it pursued disastrous policies with confident dogmatism, then it could not be forced to change its policies by crusading newspapers or effective political opposition pressure, as in India (Sen 1983a; Sen 1983b; Sen 1986; Sen 1987).

Our political economy approach, however, analyses the behaviour of ruling élites during periods of Darwinian pressures and food crises. This approach goes beyond the Sen approach, to examine ruling élites' deliberate withholding of entitlement, or even use of violence, to achieve their goals of acquiring or maintaining power, which often involves benefits at the expense of other segments of the population. Thus, according to our political economy analysis, Mao's effort to increase control through collective labour-intensive water projects during the 1958–60 Great Leap Forward contributed to China's famine, in which per capita food production from 1957–59 to 1959–61 dropped 25 per cent. Indeed in the midst of Mao's campaign for increasing collectivization in 1959, the pressure of the party establishment contributed to false reports of bumper crops (Prybyla 1970; Lardy 1983; Putterman 1993; Ravallion 1997).

Sen turns a blind eye to the possibility that the state may be the cause of famine through deliberate policy to transfer resources and food entitlements from a politically marginal group to a politically favoured one. To be sure, Drèze and Sen (1989: 5–6) point out that, 'The dependence of one group's ability to command food on its relative position and comparative power *vis-à-vis* other groups can be especially important in a market economy'. But for the two authors, famines and food shortages result from entitlement and state policy failure, and not from state action to damage the food entitlements of a group. They attribute the Soviet famines of the 1930s and the Kampuchean famines of the late 1970s to inflexible government policies that undermine the power of particular sections of the population to command food. Drèze and Sen's emphasis is on the need for public action by a benign state, making decisions about more or less food entitlements, rather than an ill-intentioned state making decisions to intervene in favour of one group at the expense of another and its food entitlement. For Drèze and Sen (1989: 17–18), avoiding famine involves the 'division of benefits [from the] differential pulls coming from divergent interest groups,' not stopping the denial of groups' entitlements.

As Keen (1994: 5) contends, in Drèze and Sen's view, 'There are victims of famine, but few immediate culprits or beneficiaries'. Drèze and Sen do not consider the possibility that states or politically powerful groups which control states may obstruct relief and contribute to famine for rational purposes of their own. Indeed, the Drèze and Sen conception of the state is essentially a liberal one, in which the failure to factor in the public interest is perceived as a failure of public policy. Most scholars and international agencies share the Drèze–Sen view, widely perceiving famine as relief 'blunders' and the result of poverty and market forces, and failing to see how markets are shaped or forced by state-condoned raiding, collusion, and intimidation.

For ruling élites to organize war and conflict involves shifting alliances with groups and individuals in authority at the local level. Where the centre lacks the resources to 'buy' the loyalty of local élites, it may procure their loyalty by tolerating exploitation at a local level. In political conflict, the need to form alliances with local groups and élites may contribute to increased levels of abuse of civilians and the natural environment. Even civilians may find it safer and more advantageous to join armed exploiters rather than risk becoming one of the unarmed exploited (Keen, Chapter 8).

The political economy approach to famine, associated with the emphasis by de Waal (1989), Duffield (1994), and Keen (1994) on famine as an outcome of government's forcible asset transfer from the politically weak to the politically strong, contrasts with that of Sen's economistic approach. Duffield and Keen point out that in the 1980s, the Sudanese government, under pressure from a shrinking economic pie, stripped the politically marginal Dinka of cattle and other major assets, distributing these to more favoured ethnic groups (Keen 1994; Duffield 1994). De Waal contends that marginalized communities in southern Somalia became destitute not only from drought, but from forcible alienation of farmland and pasture. Victims usually lacked lobbying power, not purchasing power (Keen 1994; Duffield 1994; de Waal 1994).

As Duffield (1994: 55) asserts:

The emergence of a political economy that includes asset transfer is extremely destructive and creates ever-deepening poverty and misery. Moreover, since subsistence assets are a finite resource, once such an economy is established it demands fresh inputs as the wealth of different groups is exhausted. Asset transfer becomes a moving feast on an ethnic table . . . [and] once systemic, becomes synonymous with cultural genocide and the destruction of group rights.

Famine is an extended economic and political process, usually a result of the disruption of a way of life, involving hunger and destitution and not just death, and often long-term rather than just transitory. The state may withhold relief from famine victims, allowing more politically influential groups to appropriate the food and resources.[27] Belligerents, such as Nigeria and Biafra in 1967–70 and the Sudanese government in the 1980s, are especially likely to block food supplies in a civil war. And even international agencies, non-governmental organizations, and other donors, facing government obstruction of relief and under pressure to cooperate with national authorities to provide at least relief in government-held areas, may discount independent accounts of famine that reflect on their negligence (Keen 1994; de Waal 1989). Contrary to Sen's entitlement approach, the political economy approach emphasizes that famine and humanitarian emergencies arise not only from policy errors but, and perhaps more importantly, from deliberate policy choices by ruling élites, who are trying to preserve or enhance power, thus requiring the analyst to examine the benefits and costs of famine and emergencies to major players in the conflict.[28]

---

[27] Indeed Kofi Annan (1996: 178) contends that 'In Somalia, . . . it became patently clear that continuing high death rate was being caused not so much by the absence of food and the presence of natural disaster as by a group of ambitious armed men who prevented food from reaching the needy'.

[28] In this vein, Keen's book (1994) about Sudan in the 1980s is entitled *The Benefits of Famine*.

9. Military Centrality

In Auvinen and Nafziger (1999), military centrality, as indicated by military expenditures per GNP, turned out to be the strongest and the most robust correlate of humanitarian emergencies. We say correlate, as there is a two-way causal relationship between military expenditures and emergencies. Especially violent and protracted emergencies necessitate high military spending. We emphasize the reverse dynamic, explaining how military centrality contributes to complex humanitarian emergencies through four different dynamics.

Prolonged repressive authoritarian rule is likely to create a sense of injustice and deprivation within the opposition, eventually transforming it to 'desperate underdogs', who, with nothing to lose, will fight regardless of the consequences. South Africa's black population was driven to such a position by the apartheid regime. Moreover, a strong military is apt to overthrow either democratic or authoritarian regime, which may lead to political instability and humanitarian crises. For civilian regimes in less developed countries, powerful armed forces constitute constant threat. Particularly during economic austerity they are afraid to cut back military spending. Furthermore, they may strengthen the military in order to stave off threats from the opposition. This, in turn, entails heavy socio-economic costs for the population, inducing further discontent and increasing the risk of rebellion. In very poor countries, budget allocations for the military may produce downright starvation and destitution.

First, military expenditures are needed to support authoritarian political structures, which are susceptible to violent and destructive forms of conflict. Prolonged repressive authoritarian rule is likely to create a profound sense of injustice and deprivation within the population and the opposition. Political deprivation arises from a lack of meaningful participation in making political decisions, whether this participation is prevented by law or through repression. In effect, a constant and frequent use of repression indicates lack of legitimacy and political capacity (Jackman 1993). Efficient repression may prolong authoritarian rule, as demonstrated for example by Augusto Pinochet's Chile and Hastings Kamuzu Banda's Malawi, but eventually the people are likely to challenge the regime from a 'desperate bargainer' position. Desperate underdogs will fight regardless of the consequences if they feel they have nothing to lose.

According to students of the South African transformation (du Toit 1996; Nel 1996; Friedman 1995; Auvinen and Kivimäki 1997), supported by opinion polls in 1986 and 1987,[29] the black community of South Africa

---

[29] Opinion polls of primarily urban, male, professional blacks in 1987 indicate that attitudes towards violence had become more radical despite the fact that very few people believed violence would bring about a solution to the conflict (Hirschman 1987).

could be regarded as a desperate underdog. The desperate uprisings of 1963 and 1976 and the violent popular upsurge after 1984 as well as comments by Cyril Ramaphosa, later to become the African National Congress's chief negotiator (Fisher and Albeldas 1987) reinforce the view that South Africa would have lapsed into civil war no matter how strong the repressive machinery of the white establishment was and no matter how little hope there was for the African National Congress coalition to win militarily (Auvinen and Kivimäki 1997).

Military centrality may intensify conflicts and spark new ones. Given a strong military, a government is likely to deploy it to contain various kinds of challenges. Scant military resources indicate that the government is predisposed to solving crises by other, more pacific means. A strong military is likely to exert power over government decisions and favour strong over weak responses to suppress conflict. Excessive force and fire power against peaceful demonstrations are likely to trigger further violence, as happened in South Africa in 1990–92 and in Pinochet's Chile. According to Gurr (1994), ethnopolitical conflicts tend to begin with limited protests and clashes that escalate into sustained violence.

Second, since authoritarian rule relies on military power, one usually needs considerable military resources to challenge it. Provided that repressive rule has not (yet) generated an opposition of desperate underdogs, political opponents will not attempt to challenge the regime until they have managed to collect enough military capacity. As in the case of desperate bargaining, the resulting conflict is likely to be bloody and intense. Military centrality thus has an impact on the form of conflict: large military resources may deter popular protest but encourage opponents to build up resources for large-scale warfare; rebellion promises a better chance of success than protest, or the only chance.

Third, military centrality is conducive to irregular executive transfers, which can lead to humanitarian emergencies. Jenkins and Kposowa found military centrality the most consistent independent force behind coups. The greater the resources of the military, the more likely were military interventions. While this finding was based on Africa, it is supported by earlier studies (Jenkins and Kposowa 1990; Kposowa and Jenkins 1993). In many LDCs, military takeovers of governments have occurred routinely (see Johnson, Slader and McGowan 1984), although in most of Latin America they seemed to have discontinued during the 1980s.[30]

Frequently these coups have led to humanitarian crises. To illustrate, the military has traditionally occupied a central position in Haitian politics. From the late 1930s until 1957, when Francois Duvalier (better known

---

[30] Hunter (1994) points out, though, that even in the 1990s civil-military tensions persisted in Latin America. In Venezuela, Argentina, Brazil and Chile, the military has intervened in politics as a reaction to domestic and international challenges to their professional standing and corporate integrity.

as Papa Doc) assumed the presidency, 'the army exercised the effective power and decided for how long the sitting president would be able to retain power' (Lundahl, Chapter 11, Volume 2). Duvalier was able to undermine the military's power with the help of his own paramilitary force, the *tonton macoutes*. The Duvaliers were able to stave off the threat of the military until 1986, when Francois's son, Jean-Claude Duvalier, was finally ousted in a coup. When the army reconstituted itself in Haitian politics, a new wave of coups and counter-coups followed. In September 1991, the military overthrew President Jean-Bertrand Aristide, as it felt threatened by his plans to return the police force from the military to civilian control 'since this struck at the heart of their [the military's] illegal activities' (Dupuy 1989: 116–18). This move led to a humanitarian crisis in Haiti with notorious consequences (see Lundahl, Chapter 11, Volume 2). Other instances include Nigeria's two coups in 1966, which set the stage for the 1967–70 civil war, and Pakistan's military coups in 1958 and 1969, which contributed to the conflict between East and West Pakistan in 1971.

Military coups have often been economically motivated. Jenkins and Kposowa (1990) found that debt dependence was a major predictor of coup activity in black Africa, 1957 to 1984. O'Donnell's (1973 and 1978) bureaucratic-authoritarian thesis suggests that Latin American militaries intervened in politics during periods of economic hardship, legitimizing the action by the need to establish order amid social unrest. Even more generally, economic crisis periods tend to strengthen the military's position. Civilian governments avoid cutting back military budgets and privileges to keep the armed forces satisfied (Kimenyi and Mbaku 1993). African governments favoured defence in budgeting during periods of austerity (although they discriminated against defence when budget resources were increasing) (Gyimah-Brempong 1992).

There is a vicious circle: during economic hardship, the repressive machinery needs to be strengthened, or at least not to be cut back in proportion to other sectors, in order to withstand the opposition's potential mobilization against austerity. The inability to reduce military spending, in turn, is a further economic burden on the citizens. Where per capita incomes are low, even small changes in budget allocation have great distributive impact on the peoples' welfare. Money for the military allocates funds away from other goods and services, including health care, clean water, and housing. In extremely poor countries such as Sudan, Ethiopia, and Chad, more funds for defence contributed to increased hunger (Gyimah-Brempong 1992).

The vicious circle indicates a fourth dynamic: military centrality reduces a population's welfare and dampens economic growth. Most empirical evidence supports an inverse association between military expenditure and growth—'the tank-tractor trade-off'. Deger and Smith (1983: 352) found that military spending had a small positive effect on growth through modernization effects but larger negative effects through reduced savings, which resulted in a net negative effect of military expenditure on growth. In Sudan, military expenditure had substantial economic costs, particularly on investment, human resource accumulation, trade balance, and economic growth, although Mohammed (1992) also mentions some limited positive spin-offs to the productive sectors. In conclusion, there are several mechanisms through which military centrality causes or exacerbates complex humanitarian emergencies, whether by generating violent conflicts or economic destitution.

10. Conflict Tradition

Not all economically-destitute countries with inegalitarian income distributions and predatory political structures supported by a strong military establishment were subject to humanitarian emergencies. In our econometric analysis, we found a connection between violent conflict in the 1960s and 1970s (specifically 1963 to 1977) and humanitarian emergencies in the 1980s and 1990s. Conflict cultures vary from one country to another and have been shaped by history. Certain forms of conflict are institutionalized in some countries, and would never occur in other countries.

Gurr and Duvall used conflict traditions as an indicator of the justifications for political violence. 'Tension', a multiplicative term incorporating stress, strain, and conflict traditions, 'is the primary driving force behind manifest conflict' (Gurr and Duvall 1973: 157). Gurr and Lichbach's (1986) pure 'persistence of conflict model' also explained some of the variance in political conflict. Citizens adapt to a certain, acceptable level of violence through the cultural experience of violence (Gurr 1970). A tradition of intensive political violence makes societies more susceptible to war and humanitarian emergencies. Countries with a history of mass political mobilization for conflict, such as Colombia, Burundi, and Rwanda, are likely to be more susceptible to new conflict components of complex humanitarian emergencies than other, historically more peaceful countries.

The histories of Latin America and Africa abound with irregular executive transfers. Haiti is a prime example. Despite the army's political weakness and the consequent absence of irregular executive transfers between 1957 and 1986, Haiti has nevertheless had twelve successful coups since 1956 (Brogan 1992). This is a continuation of the trend in the late 19th and early 20th centuries. According to Heinl and Heinl (1978), Haiti experienced more than a hundred more or less successful uprisings between 1843 and the landing of the US Marines in 1915. As many as 17 of the 22 presidents during this period were deposed by a coup d'état or revolution (Lundahl, Chapter 11, Volume 2).

Although Asia has experienced relatively fewer coups, some countries such as Thailand stand out. Typical features of conflict behaviour in South Korea have been self-immolations by fire and huge riots with a very small number of deaths. A war-induced humanitarian emergency would be unlikely in such a country. In Chad, a civil war involving several foreign interventions has continued, with only three short interruptions, since the late 1960s (Brogan 1992). The selection of the forms to express grievances is strongly affected by the conflict culture.

Intensity of past conflicts, as indicated by a large number of casualties, indicates that violence is not atypical for a conflict culture. Colombia is a violent society. During *La Violencia* in 1946–57, some 300,000 people were killed in the fighting between partisans of the Conservative and Liberal Parties. In 1988, when the country was not involved in active warfare, it experienced about 20,000 murders—about six times the murder rate in the United States (Brogan 1992: 513). Past violence is likely to lower the threshold for using violence as a means of expressing dissent, making intensive forms of political conflict normatively justifiable.

11. Conclusion

This chapter analyses the political economy of complex humanitarian emergencies, multi-dimensional crises characterized by warfare, disease, hunger, and displacement. A major factor responsible for the increase in emergencies in the 1990s is the developing world's stagnation and protracted decline in incomes, primarily in the 1980s. Economic decline leads to relative deprivation, or the actors' perception of social injustice arising from a growing discrepancy between goods and conditions they expect and those they can get or keep. Relative deprivation spurs social discontent and sometimes anger, which provide motivation for potential collective violence. Poor economic performance undermines the legitimacy of a regime, increasing the probability of regime turnover. Political élites may use repression to forestall threats to the regime and capture a greater share of the majority's shrinking surplus. Repression and economic discrimination may trigger further discontent and socio-political mobilization on the part of the groups affected, worsening the humanitarian crisis. Protracted economic stagnation can increase the probability of population displacement, hunger and disease. Protracted stagnation may also spur élites to expropriate the assets and resources of weaker communities violently.

A major contributor to slow growth is agricultural stagnation. Slow or negative per capita growth, which is often accompanied by a chronic external disequilibrium, necessitates stabilization and adjustment; those countries whose adjustment policies fail so that they do not qualify for the IMF 'good housekeeping seal', are more vulnerable to humanitarian disaster.

A second factor, high income inequality, contributes to regional, ethnic, and class discrepancies that engendered crises. A third contributor, inflation, increases popular discontent, especially among low-income classes. A fourth factor, the strategies of political élites in response to stagnation, inequality, inflation, and adjustment, and mass reaction to these changes, is instrumental in determining the potential for political conflict and humanitarian emergencies. A fifth explanation for emergencies is military centrality, which can spur conflicts as well as increase poverty. A sixth factor, the tradition for violent conflict, in which violence becomes normatively justifiable in a society, increases the probability of conflict-driven humanitarian crises. These factors suggest that to reduce complex humanitarian emergencies, the international community needs to facilitate widespread growth, support developing countries in reducing disparities in income and wealth, assist poor countries in adjusting to external and internal equilibria, promote good governance, and reduce trade in arms and weapons.

Appendix I. Indicators

A1. The components of humanitarian emergencies

A1.1. War

We selected the number of battle-related deaths per population as the proxy for war. Two sources were identified: the Correlates of War (COW) database for civil wars (Singer and Small 1994) and the Stockholm Peace Research Institute's database on battle-related deaths in major armed conflicts (SIPRI Yearbook 1989–96). The information yielded by the two sources was compared with each other.

The Correlates of War database includes major civil wars, where (i) military action was involved, (ii) the national government at the time was actively involved, (iii) effective resistance (as measured by the ratio of fatalities of the weaker to the stronger forces) occurred on both sides, and (iv) at least 1,000 battle deaths resulted during the civil war. Also a minimum population of 500,000 and either diplomatic recognition by at least two major powers or membership in the League of Nations or United Nations were required. A total number of 150 such wars occurred in 1816–1988 (The Correlates of War Project, 1994), whereas 38 such wars were recorded during the period under observation, 1980–95. Furthermore, the Ogaden (1976–83) and the Tigrean (1978–91) wars were extracted from the Correlates of War Dataset on *International* Wars and classified under Ethiopia as civil wars. Besides Ethiopia, six other countries experienced two civil wars in 1980–95.

The problem with the COW dataset is that casualties are reported from the entire war, not per annum. To obtain annual figures for the pooled dataset, the deaths were divided by the number of years that the conflict endured. Consequently the number of deaths is invariant from year to year, unless one war was replaced by another with a different death-rate. This is unfortunate, but of course the pool's cross-sectional variation remains.

The civil war in El Salvador will serve as an example of how the figures were arrived at. The war lasted for 14 years, from 1979 until 1992. According to the COW data, 25,000 lives were lost in fighting. The number of 25,000 battle-related deaths is divided by 14 years, which gives 1,786 deaths during each year, 1980 to 1992. The year 1979 falls out of the period under investigation. The number of deaths is then divided by the annual population estimate, and the resulting score is finally multiplied by 100 to eliminate a high concentration of figures close to zero. For example, the country's population was 4.52 million in 1980, yielding the score 3.95, and 5.04 million in 1992, yielding the score 3.31, for battle-related deaths per population (DEATHPOP).

SIPRI provides estimates of battle-related deaths for 36 countries in the present sample. However, information is missing for a total of eight years, 1980–87. In addition, the coding procedure seems to be more conservative than that of the Correlates of War Project. Even during the period 1988–95 SIPRI fails, in many cases, to report any estimate of the death toll even if a major conflict was underway during a given year. Besides the numerous cases of 'not available' data, SIPRI does not report the conflicts of Armenia (1992–), Burundi (neither the 1988 nor the early 1990s' war), Georgia (1991), Romania (1989), and Russia (1991)—which fulfil the criteria applied by the COW project. For the SIPRI data, deaths per population were multiplied by 10,000 in order to avoid a concentration of observations very close to zero.

The basic problem of the COW dataset is less dramatic: it does not contain data for the year 1995, which leaves out the conflicts in Sierra Leone and Russia (Chechnya). Because of its superior coverage, the COW figures were adopted as a basis for indicator construction. It should be noted, however, that, as compared to SIPRI statistics, COW does not record the conflicts in Algeria (1993–), Bangladesh (1989–95), Cambodia (only) (1992), Chad (only) (1989–92), Georgia (1993–94), Guatemala (1988–95), Indonesia (1988–95), Iran (1988–93), Mauritania (1988–89), South Africa (1988 and 1990–93), Turkey (only) (1989–90), Uganda (1989 and 1991), and Yemen (1994).

A1.2. Displacement

As discussed in detail by Melkas (1996), the statistics for internally displaced populations are particularly unreliable. Therefore, the number of refugees by origin adjusted for the source country's population (REFUPOP) was chosen as a proxy for displacement. (The score was multiplied by 100 in order to avoid concentration of observations close to zero.) Source: USCR: *World Refugee Survey* (1980–96, successive years).

In collecting the information, refugees from the former Soviet bloc to the Western countries before the 1980s were excluded from the dataset since neither their sources or living conditions are related to humanitarian emergencies in the 1980s and 1990s. Cuban refugees to the United States were excluded for the same reason. Several annual figures had to be estimated on the basis of previous or adjacent years because of lacking data. Normally this was unproblematic, as the *status quo* was the typical condition. The *Survey's* reporting of any significant repatriations was helpful in changing circumstances. In some other cases, estimation was more difficult, for example, when the number of refugees was reported from a group of countries such as from 'Indochina'. The statistics for individual countries (in this case Cambodia, Laos and Vietnam) would be calculated from the adjacent years' data, giving each country the average proportional share of the total number of refugees from Indochina one year before and after. Another example of the difficulties involved is the change from reporting the number of refugees by country of origin in 1980 to reporting by country of asylum in 1981. In one case the figures simply provided no basis for judging, and the number of refugees from Zambia in 1981 was estimated at 2,000.

A1.3. Hunger

The measure selected to indicate hunger is the annual calorie supply per capita (FAO 1995). Although 'starvation' is rarely the 'cause' of famine deaths, food shortages may provoke people into actions which increase their exposure to other risks, such as death from disease (Seaman 1993). A low calorie supply is an indicator of poverty rather than humanitarian emergency. One should look at changes in calorie supply rather than levels. Looking at the trend of calorie supply from 1980 to 1995 one observes an encouraging, albeit weak, upward trend in the countries under study. Any downward deviation of this general trend could be indicative of a humanitarian emergency. The indicator of hunger (CALAVE) is expressed as a deviation of calorie supply from the annual average change in the whole sample:

CALAVE = CALINDEX – AVERAGE (CALINDEX),

where AVERAGE (CALINDEX) = average annual change in the index of calorie supply in the whole sample; CALINDEX = LAG (CALINDEX) + ((((CALSUPP – LAG (CALSUPP))/LAG (CALSUPP)) * 100), or index of change in the calorie supply for $N_1, \ldots N_k$; 1980 = 100. Source: FAOSTAT TS 1995 Database. Rome: Copyright by the United Nations Food and Agricultural Programme. Software by the United States Department of Agriculture, Economic Research Service.

Negative values indicate that a country is below the general trend towards increased calorie supply, which is hypothesized to be an indicator of a potential complex humanitarian emergency. The data on calorie supply were extrapolated for all countries for 1993–95.

A1.4. Disease

Since infants are highly susceptible to disease, we used the infant mortality rate per 1,000 live births as a proxy for disease. Disease claims human lives during emergencies due to lack of food and sanitation. Seaman (1993) points out that the immediate cause of death is generally from infection, electrolyte imbalance or a range of other biological events. As with calorie supply, infant mortality in itself is also an indicator of poverty. For instance, poor countries cannot afford health services that would prevent diseases. There is a need to resort once again to a measure indicating a deviation from the general trend. Encouragingly, during 1980–95, we observe a clear reduction in infant mortality during 1980–95 in the countries under study. The indicator is constructed as follows:

INFAVE = INFINDEX – AVERAGE (INFINDEX),

where AVERAGE (INFINDEX) = average annual change in the index of infant mortality; INFINDEX = LAG (INFINDEX) + (((INFMORT – LAG (INF-MORT))/LAG (INFMORT)) * 100), or index of change in the infant mortality rate for $N_1, \ldots N_k$; 1980 = 100. Source: World Tables Database 1993 Update. Socio-Economic Access and Retrieval System, vers. 2.5, April 1992. Washington, DC: The World Bank.

The data on infant mortality were extrapolated for 1993–95 for all countries and for 1980–81 for Lithuania, Belize and Slovenia.

A2. The sources

CPIDIFF: Consumer price index, annual change.
Source: Social Indicators of Development (SID) 1995 Database. Socio-Economic Access and Retrieval System (calculated). Washington, DC: World Bank.

DEATRAD: 'Death tradition': number of deaths from political violence, 1963–77.
Source: Taylor, Charles Lewis, and David A. Jodice (1983). *World Handbook of Political and Social Indicators. 3rd edition. Vol. 2: Political Protest and Government Change*. New Haven and London: Yale University Press.

GDPGRO: Gross domestic product (average annual growth, %), 1980–92.
Source: World Tables Database 1993 Update. Socio-Economic Access and Retrieval System, vers. 2.5, April 1992. Washington, DC: The World Bank.

GINI: Gini index as defined by Deininger and Squire (1996), requiring that observations be based on household surveys, on comprehensive coverage of the population, and on comprehensive coverage of income sources.
Source: Deininger, Klaus, and Lyn Squire (1996). 'A New Data Set Measuring Income Inequality'. *The World Bank Economic Review*, 10 (3): 565–91.

GNPCAP: Gross national product per capita, 1980–93 (US$, Atlas method).
Source: Social Indicators of Development (SID) 1995 Database. Socio-Economic Access and Retrieval System. Washington, DC: World Bank.

FOODGRO: Annual growth of food production per capita.
Source: World Tables Database 1993 Update. Socio-Economic Access and Retrieval System, vers. 2.5, April 1992 (calculated). Washington, DC: World Bank.

IMFGNP: Use of IMF credit as a percentage of GNP: The use of IMF resources except those resulting from drawings in the reserve tranche.
Source: World Debt Tables 1996 Database. Socio-Economic Access and Retrieval System, vers. 3.0, May 1993 (calculated). Washington, DC: World Bank.

MILCENT: 'Military centrality': Annual military expenditures as a percentage of GNP.
Source: SIPRI Yearbook (1986–95, successive years) World Armaments and Disarmament. Stockholm International Peace Research Institute (SIPRI). United States: Oxford University Press.

ODAPOP80: Official development assistance per capita index (1980 = 100).
Source: World Development Report (successive years; calculated from 'Official

Development Assistance: receipts'). Washington, DC: World Bank and Oxford University Press.

ODAPOGRO: Official development assistance per capita growth.
Source: World Development Report (calculated from ODAPOP80). Washington, DC: The World Bank and Oxford University Press.

POLRI: Summary index of 'political rights grievances', that is, demands for greater political rights other than autonomy, sum of codings on five ordinal scales:
POL1   Diffuse Political Grievances
POL2   Seek Greater Political Rights
POL3   Seek Greater Central Participation
POL4   Seek Equal Civil Rights
POL5   Seek Change in Officials/Policies
POL6   Other Political Grievances
Source: Gurr, Ted Robert (1993). *Minorities at Risk. A Global View of Ethnopolitical Conflicts*. Washington, DC: United States Institute of Peace Press.

TOT80: Terms of trade index (1980 = 100, US$-based).
Source: World Tables Database 1993 Update. Socio-Economic Access and Retrieval System, vers. 2.5, April 1992 (converted from 1987 = 100). Washington, DC: The World Bank.

TOTCHANG: Terms of trade index, annual change.
Source: World Tables Database 1993 Update. Socio-Economic Access and Retrieval System, vers. 2.5, April 1992 (calculated from TOT80). Washington, DC: The World Bank.

A3. Indicators of the dependent variable

We constructed continuous indicators for our dependent variables, thus not losing information on annual variations or facing problems of setting thresholds, as with dichotomous indicators. Because of the complexity of humanitarian emergencies, we tested our hypotheses on three different measures of the dependent variable. Our first, most simple measure, is based on the information that battle deaths and refugees per population are closely related:

(1) DEATHREF = (DEATHPOP + 1) * (REFUPOP + 1),
where DEATHPOP, REFUPOP = battle-related deaths and refugees per population, respectively (except if both DEATHPOP and REFUPOP = 0, then DEATHREF = 0 instead of 1).

The variable combines two important components of complex humanitarian emergencies, but for a positive score both components do not have to be present (the reason for adding two constants in the equation). The variable thus gets positive values not only when there are both deaths and refugees, but also when there are deaths but no refugees or refugees but no deaths. The inclusiveness of this variable increases the number of non-zero observations, which increases the variability of the dependent variable. However, a second equation assures that a humanitarian emergency comprises both components, that is

(2) HUMEMERG = DEATHPOP * REFUPOP.

We constructed a composite indicator that also includes malnutrition and disease as parts of complex humanitarian emergencies:

(3) COHE = (1 + DEATHPOP) * (1 + REFUPOP) * ((100 – CALAVE)/10) * ((100 + INFAVE)/10),[31]

where CALAVE = deviation from trend (average annual increase) in calorie supply and INFAVE = deviation from trend (average annual decrease) in the infant mortality rate.[32]

The negative sign before CALAVE ensues because cases with below average calorie supply growth are more likely to be a part of a complex humanitarian emergency, whereas the positive sign before INFMORT indicates that below average infant mortality *reductions* are expected to increase the probability of a complex emergency. Of the three indicators, COHE is the most inclusive and HUMEMERG the most exclusive, since it only includes cases with both deaths and refugees. One point of interest is comparing the results of models using different operationalizations of humanitarian emergencies. While rejecting the 'country-list approach', we later created dichotomous variables for probit regression analyses, which enabled us to estimate the changes in the probability of humanitarian emergencies.

---

[31] By adding a constant 100 to CALAVE and INFAVE we eliminate the possibility of obtaining—what would be counterintuitive—negative composite measures of complex humanitarian emergencies. Dividing the scores of CALAVE and INFAVE by 10 avoids large scores of the composite indicators.

[32] We also created a fourth variable,

(4) COHE2 = DEATHPOP * REFUPOP * ((100 – CALAVE)/10) * ((100 + INFAVE)/10),

which added to HUMEMERG the information on hunger and disease. However, this variable suffered from lack of observations—all four dimensions had to be present in order for the variable to be registered—and was therefore dropped from the analysis.

Appendix II. Results of Regression Analyses

Table A3.1. Humanitarian emergencies: OLS regression models

Explanatory variables	(1) LDEATREF	(2) LHUMEMER	(3) LCOHE
Constant	7.31*** (2.67)	4.27** (1.85)	15.07*** (2.51)
LGDPGRO[–1]	–1.83*** (0.55)	–1.16*** (0.38)	–2.54*** (0.52)
LGINI[–1]	0.29** (0.12)	0.18** (0.08)	0.36*** (0.11)
LGNPCAP[–1]	–0.15*** (0.03)	–0.07*** (0.02)	–0.19*** (0.03)
LIMFGNP[–1]	–0.10*** (0.03)	–0.05*** (0.02)	–0.06** (0.03)
LCPIDIFF[–1]	0.26*** (0.06)	0.20*** (0.04)	0.27*** (0.05)
LMILCENT[–1]	0.18*** (0.03)	0.16*** (0.02)	0.15*** (0.03)
LDEATRAD	0.04*** (0.01)	A	0.02* (0.01)
R square	0.18	0.16	0.19
N	663	663	663
DW	0.34	0.31	0.38

Note: the figures are parameter estimates and standard errors (in parentheses), respectively. LGDPGRO = ln real GDP growth; LGINI = ln gini index; LGNPCAP = ln GNP per capita; LIMFGNP = ln use of IMF credit/GNP; LCPIDIFF= ln consumer price index, annual change; LMILCENT = ln military expenditures/GNP; LDEATRAD = ln deaths from domestic violence 1963–77; except for LDEATRAD, all explanatory variables are lagged one year [–1]; coefficient significant *** = at the 1 per cent level (2-tailed test), ** = 5 per cent level and * = 10 per cent level; a = not significant; DW = Durbin-Watson test statistic for serial correlation.

Table A3.2. Humanitarian emergencies: GLS (Prais-Winsten) regression models

Explanatory variables	(1) LDEATHREF	(2) LHUMEMER	(3) LCOHE
Constant	–2.69*** (0.81)	1.18a (0.73)	2.82*** (0.58)
LGDPGRO[–1]	B	–0.29** (0.14)	a
LFOODGRO [–1]	–0.19* (0.12)	A	b
LGINI[–1]	0.97*** (0.16)	0.14* (0.08)	0.56*** (0.14)
LGNPCAP[–1]	–0.14*** (0.04)	–0.07*** (0.02)	–0.21*** (0.03)
LIMFGNP[–1]	A	A	a
LCPIDIFF[–1]	0.16*** (0.04)	A	0.19*** (0.04)
LMILCENT[–1]	0.19*** (0.04)	0.10*** (0.02)	0.19*** (0.03)
LDEATRAD	0.05*** (0.01)	0.02*** (0.007)	0.03*** (0.01)
Rho	0.86*** (0.02)	0.88*** (0.02)	0.83*** (0.02)
N	600	753	732
DW	1.93	1.64	1.98

Note: the figures are parameter estimates and standard errors (in parentheses), respectively. LGDPGRO = ln real GDP growth; LFOODGRO = ln growth of food production per capita; LGINI = ln gini index; LGNPCAP = ln GNP per capita; LIMFGNP = ln use of IMF credit/GNP; LCPIDIFF= ln consumer price index, annual change; LMILCENT = ln military expenditures/GNP; LDEATRAD = ln deaths from domestic violence 1963–77; except for LDEATRAD, all explanatory variables are lagged one year [–1]; rho = coefficient of autocorrelation; coefficient significant *** = at the 1 per cent level (2-tailed test), ** = 5 per cent level land * = 10 per cent level; a = not significant; and b = not included in the equation; DW = Durbin-Watson test statistic for serial correlation.

Table A3.3. Probabilities of humanitarian emergencies: Probit models

Explanatory variables	(1) LDEATREF	(2) LHUMEMER
LGDPGRO[–1]	–0.82* (0.45)	–0.41** (0.20)
LGINI[–1]	0.25*** (0.10)	0.12** (0.05)
LGNPCAP[–1]	–0.13*** (0.03)	–0.03** (0.01)
LIMFGNP[–1]	–0.07*** (0.03)	–0.014 (0.011)
LCPIDIFF[–1]	0.05 (0.04)	–0.01 (0.02)
LMILCENT[–1]	0.05* (0.028)	0.02* (0.01)
LDEATRAD	0.04*** (0.01)	0.01*** (0.003)
Obs. P	0.33	0.08
Pred. P	0.30	0.05
Log Likelihood	–309.79	–136.60
Chi square	95.40	35.42
N	562	562

Note: the figures are changes in probabilities and standard errors (in parentheses), respectively. LGDPGRO = ln real GDP growth; LGINI = ln gini index; LGNPCAP = ln GNP per capita; LIMFGNP = ln use of IMF credit/GNP; LCPIDIFF= ln consumer price index, annual change; LMILCENT = ln military expenditures/GNP; LDEATRAD = ln deaths from domestic violence 1963–77; except for LDEATRAD, all explanatory variables are lagged one year [–1]; the underlying coefficient is significant *** = at the 1 per cent level (2-tailed test), ** = 5 per cent level and * = 10 per cent level; obs. P = observed probability; pred. P = predicted probability at the mean of the dependent variable. The statistical significance of the model is tested against the value of Chi square with seven degrees of freedom.

Table A3.4. GDP growth (LGDPGRO)
(1) Ordinary least squares models

LAG	LDEATREF	LHUMEMER	LCOHE
[–4]	–1.446*** (0.513)	–1.138*** (0.345)	–2.112*** (0.481)
[–3]	–1.699*** (0.521)	**–1.214*** (0.358)**	–2.304*** (0.490)
[–2]	–1.809*** (0.516)	–1.178*** (0.355)	–2.534*** (0.490)
[–1]	–1.833*** (0.547)	–1.142*** (0.380)	–2.544*** (0.517)
	–2.023* (0.576)**	–1.103*** (0.407)	**–2.720*** (0.545)**
[+1]	–1.679*** (0.581)	–0.818** (0.412)	–2.219*** (0.556)
[+2]	–1.721*** (0.580)	–0.484 (0.407)	–1.929*** (0.615)
[+3]	–1.800*** (0.648)	–0.088 (0.459)	–1.832*** (0.693)
[+4]	–1.844*** (0.703)	–0.078 (0.504)	–1.862** (0.776)

Note: the figures are parameter estimates and standard errors; coefficient significant *** = at the 1 per cent; ** = five per cent, * = 10 per cent level of significance (2-tailed test); all other variables are held constant in the models.
Strongest associations are indicated in bold.

(2) Generalized least squares (Prais-Winsten) models

LAG	LHUMEMER
[–2]	**–1.197*** (0.320)**
[–1]	–0.287** (0.142)
	–0.266* (0.157)
[+1]	–0.050 (0.168)
[+2]	–0.115 (0.182)

Table A3.5. Food production growth (LFOODGRO)

LAG	LDEATREF
[–2]	–0.105 (0.116)
[–1]	**–0.193* (0.116)**
	–0.048 (0.130)
[+1]	0.089 (0.124)
[+2]	0.039 (0.125)

Note: strongest association is indicated in bold.

Table A3.6. IMF credit/GNP (LIMFGNP)

LAG	LDEATREF	LHUMEMER	LCOHE
[–2]	–0.074** (0.032)	–0.046** (0.022)	–0.041 (0.030)
[–1]	–0.097*** (0.032)	–0.061*** (0.022)	–0.063** (0.030)
	–0.124*** (0.032)	**–0.082*** (0.022)**	–0.088*** (0.030)
[+1]	–0.127*** (0.032)	–0.079*** (0.022)	–0.101*** (0.031)
[+2]	**–0.128*** (0.032)**	–0.073*** (0.022)	**–0.106*** (0.033)**

Note: the figures for Tables A3.4(2) to A3.6 are parameter estimates and standard errors; coefficient significant *** = at the 1 per cent; ** = 5 per cent, * = 10 per cent level of significance (2-tailed test); all other variables are held constant in the models. Strongest associations are indicated in bold.

References

Adedeji, Adebayo (1989). *Towards a Dynamic African Economy: Selected Speeches and Lectures, 1975–1986*. London: Frank Cass.

Ake, Claude (1996). *Democracy and Development in Africa*. Washington, DC: Brookings Institution.

Alesina, Alberto, and Roberto Perotti (1996). 'Income Distribution, Political Instability, and Investment'. *European Economic Review*, 40 (6) (June): 1203–28.

Alnasrawi, Abbas (forthcoming). 'Iraq: Economic Embargo and Predatory Rule', in E. Wayne Nafziger, Frances Stewart and Raimo Väyrynen (eds.), *Weak States and Vulnerable Economies: Humanitarian Emergencies in Developing Countries*, Volume 2 of *War, Hunger and Displacement: The Origins of Humanitarian Emergencies*. Oxford: Oxford University Press.

Annan, Kofi A. (1996). 'The Peace-keeping Prescription', in Kevin M. Cahill (ed.), *Preventive Diplomacy: Stopping Wars before They Start*. New York: Basic Books, 174–90.

Auvinen, Juha (1996a). 'Economic Performance, Adjustment, and Political Conflict in the Developing Countries: Cross-National Statistical Analysis of the Determinants of Political Conflict with Case Study on Chile'. Sussex, UK: University of Sussex. D. Phil. dissertation.

Auvinen, Juha (1996b). 'IMF Intervention and Political Protest in the Third World—A Conventional Wisdom Refined. *Third World Quarterly*, 17 (3) (September): 377–400.

Auvinen, Juha, and Timo Kivimäki (1997). 'Towards more Effective Preventive Diplomacy. Lessons from Conflict Transformation in South Africa'. Working Paper No. 4. Series C. Rovaniemi, Finland: University of Lapland: Faculty of Social Sciences.

Auvinen, Juha, and E. Wayne Nafziger (1999). 'The Sources of Humanitarian Emergencies'. *Journal of Conflict Resolution*, 43 (3) (June).

Barro, Robert J. (1991). 'Economic Growth in a Cross-Section of Countries'. *Quarterly Journal of Economics*, 106 (2) (May): 407–43.

Bartholdy, Kasper (1996). 'Assessing Progress in Economies in Transition'. *Economics of Transition*, 4 (1) (May): 270–94.

Bienen, Henry, and Mark Gersovitz (1985). 'Economic Stabilization, Conditionality, and Political Stability'. *International Organization*, 39 (Autumn): 729–54.

Brogan, Patrick (1992). *World Conflicts. Why and Where They Are Happening*. London: Bloomsbury.

Cleaver, Kevin M. (1985). 'The Impact of Price and Exchange Rate Policies on Agriculture in Sub-Saharan Africa'. World Bank Staff Working Paper No. 728. Washington, DC: World Bank.

Collier, P. (1999). 'The Political Economy of Ethnicity', in Boris Pleskovic and Joseph E. Stiglitz (eds.), *Annual World Bank Conference on Development Economics 1998*. Washington, DC: World Bank, 387–99.

Collier, P., and A. Hoeffler (1998). 'On Economic Causes of War'. *Oxford Economic Papers* (October).

Cornia, Giovanni Andrea (1994). 'Neglected Issues in the Decline of Africa's Agriculture: Land Tenure, Land Distribution and R&D Constraints', in G. A. Cornia and G. Helleiner (eds.), *From Adjustment to Development in Africa: Conflict, Controversy, Convergence, Consensus?* Houndsmills, UK: St. Martin's Press, 217–47.

Cornia, Giovanni Andrea, and Gerald K. Helleiner (1994). *From Adjustment to Development in Africa: Conflict, Controversy, Convergence, Consensus?* Houndsmills, UK: St. Martin's Press.

Cornia, Giovanni Andrea, Richard Jolly, and Frances Stewart (eds.) (1987). *Adjustment with a Human Face: Protecting the Vulnerable and Promoting Growth*. 2 vols. Oxford: Clarendon Press.

Daley, Patricia (1992). 'The Politics of the Refugee Crisis in Tanzania', in Horace Campbell and Howard Stein (eds.), *Tanzania and the IMF: The Dynamics of Liberalization*. Boulder, CO: Westview.

Davies, James C. (1962). 'Toward a Theory of Revolution'. *American Sociological Review*, 27 (1) (February): 5–19.

de Waal, Alex W. L. (1989). *Famine That Kills: Darfur, Sudan, 1984–1985*. Oxford: Clarendon Press.

de Waal, Alex W. L. (1994). 'Dangerous Precedents? Famine Relief in Somalia 1991–93', in Joanna Macrae and Anthony Zwi (eds.), *War and Hunger: Rethinking International Responses to Complex Emergencies*. London: Zed Books, 139–59.

Deger, Saadet, and Ron Smith (1983). 'Military Expenditure and Growth in Less Developed Countries'. *Journal of Conflict Resolution*, 27 (2) (June): 335–53.

Deininger, Klaus, and Lyn Squire (1996). 'A New Data Set Measuring Income Inequality'. *The World Bank Economic Review*, 10: 565–91.

Drèze, Jean, and Amartya Sen (1989). *Hunger and Public Action*. Oxford: Clarendon Press.

Duffield, Mark (1994). 'The Political Economy of Internal War: Asset Transfer, Complex Emergencies and International Aid', in Joanne Macrae and Anthony Zwi (eds.), *War and Hunger: Rethinking International Responses to Complex Emergencies*. London: Zed Books, 50–69.

Dupuy, Alex (1989). *Haiti in the World Economy: Class, Race, and Underdevelopment since 1700*. Boulder, CO: Westview Press.

Du Toit, Pierre (1996). Associate Professor, Department of Political Studies, Cape Town University. Interview, January.

Economic Commission for Africa (1989). *South African Destabilization: The Economic Cost of Frontline Resistance to Apartheid*. Addis Ababa.

Eicher, Carl K., and Doyle C. Baker (1982). 'Research on Agricultural Development in Sub-Saharan Africa: A Critical Survey'. International Development Paper No. 1. East Lansing: Michigan State University.

Esterhuyse, W. (1992). 'Scenarios for South Africa—Instability and Violence or Negotiated Transition?' *Long Range Planning*, 25 (3): 21–6.

Fisher, A., and M. Albeldas (1987). *A Question of Survival: Conversations with Key South Africans*. Johannesburg: Jonathan Ball Publishers.

FAO (Food and Agriculture Organization of the UN) (1995). The State of Food and Agriculture. Rome.

Franzosi, Roberto (1989). 'One Hundred Years of Strike Statistics: Methodological and Theoretical Issues in Quantitative Strike Research'. *Industrial and Labor Relations Review*, 42 (3) (April): 348–61.

Friedman, Stephen (1995). Director, Centre for Policy Studies, Johannesburg. Interview, December.

Gaffney, Patrick D. (1996). 'Binding up the Broken Promises of Democracy in Burundi: Causes, Results, and Prospects for Overcoming Cycles of Ethnic Violence'. Unpublished paper. Notre Dame, IN: University of Notre Dame.

Ghai, Dharam, and Samir Radwan (eds.) (1983). *Agrarian Policies and Rural Poverty in Africa*. Geneva: International Labour Office.

Goliber, Thomas (1989). 'Africa's Expanding Population: Old Problems, New Policies'. *Population Bulletin*, 44 (November): 10–1.

Gurr, Ted Robert (1970). *Why Men Rebel*. Princeton, NJ: Princeton University Press.

Gurr, Ted Robert (1993). *Minorities at Risk. A Global View of Ethnopolitical Conflicts*. Washington, DC: The United States Institute of Peace Press.

Gurr, Ted Robert (1994). 'Peoples against States—Ethnopolitical Conflict and the Changing World-System—1994 Presidential Address'. *International Studies Quarterly*, 38 (3): 347–77.

Gurr, Ted Robert, and Raymond Duvall (1973). 'Civil Conflict in the 1960s: A Reciprocal Theoretical System With Parameter Estimates'. *Comparative Political Studies*, 6 (2) (July): 135–70.

Gurr, Ted Robert, and Mark Irving Lichbach (1986). 'Forecasting Internal Conflict. A Competitive Evaluation of Empirical Theories'. *Comparative Political Studies*, 19 (1) (April): 3–38.

Gyimah-Brempong, Kwabena (1992). 'Do African Governments Favor Defense in Budgeting?' *Journal of Peace Research*, 29 (2): 191–206.

Hirschman, D. (1987). 'Of Monsters and Devils, Analyses and Alternatives'. *African Affairs*, 89 (July): 341–69.

Heinl, Robert Debs, Jr., and Nancy Gordon Heinl (1978). *Written in Blood: The Story of the Haitian People 1492–1971*. Boston: Houghton Mifflin.

Holsti, Kalevi J. (1991). *Peace and War: Armed Conflicts and International Order, 1648–1989*. Cambridge: Cambridge University Press.

Holsti, Kalevi J. (1996). *The State, War, and the State of War*. Cambridge: Cambridge University Press.

Hunter, Wendy (1994). 'Contradictions of Civilian Control: Argentina, Brazil and Chile in the 1990s'. *Third World Quarterly*, 15 (4): 633–53.

Jackman, Robert W. (1993). *Power without Force. The Political Capacity of Nation-States*. Ann Arbor: The University of Michigan Press.

Jazairy, Idriss, Mohiuddin Alamgir, and Theresa Panuccio (1992). *The State of World Rural Poverty: An Inquiry into its Causes and Consequences*. Published for the International Fund for Agricultural Development. New York: New York University Press.

Jenkins, J. Craig, and Augustine J. Kposowa (1990). 'Explaining Military Coups d'État: Black Africa, 1957–84'. *American Sociological Review*, 55 (December): 861–75.

Johnson, T. H., R. O. Slater, and P. McGowan (1984). 'Explaining African Military Coup d'Etat, 1960–82'. *American Political Science Review*, 78 (3): 622–40.

Kaufman, Robert F. (1985). 'Democratic and Authoritarian Responses to the Debt Issue: Argentina, Brazil, Mexico'. *International Organisation*, 39 (3) (Summer): 473–503.

Kaufman, Robert F., and Barbara Stallings (1989). 'Debt and Democracy in the 1980s: The Latin American Experience', in Barbara Stallings and Robert Kaufman (eds.), *Debt and Democracy in Latin America*. Boulder, CO: Westview.

Keen, David (1994). *The Political Economy of Famine and Relief in Southwestern Sudan, 1983–1989*. Princeton, NJ: Princeton University Press.

Kimenyi, Mwangi S., and John M. Mbaku (1993). 'Rent-Seeking and Institutional Stability in Developing Countries'. *Public Choice*, 77 (2): 385–405.

Kposowa, Augustine J., and J. Craig Jenkins (1993). 'The Structural Sources of Military Coups in Postcolonial Africa, 1957–1984'. *American Journal of Sociology*, 99 (1) (July): 126–63.

Lafay, Jean-Dominique, and Jacques Lecaillon (1992). La Dimension Politique de L'Ajustement Économique. Texte préparé pour le Centre de Développement de l'OCDE, Paris, Septembre.

Lardy, Nicholas R. (1983). *Agriculture in China's Modern Economic Development*. Cambridge: Cambridge University Press.

Lemarchand, Rene (1972). 'Political Clientalism and Ethnicity in Tropical Africa: Competing Solidarities in Nation-building'. *American Political Science Review*, 66 (March): 68–90.

Lewis, Peter (1996). 'From Prebendalism to Predation: the Political Economy of Decline in Nigeria'. *Journal of Modern African Studies*, 34 (1) (March): 79–103.

Lukic, Reneo, and Allen Lynch (1996). *Europe from the Balkans to the Urals: The Disintegration of Yugoslavia and the Soviet Union*. Oxford: Oxford University Press.

Lundahl, Mats (forthcoming). 'Haiti: Towards the Abyss? Poverty, Dependence, and Resource Depletion', in E. Wayne Nafziger, Frances Stewart and Raimo Väyrynen (eds.), *Weak States and Vulnerable Economies: Humanitarian Emergencies in Developing Countries*, Volume II of *War, Hunger and Displacement: The Origins of Humanitarian Emergencies*. Oxford: Oxford University Press.

Macrae, Joanna, and Anthony Zwi (eds.) (1994). *War and Hunger: Rethinking International Responses to Complex Emergencies*. London: Zed Books.

Melkas, Helinä (1996). 'Measurement of the Seriousness and Dynamics of Complex Humanitarian Emergencies: Prospects and Limitations'. RIP United Nations University/World Institute for Development Economics Research, Research in Progress.

Mills, Cadman Atta (1989). 'Structural Adjustment in Sub-Saharan Africa'. Economic Development Institute Policy Seminar Report No. 18. Washington, DC: World Bank.

Mohammed, Nadir A. L. (1992). 'Tank-Tractor Trade-off in the Sudan: The Socio-Economic Impact of Military Expenditure'. Paper prepared for CODESRIA Research Network on 'The Military and Militarism in Africa'. Dakar, Senegal, 16–19 December.

Möller, V., L. Schlemmer, and S. H. C. du Toit (1989). *Quality of Life in South Africa: Measurement and Analysis*. Pretoria: Human Sciences Research Council.

Morrisson, Christian, Jean-Dominique Lafay, and Sebastien Dessus (1994). 'Adjustment Programmes and Politico-Economic Interactions in Developing Countries: Lessons from an Empirical Analysis of Africa in the 1980s', in G. A. Cornia and G. Helleiner (eds.), *From Adjustment to Development in Africa: Conflict, Controversy, Convergence, Consensus?* Houndsmills, UK: St. Martin's Press, 174–91.

Myrdal, Gunnar (1968). *Asian Drama: An Inquiry into the Poverty of Nations*. 3 Vols. Middlesex, England: Penguin Books.

Nafziger, E. Wayne (1983). *The Economics of Political Instability: The Nigerian-Biafran War*. Boulder, CO.: Westview Press.

Nafziger, E. Wayne (1986). *Entrepreneurship, Equity, and Economic Development*. Greenwich, CN: JAI Press.

Nafziger, E. Wayne (1988). *Inequality in Africa: Political Élites, Proletariat, Peasants, and the Poor*. Cambridge: Cambridge University Press.

Nafziger, E. Wayne (1993). *The Debt Crisis in Africa*. Baltimore: Johns Hopkins University Press.

Nafziger, E. Wayne (1995). *Learning from the Japanese: Japan's Prewar Development and the Third World*. Armonk, NY: M. E. Sharpe.

Nafziger, E. Wayne (1997). *The Economics of Developing Countries*. 3rd edition. Upper Saddle River, NJ: Prentice Hall.

Nafziger, E. Wayne, and Juha Auvinen (1997). 'War, Hunger, and Displacement: An Econometric Investigation into the Sources of Humanitarian Emergencies'. UNU/WIDER Working Paper. Helsinki: World Institute for Development Economics Research (UNU/WIDER).

Nafziger, E. Wayne, and Juha Auvinen (1999). http://www.wider.unu.edu/emerg981.htm.

Nafziger, E. Wayne, Frances Stewart, and Raimo Väyrynen (eds.) (forthcoming). *Weak States and Vulnerable Economies: Humanitarian Emergencies in Developing Countries*, Volume 2 of *War, Hunger, and Displacement: The Origins of Humanitarian Emergencies*.

Nel, R. P. (1996). Professor, Department of Political Science, Stellenbosch University. Interview, January.

Nelson, Joan M. (ed.) (1990). *Economic Crisis and Policy Choice. The Politics of Adjustment in the Third World*. Princeton, New Jersey: Princeton University Press.

O'Donnell, Guillermo (1973). *Modernisation and Bureaucratic Authoritarianism: Studies in South American Politics*. Berkeley, CA: University of California Press.

O'Donnell, Guillermo (1978). 'Reflections on the Patterns of Change in the Bureaucratic Authoritarian State'. *Latin American Research Review*, 12 (1).

Pastor, Manuel, and James K. Boyce (forthcoming). 'El Salvador: Economic Disparities, External Intervention, and Civil Conflict', in E. Wayne Nafziger, Frances Stewart and Raimo Väyrynen (eds.), *Weak States and Vulnerable Economies: Humanitarian Emergencies in Developing Countries*, Volume II of *War, Hunger and Displacement: The Origins of Humanitarian Emergencies*. Oxford: Oxford University Press.

Peters, Pauline E. (1999). 'Comment on "The Political Economy of Ethnicity" ', in Boris Pleskovic and Joseph E. Stiglitz (eds.), *Annual World Bank Conference on Development Economics 1998*. Washington, DC: World Bank, 400–05.

Pirttijärvi, Jouni (1995). 'Zapatistit—uudenlainen kapinaliike' (Zapatistas—a new kind of rebellion movement?). *Kosmopolis*, 25 (3): 37–52.

Platteau, J. P. (1996). 'The Evolutionary Theory of Land Rights as Applied to Sub-Saharan Africa: A Critical Assessment'. *Development and Change*, 27 (1) (January): 29–86.

Pleskovic, Boris, and Joseph E. Stiglitz (eds.) (1999). *Annual World Bank Conference on Development Economics 1998*. Washington, DC: World Bank.

Prybyla, Jan. S. (1970). *The Political Economy of Communist China*. Scranton, PA: International Textbook.

Putterman, Louis (1993). *Continuity and Change in China's Rural Development: Collective and Reform Eras in Perspective*. New York: Oxford University Press.

Ravallion, Martin (1997). 'Famines and Economics'. *Journal of Economic Literature*, 37 (September): 1205–42.

Reno, William (1995). 'Reinvention of an African Patrimonial State: Charles Taylor's Liberia'. *Third World Quarterly*, 16 (1) (March): 109–20.

Reno, William (1996). 'Ironies of Post-Cold War Structural Adjustment in Sierra Leone'. *Review of African Political Economy*, 67 (March): 7–18.

Reno, William (forthcoming). 'Liberia and Sierra Leone: The Competition for Patronage in Resource-Rich Economies', in E. Wayne Nafziger, Frances Stewart and Raimo Väyrynen (eds.), *Weak States and Vulnerable Economies: Humanitarian*

Emergencies in Developing Countries, Volume 2 of *War, Hunger and Displacement: The Origins of Humanitarian Emergencies.* Oxford: Oxford University Press.

Rummel, Rudolph J. (1994). *Death by Government.* New Brunswick, NJ: Transaction Publishers.

Schlemmer, Lawrence (1994). 'Sustainable Development for South Africa: Proposition and Scenarios for Debate', in Herman Giliomee and Lawrence Schlemmer (eds.), *The Bold Experiment. South Africa's New Democracy.* Halfway House: Southern Books, 99–111.

Schlemmer, Lawrence, and Herman Giliomee (1994). 'Introduction: In the Throes of a Brave and Bold Experiment', in Herman Giliomee and Lawrence Schlemmer (eds.), *The Bold Experiment South Africa's New Democracy.* Halfway House: Southern Books, 1–3.

Seaman, John (1993). 'Famine Mortality in Africa'. *IDS Bulletin,* 24 (4): 27–31.

Sen, Amartya K. (1981). *Poverty and Famines: An Essay on Entitlement and Deprivation.* Oxford: Clarendon Press.

Sen, Amartya K. (1983a). 'Development: Which Way Now?' *Economic Journal,* 93 (December): 757–60.

Sen, Amartya K. (1983b). *On Economic Inequality.* Oxford: Clarendon Press.

Sen, Amartya K. (1986). 'The Causes of Famine: A Reply'. *Food Policy,* 11 (May): 125–32.

Sen, Amartya K. (1987). 'Reply: Famine and Mr. Bowbrick'. *Food Policy,* 12 (February): 10–14.

Sen, Amartya K. (1995). 'Food, Economics, and Entitlements', in Jean Drèze, Amartya Sen, and Athar Hussain (eds.), *The Political Economy of Hunger: Selected Essays.* Oxford: Clarendon Press, 50–68.

Sheahan, John (1980). 'Market-oriented Economic Policies and Political Repression in Latin America'. *Economic Development and Cultural Change,* 28 (January): 267–91.

Singer, Hans (1990). 'The Role of Food Aid', in James Pickett and Hans Singer (eds.), *Towards Economic Recovery in Sub-Saharan Africa: Essays in Honour of Robert Gardiner.* London: Routledge, 178–81.

Singer, J. David, and Melvyn Small. *Correlates of War Database,* 1994 update.

Stewart, Frances (1993). 'War and Underdevelopment: Can Economic Analysis Help Reduce the Cost?' *Journal of International Development,* 5(4) (July-August): 357–80.

Stewart, Frances, Frank P. Humphreys, and Nick Lea (1997). 'Civil Conflict in Developing Countries over the Last Quarter of a Century: An Empirical Overview of Economic and Social Consequences'. *Oxford Development Studies,* 25 (1) (February): 11–41.

SIPRI (Stockholm International Peace Research Institute) (1996). *SIPRI Yearbook, 1996: Armaments, Disarmament and International Security.* Oxford: Oxford University Press.

Taylor, Charles Lewis, and David A. Jodice (1983). *World Handbook of Political and Social Indicators.* 3rd edition. Vol. 2: Political Protest and Government Change. New Haven and London: Yale University Press.

UNDP (United Nations Development Programme) (1994). *Human Development Report 1994.* New York: Oxford University Press.

Uvin, (Peter) (forthcoming). 'Rwanda: The Social Roots of Genocide', in E. Wayne

Nafziger, Frances Stewart and Raimo Väyrynen (eds.), *Weak States and Vulnerable Economies: Humanitarian Emergencies in Developing Countries*, Volume II of *War, Hunger and Displacement: The Origins of Humanitarian Emergencies*. Oxford: Oxford University Press.

Walton, John, and David Seddon (1994). *Free Markets and Food Riots. The Politics of Global Adjustment*. London: Basil Blackwell.

Weinberg, Bill (1995). 'From an antiauthoritarian perspective: interview with insurgent subcommander Marcos of the Zapatista National Liberation Army (EZLN). Love and Rage'. New York News Bureau, Newsgroup Soc.culture.mexican, 3 April.

Widner, Jennifer (1999). 'Comment on "The Political Economy of Ethnicity" ', in Boris Pleskovic and Joseph E. Stiglitz (eds.), *Annual World Bank Conference on Development Economics 1998*. Washington, DC: World Bank, 406–09.

Woodward, Susan L. (1995). *Balkan Tragedy: Chaos and Dissolution after the Cold War*. Washington, DC: Brookings Institution.

World Bank (1982). *World Development Report, 1982*. New York: Oxford University Press.

World Bank (1993). *World Development Report, 1993*. New York: Oxford University Press.

World Bank (1994). *World Development Report, 1994*. New York: Oxford University Press.

World Bank (1996a). *African Development Indicators, 1996*. Washington, DC: World Bank.

World Bank (1996b). *Global Economic Prospects and the Developing Countries, 1996*. Washington, DC: World Bank.

World Bank (1996c). *World Development Report, 1996*. New York: Oxford University Press.

USCR (The United States Committee for Refugees) (1986–96 successive years). *World Refugee Survey*. World Refugee Statistics. Washington, DC: Immigration and Refugee Services of America.

4

The Conflict over Natural and Environmental Resources

JAMES FAIRHEAD

1. Introduction

When linking complex humanitarian emergencies with environmental issues, there is a temptation to pursue the often-supposed links between poverty and environmental decline (the downward spiral) to more violent conclusions. A narrative linking popular readings of Malthus and Hobbes is pre-formed, merely awaiting expansion and exemplification in the conflict arena—as if conflict was merely the end game of poverty, and poverty the consequence of environmental decline. Such reasoning exists in the popular press, exemplified not only in the notorious work of Kaplan (1994) to which, fortunately, many critics have since responded (cf. Richards 1996; de Waal 1996; Keen 1997), but also in the tomes of other modern day catastrophists like Myers (1996), King (1986) and Timberlake and Tinker (1984).

Twose terms this the 'greenwar' factor (1991: 1), a nomenclature that I shall adhere to. He characterizes it thus:

The cycle is repetitive and truly vicious. Environmental impoverishment, increasing conflict over resources, marginalization of rural people, social and political unrest, displacement and uncontrolled migration lead to further conflict and the outbreak of wars within and between states. When hostilities grow into organized warfare, the environment inevitably undergoes further degradation. The insidious pattern comes full cycle, as a peacetime population and government struggle to cope with a land left environmentally bankrupt. The seeds are sown for further tension and conflict (1991: 8).

In this chapter, I want to offer a critique of the way that 'environmental degradation' has become incorporated into the international discourse on conflict. First, I shall outline what I see as *prima facie* reasons for being cautious in examining the causes of conflict in relation to the environment. Then I should like to consider several alternative conceptual frames through which to consider links between environment and conflict, and illustrate these in relation to certain cases. In particular, I shall pursue the

argument that conflicts are less generated by resource poverty and bankruptcy, than by resource value and wealth. This will permit, I would
argue, more refined analysis in several arenas. First it enables better analysis of the environmental components influencing the dynamics of warfare
itself. It enables more than just an examination of the 'causes' of conflict,
helping to resolve impacts of environmental issues throughout a conflict's
story. It thus enables us to consider the conditions in which warfare can
lead on to the displacement, hunger, and disease which characterize 'complex humanitarian emergencies'.[1] Second, a resource wealth approach to
environment will permit us to consider how the relationship between
environmental degradation and conflict is linked to international political
economy. Third, in this, it can help resolve differences in environment-
conflict dynamics between valuable immobile resources (notably land)
and mobile ones (oil, water, diamonds, timber) in this analysis. Fourth,
conflicts might be about control over valuable resources themselves, or
over the labour, capital, technology, trade routes, market access, and other
factors necessary to make them valuable. Fifth, it may not be environmental decline 'on location' that stimulates conflict, but the effective demand
present elsewhere for what that territory has to offer. And that demand
elsewhere may well be generated through environmental depletion or
other causes of supply failures in other historically significant sources. In
short, this framework suggests that *the environmental causes of conflict when
considered at all, need to be traced in a global, rather than local frame.* This is not
the spirit of either the 'greenwar' position, or 'environmental scarcity'
analysis. This is important, as the major destinations for the resources
which, it can be argued, have been fuelling conflicts in Africa tend to be
the industrialized nations.

The chapter therefore attempts to 'put environment in its place'. The
strategy taken is to focus on the many political and economic causes of
complex humanitarian emergencies, and then try to see where environmental phenomena fit in, rather than looking at environmental phenomena and trying to see how they might contribute (or not) to understanding
CHEs. In much of the chapter, I therefore treat environmental components
in a decentred way. This approach will provide an alternative perspective
from which to assess briefly the greenwar concept. I suggest that it
obscures more than it reveals in the analysis of the causes of war. In fact I
shall suggest that even those who promote the idea of greenwar and its
contemporary relevance, do not actually find it useful in their own analysis. Worse, I shall hint that the concept of greenwar—in its ideological cir-
culation or strategic deployment—may itself more fuel conflicts, than
assist in defining policies to address them. Like the idea of desertification,

---

[1] In the definitions of CHEs in this volume, emergencies are complex not in origin, but in
effect on civilian populations.

the concept is both useless yet somehow so necessary as to be so repeatedly coined and elaborated that it must be taken seriously.

Many studies assuming the greenwar position might best be considered popular, rather than academic. Yet popular works are written not only for popular audiences, but also to influence policy. The greenwar message has indeed become influential to strategic policy, and academic research into the popular question of environmental causes of conflict is now attracting large funding. Here, I shall argue that the questions being researched need reframing.

The popular analysis relating conflict to environmental causality has already been reframed once in the more sophisticated research of Homer-Dixon and colleagues (for example, 1991, 1994, 1995). He sets the analysis of conflict within the broader nexus of not only environmental change, but also population growth and unequal social distribution of resources. Together these conditions can comprise what he terms 'environmental scarcity', and it is this which his research suggests:

... can contribute to diffuse, persistent, subnational violence, such as ethnic clashes and insurgencies. In coming decades, the incidence of such violence will probably increase as environmental scarcities worsen in some parts of the developing world. This subnational violence will not be as conspicuous or dramatic as interstate resource wars, but it may have serious repercussions for the security interests of both the developed and developing worlds (Homer-Dixon 1995).

But the concept of environmental scarcity is, I would argue, deeply misleading. It obfuscates environmental degradative components (or lack of them) in conflicts by lumping them together with issues of increased demand and inequality of resource access. Once again issues which have little, if any, link with environmental degradation come to be glossed as 'environmental', depoliticizing them, and in Homer-Dixon's case, isolating them from international political economy.

The aim of this more conceptual chapter is to sketch out what might form another approach through which to examine environmental components (or lack of them) causing conflicts and complex humanitarian emergencies, and to illustrate its analytical power. This chapter does not examine the environmental consequences of conflict. Nor does it examine the political economic, and associated techno-economic reasons for environmental degradation.

2. Some Reasons for Caution in Linking Conflict Directly to Environment

Today, more than ever, we must approach the consideration of environmental components of conflicts with extreme caution. This is for at least three reasons. First, both environmental and conflict issues have become central within development circles, funding agendas and research, but each has gained analytical priority as a result of very particular and (seemingly) unrelated histories. The will to know their relationship may be little more than the accident of historical conjuncture rather than the result of compelling association.

A second reason for caution is common to all 'double issue' reviews and research (gender and environment; poverty and environment; gender and conflict; governance and environment; structural adjustment and environment, etc. etc.). There is, in all such works, a temptation to overstate reductive cases to the exclusion of more relevant/priority issues, and to suggest *a priori* connections for which there may be little or no evidence (Mearns 1991).[2]

Third then, causal ascriptions of conflict (like famine) to environmental factors appear to have an effect of 'depoliticizing' the causes of conflict. Considering conflicts to be 'environmental-population' in origin might obscure the political origins of what are so definitively political events. A literature criticizing causal ascription of famine to neo-malthusian and environmental factors has long shown how such analyses not merely misrepresent the causes and dynamics of famine (Devereaux 1993) but can also, through their effect on policy, contribute to the problem (de Waal 1989; Keen 1994; Macrae and Zwi 1994). Similarly, obfuscation of political causes of conflict within depoliticized environmental and neo-malthusian explanatory frames may impede moves towards resolving conflicts. Worse, for this reason such environmental arguments can usually be wielded intentionally as a political weapon on behalf of one side or another—in a way that will fuel the conflict. Moreover, environmental reductivity not only diverts attention away from actors in the conflict, but also implies that mediators should 'keep their distance' in what might be an essentially irresolvable set of affairs, or act only indirectly on the 'root environmental causes'. So greenwar reasoning might not only depoliticize conflict, but may do so in a way that strongly orientates how outside parties consider their role in conflict resolution—and their role in contributing to conflict.

A fourth reason is more personal. One needs to be cautious in engaging with the conceptual and methodological reflections suggested by any particular author, including myself. Each will be affected by the specificities of the wars with which they have more engaged experience. I am no exception, and my analysis will surely be inflected by the conflicts in Congo and Rwanda, and in the Sierra Leone and Liberia nexus. Given the paucity of data of a reliable sort, and given the immensity and complexity

---

[2] For a protracted discussion of this methodological problem in relation to conflict-environment links, see Homer-Dixon (1995).

of war as political event, the work of comparison is inevitably a rather subjective, interpretative enterprise.

3. Primary Hypothesis

I should like to present several hypotheses around which to reframe consideration of environment-conflict linkages. The first of these is that conflicts are less generated by resource poverty than by resource wealth. It is the very wealth that the environment offers—its potential value—that drives conflict. Conflicts are environmentally caused, from this perspective, less from the push of their impoverishment than from the wealth they do, or can provide. This perspective does not preclude attention to environmental scarcity, but sets its analysis within a rather more political-economic framework.

To take an example of the analytical contrast, consider the different way these positions frame migrancy. Migrants are often blamed in greenwar arguments as the harbinger of violence (ethnic or predatory) where they settle, following their flight from areas of environmental decay. It is such reasoning, for example, which tempts Myers (1996) and others to depict West African migrants (and the political tensions they supposedly engender) as environmental refugees. 'In the Ivory Coast, at least one-fifth of the population are unofficial immigrants from the Sahel following its desertification' (Myers 1996: 80). Yet characterizing such people as environmental refugees overlooks how land in the Ivorian forest zone was available on reasonable tenure arrangements at a reasonable cost, so that migrants could (in times of cocoa and coffee boom) perhaps grow their own tree and food crops profitably, or work as well remunerated labourers on others' plantations. It overlooks how those remaining in the regions which migrants leave, bemoan the loss of labour to the south as a problem for their livelihood, rather than seeing the migrant's departure as the only alternative for livelihood. It overlooks the questionable evidence for 'desertification' (cf. Swift 1996; Hellden 1991). In short, it prevents us considering how migration says less about environmental change than economic change, and (perhaps) land scarcity. Rather than consider migrants (and the conflicts they are associated with) in relation to the environmental impoverishment of their first home, policy analysis should focus on the political economy of impoverishment there (perhaps with scarcity as a factor generating value and generating violence), but more significantly, on the economic conditions where people settle.

Whilst it is tempting for environmental theorists to consider environmental depletion as a cause of conflict, with people driven to struggle for the meagre entrails of a slaughtered earth, it is instructive to begin by observing that areas of major conflicts, and especially those resulting in enduring complex humanitarian emergencies, tend to be in areas of high value 'environmental' (primary) resources (diamonds, gas, timber, oil, metals, nuclear and space age elements), or in areas which impinge on their profitable extraction. Table 4.1 illustrates this in a basic way, reminding us of the natural resource struggles which have oriented the majority of recent African conflicts. Subsequent examples will drive the analysis home. Although each of these wars has domestic elements, it is inconceivable that the cause and course of these wars—their endurance, their arming, and their impacts on civilian populations—could be understood without considering these broader resource issues. Understanding how latent, nascent or low-intensity conflicts develop into complex humanitarian emergencies thus requires consideration of the country's resource base, and most notably its strategic and financial appeal to international governments and corporations, and the leverage that can be applied by the latter over governments and oppositions. One must consider whether or not the resources can be profitably exploited through extraction[3] in times of conflict (FitzGerald personal communication).

Table 4.1. Complex political emergencies and their key resources

Conflict	Gems	Minerals	Carbons
Angola	Diamonds	Uranium	Gas and oil
Nigeria (Biafra 1967–70)			Oil
Ethiopia–Somalia (Ogaden 1977)			Oil-trade routes
Algeria (1954–62)			Oil
Chad (circa 1985)		Uranium	Oil and gas
Sierra Leone (1991–present)	Diamonds	Gold, rutile	Timber
Sudan (1982–present)			Oil
Liberia (1989–present)	Diamonds		Timber
Congo (Shaba 1978)		Cobalt	
Congo	Diamonds	Gold	Gas
		Niobium	Oil
		Rubidium	Timber
		Uranium	
		Copper	
Namibia	Diamonds	Gold	
		Vanadium	
Western Sahara (Kilgore 1981)		Phosphates	

4. Resource Issues in the Dynamics of War

That it may be not what lands have lost, but what they still have that links environments to conflict is shown in the dynamics of warfare itself. In each

---

[3] Or as we shall see, non extraction making extraction of the same minerals elsewhere more profitable.

war, factions frequently fight for the resources which will finance the fight; for the diamond producing areas, for the timber regions, and so on. Arguably it is such resources, not the lack of them, that enables many conflicts to endure, and develop into complex emergencies. Several cases will illustrate this.

4.1. Sierra Leone and Liberia

Several recent African conflicts show how the course of a conflict, and its dynamics have been shaped by resource wealth. In Liberia, Charles Taylor's NPFL (National Patriotic Front of Liberia) fought to gain control over the railway line to the coast, the railway port and diamond rich regions. For some time NPFL was able to export timber onto the international timber markets, and used this to finance the war. Preventing this export, whether by disrupting the rail network or the port, was a strategy pursued by his opponents.

In Sierra Leone as well as Liberia, the capacity of each of the many factions to finance their struggles was largely linked to diamond mining. The RUF (Revolutionary United Front) in Sierra Leone originally captured the diamond region in the east of the country in 1991 and those in the Kono region in 1992, and their fortunes waxed and waned with their success or otherwise in maintaining these resources in the war until the fragile peace settlement in 1996. Many government army units also operated as soldier-rebels, tempted to go freelance when in control of diamond mining zones. The government's eventual counter strategy against the RUF and its own renegade soldiers was to secure the major diamond and rutile regions by hiring the international security (mercenary) firm, Executive Outcomes. Just how Executive Outcomes' operations were financed by linking success to control over future revenue flows from these resources is brilliantly described by Reno (1997: 181).

4.2. Biafra

The Biafra war of 1967 shares similar resource elements. The industrially developed eastern region of Nigeria seceded as 'Biafra' in 1967 following ethnic violence rooted in Nigerian political, religious and colonial history. Yet as Arbatov (1986) argues, whilst these tensions were necessary for the war, they were not sufficient (cf. Nafziger 1983). The war was also fuelled by mineral competition. The eastern region is rich in oil. Nigeria launched an armed counterattack against secessionists in July 1967 'only after Shell (which was extracting oil in the contested region) agreed to pay its royalties to Biafra rather than to Nigeria' (Arbatov 1986: 34). When Arab states imposed an oil embargo on US and Europe during the Arab-Israeli war of June 1967, Nigerian oil suddenly had heightened strategic interest and greater value. The Nigerian state prevented exports from Biafra by imposing a sea blockade. The UK, which had much to profit from Nigerian oil, first withheld support to Biafra, then gave military and other support to Nigeria. France, on the other hand, gave public and military support to Biafra. A French owned oil company had obtained huge oil rights from Biafra, indeed the House of Rothschild Bank had obtained from Biafra exclusive rights for 10 years to all its deposits of niobium, uranium, coal, tin, oil and gold. Those in the US lobbying for Biafra were supported by Mobil Oil and other US companies (Cervenka 1971, in Arbatov 1986: 35).

4.3. Congo (formerly Zaire)

In Congo, the first decades of Laurent Kabila's 'liberation struggle' were financed by gold mining. His rebel movement was able to gain and maintain control of a gold rich region in South Kivu. Mined in an artisanal way, much of the gold was then sold to elements of the corrupt national army which he was allegedly fighting, in exchange for the 'capture' of arms which he needed to continue the fight and to guarantee the supply of mining labour (Schatzberg 1988).

More recently, the astonishing speed with which the AFDL (Alliance des Forces Démocratiques pour la Libération du Congo) headed by Laurent Kabila routed the national army is linked not only to the corrupt inefficiency of the latter and to the unpopularity of the Mobutu regime, but also to the huge mineral wealth that AFDL—if successful—would control. The war was completed swiftly, in contrast with the enduring conflicts of earlier cases, but it nevertheless resulted in a complex humanitarian emergency. I shall dwell on this case at some length to illustrate the broader political economic issues involved in this conflict. The wealth accruing to Kabila was forthcoming not only because the AFDL captured the mineral reserves as it crossed the country from Kivu to Kinshasa but also because multinational mineral firms became confident that the AFDL campaign was likely to be successful on the international stage.

Crucially, the AFDL had the backing of the US (which it has since thanked). The USA provided political, logistical, surveillance and it is rumoured, on the ground military support to the movement, and used its influence in Zaire to limit the capacity of the national army.[4] The coopera-

---

[4] The New Congolese Foreign Minister admits that foreign support was essential to the ADFL and that the support from the United States was especially helpful (Marek 1997 http://www.marekinc.com/ZWNews060797.html). Reports suggest that the CIA were operational in support of Kabila early in the rebellion (Marek, http://www.marekinc.com/ZWIntell05309702.html) According to Thomas Kanza (former Minister of International Cooperation) the rebellion of 1997 was under preparation with US support from 1993 (pers. comm. April 1997). There are many unconfirmed reports of American and British military assistance (lethal and non-lethal) which has effectively assisted the RPA/ADFL forces both

tive link between the US and elements of the AFDL movement dates back
at least to 1993.[5] US foreign policy in Congo has been backing (or 'hitch-
hiking' on) a Uganda/Pan Africanist alignment in southern African politics since the days of the Bush administration in the USA, and of Mulroney
in Canada. As an indication, Paul Kageme, the army commander who
masterminded (i) the Rwandan Patriotic Front invasion of Rwanda (and
now its vice president), (ii) the ADFL campaign in Zaire, and (iii) aspects
of Museveni's campaign taking Uganda (in 1986), and who was minister
of procurement in Uganda, had been studying at the US Army Command
and General Staff College at Fort Leavenworth, Kansas, in 1990. He flew
from this training to spearhead the October uprising in Rwanda when
Rwigema, the first RPF general was killed.

Certain multinational corporations were well poised to know US strategy and its likely impact on the dynamics of the war. Indeed, North
American mineral companies which signed mineral agreements with
Kabila to the tune of US$ 3 billion during the military campaign had
chosen their advisors with care. Barrick Gold corporation which was one
of the first to sign contracts with Kabila counts among its international
advisory board, George Bush (former CIA director and former President
of USA), Brian Mulroney (former Prime Minister of Canada), Richard
Helms (former director of the US CIA) and Karl Otto Pohl (former director of German Bundesbank).[6] The influential consultancy firm, Cohen and
Woods, which lobbied internationally on behalf of AFDL and eventually
for the regime of Laurent Kabila (from April 1999) and which is associated
both with mineral deal making, and with linking AFDL with Angolan
interests (Reno 1997), is run by Hermen Cohen, a former assistant secretary of state for foreign affairs, and James Woods, a former assistant secretary of state of US defence.[7] American Mineral Fields, even more
successful in gaining mineral contracts during Kabila's campaign, was
lending Kabila its executive Lear jet among other things, to assist the
rebels' logistics.

It would be disingenuous to ignore that several firms (AMF, Tenke,
Iscor) had also recently signed large contracts with the Mobutu regime
which Kabila overthrew. As with the US government, they did not risk
backing only one side. Such deals also gave legitimacy for concessions
desired in the looming post-Mobutu era. Yet earlier contracts did not

during the initial campaign to close the refugee camps on the Zaire border, and later, during
Kabila's campaign to take Zaire. There have been reports of special Afro-American units of
the US special Delta Force in operation within the rebel lines, of US military transport (flying
under other corporate guises) assisting the campaign logistics, and indeed of American casualties linked to these activities. The latter were reported in the Belgian press. Certain journalists (pers. comm., names withheld) are convinced that there was continuous surveillance
of satellite based communications emanating from Zaire, and that this was at the disposal of
AFDL forces.

[5] Thomas Kanza, pers. com.   [6] *Africa Confidential.*   [7] *Africa Confidential.*

revive existing mining which had slumped.[8] In April, the AFDL called on all mining companies to enter into negotiations with it, or risk losing control of their concessions. They negotiated protection of staff and equipment, and began to pay tax and royalties to AFDL. At this time, the AFDL also acquired diamonds, already mined, selling one stockpile they seized to de Beers for US\$ 5 million. Mobutu had inside information gleaned from 30 years of experience when he hypocritically, but correctly, noted on 25 April 1997 that, 'It is because of copper, cobalt, gold, and diamonds that they are in the process of arming Kabila. It is not because they like DRC.'

Cynically, one must suppose that it is such commercial-state interests which contributed to one of the most disturbing events of modern times. US aerial reconnaissance photogrammetry confirmed the existence of over 500,000 displaced people in three major concentrations fleeing before AFDL forces, according to UN and Oxfam observers who saw these data on 20 November 1997. Yet when the figures were released in a press conference in Kigali three days later, the US military claimed that they had located only one significant cluster of people, and that these were armed forces, not refugees (Stockton 1997: 2). As Stockton argues, 400,000 people were effectively 'airbrushed from history' (1997: 2) for political reasons linked to US interests.

The involvement of foreign interests in this war might seem somewhat far fetched. Yet those championing the way contemporary conflicts sweeping central Africa are bringing African solutions to African problems, should be cautious not to overlook the commercial and strategic mineral dimensions to the conflicts (cf. Reno 1995, 1997). Certain journalists are heralding the military-political shifts best characterized perhaps as the 'Uganda alignment', or the 'Pan Africanist' Alignment, as a part of a new 'wind of change' sweeping the continent.[9] Yet other journalists such as Sam Kiley in *The Times* (22 April 1997: 18) dub the same process as 'the second scramble for Africa', quoting 'a mining magnate based in Johannesburg' who suggests that 'Cecil Rhodes must be spinning in his grave at the opportunities he is missing'. As *The Economist* puts it, 'Zaire is the biggest prize since the new mining scramble for Africa started some four years ago' (3 May 1997: 62). Whilst spokespeople for the pan-Africanist movement suggest that it is they who are using the US and minerals firms, not vice versa, this is not the view held by all. Subsequent events bear this out. While Kabila soon turned against his older pan-Africanist allies, he could continue to count on the support of the North American minerals firms that helped him to power as a second rebellion

---

[8] Copper production fell from 500,000 tons per year in 1980 to 30,000 tons per year in 1996. Cobalt dropped from 17,000 tons per year to 3,000 tons per year, and the world price shot up from \$6/lb to £25/lb.

[9] Lindsay Hilsum, Channel 4 News, reporting from South Sudanese SPLA (Sudan People's Liberation Front) lines only days after Kabila took power in Kinshasa.

flared up. And how long he can count on this is an open question as we go to press.

In Africa, as elsewhere, when considering conflict in relation to environmental wealth, it is useful to distinguish between (i) immobile materials, notably land which we shall consider later, (ii) valuable mobile materials (gold, diamonds, etc.), and (iii) strategic materials, that is, minerals vitally needed for military, political, or economic reasons. The most significant strategic minerals are those for which supply is highly concentrated in a limited number of states from whom major military-industrial powers must import. Only a few elements can claim this status. As Hveem notes, for example, only three countries account for 100 per cent of known global platinum reserves, two countries share 98 per cent of known chromium reserves (South Africa, Zimbabwe), and three countries control 90 per cent of known manganese reserves. Three countries share 90 per cent of molybdenum production, and three countries (Congo and Zambia) share 80 per cent of cobalt exports (1986: 61–4). According to Hveem, all five major capitalist countries (France, Germany, Japan, UK, USA) are critically[10] dependent on chromium and cobalt. Other critical minerals include the two elements niobium[11] used in super-conducting alloys, and tantalum,[12] used in electric and aerospace applications, which are often found together.

Changing patterns of international resource demand have led to a decrease in mineral self-sufficiency, and increased import dependence on many minerals, making more minerals strategic, and more of these, critically so. This is the trend into the twenty-first century. For example, whilst the US was self-sufficient for most of its industrial raw materials in the 1960s, the National Materials Policy Commission suggests that by the turn of the century, it will depend on imports for more than 80 per cent of materials. This trend preoccupies many military and economic strategists the world over. Demand is rising due to increased industrial and consumer demand, and to the development of new technologies giving minor minerals key roles (for example, cobalt in the expanding superalloys market is important in aero-space; in the battery industry, including new generation vehicle batteries, growing at 40 per cent per year, and in the electrical and chemical industry).

All analysts aware of struggles for strategic minerals single out the southern African region, which 'occupies a prominent position in the strategic thinking of several, if not all, of the major powers' (Hveem 1986). The region supplies Western powers and Japan with several of the most critical minerals including chromium and cobalt:

[10] That is, when supplies come from few suppliers, over long distances, or from a country of different ideology.

[11] Otherwise known as colombium or colombite, atomic no. 41.

[12] Ta., atomic no 73.

which are particularly critical to the vulnerability of the USA, Japan, and Western Europe. Manganese should be classed with these also because of its importance in the ferro-alloy industry, as should platinum and vanadium. Southern Africa is the largest source of supply for these minerals. If to this brief list are added gold and uranium, then the strategic importance of southern Africa becomes even more evident (Hveem 1986: 73).

Such analysis, dating from the last days of the cold war, should be tempered by subsequent events, but how, and how much, the operation of state-commercial strategizing has altered remains debatable, as we shall see. Ex-Zaire monopolizes southern Africa's cobalt reserves, having 1.36 million tons of proven reserves, reputedly circa 60 per cent of global reserves.[13] Its competitors are Cuba (with perhaps 1.04 million tons) and Canada. Add to this Congo's uranium reserves the more recently discovered, and reputedly phenomenally rich deposits of niobium, rubidium and tantalum mined in secret (and not registered in official statistics) in Kivu during the last six years, and one begins to understand the global strategic and commercial interest of this nation (itself as large as Western Europe). Add to this also the huge reserves of non-critical but valuable conventional resources (copper, gold, diamonds, zinc, and timber). Moreover, the copper, cobalt, zinc, niobium reserves are reputedly the best quality in the world.

Strategic minerals tend to be price inelastic: that is, if prices rise, the amount demanded does not fall off. Rather, if supply can be assured, the buyer is often willing to pay a very high price. As Hveem (1986) notes, in strategic terms, embargoes are worse than price increases. Under such conditions, there is huge potential for monopolistic behaviour, and conglomerates controlling strategic elements can make massive profits (in forming cartels and in intra-firm trade, etc.). At several times, neither chromium, cobalt, niobium or tantalum has had a traded world price. Prices tend to be set by producers or negotiated in contractual arrangements. Those who control these minerals can exert huge leverage ('rents') over industries dependent upon their minerals—especially if they form cartels. Control over chromium and cobalt is highly concentrated at the corporate level.[14]

In the 1990s, the reduction in the then Zaire's cobalt output (from 10,000 tons per annum in 1992 to circa 2–3,000) forced the price up from about US$ 6 per pound to US$ 25–$33 per pound. This makes access to Congo's cobalt reserves worth more to corporations which control the rest of the world's supply (principally American Mineral Fields, and Tenke which

---

[13] Robert Block, Staff Reporter, *Wall Street Journal* ('Mining Firms Want a Piece of Zaire's Vast Mineral Wealth'). 1 May 1997. e-mail circular.

[14] In 1986, Anglo-American held the key decision-making position in the global chromium industry, and Belgium's Societe Generale, Anglo American, INCO Canada, Falconbridge Nickel Mines Canada held the key to cobalt (Hveem 1986).

control much of Canada's reserves). Informed analysts predict that if Congo's cobalt production picks up again, the price of cobalt may drop from US$ 25 per pound to US$ 7 per pound (*The Economist* 3 May 1997: 62) massively reducing, for example, the value and extraction profitability of American Mineral Field's Canadian reserves. It is not surprising, therefore, that the principal firms competing for Congo's cobalt reserves are AMF and Tenke which control much of the Canadian reserves, and which could maintain the value of these by limiting Zaire's supply. Cuba, the other major cobalt producer, is presently embargoed internationally.

Entrepreneurs will go to some length to secure reserves. Those already with reserves remain undaunted by backing both sides of conflict (even brokering peace negotiations, as Anglo-American did in South Africa). On the other hand, non-established firms seeking to capture reserves can back one side, perhaps hoping—in the event of victory—of displacing competitors. In Congo, the established major mining corporations were largely Francophone, but following the conflict, Anglophones are taking over. *Africa Confidential* describes 'Considerable brawling among foreign investors' and notes that 'French and Belgians, Japanese and South Africans suspect that the advance of the Alliance's troops will mainly benefit North American mining corporations' (25 April 1997).

During the cold war, many states were willing to assist conglomerates to gain access to mineral concessions for state strategic reasons. Equally, supply governments like Zaire were able to use their resources to exert international leverage, making long-term bilateral barter/counterpurchase agreements guaranteeing mineral supply, in return for equally significant materials, often military items (Hveem 1986). Access to southern African minerals has been orienting UK, USA, French, German, Chinese, Canadian foreign policy interests for many decades. Whilst Mobutu may himself have been corrupt, it was such structures which enabled him to continue his practices over decades. The US appears to have been preoccupied for several years with the plans for the post-Mobutu era (especially given his cancer), and its support to the Pan-Africanist alliance in east and southern Africa out of which Kabila emerged was part of this strategy.

4.4. Angola

Across the border in Angola, the protracted conflicts have had cold war dynamics, which have again carried over into 'modern' times. At the risk of simplification, during the cold war, the Soviet bloc, especially Cuba, supported the MPLA,[15] whilst the Western bloc (including the Republic of South Africa) used to give its support to the opponents, the FNLA (Nacional de Libertação de Angola) and UNITA. Once again, the

---

[15] MPLA is the Movimento Popular de Libertação de Angola.

competition was ideological, but ideological differences had a dialectical interplay with strategic economic concerns, most notably over Angola's own resource reserves (oil, diamonds, and uranium), and those of its neighbours. For example, Cuban-backed MPLA lent support to SWAPO in Namibia, and to the Shaba secessionists in Zaire. When in 1978, for example, opponents of the government of Zaire, backed by Angola and Cuba, attacked mining installations in Shaba province, leading to an interruption of production, Belgium responded, backed by France by deploying a military force in Shaba. Apart from Zaire, Cuba, one should recall, at that time dominated world cobalt reserves. During the cold war, it stood to gain as massively from depriving the USA access to this strategic mineral.

Reno (1997) documents how the end of the cold war has influenced the dynamics of the Angolan conflict. He documents how South African security firms, principally Executive Outcomes (EO), now assist the Angolan government in its fight against UNITA (using mercenaries who had, as South African soldiers, been working alongside UNITA during the cold war). It has helped transfer from UNITA to government forces 'about US$ 1 billion of earnings from gemstone exports', and guarded the Soyo oil installations, under attack from UNITA in 1993 (Reno 1997: 176–8). EO's business partners came to control huge oil concessions. Oil generates circa US$ 0.8 billion annually, and resource sales enabled the Angolan government to purchase the US$ 0.35 billion needed to prosecute the war. EO also helped the Angolan leader stop his own generals going freelance by using diamond revenues to build an independent powerbase (Reno 1997: 179). Yet as Reno documents, the US put pressure on the Angolan government to end its contracts with EO, and a US firm, Military Professional Resources (MPRI), stepped in. MPRI's board of directors includes retired US military officers including Soyster, ex-director of Defence Intelligence Agency, and 'presented its bid to the Angolan government through a private firm run by Herman Cohen' (Reno 1997: 179).

It has been argued that following the end of the cold war, several relationships central to these dynamics have changed. First, it is held that the relationship between governments and people have changed, as rulers can no longer seek unlimited support from foreign patrons (for example, de Waal 1996). Second it is held that the relationship between state and corporations has altered from a cold war position in which governments assisted corporations in endeavours of joint strategic-commercial interest (for example, with oil and other minerals) to a situation in which businesses operate with political connections. Well-connected firms profit from their knowledge of government policy, and their influence over it.

But the relevance of these transformations can be exaggerated. First, the ideological conflicts of the cold war, and superpower policy itself, were fuelled not only by strategic resource requirements but also by well connected commercial interests. Second, the effect of superpower political withdrawal on the national politics of weak states may not be as dramatic as anticipated. In the new climate, as Reno (1997) argues, rulers of weak states are finding ways other than superpower backing to preserve their regimes. As explicit external superpower support dwindles, multinationals, NGOs, and international development agencies step in. Leaders of weak governments who had perhaps relied on superpower state support to maintain external and internal security against 'strongmen inside state boundaries' now turn to more or less clandestine international commercial ties to do the same task. The internationally condoned sale of national assets (generally to foreign interests) raises international funding and also keeps national resources out of reach of internal opposition,[16] and one can even sell resources controlled by rivals. Asset sales suit creditors, satisfying their demands for revenue generation. Often, therefore, weak states can, in the same old way, continue to use state bureaucracy for patronage and co-optation rather than move to serve popular needs in exchange for popular support. These patterns of continued patronage also often suit aid agencies. Better the weak state you know and can work with than the 'failed state', overwhelmed by warfare between local strongmen. Crucially, relations with foreign companies and aid agencies enable weak governments to acquire both foreign exchange liquidity and weapons, despite huge debts and their systemic defaults (Reno 1997).

Links between weak states and international corporate (and development) interests are thus strengthening. But the extent to which these interests are themselves independent of external state support (for example, of USA, South Africa, UK, France, Japan, China, etc.) is highly questionable. Companies and development organizations (multilateral, NGO, and bilateral) are providing good proxies (even covers) through which strategic state interests can be pursued ruthlessly. Certainly, it would appear from the evidence in Congo and Angola that there are strong links between US state and commercial interests. And as Reno (1997) demonstrates, the new South Africa is also assisting its investors in moving north, satisfying the needs both of its internal policy (sending belligerent former internal security forces abroad) and its external policy, encouraging South African-based investment in what are very profitable enterprises. As Reno comments, South Africa, far from showing the way towards stability, as a strong country might support a weaker one, is profiting hugely from enduring warfare in the region. There has been an expansion in the demand for security contracts for its security firms well poised to enter this market, and for the armaments to fight the wars, as well as opportunities to gain linked commercial resource concessions. Indeed, South African firms have a competitive advantage in this market (Reno 1997).

[16] In Sierra Leone, as Reno (1997) notes, this includes oil refinery, customs, fisheries, banks, the lottery . . .

It is certain that the demise of the cold war has been taken as an opportunity for multinationals (with or without dominant state interests) to gain access to prospecting and reserve rights to which they had earlier been denied. This is the 'second scramble for Africa'. As with the first, it is not being conducted independently of the national interests of major world powers.

Modern orthodoxy now holds that the whole concept of strategic resources is defunct, arguing that critical minerals have been stockpiled in the industrialized nations, and that there are no longer any strategic communication lines at stake. Yet, is this true? Mineral dependency is increasing, not decreasing, and mineral strategizing cannot have fallen off the agenda. The cold war may be over, but many rival commercial superblocs are present or forming, and the USA is certainly not the last remaining superpower. None of this can be lost on its strategists. In short, the 'end of the cold war' may be a nice myth behind which powerful nations can get on with furthering their strategic interests in other ways.

5. Secondary Hypothesis

If conflicts are linked to resource wealth rather than to their depletion, then we can forward several further secondary hypotheses. Conflicts might be fought for control over resources themselves, but they could equally well concern struggles over the means to exploit resources such as control over (i) a labour force ('tied labour' and shackles of assorted physical and economic sorts), and (ii) capital, such as access to international capital markets—balanced perhaps by problems in acquiring responsibilities for national debt. Equally, conflicts occur over the means to make resources valuable, such as control over (i) means of communication and trade routes; and (ii) political means to 'access' markets, or (iii) the markets themselves. Thus, it is instructive to examine certain case studies of conflict dynamics in relation to factors of production other than the primary resource, and in relation to market access.

In several of the examples already encountered, conflicts have not merely been over the resource *per se*, but over the means to exploit the resources. In many cases, this translates into control over a labour force. In Liberia and Sierra Leone, warlords are able to profit from the climate of conflict, using the conflict to recruit labour, either by force (by enslavement, creating slaves as 'political outlaws' by forcing them to commit atrocities, or by physically branding captured populations with the distinctive mark of those who commit such atrocities). Equally recruits were enticed to join up, offered 'ways of life' and a future (job/drugs/videos/educational programmes/food security) in an otherwise difficult climate in which to derive a livelihood (cf. Richards 1996).

In economic conditions which favour gaining control of tied labour, the distinction between war and peace fades. As Keen writes, 'war can usefully be seen as a deepening of exploitative processes already existing in "normal" times, a continuation and exaggeration of long-standing conflicts over resources [such as labour . . .] and a means—for certain groups—of maximizing the benefits of economic transactions through the exercise of various kinds of force against groups depicted as 'fair game' in the context of civil (or 'holy') war (Keen 1997: 2).

In the Kivu region of Zaire, conditions emerged in which gaining tied labour was a central strategy for employees during peacetime, and this carried over into rebel recruitment in the early stages of the conflict. During the 1970s and 1980s, powerful coalitions had emerged between state administrators, traditional administrators, the 'freelance' army and police and large landholders which made it possible for large landlords to expropriate land from its poorer claimants. New landholders were able to extort heavy labour dues from those who had been living on the lands. It was this which enabled employers (merchants, plantation owners, and even smallholders) working in increasingly unprofitable circumstances to pass their problems on to their work force. So as wages slumped,[17] and labourers were reluctant to work for real wages less than 6 per cent of 1960 levels, employers found it necessary either to draw on tied labour (forcing those who squatted on their land to work for them for free), or to rely on the labour of the desperate and land destitute. Under such conditions, employers were also able, given conditions of personal insecurity, to recruit labour by 'giving protection' to employees. Realizing this, employers were not encouraged to reduce levels of violence and insecurity, as their protection-racketeering assisted their recruitment of cheap labour. In many cases, landlords were behind the deployment of violence which became endemic. There was a time when men migrated to work in Zaire's mines, or in Uganda, Tanzania, and Kenya. Now the alternatives are only speculative gold digging, paid work as 'rebels', or settling in regions in the forest. Those taking any of these avenues do not escape Kivu's predatory political economy. They become subordinates to the mine owners, the rebel leaders or the land chiefs of the forest tracts. Such conditions make it easy to recruit a rebel army.

Conflict can occur over the capital required for investment in natural resource exploitation; a second factor of production other than the primary resource which might be driving resource wars. In Sierra Leone in the mid-1990s, the RUF rebels (among others) sought to occupy government mining areas, thus threatening the government's ability to repay international debt, and indeed, its ability to be supplied further credit at

---

[17] By 1977, the index of real salaries was only 16 per cent of what it had been in 1960; by 1979 it was only 6 per cent, and since then it has declined further.

the Paris Club debt negotiations. As Reno (1997) argues, it was partially this that prompted the government to engage Executive Outcomes, which secured not only the resources, as described above, but also the government's creditworthiness. It has been argued that, across the border the Liberian conflict has been prolonged by the problems which warlords such as Charles Taylor would have if they were to become the legitimate state leader. In so doing, they would acquire the liabilities of state debt which can cripple the dynamics of financing a war machine which had been flush with money when acting as an autonomous rebel faction. In acquiring state status, rebel movements also succumb not only to the financial, but also the political conditionalities associated with it. In this way, rebels may be hesitant to pursue profitable conflicts to their less profitable termination. Indeed, as Keen puts it in the Sudan context, '"Winning the war" was not the sole, or even the most important, objective of many of those engaging in violence. The primary goal for many was to manipulate violence in ways that achieved economic goals' (Keen 1997: 2).

Wars are also fought over the means to make resources valuable, including control over means of communication and trade routes. At a microlevel, this includes conscription of porterage and headloading as occurred in Sierra Leone as much during the recent civil war as during the colonial wars 100 years earlier. At the macrolevel, transport and communications have contributed to many protracted conflicts in the 'horn' of North East Africa during the cold war. At the junction of Asia and Africa, and commanding the Suez shipping channel, these states control the sea routes linking the oil producing countries to America and Europe through which 70 per cent of oil and other raw materials are imported by Western Europe. During the cold war, superpower rivalry left the USSR assisting the then Somalia with US$ 181 million in military assistance, and US$ 154 million in economic assistance, having designs on the port of Bereba. By 1977, they had delivered US$ 1 billion of arms to Greater Ethiopia. This situation enabled Ethiopia to build up a formidable defence capability against its enemy, Somalia, and in its own internal struggles against separatist forces and domestic foes. As Thiam and Mulira sum up, 'the fact is that the massive military aid granted to Ethiopia and Somalia by both Warsaw Pact and NATO countries encouraged the two neighbouring states to settle their differences on the battlefield' (Thiam and Mulira 1993).

This highlights the international dimensions to African resource conflicts. It is, of course, not merely primary wealth and international/corporate interest that drives conflict. The spoils of war—requisitioning and looting of consumer durables (televisions, cars, etc.), also enables wars to be fought, whether in financing the purchase of armaments, or subsidizing the pay and increasing incentives to soldiers.

Attributing conflicts and CHEs to environmental values can be overstated, at the expense of broader political and ideological agendas shaping conflicts. Yet whilst causality should not be reduced to these economic issues, it would be equally incorrect to ignore them, and the complex dialectical interplay between political economy and ideology. And whilst I have downplayed this dialectic in discussion this far, it is considered more centrally in relation to land issues.

6. Land

Land in contrast with the mobile resource focused on above, is definitively immobile, and is clearly incorporated in different ways to other resources into the regional and world economy and into the international politics of conflict. It need not be so, as such countries, without resources themselves, can still be strategic for all the other reasons discussed above, whether due to control over trade routes, or political activity beyond their borders. US support to the Uganda/Rwanda alliances, and French support to the old regime in Rwanda have, thus, been a important key aspect of their broader regional policy covering Zaire. In the same way, cleavages in the international political economy hitch onto, and exacerbate existing social cleavages in those countries.

Yet even where international concerns are relatively minimal, the argument that the origin of conflict may relate less to the impoverishment of resources than to their value is still instructive to pursue, throwing into focus problems with the greenwar approach. As Väyrynen (Chapter 2) notes, several complex humanitarian emergencies have occurred in countries with few natural or renewable resources, and high, predominantly rural populations (Rwanda, Burundi). In these locations, land itself can be immensely valuable. In Rwanda, average farmland was exchanging hands at more than £2,500/ha in the late 1980s, and there was a thriving commercial land market despite regulation (for example, André and Platteau 1996/7); this, at a time when incomes rarely topped £300 a year. For many smallholders, their land thus represents a massive financial asset, leaving aside how people value the cultural and emotive meanings of land, of particular lands, and of the livelihood security it offers. Land acquisition is unrepeatable for the majority given their present incomes, with only the salaried classes with access to off-farm income and employment related credit schemes in a position to accumulate land (cf. André and Platteau 1996/7, Murton 1997). Land is worth fighting for, and defending.

It is argued in 'greenwar' logic, that land is valued because of scarcity, and scarcity brings over-use, land degradation, and the poverty associated with scarcity encourages nutrient mining. Yet evidence from the central African region suggests that this reasoning is flawed. Despite high and increasing population densities, where land shortage clearly undermines the livelihoods of a predominantly (90 per cent) rural population, land

improvement and improved productivity—not degradation—have sometimes been observed. A relative abundance of labour can lead to more
investment in land's productivity such that livelihood decline need not be
associated with environmental decline (for example, Murton 1997; Tiffen,
Mortimore and Gachuki 1993; Lindblane, Carswell and Tumuhairwe
1997). Certainly the balance between investment and disinvestment in
land productivity will vary with place, time, technology, tenure conditions,[18] national policies, and individual circumstances to name but a few
factors.

That land values can increase not only due to scarcity, but also due to
the productive legacy of past users is recognized in indigenous economic
thought throughout much of Africa (for example, Pavanello 1995;
Fairhead and Leach 1996). It runs counter to the idea driving 'greenwar'
reasoning that more intensive land use leads to land degradation. In short,
one should not confuse scarcity with degradation, which—as we shall see
as the essay progresses—is written into both the 'greenwar' concept, and
Homer-Dixon's concept of 'environmental scarcity'. Environment can
improve even whilst scarcity, poverty, and destitution deepen.

To explore the relationship between land scarcity, land value, and conflict further, it is important to consider not only economic valuation, but
also issues of identity linked to land and its economy, if only to overcome
the rather 'instrumentalist' reasoning in which analysis of political economy such as that presented above is couched. Once again, we can turn to
examples from central Africa.

For many years, analysis of conflict history in terms of ethnic migration
and ethnic conflict has been strongly criticized. Ethnicity, even in the
forms it takes today, is but one of many sources of identity and alliance. As
Newbury (1988), among others, outlines for Rwandese, and as I do for
Zaire (Fairhead 1990)—and as is perhaps the one social universal—people
find their identity and interests represented within a large number of
social milieus; in religious associations, family, friendship networks, col-
legiate or initiation fraternities, and workplace, as well as ethnic and
party-political fora, nationality and so on. A sense of community and identity articulated by these and other social institutions overlap in a confusing array which usually defies and confounds anthropological and
sociological representation, much to the annoyance of analysts who would
like society and social and intellectual allegiances to be more rational,
knowable and predictable. Indeed that these arenas of social life all confer
a sense of identity is perhaps their only point of comparison. And many
would argue that it is their very overlap, and their confusion of identity,
which diffuse potentially divisive tendencies (us and them styles of other-
ing) potentially inhering in each institution.

---

[18] For example, Rossi (1991); Clay and Lewis (1990).

As Berry (1989, 1993) has argued, where economic and political rights are insecure, in the modern world, where the state apparatus is either weak, or very partial towards certain groups, it is important for people to invest more time, money, and energy not only into their productive activity, but also in the various affiliations which uphold their own rights to the resources they control—or would like to. In Kivu, in former Zaire, for example, the church, the state, ethnic associations, family associations and refugee associations can be counted among the institutions which strive to uphold very different (and competing) sorts of land claims on behalf of (protecting) very different people (Fairhead 1990). A weak or partial state, and conditions of economic and political insecurity encouraged the emergence of strong loci of affiliation which competed to provide protection for property and personal security, and to provide a domain for advancement. Such loci came to form conflicting axes of patron-clientage. The potential for overlap of affiliations declined, to be replaced instead by certain mutual exclusivity in the sorts of affiliations one follows—a process which was enhanced by those in influential positions, but in a process which could not be reduced to their actions.

Ironically, in such circumstances, the job of the anthropological analyst becomes much easier, as different political and economic interests become more clearly locked into their respective supportive institutions. Put another way, it becomes easier to map the politics of identity on to the politics of resource access. Social institutions, and the oppositional, bipolar discourses they come to produce acquire the power to define people more completely and exclusively. They come to constitute the ethnic subject, the national subject, god's subject or whatever. Each offers not only an economic position, but also a vision for modernity and of the 'good' and 'bad'.[19]

Unfortunately, under these conditions—which popular and academic writers alike might refer to as social fragmentation—the downfall of institutions with which one is affiliated can result in an absolute loss in resource control. Such forces driving political fragmentation and polarization are perhaps to be expected during periods of warfare, where it is harder to sit on political fences, and where economic security including land holding is clearly dependent upon political allegiance (and victory). Nevertheless (echoing Berry 1989), political observers such as Ake generalize for Africa that this political form is not just a feature of wartime conditions, but characterizes present conditions of political mobilization more generally. He argues that rather than consider the state as an impartial guarantor of rights, it is best characterized—for political economic and historical reasons—as an enormous power resource, 'as beneficial to those

---

[19] Concerning land, each might have much to say about the supposed land degrading activities of others (Biot 1992; Beinart 1996).

who control it as it is dangerous to those who are in no position to control it' and that 'political society is contested terrain where alien social groups go to fight for the appropriation of state power or to limit their exposure to its abuse' (Ake 1997: 5).[20] Ake's arguments are all the more powerful in predominantly rural societies, where access to non-farm employment opportunities (which as argued above often also holds the key to rural prosperity) tends to be via the administration, which controls jobs in ministerial bureaucracies and only quasi-autonomous business. Such states also extract wealth from rural areas (via taxes, price policies, etc.), and derive wealth from controlling aid to rural development. Thus, victors in conflict need not even dispossess land by force, to acquire wealth emanating from land, if they can control the dynamics of land transfer, extract surpluses, and exert control over external assistance.

The pattern of identity genesis linked to insecure political and economic rights, and to the 'all or nothing' state is exemplified in recent Rwandan politics. In Rwanda, after the RPF invasion of 1990, Rwandan faction-driven ethnic discourses once again gained ascendancy, such that ethnicity came to define more completely than ever before people's inner nature. Ethnicity was everywhere present in an individual, with the ethnic character put together as a psychological category—drawing on ethnic myths of capability. One ethnic identity created a completeness: a past—a history—a childhood—a type of life. The idea is consolidated by oppositional discourse (and war) in which it was harder and harder to sit on the fence. True, the forging of such unipolar identity is never complete. During the genocide, many Rwandese had ambiguous ethnic identity perhaps as a result of their own or their parents' marriage, or even their looks. For many, political affiliations (to non-Habyarimana factions) continued to be more significant in defining future aspirations than ethnicity. Some Bahutu did hide and protect some Batutsi. But no one should forget that real political events made life very difficult for the ethnically ambiguous, many dying for one-half of their ambiguity. The same fate befell many of those professing party, rather than ethnic futures. And many of those who protected across ethnic lines and became heroic because of the risks they took, died for their heroism. Some, indeed, at times had to kill to maintain their 'heroic' protection of others.

How this came to occur has become, and should remain the subject of intense analysis, not least in the Arusha trials. Certainly elements of the state regime (more particularly a group of radical Hutu ideologues known as the *Akazu*) who orchestrated the militia and media bear huge responsibility. Yet, however much this group may be found legally criminally responsible, the event of the 'final solution' which they came to advo-

---

[20] One can exaggerate the novelty of this in African polities—it has been the stuff of colonial regimes in which colonial entrepreneurs and agents of indirect rule were able to amass vast personal wealth.

cate—its occurrence, its form and extent—can only be understood within the wider social, political, and economic field in which they participated, and which they manipulated. It is reasonable to argue, I think, that the roots of the conflict lie in tensions over resource control, structured by the resource claims made by (articulated by) poles of social identity. The economic-identity dialectic during the conflict generated a kind of ethnicity not earlier seen in Rwanda (cf. Turton 1996).[21] International policies such as structural adjustment and the conditionalities linked to international financing, coupled with a 'tolerance of prospect of state disintegration after the cold war' (Ake 1997) have contributed to such fractured political activity.

The economy-identity dialectic important to considering the dynamics of warfare in agrarian economies is little different to the interplay of ideology and international political economy surrounding African conflicts; whether these be the old 'socialist-capitalist' ideologies of the cold war, or modern equivalents, incorporating tensions between democratization/ good governance on one hand, and prioritizing stability and the developmental state on the other; between environmental concern and economic development, and between individualistic human rights and social and economic rights.

7. Conflict, Resource Scarcity, and 'Greenwar'

We are now in a better position from which to evaluate the 'Greenwar' concept and associated arguments concerning environmental causes of conflict and complex humanitarian emergencies. First, in evaluating environmental degradation as a possible cause of conflict, it is important to look beyond environmental change in the vicinity of the conflict, to explore how resource degradation elsewhere alters demand for what any territory has to offer. That is, of course, if 'supply failure' can even be traced to absolute depletion, as opposed to economic supply failure—for example, changes in labour costs relating to supply in other producing regions, or indeed to warfare in that area of supply.

Cases abound where supply failure in one region generates increased demand in another. The Allied forces in the Second World War faced quinine and rubber shortages when South East Asian supply failed under Japanese occupation. Production was stepped up in Allied Africa leading

---

[21] Other modern movements such as the Lord's Resistance Army, the West Nile Liberation Front, and the Ruwenzu movement in Uganda, the Mayimayi and Banyilima in Zaire, can be considered from this perspective—despite their support from foreign governments that hitch-hike on their cause. So, indeed can the more ancient movements such as the possession cult of Nyabingi (Biheeko) around which opposition to the pre-colonial Rwandan state, and then the colonial Ugandan state was organized (Berger 1976; Freedman 1984).

to encroachment by industrial plantations on forest reserves. In the Biafra war, supply problems caused by the Arab–Israel war rendered Nigerian oil reserves more valuable and strategic. Resources also gain value through increased global and regional demand and are not merely problems linked to reduced supply or degraded resources. The central issue when relating water scarcity to conflict is generally such extra demand, not aquifer degradation.

This framework, therefore, suggests that *the environmental causes of conflict when considered at all, need to be traced in a global frame.* This has certainly not been the spirit of greenwar and 'environmental scarcity' analysis. The lack of a global frame is symptomatic in the analytical vocabulary which 'environmental scarcity' theorists deploy: a vocabulary of 'groups' and 'societies', arguing, for example, that 'societies that adapt to environmental scarcities can avoid undue suffering and social stress', and that if social and ecological adaptation is unsuccessful, environmental scarcity constrains economic development and contributes to migrations and other stressors of conflict (Homer-Dixon 1995). Equally indicative is the focus on 'intrastate', and 'interstate' dynamics of warfare, but not international political economic concerns which render such terms simplistic.[22]

The major destinations for the resources which, it can be argued, have been fuelling the conflicts in Africa tend to be the industrialized nations. African industrial demand hardly features in the world demand for diamonds, gold, oil, high grade timber, niobium, uranium, copper, rutile, bauxite, cobalt, chromium, and others. The cases have illustrated the importance of international capital in modern conflicts (as has been the case in European and colonial wars in procuring resource contracts during and immediately following conflicts).

Where does this leave the greenwar thesis that, 'In the complex web of causes leading to social and political instability, bloodshed and war, environmental degradation is playing an increasingly important role' (Twose 1991). Curiously, when read carefully, even those popularizing the 'greenwar' concept would agree that few (if any) conflicts can be attributable to environmental degradation. In the book entitled *Greenwar* (Bennett 1991) where one would expect to find evidence of environmental degradation linked to war, the content does not support the general thesis. The edited chapters concentrate on (i) social attachment to and increasing competition for resources, (ii) government partiality in resource allocation, and official neglect of rights of certain elements in society, including dispossession, and economic marginalization, (iii) differential political voice, and

---

[22] Homer-Dixon argues that environmental scarcity often encourages powerful groups to capture valuable environmental resources and prompts marginal groups to ecologically sensitive areas. These two processes—called 'resource capture' and 'ecological marginalization' in turn reinforce environmental scarcity and raise the potential for social instability (Homer-Dixon 1995).

(iv) availability of arms. These are political-economic issues, not those of environment *per se*. Only in Chapter 7 of this work is greenwar faced more directly. As it is summarized in the introduction,

Another kind of social breakdown is suffered by people who have been forced to give up their traditional livelihoods because of drought, eroded land, or conflict. They have to move to shanty towns, to camps for the displaced or to new settlements, where their presence can cause more tension and conflict, as they compete with the local population for work and resources, and put further pressure on the surrounding environment. So the vicious circle continues (1991: 7).

Such displacement, within Homer-Dixon's analysis, would create 'group identity conflicts' (1994: 20). But again the examples given in Bennett do not substantiate the 'greenwar' argument, focusing as they do on the social and economic difficulties faced by displaced women in Sudan and those displaced *by the Ethiopian government's resettlement policy*.

In the preface to that volume, Twose notes the weakness of the greenwar thesis.

The authors do not argue that environmental degradation *is ever the sole cause* of conflict in the Sahel, *or even* always the major cause. They do insist that the environment is an *increasingly* important factor, and that if the implications are not recognized, the *prospects* for the Sahel's future stability are bleak (1991: 4, my emphasis, cf. Myers 1996: 81).

In short, in a book called 'greenwar', the greenwar problem is not yet evidenced.

Homer-Dixon explicitly confuses issues of environmental *degradation* with issues of natural resource *scarcity* when forwarding the concept of environmental scarcity. In his analysis, environmental degradation is only one of three main sources of scarcity of renewable resources. The others, in his analysis, are population growth and unequal social distribution of resources. The concept of 'environmental scarcity' thus encompasses all three sources (1994: 8) and 'allows these three distinct sources of scarcity to be incorporated into one analysis' (1994: 8). But why do this? Why conflate these very distinct issues into one concept? As the examples above demonstrate, examining issues of resource scarcity, degradation, and population in one concept is tantamount to analytical obfuscation. Land scarcity leading to poverty and arguably conflict (André and Platteau 1996/7) can be co-extensive with land improvement and rehabilitation. Water scarcity can be co-extensive with improved water economy and distribution. It is wrong to conflate pressure on natural resources with their 'degradation'. These three components of 'environmental scarcity' are not facets of the same thing.

Indeed, if by 'environmental scarcity' we also mean unequal resource distribution, it becomes absolutely banal to suggest, as Homer-Dixon does, that 'environmental scarcities are already contributing to violent conflict'. Analysts have long been tracing conflicts to issues of the social distribution of resources. One could profitably revert to the more classic concept of resource war, a concept as germane to peace, conflict, and strategic studies as the examples above probably are. What is the 'environmental' issue in this? Why conflate into one concept, the very relationships which are interesting to explore? A conflict with its causes in environmental scarcity need have absolutely nothing to do with the environment. So why call it environmental? It is only by a sleight of hand that these scarcities are so termed, and that conclusions can be forwarded that we should focus our attention on 'environment' when considering conflict prevention, mitigation, and resolution. It takes attention off more pressing issues.

Whilst one can easily accept that environmental scarcity, as he defines it, can be causal of conflict, in no case do Homer-Dixon and colleagues show that resource degradation was a causal component. Take the conflicts in the Senegal river valley. It is argued, with justification, that the conflict relates to powerful classes gaining control over land which had been newly irrigated at public expense. Homer-Dixon's research team renders the conflict environmental by suggesting that the land was itself irrigated by agricultural development programmes to offset reduced productivity from desertified lands elsewhere. This connection is both tenuous and forced. It overlooks all of the political economic and developmental reasons why dams get built, and overplays 'desertification'.

This case exemplifies how, to the extent that greenwar arguments do maintain that degradation provokes conflict, there is a clear tendency to exaggerate the extent of ecological deterioration. There are many structural political and economic reasons why perceptions of environmental degradation have been exaggerated by colonial and post-colonial states (Fairhead and Leach 1995, 1996, 1997; Swift 1996; Hellden 1991). Linking conflict to environment is adding to this tendency. We are now left deducing that, 'if there are conflicts, then there must have been degradation.'

Myers forges this deduction in a classic example of argument by innuendo and association:

Sub-Saharan Africa is racked with political turmoil and violence. There have been more than 200 coups or attempted coups since 1950. We have seen how Ethiopia has endured prolonged war; the same goes for several other countries, notably Sudan, Chad, Angola, and Mozambique. Each of these countries also suffers widespread environmental travails in conjunction with wall to wall poverty. Can it be coincidence? (Myers 1996: 71).

In short, greenwar and 'environmental scarcity' approaches have a tendency to confuse, not clarify the origins of conflict. This is not conducive to creating policies for peace. The crux of the greenwar position is that governments are failing to concentrate on conservation as a means of defusing conflict. It puts conservation on the peace agenda and on an equal footing with allocation issues. Drawing on the greenwar concept, Germany's environment minister, Angela Merkel now argues that 'the greenhouse effect, desertification, and increasing scarcity of water are likely to cause violent conflicts and millions of environmental refugees' (noted in Robins and Pye-Smith 1997).[23] Yet the case has, I would argue, never been made convincingly.

The implication is that environmental mitigation is an issue for national security. 'If environmental stress is a root cause of conflict, this makes issues of sustainability, or environmental protection, and of the distribution of wealth and resources' a central element of peace building (Homer-Dixon, pers. comm. to Robins and Pye-Smith 1997). In the interests of peace, governments should be investing in such things as sustainable forestry and water conservation.

8. Conclusion

This chapter has not attempted a systematic review of work relating to conflict and CHEs to environmental causes. It has attempted to provide an alternative framework by displacing the focus off environment in the analysis of broader CHE causes, and then seeing how environmental issues may or may not fit in, and by focusing less on environmental impoverishment than on environmental value.

Approaches using concepts such as 'environmental scarcity' or 'greenwar' in linking conflict to environment are, it has been argued, deeply flawed. Given their popularity in quasi-academic circles, it is necessary to examine certain effects linked to the deployment of 'greenwar' arguments. This is the meta issue in which the relationship between environment and conflict needs to be discussed, not focusing on the relationship between environment *per se* and conflict, but on environmental discourse and conflict. It could be argued that the way in which concern with the environment has been framed historically and within present political configurations, is not irrelevant for considering present patterns of conflict. Returning to the point made in the introduction, causal ascription of conflict to environmental factors appear to have a depoliticizing effect. Considering conflicts to be 'environmental' in origin can obscure the political and political-economic origins of what we have noted are definitively

---

[23] 'Interstate tension, refugees, revolutions, civil wars, urban riots and rural unrest are clearly connected to environmental bankruptcy; to deforestation, overgrazing, to soil erosion, and landlessness, to drought and hunger and migration to cities, as well as to disputed rivers and underground aquifers. The UN, foreign aid agencies and African governments must tackle the environmental causes of violence if they wish to move towards a peaceful continent' (Timberlake 1985: 198).

political events. We are led to see causes of conflict as internal to nations, and 'groups' which either 'adapt' or do not to emergent environmental conditions. In so doing, we take attention off the brutal reality depicted in Table 4.1.

Deploying environmental arguments, whether fortuitously or strategically, can play to the advantage of certain protagonists in the conflict on the international stage, as it deflects analysis away from international commercial concerns, and indeed national politics, on to those who are environmentally marginalized. Examples will be found where environmental arguments are, thus, wielded as a political weapon on behalf of one side or another.

The importance of environmental issues as a mobilizing force in the discourse of international assistance is further obfuscating the origins of conflict in other ways. As Salih argues, state, commercial and indeed development ventures have often been 'insensitive to peasants and pastoralists property rights and to the fragility of the ecosystems in which they live. People lose their land, its productivity, and its resources without receiving compensation' (Salih 1997). To the extent, however, that such policies contribute to resource depletion, to poverty, and to conflict, it would be erroneous to suggest that it was the resource depletion and the poverty it engendered which led to conflict.

In other cases, many people are so marginalized from the benefits of resource extraction that their only experience of it is of the 'negative externalities' (pollutants) that its extraction and processing generate. In both these circumstances, and especially given the position of environmental agendas in international and national politics, forms of resistance can be articulated in environmental idioms. Resistance in Ogoni, South East Nigeria, and the Chikpo movement in India are cases in point.

So as Salih (1997) argues, it is worth asking whether it is proper to consider these 'environmental movements' as dissent about mitigating the environmental destruction and externalities of resource use, or as movements about rights to resource control and revenue streams. If the latter, despite dissent being articulated in the environmental idiom, these should not be treated as environmental movements:

If environmental conflicts constitute a contestation or a response to the lack of entitlement to income, consumption, and welfare militated by social injustice, inequality, ill distribution of resources, etc., the question then is why a social or political movement whose objective is to regain, maintain or retain a degraded or compromised natural resource, assets and/or values be called an environmental movement engaged in environmental conflicts. If the majority of those who support a movement or liberation movement are poor peasants or pastoralists fighting for the natural resources which they lost to a multinational or private capital, can that movement be called an environmental movement? Why shouldn't it be called simply a peasant movement? (Salih 1997: 4–5).

To make such arguments does not devalue people's concern for the non-material value of environmental welfare, but it avoids obfuscating the importance of this by compounding it with struggles for resources when all resource struggles are deemed environmental struggles.

This chapter has considered conflict in relation to the political-economy of resource wealth. With a focus on wealth, there is a clear need to examine the scarcities which generate it, and a component of scarcity is environmental degradation. But, I have argued, to conflate scarcity and environmental degradation within the encompassing term 'environmental scarcity' or 'greenwar' is at best unhelpful, and is often dangerously obfuscatory, giving the exaggerated impression that conflicts are somehow 'green' in origin. This effect, of course, is the implicit or explicit aim and effect of such analysis. It would support policies and their financing in the emergent development arena of 'conflict and complex emergencies' which integrate with environmental programmes, a position which is attractive to international development agencies when responding to their domestic constituencies.

Ultimately, environmental concerns are, I would argue, a distraction in the analysis of conflict and CHEs. Those seriously engaged in conflict prevention and mitigation should seek to understand *and respond to* the new and transforming international political economic configurations. And it is important to consider how these have been articulating with national political processes and their specific social, political and economic histories, and in doing so are productive of the identities of the people who make war, and the ideologies which make them fight. If international policies concerning conflict prevention and mitigation, and concerning social and economic rejuvenation following cessation of hostilities revert to a concern with 'the environment', and if this engenders a spate of conservation and environmental rehabilitation programmes as it is poised to, it will be an indictment of international development discourse and action.

References

Ake, C. (1997). 'Why Humanitarian Emergencies Occur: Insights from the Interface of State, Democracy and Civil Society'. UNU/WIDER Research for Action 31. Helsinki, Finland: UNU/WIDER.

André, C. and J-P. Platteau (1996/7). 'Land Tenure under Unendurable Stress: Rwanda Caught in the Malthusian Trap'. Série Recherche 164. Namur: Cahiers de la Faculté des Sciences Economiques et Sociales de Namur.

Arbatov, A. (1986). 'Oil as a Factor in Strategic Policy and Action: Past and Present', in A. Westing (ed.), *Global Resources and International Conflict: Environmental factors in Strategic Policy and Action*. Oxford: Oxford University Press, 21–37.

Beinart, W. (1996). 'Soil Erosion, Animals and Pasture over the Longer Term', in M. Leach and R. Mearns (eds.), *The Lie of the Land: Challenging Received Wisdom on the African Environment*. Oxford: James Currey, 54–72.

Bennett, O. (ed.) (1991). *Greenwar: Environment and Conflict*. London: Panos.

Berger, I. (1976). *Religion and Resistance: East African Kingdoms in the Precolonial Period*. Tervuren: Musée Royal de l'Afrique Centrale.

Berry, S. (1989). 'Social Institutions and Access to Resources'. *Africa*, 59 (1): 41–55

Berry, S. (1993). *No Condition is Permanent: the Social Dynamics of Agrarian Change in Sub-Saharan Africa*. Madison: Wisconsin University Press.

Biot, Y. (1992). 'What's the Problem? An Essay on Land Degradation, Science and Development in Sub-Saharan Africa'. UEA/SDS Discussion Paper.

Cervenka, Z. (1971). *Nigerian War 1967–70: History of the War, Selected Bibliography and Documents*. Frankfurt AM: Bernard and Graefe Verlag fur Wehrwesen.

Clay, D. D., and Laurence A. Lewis (1990). 'Land Use, Soil Loss and Sustainable Agriculture in Rwanda'. *Human Ecology*, 18 (2):90.

Devereaux, S. (1993). *Theories of Famine*. Hemel Hempstead: Harvester Wheatsheaf.

de Waal, A. (1989). *Famine that Kills: Darfur, Sudan, 1984–1985*. Oxford: Oxford University Press.

de Waal, A. (1996). 'Contemporary Warfare in Africa: Changing Context, Changing Strategies'. *IDS bulletin*, 27 (3): 6–16.

Fairhead J. (1990). 'Fields of Struggle: Towards a Social History of Farming Knowledge and Practice in a Bwisha Community, Kivu, Zaire'. London: SOAS, University of London. Ph.D. thesis.

Fairhead, J., and M. Leach (1995). 'False Forest History, Complicit Social Analysis: Rethinking Some West African Environmental Narratives'. *World Development*, 23 (6): 1023–36.

Fairhead, J., and M. Leach (1996). 'Misreading the African Landscape: Society and Ecology in a Forest-Savanna Mosaic'. African Studies Series. Cambridge and New York: Cambridge University Press.

Fairhead, J., and M. Leach (1997). 'Deforestation in Question: Dialogue and Dissonance in Ecological, Social and Historical Knowledge of West Africa— Cases from Liberia and Sierra Leone'. *Paideuma*, 43.

Freedman, J. (1984). *Nyabingi: The Social History of an African Divinity*. Butare (Rwanda) INRS.

Hellden, U. (1991). 'Desertification: Time for an Assessment?' *Ambio*, 20 (8): 372–83.

Homer-Dixon, T. (1991). 'On the threshold: Environmental Changes as Causes of Acute Conflict'. *International Security*, 16 (2): 76–116.

Homer-Dixon, T. (1994). 'Environmental Scarcities and Violent Conflict: Evidence from Cases'. *International Security*, 19 (1): 5–40.

Homer-Dixon, T. (1995). 'Strategies for Studying Causation in Complex Ecological Political Systems'. Occasional Paper. Project on Environment, Population and Security. Washington, DC: American Association for the Advancement of Science.

Hveem, H. (1986). 'Minerals as a Factor in Strategic Policy and Action', in A. Westing (ed.), *Global Resources and International Conflict: Environmental Factors in Strategic Policy and Action*. Oxford: Oxford University Press, 55–84.

Kaplan, R. (1994). 'The Coming Anarchy: How Scarcity, Crime, Overpopulation, and Disease are Rapidly Destroying the Social Fabric of Our Planet'. *Atlantic Monthly*, (January): 44–76.

Keen, D. (1994). *The Benefits of Famine. A Political Economy of Famine and Relief in Southwestern Sudan, 1983–1989*. Princeton: Princeton University Press.

Keen, D. (1997). 'Conflict and Rationality in Sudan'. Paper presented at Queen Elizabeth House Workshop on Economies during Conflict. June 1997.

King, P. (1986). *An African Winter*. Penguin: Harmondsworth.

Lindblane, K., G. Carswell, and J. K. Tumuhairwe (1997) (forthcoming). 'The Mediating Effects of Land Use and Land Management on the Relationship between Population Growth and Land Degradation in Southwestern Uganda'. *Ambio*.

Macrae, J., and A. Zwi (eds.) (1994). *War and Hunger: Rethinking International Responses to Complex Emergencies*. London: Zed Press.

Mearns, R. (1991). 'Structural Adjustment and the Environment: Reflections on Scientific Method'. IDS Working Paper 284. Sussex: IDS, University of Sussex.

Murton, J. (1997). 'Coping with More People'. Cambridge: Dept. of Geography, University of Cambridge. Ph.D. thesis.

Myers, N. (1996). *Ultimate Security: The Environmental Basis of Political Stability*. New York: Norton.

Nafziger, W. (1983). *The Economics of Political Instability: The Nigerian-Biafran War*. Boulder, CO: Westview Press.

Newbury, C. (1988). *The Cohesion of Oppression: Clientship and Ethnicity in Rwanda 1860–1960*. New York: Columbia University Press.

Pavanello, M. (1995). 'The Work of the Ancestors and the Profit of The Living: Some Nzema Economic Ideas'. *Africa*, 65: 36–57.

Reno, W. (1995). *Corruption and State Politics in Sierra Leone*. Cambridge: Cambridge University Press.

Reno, W. (1997). 'African Weak States and Commercial Alliances.' *African Affairs*, 96 (383): 165–86.

Richards, P. (1996). *Fighting for the Rainforest: War Youth and Resources in Sierra Leone*. Oxford: James Currey.

Robins, N., and C. Pye-Smith (1997). 'The Ecology of Violence'. *New Scientist*, 8 March: 12–3.

Rossi, G. (1991). 'Croissance de la Population, Mise en Valeur et Equilibre des Versants: Quel avenir pour le Rwanda?' *Cahiers d'Outre Mer*, 44 (173): 29–45.

Salih, M. (1997). 'Politics of Poverty Management and Environment: Displacement by Conservation'. Paper presented at Workshop on Politics of Poverty and Environmental Interventions. Nordic Africa Institute. May (Institute of Social Studies, The Hague, Netherlands).

Schatzberg, M. (1988). *The Dialectics of Oppression in Zaire*. Bloomington: Indiana University Press.

Stockton, N. (1997). 'Rwanda: Rights and Racism'. Paper presented at the conference: Towards Understanding the Crisis in the Great Lakes Region, 1 February, Nissan Centre and Queen Elizabeth House, Oxford.

Swift, J. (1996). 'Desertification: Narratives, Winners and Losers', in M. Leach and R. Mearns (eds.), *The Lie of the Land*. Oxford: James Currey and London: International African Institute.

Thiam, I. D., and J. Mulira (1993). 'Africa and the Socialist Countries', in A. Mazrui (ed.), *General History of Africa*, Volume VIII. Berkeley: UNESCO and Heinemann, 798–828.

Tiffen, M., M. Mortimore, and F. Gachuki (1993). *More People: Less Erosion*. London: Wiley.

Timberlake, L., and J. Tinker (1984). *Environment and Conflict*. Earthscan Briefing Document 40. London: IIED.

Timberlake, L. (1985). 'Conflict, Refugees and the Environment', in L. Timberlake and Tinker (eds.), *Africa in Crisis: The Causes, the Cures of Environmental Bankruptcy*. London: Earthscan, 185–98.

Turton, D. (1996). 'War and Ethnicity: Global Connections and Local Violence in North East Africa and Former Yugoslavia'. *Oxford Development Studies* 25 (1): 77–94.

Twose, N. (1991). 'Introduction: What is Greenwar?', in O. Bennett (ed.), *Greenwar: Environment and Conflict*. London: Panos, 1–8.

Westing, A. (1986). 'Environmental Factors in Strategic Policy and Action: An Overview, in A. Westing (ed.), *Global Resources and International Conflict: Environmental Factors in Strategic Policy and Action*. Oxford: Oxford University Press, 3–20.

5

Water Scarcity as a Source of Crises

ASHOK SWAIN

1. Introduction

Water is critical for human survival, economic development, and the environment. Certainly, few other resources affect so many areas of the economy or of human and environmental health (Feder and Moigne 1994). We require water to grow foodgrains, to get energy, and to run industries. Water can mean the difference between life and death. It can be the cause of cooperation or conflict and it can bring prosperity or poverty. Much of human history is caught up in the struggle for water. Despite its importance, water is rarely seen as a resource in the same manner as many other natural resources. In most parts of the world, its availability is simply taken for granted.

More than 80 per cent of the total global runoff is concentrated in the northern temperate zone which hosts a small portion of the world's population. In the tropical and arid areas, where most of the population lives, the remaining limited flowing water resources are also distributed unevenly. Almost all of the developing countries are in the arid, semi-arid, and tropical regions; many of them are facing severe water shortages. The world's population is now increasing by about 90–100 million people every year. As the World Bank Report (1992) states, 95 per cent of future growth will take place in the developing countries of Africa, Asia and Latin America. This high population growth in the developing countries has multiplied pressure on freshwater. This problem is further intensified in these regions due to their strive towards rapid industrialization, massive urbanization, and agricultural intensification.

Some sobering statistics illustrate that water scarcity has become a crucial issue. The 'water barrier' concept of Malin Falkenmark is frequently used to measure the water adequacy of different countries. This concept uses a simple index of annual per capita freshwater availability for each country. The countries having an index value of more than 1,700 cubic metres are treated as water sufficient. These countries face only occasional water problems of a localized nature. When the index lies between 1,000 and 1,700 cubic metres, the country confronts 'water stress'. In these countries proper water management is required to address widespread shortage problems. When the index falls below 1,000 cubic metres, the country reaches 'water scarcity'. In these countries, water scarcity threatens public health and affects socio-economic development. If the index drops down to 500 cubic metres, the country reaches 'absolute water scarcity'. After crossing this red line, the country is almost certain to face inherent water deficit problems, with often outright shortages and acute scarcity.

According to the water barrier index, eight countries were in the 'water stress' category in 1990, while eight had reached a 'water scarcity' situation, and twelve countries already had water resources below 500 cubic metres per capita (see Table 5.1).

Table 5.1. Countries facing major water barriers

Country	Per capita freshwater availability in 1990 (in cubic metres)
Absolute water scarcity	
Djibouti	23
Kuwait	75
Malta	85
Qatar	117
Bahrain	179
Barbados	195
Singapore	221
Saudi Arabia	306
United Arab Emirates	308
Jordan	327
Yemen	445
Israel	461
Water scarcity	
Tunisia	540
Cape Verde	551
Kenya	636
Burundi	655
Algeria	689
Rwanda	897
Malawi	939
Somalia	980
Water stress	
Libya	1,017
Morocco	1,117
Egypt	1,123
Oman	1,266
Cyprus	1,282
South Africa	1,317
South Korea	1,452
Poland	1,467

Source: Engelman and LeRoy (1993: 48).

The growing population is further shrinking the amount of water available per capita in many countries. The growth in population has reduced the global per capita water availability from 33,300 cubic metres per year in 1850 to 8,500 cubic metres per year in 1993 (Shiklomanov 1993: 18). With the current population growth projection, per capita water supply is projected to decline at a much faster rate than this. It is anticipated that between 44 per cent and 65 per cent of the world's population will experience conditions of water scarcity or water stress by the middle of the twenty-first century (Lonergan 1996).

The 'water barrier' approach provides a simple and comprehensive global view of the water situation. However, it does not address the water availability to a country from transboundary sources. Besides, its emphasis is on population, while the per capita demand for water depends on economic activities, type of agriculture, livestock practices and lifestyle (Raskin, Hansen and Morgolis 1995). The approach also hides the seasonal and local nature of water scarcity. Moreover, the concept fails to capture the different forms of water use among the various regions of the world.

There are many countries that are not captured by the water barrier concept, but have serious water shortages for various reasons: difficult geographical terrain, seasonal precipitation, unequal water distribution within the country, lack of economic and technological infrastructure to tame nature, and so forth. The most illuminating example of a seasonal water scarcity is Cherapunji in north-eastern India. This area holds the world record of annual precipitation (more than 10 metres). After a few months of the heavy monsoon season, a severe water problem occurs in this region (Lundqvist 1992: 41). On a global scale the large variations in precipitation and evapotransportation produce large differences in the actual availability of water.

In this context, it may also be useful to look at the per capita water use rather than only its availability in various countries. As Gleick (1996: 88) points out, the statistics on the per capita water use are 'more representative of actual human well-being'. Moreover, with this approach we can more readily identify the regions which are vulnerable to problems caused by water scarcity. This is because (i) this index helps to locate the regions which are going to undertake intensive water resource development in the future to meet the demand for water, and (ii) reflects the capacity of the society to address various issues arising from water scarcity.

As water is a basic condition for life, a minimum amount of water is required for human survival. While the availability of water in a country is important, but the amount of water being provided for the use of the people is even more important. In Gleick's calculations, 50 litres per person per day (l/p/d) is the basic water requirement standard for human needs: drinking water for survival, water for human hygiene, sanitation services, and modest household needs for preparing food. There are 55 countries where the 1990 per capita water withdrawal for domestic needs falls below 50 litres (see Table 5.2).

Most countries that use less than 50 litres domestic daily water per capita are in Africa. The rest are in the developing regions of Asia and Latin America. While many of these countries are not listed as those with water scarcity, in reality, the people of these lands have too little water to meet basic needs. This has been primarily due to geographical barriers, an underdeveloped economy, and the failure of the state and its institutions.

Table 5.2. Countries failing to meet basic water needs

Country	Total domestic water use (litres per person per day)
Gambia	4.5
Mali	8.0
Somalia	8.9
Mozambique	9.3
Uganda	9.3
Cambodia	9.5
Tanzania	10.1
Central African Republic	13.2
Ethiopia	13.0
Rwanda	13.6
Chad	13.9
Bhutan	14.8
Albania	15.5
Zaïre	16.7
Nepal	17.0
Lesotho	17.0
Sierra Leone	17.1
Bangladesh	17.3
Burundi	18.0
Angola	18.3
Djibouti	18.7
Ghana	19.1
Benin	19.5
Solomon Islands	19.7
Myanmar	19.8
Papua New Guinea	19.9
Cape Verde	20.0
Fiji	20.3
Burkina Faso	22.2
Senegal	25.4
Oman	26.7
Sri Lanka	27.6
Niger	28.4
Nigeria	28.4
Guinea-Bissau	28.5
Vietnam	28.8
Malawi	29.7
Congo	29.9

Country	Total domestic water use (litres per person per day)
Jamaica	30.1
Haiti	30.2
Indonesia	34.2
Guatemala	34.3
Guinea	35.2
Côte d'Ivoire	35.6
Swaziland	36.4
Madagascar	37.2
Liberia	37.3
Afghanistan	39.3
Uruguay	39.6
Cameroon	42.6
Togo	43.5
Paraguay	45.6
Kenya	46.0
El Salvador	46.2
Zimbabwe	48.2

Source: Gleick (1996: 89).

The increasing use of fertilizers and pesticides in order to achieve food security is contaminating the available water supply in many developing countries. Table 5.2 does not indicate the quality of water. Not only do all these countries have less litres per person than Gleick's basic water requirement, but also much of this water is polluted or contaminated in other ways. In addition to water scarcity, water quality poses a serious problem.

Until recently, irrigation contributed little to the pollution of water systems. Due to increased food demand, there is now widespread use of fertilizers and pesticides, which has heavily polluted irrigation return flows. Drainage and run-off from fertilized crops bring high concentrations of nitrogen and phosphorous nutrients and the infusion of nitrates into drinking water leads to various human health hazards. Industrial pollution also is a common phenomenon. Domestic pollution from untreated water sewage contaminates water. In developing countries, most drinking water is contaminated and most sewage is left untreated. According to the report of the Global Environment Monitoring System (GEMS), untreated water is the most commonly encountered health threat in developing countries and causes an estimated 25,000 deaths a day (UNEP 1991: 4).

The increasing scarcity of freshwater and its growing demand can spur conflict among users. This conflict may escalate, culminating in physical force. Violent conflict is not the only consequence of water scarcity. To meet the increasing water demand, authorities generally tend to rely on massive water projects. These large projects bring immediate respite to the

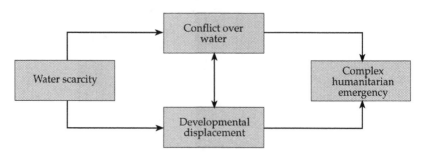

Fig. 5.1. Water scarcity, conflicts, population displacement, and humanitarian emergencies

water scarcity problem of a particular group or region but at the same time displace many people from their homes. Moreover, water projects also generate conflicts in the society over the retention or acquisition of the scarce resource. Displaced people protest against being uprooted. And, in the conflict, the state response is often inadequate and may sometimes be negative.

A complex humanitarian emergency is defined as a man-made crisis in which a large number of people die and suffer from war, disease, hunger, and displacement (Väyrynen, chapter 2). The increasing drop in the quantity and quality of water resources, of course, has the potential to affect food production and human health. But in this chapter, the focus is primarily on violent conflicts and population displacement, which can be the direct outcome of water scarcity. The increasing number of water conflicts having a strong potential for violent escalation, and water projects causing massive population displacement increase the possibility of death and suffering for large numbers of the population and can lead to a complex humanitarian emergency.

2. Water Scarcity and Conflicts

The gap is gradually widening between the real need for water and its actual availability. As the population increases while the total of available water resources remains constant, the maximum per capita demand that a country can support decreases correspondingly. Moreover, increasing demand for water from rapid industrialization, urbanization, and expanding agriculture may lead to a situation where a previously adequate water supply is no longer sufficient. In this scenario, it becomes impossible for all the actors in society to remain content with the present or future prospects of water availability. They therefore undertake purposeful actions to increase their share of the water supply.

In many cases these actions have destroyed the existing arrangements regarding water distribution. The increasing competition has witnessed the emergence of organized actors in conflict over water sharing. Conflicts over water can be observed at all levels of society, occurring not only between nation-states, but also within the nation-state at different levels within society. If these conflicts escalate further, they may turn into violent wars (Beschorner 1992/93; Clarke 1991; Cooley 1984; Gleick 1993; Homer-Dixon 1994; Myers 1989; Starr 1991; Swain 1996c).

International rivers demonstrate this delicate situation very well. More than forty per cent of the world's population is directly dependent on freshwater from rivers. About two-thirds of these people live in developing countries. Approximately 250 of the world's largest rivers are shared by two or more countries. When a number of countries are jointly dependent on the same river systems, upstream withdrawal and pollution can potentially lead to 'upstream/downstream' conflicts. The increasing scarcity of water and the unequal and multilateral distribution of this resource suggest a potential for a greater number of water conflicts.

Not only does the prognostication project a gloomy picture of rising water conflicts in the future, but the present number of these conflicts has also become a matter of serious concern. There are many interstate conflicts active among the users of international river basins in different parts of the world. Some international rivers inducing conflict are the Jordan, Nile, Euphrates-Tigris, Danube and Ganges. With the exception of the Jordan basin (Cooley 1984), most such international water conflicts have not led to physical violence, although the threats of the use of arms in these cases are not uncommon. As early as the mid-1980s, US intelligence services estimated that there were at least ten places in the world where war could break out over the shortage of supply of freshwater and the majority were in the Middle East (Starr 1991).

Conflicts over water can be observed at different levels of society. Water issues can create new conflicting groups within a state, and in other cases, infuse incompatibility among the existing administrative units as well as between ethnic groups. If a particular group is involved in exploiting more than its 'perceived' share of water with the backing of the state, then this may lead to a conflict between the exploited group and the state itself. In some cases, the dispute over sharing or using water resources may begin with the competing groups inside a state, but the state's perceived favour of a particular group makes the state a party to the conflict.

There are several examples of violent intra-state conflicts over the issue of water. One of the clear cases is the Cauvery River water dispute which resulted in a violent riot between Tamils and Kannadigas in the southern part of India in late 1991, resulting in several deaths and massive population displacement (Swain 1998a). South Asia is presently witnessing a number of violent intra-state conflicts over river water sharing. For example, a dispute over the sharing of river water has contributed to the on-going violent separatist movement in the Punjab province of India. The Indus river water also plays a critical role in the Sind separatist movement in Pakistan. Many developing countries suffering a growing water short-age as well as a weak state and strong ethnic divisions will be predisposed to similar conflicts in the near future. As the statistics suggest, countries with a low supply of freshwater provide a more serious potential for civil war than countries with a high supply of freshwater (Hauge and Ellingsen 1998).

It is not only 'violent water conflicts' which can cause human death and suffering and potentially lead to humanitarian crises. To meet the increas-ing demand for water, several large water projects are being undertaken in developing countries. Such projects can cause immediate or potential large-scale population displacement, which in turn many result in con-flicts and violence in society, as well as suffering to the large number of people displaced.

3. Water Scarcity and Population Displacement

Developing countries are increasingly meeting growing water demand by building reservoirs for water storage, using a canal to divert water from one area to another, or extracting groundwater. The requirement of hydro-energy and commercial fishing has also contributed towards human inter-vention in water. A large number of these water development projects create conflicts in the society over water ownership. There is, however, another side to the coin of water resource development projects—envi-ronmental destruction and population displacement.

3.1. Building big dams

The first recorded human-built dam was constructed in Egypt some 5,000 years ago. However, in the twentieth century the construction of dams increased tremendously to meet the growing water demand. In 1997, there were more than 36,000 dams in the world. Dam building, which has already become out of fashion in North America and Western Europe, is still considered the panacea for water shortage prob-lems in many developing countries. Moreover, these dams and reser-voirs are becoming larger. In 1992, 60 per cent of the dams being constructed were more than 30 metres high, compared with only 21 per cent of existing dams in 1986. The construction of dams higher than 100 metres increased by nearly 27 per cent between 1991 and 1993. This new tendency is due to the increasing scarcity of water and reduced avail-ability of suitable dam sites.

In the 1930s, the Hoover Dam in USA was by far the tallest in the world with a height of 221 metres. By the early 1980s, this height was exceeded by at least 18 other dams. Today, worldwide, there are more than 100 'superdams' with a height of more than 150 metres. Lake Mead, behind the Hoover Dam was the largest in the world in 1936, with 38 billion cubic metres of water. By the 1970s, it was dwarfed by a series of dams in developing countries: the Kariba Dam in Southern Africa with 160 billion cubic metres, Aswan's Lake Nasser with 157 billion cubic metres and Ghana's Akosombo with 148 billion cubic metres. The reservoirs created by these 'superdams' together cover almost 600,000 square kilometres, roughly the size of the North Sea.

However, these huge dams and their reservoirs have brought a series of environmental consequences to their sites. Besides triggering earthquakes, they build up soil salinity, change groundwater levels and create water logging. The problem does not end there. Dams extract a high human toll as well. The dam projects submerge vast areas of land and forest and displace their inhabitants. There are millions of people who have lost their homes and livelihoods due to these projects (Swain 1996d). By blocking the migration path, these dams also reduce the fish population and that results in the loss of the source of the livelihood for many people.

The construction of big dams has led to large-scale population displacement. In many cases, there has been massive popular opposition against such dislocation. In India alone, one author adopting conservative assumptions, estimates that the number of dam-related displaced people from 1951 to 1990 is 14 million (Fernandes 1993). Several movements have arisen in India recently to protest against these displacements. The dam-displaced people are gradually becoming organized and have taken their struggle to the streets (Swain 1997a). But dam building and its consequent population displacement are still going on in a big way in India.

Currently the largest dam in the world is the Itaipu Dam on the Paraná River, which forms the border between Paraguay and Brazil (Pearce 1992). However, China's Three Gorges Dam project (Sanxia), under construction, is going to a break a few records. If all goes as planned, the dam and associated constructions will be the biggest public-works project in China since the Great Wall. It aims to be completed in 2009 and the 185 metres high dam on the Yangtze River, just downstream from the scenic Three Gorges, will create 632 square kilometres of reservoir (*Far Eastern Economic Review*, 20 October 1994). After thirty years of deliberation, this project was finally approved by the National People's Congress (NPC) in April 1992. The huge project aims to increase the discharge flow of the river in the dry seasons to meet the need for water. However, approximately 30,000 hectares of farmland will be inundated. Moreover, the dam will adversely affect the aquatic life of the river. But, most importantly, this project will directly displace more than a million people (Heggelund 1993). For the displaced population, the problem of uprootment is further exacerbated by inadequate compensation and poor rehabilitation measures (*South China Morning Post* (Hong Kong) 3 May 1997). The authoritarian regime in China is using force to evict the people and clear the project area.

President Suharto guided Indonesia to be the top dam-building nation in Southeast Asia (Aditjondro and Kowalewski 1994). The repressive regime has carried out many water development projects in the water scarce islands without being responsive to the plight of the displaced population. The construction of the dams has evoked a number of protests in Indonesia in recent years, without achieving much success (Aditjondro and Kowalewski 1994). Even the country's Supreme Court has sided with the government in denying basic rights to the displaced people. The Kedung Ombo Dam has displaced more than 5,000 families, but the authority has failed to rehabilitate them (McCully 1994: 85).

The 4,200 kilometre long Mekong River is the life-line of the main part of Southeast Asia. It originates from the Himalayas and runs through southern China, Burma, Laos, Thailand, Cambodia to the delta in Vietnam. Due to the increasing demand for water and energy, a series of 30 dams has been proposed on the mainstream with another 200 sites identified on tributaries. In 1991, the Lao government announced its plan to build at least 23 dam projects by the year 2020, costing about US$ 7 billion. Swedish and Norwegian firms are involved in building a dam on the Theun River, a tributary of the Mekong (Usher 1996). This Nordic-led Theun Hinboun Dam was constructed despite the lack of a complete impact assessment. The dam has displaced a large number of people and many fishermen have lost their traditional source of livelihood. The next dam in line is the Nam Theun 2, which an Australian-led consortium is expected to build (*The Nation* [Bangkok], 27 December 1996). Due to popular opposition to dam building, these firms have lost their market in their home countries, and are presently moving their operation to developing countries in a big way. The Nam Theun 2 Dam will alter the course of two major tributaries of the Mekong River, flooding an area the size of Singapore, disrupting a rich ecosystem, and uprooting about 4,500 village people (*Wall Street Journal*, 12 August 1997).

The Mekong fish, on which a large number of people are directly dependent for their livelihood, have complex migratory patterns both for spawning and feeding, which are threatened by the dams in the Mekong. The recently built Pak Mool Dam in Thailand, on the Mekong's largest tributary, the Mool River, has resulted in a massive decline in the wild fish catch. A fishing community of over 3000 households has lost its livelihood and is still fighting for compensation from the government (Tangwisutijit 1996). Another major dam project, recently undertaken in the region, is the Bakun Dam in Malaysia. The contract to build this dam has been given to ASEA Brown Boveri AB (ABB), whose home countries are Sweden and

Switzerland. Both these countries have long abandoned the policy of building large dams in their own territories. Once the Bakun Dam is completed, it will displace more than 9000 indigenous people and submerge 69,000 hectares of rain forest.

A number of big dam projects were undertaken in India after independence in 1947 to meet the increasing demand for water for irrigation. They included Bhakra Nangal project on the Sutlej River in the north, Damodar River Valley project and Hirakud Dam on the Mahanadi in the east and the Nagarjunasagar project on the Krishna in the south. Even today, these projects continue to be among the largest and highest in the world (Shah 1993).

These large river valley projects submerged vast areas of forest and agricultural land. Besides a litany of environmental problems, their construction resulted in massive population displacement. The displaced population frequently included a sizeable number of tribal people who belong to lower strata of the society politically and economically (Swain 1997a). India is presently building a series of large dams on the Narmada River to supply water to its western part, which is facing severe water scarcity. The Sardar Sarovar Dam project (SSP) is the terminal dam of this huge project. The SSP will be the second largest concrete gravity dam in the world and will form a reservoir that will submerge a total of 34,996 hectares in three Indian states, Madhya Pradesh, Maharashtra, and Gujarat, including 248 villages with a population of 66,593 (Wood 1993). The state is using brutal force to suppress the resistance of these displaced populations (Kumar 1996). There are claims that if the total Narmada Project gets completed, it may displace over two million people (Kothari and Parajuli 1993).

The other on-going dam project in India which is going to displace a large number of people is the Tehri Dam. Once the construction of this project is complete, it will submerge one township and 32 villages in the Himalayan region. The potential oustees of these two dams are now in a struggle with the state to protect their homes and sources of living but without much success. Authorities are determined to carry out this project in order to provide water to the highly populated state of Uttar Pradesh and rapidly expanding national capital region of New Delhi, which are facing chronic water shortages.

Water scarcity also led to the construction of the Kaptai Dam in Bangladesh and the Mahavali project in Sri Lanka. Both these projects displaced a large number of people. As those displaced belong to ethnic minorities in the respective countries, the dam constructions have also fuelled on-going ethnic conflicts (Swain 1996c).

Due to increasing water scarcity, there are very few rivers left in the world which run freely towards the sea. While the slow flowing Amazon has been saved from dam construction until now, the Brazilian government in its 'Plan 2010' envisages 80 dams on its tributaries in order to meet future demand for water. The other important river basin of the South America, the Rio de la Plata, is threatened with a series of dam constructions, the construction of which will displace many people.

The Akosombo Dam on the Volta River in Ghana submerged an area of about 9,000 square kilometres and displaced 78,000 people. Likewise, the Kariba Dam on the Zambezi River displaced 57,000 tribal people in Zambia and Rhodesia (presently Zimbabwe). The Egyptian pride, Aswan High Dam on the Nile River, led to the evacuation of 100,000 people. These large dams were built in Africa in its post-colonial period for energy production and in order to increase food production to meet the growing demand.

Water scarcity in Euphrates–Tigris River basin has led to the construction of a series of dams on this river. The construction of the Keban Dam in 1970s displaced 30,000 people in Turkey. Now, Turkey is building a number of large dams on the Euphrates River. This Southeast Anatolia project, known by the Turkish acronym of GAP, includes 22 dams. Its construction began in 1983 and is expected to be completed by the end of this century. The centrepiece of GAP is the Attaturk Dam, whose construction was finished in 1989 and it is the fifth largest rockfill dam in the world. Turkey is now building other dams of this huge project. Nearly 336 villages and 200,000 people are, or will be, directly affected by the GAP project. Between 1923 and 1950, Turkey constructed three dams, in 1950s six more, but now it houses 140 dams. After China, Turkey comes in the list of the countries in building large number of big dams (over 10 metres) in the 1990s. These dams in Turkey, besides creating conflicts with downstream Syria and Iraq, have also displaced a large number of people from the submerged areas.

In the twentieth century, significant advances in the design and construction of dams were achieved. Factors of safety have been refined, human errors reduced, and design criteria have found international consensus (Veltrop 1993). But, the three most detrimental effects of the big dams are still haunting policy-makers and engineers: (i) displacement and resettlement of the population, (ii) salinization and waterlogging, and (iii) health issues resulting from water-related diseases. The range of such social and environmental effects are gradually becoming apparent.

The dams are being built to store water to provide irrigation and electricity for people in distant locations and to supply water to the cities, but at the same time these dams displace substantial populations and threaten their livelihoods. It is difficult to get a global figure of the dam-displaced people, but certainly the number is not small. Millions of people have lost their homes and livelihood due to the construction of the dams.

Usually those displaced are rural and illiterate people. In India, the tribal population living in the forest constitutes 60 per cent of the total dam-displaced population (Fernandes 1993). In many developing countries, dam projects are heralded by post-colonial nationalist leaders as a harbinger of future development. To promote the national interest, rural poor are asked to sacrifice their interests. However, it is usually the poor who made the sacrifice that lose from these projects, which primarily benefit the educated élites.

Displacement from home and resettlement to a new place, which are always difficult, are usually disastrous in developing regions. Very few people get government support for rehabilitation. Most of those displaced are left to find their own means of survival. Even for the few 'lucky' ones, inadequate planning, insufficient budget, incomplete execution of the plan and little appreciation of their problems prevent proper resettlement (Biswas 1978). Corruption of the bureaucracy further adds to the problem. The promised compensation, land, which becomes more scarce over time, is usually not available for authorities to provide to the displaced. When land is available, it is usually less than the amount lost, and often inferior and unproductive. Generally landless agricultural labourers and tribal people in the forest do not get land as they lack any record of land holding. Moreover, corruption and exploitation prevents most from receiving their full cash compensation.

The trauma of displacement begins well before the process actually takes place. As soon as a dam project is officially discussed, the area becomes 'untouchable' to the government as well as to private investors. Banks withdraw their operations, and schools, government offices and hospitals move elsewhere. Moreover, authorities do not provide proper and sufficient information for the people affected. The oustees are involved in the rehabilitation process in only a very few cases. Usually they remain in the dark about the project and their future. The displaced person has to go through an entire process of resocialization and adjustment in an alien environment. In many cases, the people from small villages or the forest are forced to live in big resettlement colonies. The breakdown of social community and family networks due to displacement bring further miseries. After being displaced, some migrate to the cities in search of work but due to a lack of skills, they end up working at the lowest-paid manual jobs. For most, displacement coupled with landlessness creates joblessness and food insecurity and increases morbidity (Thukral 1992). All these bring suffering and create serious survival problems for large numbers of people displaced by the construction of dams.

3.2. Diverting rivers

To meet increasing water demand, many diversion canals are being constructed to transport water to cities, to farmlands, and from one region to another. By altering the natural water courses, these diversion projects create conflict between water receivers and water contributors. Water diversion schemes also require dam and canal building, which directly contributes to population displacement. Moreover, the areas whose water is diverted by the projects suffer various adverse environmental effects. Water diversion may result in the gradual loss of livelihood of many people living in the affected areas and force them to migrate to other areas in the search for survival.

There are several forms of water diversion schemes being implemented throughout the world. Many long-distance water transfer projects remain in the planning stage for some time. High infrastructure and maintenance costs are the major deterrents for their execution. Such endeavours become more problematic when the diversion routes have to pass through several political units. Thus water diversion projects are usually carried out within a single freshwater basin. By using dams and canals, the core area gets preference over the others and receives the major supply of water. This mostly takes place when a river is shared by more than one country. The region whose water gets diverted faces many environmental as well as human problems. There are several cases of this type of 'water apartheid'. In this section, we will discuss a few of these water diversion schemes at length.

3.2.1. The Ganges River   The Ganges River flows through India and Bangladesh. The flow of this river is subject to great seasonal fluctuations. While the monsoon flow is more than enough to meet the needs of this highly populous belt in its two riparian countries, the river runoff in the dry seasons is quite inadequate. Since 1975, India has diverted a large portion of the dry season flow of this river to one of her internal rivers, Bhagirathi-Hooghly, before it reaches Bangladesh, to meet India's own water requirements. This has been the major source of tension between these two neighbours for more than two decades. In spite of the official agreement of December 1996 between India and Bangladesh to share the Ganges water, water-sharing remains at the top of the bilateral agenda due to increasing scarcity of the water in the region.

About 40 million people in nearly one-third of the total area of Bangladesh are directly dependent on the Ganges basin for their livelihood. The Indian water diversion at Farakka was bound to have an impact as it was an attempt to introduce a new ecological system against the course of nature. This diversion has affected agricultural and industrial production, disrupted the domestic water supply, fishing and navigation, and changed the hydraulic character of the rivers and the ecology of the delta in the downstream areas of Bangladesh. It has reportedly brought much misery and hardships to the people of the affected south-western part of Bangladesh.

The loss in the agricultural sector has seriously affected a large number of agricultural labourers and small landowners, resulting in the loss of their source of livelihood. Fishermen have been similarly affected. Most of the fishing villages in the Kushtia district of Bangladesh have virtually disappeared in recent years. Besides the agriculture and fishing sectors, the drop in the production of forest products and the closure of industries and navigation routes have also led to a loss of source of living. Moreover, the increasing number of high floods and the river bank erosion, to which the Farakka diversion has made a significant contribution, have resulted in displacing a large number of the Bangladesh population.

These people who belong to the lowest social stratum of the Farakka-affected region have been forced to move away from their homes as a result of the loss of their livelihood. Given the limited opportunities in other parts of their own country, many were forced to cross the porous border and migrate into India. According to the findings of this author's research, from the late 1970s, nearly two million Bangladeshis have been forced by Farakka-induced environmental problems to leave their homes and migrate to different parts of India in search of sustenance. The migration of these Muslim Bangladeshis to Hindu-majority India has elicited violent opposition from the host population, multiplying the suffering of these large numbers of uprooted people (Swain 1996a; 1996b).

3.2.2. The Aral Sea Since 1960, Central Asia has witnessed a dramatic increase in the demand for water resources. Water withdrawals for irrigation have become enormous. The extreme specialization of cotton monoculture and its irrigation practices led to an almost total diversion of the Amu Dar'ya and Syr Dar'ya Rivers, whose run-offs originally reached the Aral Sea. In 1988, water withdrawals in the Aral Sea basin for all purposes were 125 per cent of the average annual water resources—so substantial because the return flows were used repetitively downstream (Klötzli 1994).

In Soviet times, waters of feeder rivers were allocated according to the 'irrigation-optimal' scenario. In summer, when the demand for irrigation for the cotton fields was at a peak in Uzbekistan, the flow from the reservoirs of rivers in Kyrgyzstan was substantially increased. In winter, the reservoirs were almost empty and to cover the peak energy demand of Kyrgyzstan, the Soviet authority compensated by supplying thermal energy from outside. After the Soviet disintegration, Kyrgyzstan's efforts to conserve the water for the winter to achieve 'electricity optimality' led to a serious dispute with Uzbekistan. As a result of economic inducements, Kyrgyzstan finally agreed in 1995 to follow the old formula. In April 1996, Kazakhstan also expressed its desire to be a party to this type of agreement to receive water for its own irrigation (Klötzli 1996). According to this barter arrangement of 1995 and 1996, Kyrgyzstan supplies both Uzbekistan and Kazakhstan with water during the summer months in return for gas and coal, respectively, during the winter months.

Whether it is for energy production or irrigation of cotton fields, the water from the Amu Dar'ya and Syr Dar'ya no longer reaches the Aral Sea. In the 1960s, the Aral was the fourth largest freshwater lake in the world. As a result, the Aral Sea surface has fallen by 40 per cent and volume by 60 per cent, while the salinity level has tripled since 1960. To meet the Aral Sea crisis, the authorities of the former Soviet Union considered diverting some the Siberian rivers to augment the flow in the central Asian region. Objections from environmental groups forced President Gorbachev to shelve the proposal in 1986. Now, the decimation of the Aral Sea in Central Asia has brought a major ecological catastrophe in that region.

The human tragedy associated with these developments is also now emerging (Hinrichsen 1995). Poor drinking water quality and airborne toxic salts have posed major health hazards to the people living in the lower reaches of the feeder rivers or near the Aral Sea. Contaminated drinking water has led to diseases like hepatitis, typhoid, throat cancer, liver ailments, kidney failure, and birth defects. The poor water quality has also contributed to the high infant mortality rates in the region. Severe dust storms carrying toxic salts now affect health through diseases of the respiratory tract. Due to the high salinity in its water, 20 of the Aral Sea's 24 fish species have disappeared. The fish catch, which had provided 60,000 jobs, was depleted so much that fishermen have been forced to move to other areas. Many have migrated to other areas in search of survival (Klötzli 1994). The population in Muynak alone has dropped from 40,000 several decades ago to just 12,000 in 1996 (Postel 1996). People have been forced to migrate on a large scale from the Aral Sea coast to other areas to survive.

3.2.3. The Jonglei Project   The Sudd wetlands on the White Nile River in southern Sudan is one of the largest swamps in the world. Egypt wanted to divert water from the wetland to the Nile through a canal system, the Jonglei Project, to augment the supply to Lake Nasser in order to meet its growing problem of water scarcity. By helping President Numayri to remain in power in Sudan, Egypt received a concession from Sudan to carry out the Jonglei Canal project in 1976 (Swain 1997c). The construction of the canal began in 1978 as a joint Sudanese-Egyptian project in collaboration with the French CCI company.

It was widely believed in the south of Sudan that the Jonglei Project was being carried out to bring benefits to the people of the northern Sudan and Egypt at the cost of the south. A series of attacks on the site by the Sudanese People's Liberation Army led to the suspension of canal construction in 1984, with only 250 kilometres of the proposed 360 kilometres complete (Suliman 1992). This project, if completed, will have a damaging impact on the 40,000 pastorialists living in the Sudd swamplands. In the meantime, the incomplete Jonglei Canal has now become a dangerous ditch for humans and wildlife.

Water diversion also frequently occurs within individual countries. Hundreds of urban centres in arid regions of Africa, Asia and Latin America have grown beyond the point where adequate water supplies can be drawn from local sources. Poor management and distribution systems also contributes to the problems of water scarcity in these urban centres. So water is being diverted from distant rivers and lakes to feed these cities (Satterthwaite 1993).

Some of the deepest divisions are between rural and urban areas, with both having different priorities of water use. For political and economic reasons, urban and industrial water demands usually take precedence over rural and agricultural needs. These forms of water transfer lead to water scarcity in the rural areas and economic hardship for the rural population. The diversion of water towards cities and industrial centres endangers fish habitats, creates loss of wetlands, erodes river banks and, moreover, pollutes the water source. Most importantly, it adversely affects agricultural production, which provides the source of survival for a large population.

The rising demand for urban and industrial water supplies poses a serious threat to irrigated agriculture. In 1990, irrigation represented 68.9 per cent of the total water demand, while industry and municipal water demand accounted for 27.5 per cent. It was projected that by 2000 the share of industry and municipal water would increase to 32.2 per cent compared to irrigation's share of 62.6 per cent (Wallensteen and Swain 1997). This indicates the growing competition between various water demands, particularly in arid and semi-arid regions. In general, the developing regions need more water for irrigation for fibre and cash crops to meet the objectives of self-sufficiency, employment creation, poverty alleviation and development.

The diversion of water from agriculture to other sectors is likely to undermine the livelihoods of a large number of people.

Water-diversion projects lead to conflicts between the receiver and the contributor, arising from disagreement over the distribution of the benefits of the water resource. Such conflicts may escalate into a violent form, where other predisposing factors are present. When diversion projects displace populations, they are rarely covered by compensation or rehabilitation schemes.

3.3. Draining the aquifers

Throughout history, groundwater has been an important source of water for human consumption and agricultural production. However, recently, groundwater withdrawal in the arid and semi-arid areas to meet the increasing scarcity situation has become unsustainable. The extraction of water from the ground has two effects: a reduction in the water-table, and, in the coastal areas, the intrusion of salt water to replace freshwater. Besides drying up freshwater sources, these effects lead to ground subsidence and soil salinization (Goudie 1990: 179). Various human activities like unsound waste disposal, inadequate sewage treatment and inefficient irrigation practices could also impair the quality of groundwater for future use (Biswas 1992). However, the major threat to groundwater is its massive mining to reduce the shortage of water.

The most important complication ensuing from the use of groundwater is that it renews much more slowly than other water sources. On average, while moisture in the atmosphere renews every eight days, stream water in 16 days, soil moisture in one year, swamp water every five years and lake water every 17 years, groundwater is renewed only once every 1,400 years (Korzoun and Sokolov 1978). Groundwater has to be used in an environmentally sustainable manner, meaning that the rate of withdrawal should be equal or less than the rate of recharge. But when the extraction rates from underground basins exceed renewal rates, the result is a falling watertable and surface level. The falling of the water-tables of coastal aquifers increases the likelihood of the infiltration of saline water, making water unsuitable for human use. Away from the coastal areas, overconsumption of the aquifers leads either to their drying up completely, or the water-table being lowered so much that it greatly increases the cost of pumping.

In many parts of the world, underground water pumping is now being carried out on a massive scale to stem the increasing water scarcity. This water withdrawal in an unsustainable manner makes it certain that freshwater from the aquifers will be finished in the near future. The termination of this water supply will affect agriculture and even pose a threat to human survival. Thus, the unsustainable mining of groundwater sets the stage for large-scale population displacement and humanitarian crises in parts of the world.

Israel's annual renewable freshwater supply is about 1,950 million cubic metres (mcm), while the current demand (including Palestinian territories) is about 2,150 mcm. Thanks to its rapid population growth and intensified agriculture, the country's water demand is projected to exceed 2,600 mcm by 2020 (Homer-Dixon and Percival 1996). This water scarcity has compelled the country to overpump the aquifers. Because Israel's coastal aquifer has deteriorated, the mountain aquifer now constitutes the country's primary source of drinking water. During the 1970s and 1980s, the coastal aquifer was overused to such an extent that the water-table fell to less than one metre above sea level, and in some areas it fell below sea level. This led to salt water intruding into the empty aquifers.

However, the mountain aquifer of the West Bank consists of three main aquifer groups, but only one is located in Israel proper, beneath the coastal plain. The remaining two originate in occupied areas, and are the source of 40 per cent of the country's groundwater supply (Lowi 1993). The western and north-eastern section of the mountain aquifers reached their limits by the mid-1970s. In this region, the water-table fell 16 metres from 1969 to 1995 (Libiszewski 1995). Overpumping has also worsened the water quality of these aquifers. The Palestinians accuse Israel of severely overpumping from large sections of these aquifers. The Israeli authority, while restricting the drilling of the wells for Arabs, had allowed Jewish settlers to exploit the groundwater, which has been a major irritant between the two communities.

The drying of the mountain aquifer poses a serious threat to agriculture and the economic prospects of the Palestinians (Swain 1998b). The problem is not limited to the West Bank; the Gaza area is also severely affected. Gaza's limited underground water has been long overexploited, particularly since the early 1970s. The aquifer system underlying the Gaza Strip is an extension of Israel's coastal aquifer. This shallow sandy sandstone aquifer is fed primarily by direct local rainfall. The overpumping of the aquifer by Jewish settlers has reduced the water-table below sea level. The situation further worsened after self-rule, as the Palestinians are using their new-found independence to dig more wells to satisfy their water needs (Libiszewski 1995). The infiltration of saltwater from the Mediterranean has made the Gaza aquifer water unsuitable for irrigation. Farmers have already experienced declining crop yields (Kelly and Homer-Dixon 1995). The likelihood of total salinization of the aquifer in the near future does not bode well for these farmers. The looming severe water scarcity is going to force them to move away from these regions.

Many countries in the Middle East and North Africa rely heavily on non-renewable groundwater supplies to augment their meagre freshwater supplies and to create new farm lands. And these regions are very vulnerable to the drying up of their precious underground resource in the near future. This creates a highly uncertain future for the economy of these countries, and especially the people who are living on newly created agricultural lands. Many Arab regimes are using their fossil aquifers in their short-term strategy to meet the water scarcity and to increase agricultural production to meet growing food demand (Swain 1998b).

Underground water withdrawal on a large scale is being done in Saudi Arabia for domestic and agricultural use. Nearly 2,000 billion cubic metres of water are deposited in the aquifers beneath Saudi Arabia which provides 88 per cent of the country's water needs. In early 1992, King Fahd authorized payments totalling US$ 2.1 billion for the record four million ton wheat production of 1991, which he could have purchased from the global market for one-fourth of that price. But, this remarkable increase of agricultural production threatens to drain the country's underground water resources completely in 20 or 30 years. Like Saudi Arabia's oil resources, the 'fossil' water deposit is also finite, and its complete drying up is not hard to imagine.

Libya provides another example of massive underground water withdrawal. However, Libya's major fossil aquifers are found hundreds of miles south of its agricultural region. So, Libya withdraws water from the underground basin in the southern desert and diverts it to the northern part near the Mediterranean coast for agricultural purposes. The water is transported through a long and expensive pipeline link. Libya shares this vast aquifer partly with Egypt and Sudan. This massive water withdrawal has brought Libya into conflict with these two other riparian countries. The first phase of this project was inaugurated by Colonel Qaddafi, describing it as the 'eighth wonder of the world'. The project irrigates half a million hectares (1,235,500 acres) of new farmland. This sudden increase in agricultural land has not been equally matched by the availability of the labour force. So, Libya has started importing agricultural labourers since 1991, particularly from Egypt. The underground non-renewable basin is predicted to be completely dried up in 40 to 60 years depending upon the amount of withdrawal. This creates a highly uncertain future for the people who are living on these newly created farmlands.

Extensive groundwater withdrawal has also been a serious concern in many parts of South Asia. India is presently drawing half of its water supply from underground to meet the increasing demand (Clarke 1991). In most areas of India's breadbasket, Punjab, groundwater tables have dropped 20 centimetres annually, thus threatening agriculture. Groundwater withdrawal in the western part of Bangladesh has increased dramatically after India's Ganges water diversion at Farakka barrage. In the 1990s, a large number of irrigation pumps have became inoperative due to the falling groundwater table as a result of over-pumping (Majumder 1992: 13), creating further problems for the people of this region.

As groundwater is a hidden resource and not easy to estimate, its exploitation or overuse may not initially spur opposition or popular protest, which makes it easier for the authority to overuse it. It also offers a cheap way of increasing water resources. All these factors have led to excessive groundwater mining in many parts of the world. As Stephen Foster (1996: 13) states: 'The fact that they are "out of the public sight" has caused them also to be "out of the political mind" and they are too often abandoned to chance.' The salinization or drying up of the freshwater aquifers has already resulted in decreasing crop yields in the areas where groundwater is being extensively used for irrigation, and has also intensified the drinking water problem.

The drying up of the groundwater may displace large numbers of people in the future as the decreased water supply fails to meet increasing demand. This form of population displacement has already taken place in parts of the Middle East. In other regions, groundwater withdrawal has not yet resulted in significant population displacement as the falling water-table is being countered by the deeper boring of wells. Present water mining in these areas makes it easy to predict the serious threat of large-scale population displacement in the future. The 'new lands' acquired for agricultural purposes by withdrawing water from underground are bound to be deserted after the sources dry up. The 'overabstraction' of groundwater will also lead to the abandonment of wells in other areas, forcing people to move. Thus, groundwater withdrawal in an environmentally unsustainable manner is likely to create humanitarian crises in many water scarcity regions.

With the help of dams, canals and groundwater withdrawal, there is an on-going attempt to increase the supply of water to meet the growing demand. But at the same time, the price of these water resource development projects has been very high. Besides the economic and environmental costs of the schemes, the human cost is staggering. Due to massive water projects, large numbers of people have already been forced to move away from their homes, and poor rural people have been the major victims. Due to inferior political and economic strength, these poor have become early and easy targets. Persons who are displaced and migrate to another place have to undergo an entire process of resocialization and adjustment in an unfamiliar environment. Apart from psychological consequences of insecurity, the displaced people suffer economic and social consequences. A hostile host population and a climate they are not used to makes the process even more difficult.

Due to severe water scarcity, developing countries who have not been able to provide the basic water requirement standard for human needs are especially vulnerable to water conflicts and large-scale population displacement. Many of these states, furthermore, are characterized by strong ethnic identities, inefficient administration, and a weak economy, which make them particularly vulnerable to humanitarian crises.

4. Prevention and Policy Implications

As discussed, the increasing water scarcity, particularly in developing countries, can directly contribute to violent conflicts and large-scale population displacement, resulting in deaths and suffering. Unless there is an urgent and substantial effort to address the water scarcity issue, the likelihood of its contribution to a humanitarian crisis in many parts of the world is strong.

4.1. Cooperation in sharing the rivers

The increased demand for water from population growth, rapid industrialization, urbanization, and expanding agriculture is so substantial that present water availability is not sufficient. The problem is especially serious for countries in the arid, semi-arid, and tropical regions. Unfortunately, many of these countries lack the resources and administrative abilities to deal with the problems arising from water scarcity. Lack of education and ethnic divisions also easily lead to politicization and ethnicization.

However, while river systems have generated conflict among the riparian states, they have also been instrumental in facilitating cooperation. The need to control water and its improved use are important contributors to joint human construction (Barrett 1994; Biswas 1993; Lowi 1993; K. Rogers 1995; P. Rogers 1993). There have been a number of instances of cooperative arrangements for the better use of available water resources.

The agreements among the riparian countries of the River Rhine, Colorado and Paraná are some of the recent examples.

In the Colorado River basin, the increasing salinity due to agricultural pollution became an issue of contention in the late 1960s between its two riparians, Mexico and USA. Mexico was unhappy over the quality of the water coming from upstream, USA. In 1972, both countries signed an agreement for the better use of the river water resource. The US satisfied Mexico's demand mainly by putting a desalinization plant at Yuma, Arizona and a canal to divert some saline water from the Wellton-Mohawk irrigation district to the Gulf of California. Due to all these measures, the salinity level of the Colorado River in Mexico has now fallen ten times below its 1960s level.

The dispute over the waters of the Rhine came up because of salt pollution from the French mines in the 1970s. As in the case of Colorado, the downstream countries, particularly the Netherlands, objected to the quality of the water received. The four major riparians of this river, Switzerland, France, Germany and the Netherlands came together in the 1980s and shared the cost to address the upstream pollution issue. The successful cooperation among the basin states of the Rhine has now been going on for more than a decade.

The conflict over the Paraná River came up between Brazil and Argentina as a part of their competition to control the water resources in Paraguay. The bilateral agreement in the early 1970s between Brazil and Paraguay over the construction of Itaipu Dam became the source of irritation for Argentina as the country was being left out. After several years of bitter dispute, three basin states reached an agreement in 1979. Once Argentina found its place in Itaipu's regulating mechanism, all three riparian countries are cooperating over the use of the water resource of the Paraná River.

International organizations have not pursued the sharing of international river water as seriously as the situation demands. Indeed, there is not yet an internationally acceptable formula for sharing rivers. It took more than thirty years for the member-states of the UN General Assembly to agree in 1997 on a convention on the law of the non-navigational uses of international watercourses. But, this convention is unable to come into effect due to a delay in the ratification process. The lack of progress can be attributed to the inherent sensitivity of these issues (Wallensteen and Swain 1997). Even if a universal legal principle was clearly enunciated, it would not be sufficient by itself to address the problem of water sharing in different parts of the world. Every river basin has its own long history of water use and sharing in consistent with the region's culture and tradition. Each has its own social and economic interdependencies. Thus, water-sharing issues need to be addressed in the specific regional, or basin based, institutional context (Swain 1997b).

4.2. *Managing water*

Numerous large-scale water projects are being executed to increase the supply of water to meet the world's growing demand. Another approach recently undertaken is to convert seawater to freshwater. A desalinization plant has been an option in the rich areas of south-western United States, southern Europe and the oil-rich areas of the Middle East. Such projects are expensive and it is unlikely that such measures will be economically or technically viable elsewhere in the world. Thus to meet the growing water scarcity, much of the world, particularly the developing countries, must rely substantially on traditional methods to increase the volume of water availability.

Many countries in developing regions are far behind in the race to provide the basic water needs of their people. Further water resource exploitation in these developing countries is a virtual certainty. The demands for water will increase rapidly in most of these countries due to population growth and urbanization. In order to chase the mirage of water security, more superdams will be constructed. As noted, the dam builders of the west have already shifted their operations to developing countries, and there has been a gradual increase in the average height of new dams. Moreover, as almost all suitable dam sites have already been used, new dams will be placed in highly populated areas, resulting in the submergence of vast arable lands and forest, with its accompanying larger population displacements.

Increased public awareness and ethnic awakening in various parts of the world have made it difficult for governmental authorities to carry out large-scale inter-basin water transfer schemes. Inter-state water diversion is not an easy option either, particularly after the end of bloc politics in the post-cold war period. But it is likely that there will be increased water diversion from rural and agricultural sectors to urban and industrial use, which is bound to affect agricultural output and may exacerbate food scarcity in many countries. The loss of the livelihood in rural areas may lead to increased urban migration, creating further social problems.

As discussed earlier, we can expect further intensification of groundwater withdrawal, due to lower financial and political costs. As political authorities are prone to adopt short-term solutions, the further exploitation of groundwater is likely. But, as noted, it is bound to pave the way for future human disaster.

Large-scale water resource projects may not provide the right answer for meeting water scarcity. Water-resource exploitation in an environmentally unsustainable manner will not be able to meet the increasing demand; but rather this exploitation will bring further human crises. In the twentieth century, the growth in water withdrawals and use has been about three times faster than the population increase. So there is a need to change the prevailing attitude towards water resources. Water is not plentiful as commonly believed. It is a scarce resource and its use should be restricted. It should not be a free commodity.

Many people argue that water, given by God, should not be priced. For that matter, all natural resources are God-given. The pricing of water to ensure efficient and reduced use of this scarce resource is not being implemented properly for political reasons. Moreover, many countries lack institutional mechanisms to manage the distribution of water and collection of water revenues. Policy-making and administrative processes are subject to the inertia of the status quo of special interests (Howe 1996; Kirmani and Rangeley 1994).

Water needs to be treated urgently both as a social and an economic good, necessitating the strengthening of the institutional capacity of the state. There is also need for better irrigation management by developing countries to achieve food security with the limited availability of water. The management of water should be entrusted to the local institutions at the lowest appropriate levels to encourage popular participation. Unless water scarcity is handled by limiting its demand, it is going to pose serious development constraints and security concerns, not to mention more human suffering and many cases of humanitarian emergencies, in many regions of the world.

References

Aditjondro, George, and David Kowalewski (1994). 'Damning the Dams in Indonesia: A Test of Competing Perspectives'. *Asian Survey*, 34 (4): 381–95.

Barrett, Scott (1994). 'Conflict and Cooperation in Managing International Water Resources'. Working Paper WM 94–04. CSERGE (Center for Social and Economic Research on the Global Environment).

Biswas, Asit K. (1978). 'Environmental Implications of Water Development for Development for Developing Countries', in Carl Widstrand (ed.), *The Social and*

Ecological Effects of Water Development in Developing Countries. Oxford: Pergamon Press, 283–97.

Biswas, Asit K. (1992). 'Environmental Impact Assessment for Groundwater Management'. *Water Resource Development*, 8 (2) June: 113–17.

Biswas, Asit K. (1993). 'Management of International Waters: Problems and Perspective'. *Water Resource Development*, 9: 167–88.

Beschorner, Natasha (1992/93). 'Water and Instability in the Middle East'. Adelphi Papers No. 273 (Winter).

Clarke, Robin (1991). *Water: The International Crisis*. London: Earthscan Publication Ltd.

Cooley, J. K. (1984). 'The War over Water'. *Foreign Policy*, 54: 3–26.

Engelman, Robert, and Pamela LeRoy (1993). *Sustaining Water: Population and the Future of Renewable Water Supplies*. Population and Environment Program: Population Action International.

Feder, Gershon, and Guy Le Moigne (1994). 'Managing Water in a Sustainable Manner'. *Finance and Development*, 31 (2) June.

Fernandes, Walter (1993). 'The Price of Development'. *Seminar*, 412 (December): 19–24.

Foster, Stephen (1996). 'Ground for Concern'. *Our Planet*, 8 (3): 13–14.

Gleick, Peter H. (1993). 'Water and Conflict: Fresh Water Resources and International Security'. *International Security*, 18 (1): Summer.

Gleick, Peter H. (1996). 'Basic Water Requirements for Human Activities: Meeting Basic Needs'. *Water International*, 21 (2): 83–92.

Goudie, Andrew (1990). *The Human Impact on the Natural Environment* (3rd edn). Oxford: Basil Blackwell.

Heggelund, Gorild (1993). 'China's Environmental Crisis: The Battle of Sanxia'. (NUPI) Research Report No. 170 (August). Norwegian Institute of International Affairs.

Hinrichsen, Don (1995). 'Requiem for a Dying Sea'. *People and the Planet*, 4 (2): 10–13.

Hauge, Wenche, and Tanja Ellingsen (1998). 'Beyond Environmental Scarcity: Causal Pathways to Conflict'. *Journal of Peace Research*, 35 (3): 299–317.

Homer-Dixon, Thomas F. (1994). 'Environmental Scarcities and Violent Conflict: Evidence from Cases'. *International Security*, 19 (1) Summer.

Homer-Dixon, Thomas (1996). 'Environmental Scarcity and Mass Violence'. Paper presented at the NATO Advanced Research Workshop on Conflict and the Environment, Bolkesjo, Norway, 12–16 June.

Homer-Dixon, Thomas, and Valerie Percival (1996). 'Environmental Scarcity and Violent Conflict: Briefing Book'. The Project on Environment, Population and Security, American Association for the Advancement of Science and University College, University of Toronto.

Howe, Charles W. (1996). 'Sharing Water Fairly'. *Our Planet*, 8 (3): 15–17.

Kelly, Kimberley, and Thomas Homer-Dixon (1995). 'Environmental Scarcity and Violent Conflict: The Case of Gaza'. The Project on Environment, Population and Security, American Association for the Advancement of Science and University College, University of Toronto.

Kirmani, Syed, and Robert Rangeley (1994). 'International Inland Waters: Concept for a More Active World Bank role'. World Bank Technical Paper No. 239. Washington, DC: World Bank.

Klötzli, Stefan (1994). 'The Water and Soil Crisis in Central Asia—A Source for Future Conflicts? Occasional Paper No. 11. Zurich and Bern: Environment and Conflict Project.

Klötzli, Stefan (1996). 'The "Aral Sea Syndrome" and Regional Cooperation in Central Asia: Opportunity or Obstacle?' Paper presented at the NATO Advanced Research Workshop on Conflict and the Environment, Bolkesjo, Norway, 12–16 June.

Korzoun, V. I., and A. A. Sokolov (1978). 'World Water Balance and Water Resources of the Earth'. In United Nations, *Water Development and Management Proceedings of the United Nations Water Conference*. London: Pergamon Press.

Kothari, Smitu, and Pramod Parajuli (1993). 'No Nature without Social Justice: A Plea for Cultural and Ecological Pluralism in India', in Wolfgang Sachs (ed.), *Global Ecology: A New Arena of Political Conflict*. London: Zed Books, 224–41.

Kumar, Krishna (1996). 'Narmada, State and the People: Styles of Suppression and Resistance. *Economic and Political Weekly*, 31 (39): 2666–7.

Libiszewski, Stephan (1995). 'Water Disputes in the Jordan Basin Region'. Occasional Paper No. 13. Zurich and Bern: Environment and Conflict Project.

Lonergan, Steve (1996). 'Water Resources and Conflict: Examples from the Middle East'. Paper presented in the Conflict and the Environment, NATO Advanced Research Workshop, Bolkesjo, Norway, 12–16 June.

Lowi, Miriam R. (1993). 'Bridging the Divide: Transboundary Resource Disputes and the Case of West Bank water'. *International Security*, 18 (1) Summer: 113–38.

Lundqvist, Jan (1992). 'Water Scarcity in Abundance: Management and Policy Challenges'. *Ecodecision*, 6 (September): 41–3.

Majumder, Mostafa K. (1992). 'Bangladesh Keeps Priming the Pumps'. *Panscope*, 31 July.

McCully, Patrick (1994). 'Update on the Deadly Kedung Ombo Resettlement Fiasco'. *Bulletin of Concerned Asian Scholars*, 26 (4): 85–6.

Myers, Norman (1989). 'Environment and Security'. *Foreign Policy*, 74.

Pearce, Fred (1992). 'Tide of Opinion Turns against Superdams'. *Panscope,* 33 November.

Pierce, John T. (1990). *The Food Resource*. New York: Longman.

Postel, Sandra (1996). 'Dividing the Waters: Food Security, Ecosystem Health, and the New Politics of Scarcity.' *Worldwatch Paper,* No. 132 (September).

Raskin, Paul, Evan Hansen, and Robert Morgolis (1995). 'Water and Sustainability: A Global Outlook'. Polestar Series Report No. 4. Stockholm: Stockholm Environment Institute.

Rogers, Katrina S. (1995). 'Rivers of Discontent—Rivers of Peace: Environmental Cooperation and Integration Theory'. *International Studies Notes*, 20 (2) Spring.

Rogers, Peter (1993). 'The Value of Cooperation in Resolving International River Basin Disputes'. *Natural Resources Forum*, 17 (2) May.

Satterthwaite, David (1993). 'Securing Water for the Cities'. *People and the Planet*, 2 (2): 13.

Shah, R. B. (1993). 'Role of Major Dams in the India Economy'. *Water Resources Development*, 9 (3): 319–36.

Shiklomanov, Igor A. (1993). 'World Fresh Water Resources', in Peter H. Gleick (ed.) *Water in Crisis: A Guide to the World's Fresh Water Resources*. New York: Oxford University Press.

Starr, Joyce R. (1991). 'Water Wars'. *Foreign Policy*, 82.

Suliman, Mohamed (1992). 'Civil War in Sudan: The Impact of Ecological Degradation'. Occasional Paper No. 4. Zurich and Bern: Environment and Conflict Project.

Swain, Ashok (1996a). 'The Environmental Trap: The Ganges River Diversion, Bangladeshi Migration and Conflicts in India'. Report No. 41. Uppsala: Department of Peace and Conflict Research.

Swain, Ashok (1996b). 'Displacing the Conflict: Environmental Destruction in Bangladesh and Ethnic Conflict in India'. *Journal of Peace Research*, 33 (2) May: 189–204.

Swain, Ashok (1996c). 'Water Scarcity: A Threat to Global Security'. *Environment and Security*, 1 (1): 156–72.

Swain, Ashok (1996d). 'Environmental Migration and Conflict Dynamics: Focus on Developing Regions'. *Third World Quarterly*, 17 (5): 959–73.

Swain, Ashok (1997a). 'Democratic Consolidation: Environmental Movements in India'. *Asian Survey*, 37 (9): 818–32.

Swain, Ashok (1997b). 'Sharing International Rivers: A Regional Approach', in Nils P. Gleditsch (ed.), *Conflict and the Environment*. Dordrecht: Kluwer Academic Publishers, 403–16.

Swain, Ashok (1997c). The Nile River Dispute: Ethiopia, the Sudan, and Egypt'. *The Journal of Modern African Studies*, 35 (4) December: 675–94.

Swain, Ashok (1998a). 'Fight for the Last Drop: Inter-State River Disputes in India'. *Contemporary South Asia*, 7 (2) July: 167–80.

Swain, Ashok (1998b). 'A New Challenge: Water Scarcity in the Arab world'. *Arab Studies Quarterly*, 20 (1) Winter: 1–11.

Tangwisutijit, Nantiya (1996). 'Must the Mekong Die?'. *People and the Planet*, 5 (3): 10–13.

Thukral, Enakshi Ganguly (ed.) (1992). *Big Dams, Displaced People: Rivers of Sorrow—Rivers of Change*. New Delhi: Sage Publications.

UNEP (1991). *Freshwater Pollution*. Nairobi: UNEP/GEMS Environment Library No. 6.

Usher, Ann Danaiya (1996). 'Damming the Theun River: Nordic Companies in Laos'. *The Ecologist*, 26 (3) May/June: 85–92.

Veltrop, Jan A. (1993). 'Importance of Dams for Water Supply and Hydropower', in Asit K. Biswas *et al.* (eds.), *Water for Sustainable Development in the Twenty-first Century*. Delhi: Oxford University Press, 102–15.

Wallensteen, Peter, and Ashok Swain (1997). *International Fresh Water Resources: Source of Conflict or Cooperation*. Stockholm: SEI.

Wood, John R. (1993). 'India's Narmada River Dams: Sardar Sarovar under Siege'. *Asian Survey*, 33 (10) October: 968–84.

World Bank (1992). *World Development Report 1992. Development and the Environment*. New York: Oxford University Press.

6

Stabilization Programmes, Social Costs, Violence, and Humanitarian Emergencies

CHRISTIAN MORRISSON

1. Introduction

It is well known that in some countries stabilization programmes (SPs) have resulted in considerable social costs, and even heavy social costs. But these social costs cannot be compared in importance to the impact that results from an increase in the rate of unemployment, or of poverty, or a complex humanitarian emergency (CHE). According to Väyrynen (Chapter 2), a complex humanitarian emergency is a crisis 'in which a large number of people die, or suffer from war, physical violence, disease, hunger or displacement'. Consequently, two conditions are needed for a CHE to evolve: (i) a number of people suffering from war or violence or dying, and (ii) a number of people becoming victims to disease, hunger or displacement.

As will become apparent from this chapter, it is impossible to point to a specific stabilization programme that has been conducive to thousands of people dying from violence or becoming subject to disease, famine, and displacement. But it is possible to cite well known situations in which an increase in poverty and malnutrition has raised infant mortality significantly, or to point to examples of harsh repression (as in the case of demonstrations against stabilization measures) that have resulted in hundreds of people being killed. As the consequences of stabilization programmes go beyond the usual definition of social costs, the concept in this instance is confined to 'limited humanitarian emergency' (LHE), which is an emergency limited in time (it is temporary) and in space (it is local). Thus, a limited humanitarian emergency is much less serious than a complex humanitarian emergency. A good example is the 1989 events in Caracas during which an army repression of riots against a drastic stabilization programme resulted in the death of 1,000 people and numerous casualties. Although this LHE clearly exceeded the normal interpretation of social costs, it did not develop into a complex humanitarian emergency of the same magnitude as the 1994 Rwanda crisis.

It is a fact that even though stabilization programmes have induced certain limited humanitarian emergency situations, blame for the complex humanitarian emergencies of the world lies elsewhere. Moreover, in some instances, stabilization programmes can have a neutral or even a positive impact. Therefore, the focus of this chapter will adhere to stabilization programmes defined according to the following typology: those which bring about (i) net social benefits, and those that induce (ii) no social costs, (iii) social costs without LHEs, or (iv) LHEs.

According to Cornia, Jolly and Stewart (1987), stabilization programmes can increase unemployment, inequality, and poverty, i.e. social costs without LHEs. But the results of the OECD project (Bourguignon, De Melo and Morrisson 1991) prove that in some countries—as in Malaysia—social costs have been avoided. Consequently, there is always some risk of social costs, but they need not be inevitable. Cuts in public expenditures can entail social costs if education and health services decrease, but these adverse effects cannot be considered as an LHE, and the difference between social costs and LHEs needs to be defined more precisely. For example, if a pupil-teacher ratio increases from 30 to 40, it becomes a social cost, but certainly not a limited humanitarian emergency. In contrast, when cuts in health expenditures result in rural public health centres being void of medication for extended periods, this can lead to an LHE because the poor cannot afford to buy medicine, and some of the sick will die. Madagascar suffered from such a shortage in the late 1980s after a stabilization programme. A specific grant to compensate for the higher prices of imported drugs was arranged by France in 1994 after the devaluation of the franc CFA in an effort to avoid calamitous shortages of medicine. Although SPs induce social costs, they rarely give rise to LHEs, and never to CHEs.

Stabilization programmes can also have *indirect* negative effects. Various experiences of adjustment have shown that some stabilization measures run the risk of causing political instability. In many developing countries, any type of conflict can erupt in a dispute over the legitimacy of the regime, thus making the repression of demonstrations much more violent than in the developed countries. Repression can be distinguished into two different types: 'soft' repression and harsh repression. 'Soft' repression entails the closing of schools and universities, and the prohibition or banning of meetings, newspapers, political parties, or of strikes and demonstrations. Undemocratic and, in some instances, abusive of human rights, but soft repression cannot be defined as a limited humanitarian emergency. Harsh suppression makes use of detention (and, at times, torture), violence, and on-the-spot executions in the tens and hundreds to stifle demonstrations, and would definitely classify as a limited humanitarian emergency.

Consequently, the focus of this study will be on the various degrees of repression: incidents with no repression; 'soft' repression; and, harsh repression that can evolve into a limited humanitarian emergency. As pointed out above, a limited humanitarian emergency is very different from the traditional concept of CHE, such as famine or civil wars which lead to the demise of thousands of people. In Morocco, the harsh suppression of riots in June 1981 that followed the country's stabilization efforts, caused the death of dozens and casualties in the hundreds, but the crisis, limited to Casablanca, lasted a day and thus was very different from a complex humanitarian emergency.

Following this classification, the chapter will first analyse stabilization programme's direct impacts (section two) and, in section three, its indirect effects as they relate to political turmoil. The fourth section will consider the impacts of structural adjustment, and the fifth section will be devoted to examining social costs caused by the refusal to adjust. Evidence shows that in some cases, social costs of adjustment repudiation can far exceed those incurred with SP. They may even give rise to a CHE, as in Ghana prior to 1983. Thus, non-adjustment cannot be advocated as an option simply to avoid social costs (or an eventual LHE). Instead, efforts should be made to find an optimal SP which includes measures to minimize direct social costs and political turmoil. Section six briefly describes the social costs of the recent crisis in Indonesia. Finally, certain African countries verging on CHEs will also be reviewed. Although the economy of these countries was satisfactory and there was no pressing need for stabilization programmes, political instability and civil war contributed to the CHEs. The last section concludes the chapter with an examination of the correlation between stabilization programmes and social costs, limited or complex humanitarian emergencies.

2. The Direct Impact of Stabilization Programmes

OECD studies[1] are used to assess the impact of SPs on poverty and other social indicators. These studies cite several countries where stabilization programmes have caused excessive social costs without these developing into CHEs. It is, however, more difficult to point to countries in which social costs have escalated into complex humanitarian emergencies. The seven-country sample in question is too small to be conclusive and other empirical studies were reviewed for experiences of CHEs. Evidence supports the fact that in some cases, albeit rarely, stabilization programmes induced CHEs. A review of these cases will provide a more complete examination of the risks involved with stabilization programmes.

---

[1] Cf. Bourguignon and Morrisson (1992).

2.1. Results of the OECD studies

Poverty is at the heart of the debate on the consequences of stabilization programmes. Thus, the ultimate question is to determine whether SPs have increased poverty (social cost), and if so, have they increased poverty so dramatically that a CHE could develop?

Of course, it is also possible to cite examples of countries in which adjustment has reduced poverty, as in Malaysia and Indonesia in the 1980s (at least until the 1997 crisis). In Malaysia, the percentage of rural poor decreased from 25 per cent in 1984 to 22.4 per cent in 1987, while the percentage of urban poor remained stable. In Indonesia, the percentage of the poor declined from 33 to 22 per cent and the poverty gap dropped from 8.5 to 4.2 per cent. Furthermore, the intensity of poverty decreased in both countries. Data on consumption and calorie intake confirm the trend. This positive trend can mainly be attributed to agricultural growth, reflecting government capital investments to rural areas made possible by the petroleum revenue from the 1970s. But this growth was also the result of certain adjustment measures, such as devaluation and trade liberalization, which increased agricultural prices compared to manufacturing prices.[2] Furthermore, governments did not adjust social expenditures during the first adjustment programme (1984–87). Educational expenditure was increased in Malaysia by 5.7 per cent per annum and health expenditure by 3.7 per cent. The composition of these expenditures also shifted to favour the poor. Expenditures earmarked for new hospitals were cut, but rural health service funds remained intact. Similarly in Indonesia, allocations for education and health were the least affected by cuts in public expenditures. As the experiences of Malaysia and Indonesia show, it is possible to formulate stabilization programmes that do not add to the social costs of the poor.

In other countries, however, results were less satisfactory. Rural poverty decreased in Morocco, but only because of large remittances sent home by emigrants, periods of ample rainfall, and higher official agricultural prices. In towns, however, poverty increased because SPs added to unemployment, causing a severe drop in average incomes in the informal sector. Interestingly, the rate of infant mortality declined simultaneously, and the educational and health services increased. The only exception was primary schools, where enrolments fell by 10 per cent.[3] Indeed, some social

---

[2] These results are corroborated by Ravallion and Huppi (1989). In their careful analysis of household surveys, they found evidence of a net decrease in poverty between the 1984 and 1987. Three indicators—income, food expenditure share and calorie intake—show the same development and no measurement error (for example, estimate of consumer price index) can reverse this conclusion.

[3] The number of teachers increased by 14 per cent during 1983–86, but the fall in enrolment rate reflects the fact that poor families refused to send their children to school because education no longer leads to jobs in the modern employment sector.

costs can be imputed to SPs, but it is obvious that these never developed to the LHE stage.

Poverty in Côte d'Ivoire clearly grew in the capital city, but stabilized in the rural areas between 1981 and 1985. Lower income in the informal sector, large unemployment, and consumer price increases (as subsidies were cut) added to urban social costs. Social indicators confirm this trend, which showed a small increase in secondary school attendance, as well as a slight decrease at the elementary level. The declining rate of infant mortality was maintained and there was no change in the per capita calorie intake.

The World Bank studies, based on the Côte d'Ivoire Living Standards Survey, complement Schneider's research (1991). Also studying the effects of adjustment in 1980–85, Glewwe and de Tray (1988) found that adjustment had a favourable impact because of the initial living environment of the poor, most of whom lived in rural areas. Prior to 1985, adjustment policies led to an improvement in the rural-to-urban terms of trade by increasing real farm-gate prices for cash-crops and by removing export taxes on rubber, oil palm, coconut oil, cotton, and pineapple. The urban poor, on the other hand, were adversely affected by SPs, but only 4 per cent of the ultra-poor (first decile) and 14 per cent of the poor (second and third decile) were city dwellers. The reduction of subsidies on cotton and rice partially offset these gains, but the balance remained largely positive. This was not surprising because 66 per cent of the ultra-poor (first decile) and 70 per cent of the poor (first, second, and third deciles) produced cotton, coffee, cacao, or oil palm.

This optimism is negated by Grootaert (1992) in a study covering a later period (1985–88). Examining a period of declining GDP (when household expenditure per capita dropped by about 30 per cent over the period in question), Grootaert found evidence of significantly increased poverty. In three years, the number of the very poor and of the poor had risen by approximately 50 per cent. This increase in poverty was mainly explained by the falling income of smallholder farmers. Public sector employees were also affected, although to a lesser degree.

A comparison of these studies indicated that the evolution of poverty in Côte d'Ivoire is correlated with the average peasant income.[4] When SP measures improved this income, a corresponding increase was observed in urban poverty, but there was no significant deterioration in the consumption levels of the rural poor. Furthermore, as cash crop prices decline, living standards can deteriorate, regardless of whether or not a country has introduced stabilization measures.

---

[4] In this connection, a distinction needs to be made between farmers who sell cash crops, and poor peasants who have nothing or next to nothing to sell and are forced to consume their products. Cash-crop farmers benefited from the adjustment measures in the form of higher prices, but not the peasants.

The situation was worse in Ecuador and Chile. As a country with considerable inequality in its agrarian structures, Ecuador faced a serious drop in the average income of peasants and petty agricultural workers as well as individuals active in the urban informal sector, causing a large increase in poverty. In Chile, where the majority of the poor live in towns, deterioration of the living standards was mainly the result of high unemployment and wage reductions. A reduction in social expenditures further eroded living circumstances of the people. Although an aid programme targeted at the poorest (lowest decile) stabilized living conditions of these families, circumstances of families in the second, third, and fourth deciles worsened from 1982 to 1985. It is interesting to note that even though social costs of SP were high, Chile's safety net protecting the poorest sector and Ecuador's public works programmes prevented the situation from developing into an LHE.[5]

The OECD studies have thus provided examples of stabilization programmes which have been initiated *without* ensuing social costs. There are also cases with social costs which, at times, were considerable in certain Latin America countries but no there was no evidence of these developing into CHEs.

2.2. Other analyses of the social costs of stabilization programmes

There are two conflicting syntheses on the social costs of SPs. UNICEF's *Adjustment with a Human Face*, by Cornia, Jolly and Stewart (1987) was the first important and critical analysis of the social impact of SPs, and the second, the World Bank's *Social Dimension of Adjustment*, is a recent and more optimistic study (Jayarajah, Branson and Sen 1996).

The UNICEF report, examining ten nations, provides examples of countries undergoing adjustment which triggered increasing social costs, as well as evidence of exceptional situations which approached the CHE level.

The results in three countries—Botswana, South Korea, and Zimbabwe—were rather optimistic. Households in these countries, particularly in the formal sector which excludes the ultra-poor, suffered some adjustment costs, but many welfare indicators improved during adjustment and there was no significant increase in poverty.

Other countries in the survey contradict this finding. An adjustment programme with IMF assistance was undertaken in Brazil (São Paulo) early in 1983. Unemployment increased over the period 1983–85, mean income dropped, and the poorer sectors suffered the greatest hardship.

---

[5] The potential threat of misery existed, but the worst scenario was averted by the public works programmes in Ecuador—at least, this was true in the coastal areas where these programmes were instigated by President Cordero to repay his local constituents for their loyalty.

This social cost was compounded by cuts in social budgets all over the country.[6] As a result, infant mortality rate reversed its earlier declining trend and the nutritional status of many children worsened. Data from schools indicated higher rates of learning disability and drop-outs. Finally, there was a rise in child abandonment and delinquency, the most tragic consequences of the crisis.

At the beginning of 1984, the Jamaican government concluded a deflationary agreement with the IMF. As subsidies were reduced and large devaluations applied, the price of a minimum basket of goods increased more than wages. Moreover, education expenditure per head for the population aged under 14 years declined by 40 per cent, forcing the closure of some schools, and per capita health expenditure dropped by 33 per cent. The number of children showing signs of malnutrition rose. When the long-term consequences of limited education and child malnutrition are taken into account, the ensuing deterioration in the living standards of the poor exceeds the normal concept of social costs.

Similar large social costs were observed in the Philippines between 1981 and 1985, where stabilization programmes were applied in 1983–85. Education and health expenditures per capita fell by one-third. Malnutrition rose from 17 per cent in 1982 to 22 per cent in 1985 for children under five, and in the worst-affected regions infant mortality rate increased sharply. The stabilization programme was followed by setbacks in primary schooling in the form of falling participation and increased repetition rates, adding to the number of street children who were forced to beg and steal. The Philippines was hit harder than Jamaica by the aftermath of the stabilization programme because inequality and poverty were already a fact of life in the country prior to adjustment.

The effects of SPs were similar in Peru, where an adjustment package was introduced in 1977–78 and again in 1982–84. At the end of 1985, formal sector wages were equivalent to 64 per cent of their 1979 level and 44 per cent of the 1973 level. The share of total social expenditure in the national budget declined from 26 to 18 per cent. Food and fuel subsidies were cancelled without compensatory measures for the poor. Average food availability per capita declined by 26 per cent and child malnutrition increased in the south. The number of deaths due to tuberculosis increased, as did the incidence of certain other diseases. Finally, primary enrolment rates remained constant, but the quality of education declined.

In the 1950s and the 1960s, Sri Lanka was successful in meeting its basic needs, but a new policy undertaken in 1977 (devaluation, liberalization, cuts in public expenditures) clearly had social costs. Income inequality increased, the share of social expenditure declined from 33 per cent (1977)

---

[6] The city of São Paulo was an exception. Its social expenditures rose despite slashes to the nationwide social budget.

to 22 per cent (1983), as food subsidies were greatly reduced. Health and education sectors also suffered. Participation in education did not increase and the standard of basic health services fell. The worst consequence of this new policy was a decline in the calorie consumption of poor households (first, second, and third deciles) and increasing malnutrition. In Sri Lanka's case, GDP growth accelerated and the unemployment rate fell, but the experience also highlighted the fact that when social expenditures for the poor are reduced, it has adverse effects.

Based on a survey of the literature, the UNICEF study concluded that, with the exception of Asia, infant mortality rates showed an increasing trend in many countries of Latin America and Sub-Saharan Africa (north and east Brazil, Uruguay, Bolivia, Barbados, and Jamaica) (Cornia, Jolly and Stewart 1987). The same was true for malnutrition. In Sub-Saharan Africa, various indicators confirmed that between 1980–85 malnutrition was on the rise in Madagascar, Rwanda, Burundi, Lesotho, Zambia, Kenya, Cameroon, Zaïre, Tanzania, and Guinea-Bissau. There were very few indications of a similar deterioration in Asia; on the contrary, a decline in all forms of malnutrition was observed in most countries. Primary education was also affected. Evidence confirmed decreasing enrolment rates (or poorer standard of education) in countries like Mexico, Bolivia, Barbados, Nigeria, and Zaïre.

The overall conclusion of the UNICEF study was pessimistic. The majority of countries in Latin America, Africa and the Middle East experienced '. . . a sharp reversal in the trend toward the improvement in standards of child health, nutrition, and education' (Cornia, Jolly and Stewart 1987: 34).

The comprehensive evaluation by the World Bank (1996) forms a contrast to the UNICEF study. This book, using a large sample of countries, examines two important questions—the evolution of poverty during adjustment, and the impact of adjustment on social expenditures.[7] In this study, the poverty line is defined according to the headcount index, the poverty-gap index, and the squared poverty gap index,[8] and countries with two available consumption surveys (one prior to adjustment loans, the second post-adjustment) were selected. Results differed according to the different regions examined. Not surprising, a decline in poverty was apparent in ten Asian countries (five pro-adjusting and five non-compliant countries). Although the situation for households near the poverty line improved more than it did for the ultra-poor, social costs in these Asian countries cannot be imputed to adjustment. In Latin America, the results were more ambiguous. In adjusting countries, poverty was alleviated in five cases, but the reverse occurred in five others. The results were similar

---

[7] The fact that World Bank operations are evaluated by its own staff rather than external experts constitutes a minor limitation to the study.

[8] This index captures the inequality among the poor.

in countries that refused adjustment: two with increased poverty versus two with some alleviation. The same results were apparent in adjustment countries in Africa and the Middle East: in one out of two cases, poverty was alleviated. As the initial sample of eight nations was rather small for drawing conclusive results, it was extended to additional eight countries in Sub-Saharan Africa, even though only one consumption survey was available. Six of these additional case studies were adjustment loan recipients, and among them, Malawi, Rwanda, and Zimbabwe ranked among the worst performers. In all cases, income distribution was assumed to remain stable.

The results, with the exception of the Sub-Saharan African countries, are rather satisfactory. As explained in the World Bank study, two indisputable factors account for the outcome:

... most of the poor in the developing countries live in rural areas and the immediate impact of a higher agricultural growth rate was a reduction in the rural poverty rate ... adjustment programmes usually stimulate the growth of agriculture (World Bank 1996).

These two official studies might be disturbing to the average reader in the fact that their conclusions are contradictory, but these discrepancies can be explained. First, the periods of analysis were different. The UNICEF study generally referred to the years 1980–85 and World Bank study to 1985–92. This introduced different results because poverty is correlated mainly to GDP/capita growth and the beginning of the 1980s was a period of crisis in the majority of developing countries with decreasing GDP/capita, whereas the 1985–92 period was one of an economic upswing. This meant that in the early 1980s an increase in poverty would have been an inescapable factor in many countries, with or without adjustment. In addition, the World Bank study points to evidence of growing poverty in several adjusting countries in Africa and Latin America. If the analysis had included only countries which were undertaking adjustment measures, it would have been possible to conclude that a positive correlation exists between SPs and poverty.

Another difference between the studies concerned methodology. The WB study focused only on parallel household surveys, pre- and post-stabilization programme, whereas the UNICEF report combined numerous indicators, including percentage of poor households, nutritional status of children, food intake, infant mortality rate, child death rate, education attainment. But it needs to be noted that some indicators, such as education attainment, can deteriorate even as the average consumption of poor households increases. In addition, the timeframe of the UNICEF study was not strictly linked to adjustment. For example, in the case of Ghana, indicators were compared for 1979 and 1985, but adjustment was not undertaken until 1983. Furthermore, Roe and Schneider (1992) have shown that non-adjustment was in effect up to the year 1983. This had heavy social costs, but certain social indicators improved thereafter.

Third, the World Bank study utilized average data only for each particular country, for example, the average consumption of the poorest 10 per cent. However, as has been indicated, this can be misleading because average consumption can show a slight upward trend despite an increase in poverty in a particular region. The UNICEF report at times also quoted local data, and this point needs to be taken into account.

Differences aside, several conclusions can be drawn from the World Bank and the UNICEF studies:

  (i) the experience of the Asian countries proves that stabilization programmes do not necessarily entail significant social costs;

 (ii) it is easier to avoid social costs during a period of long-term growth than during recession, but social costs were apparent even in the 1985–90 period; and

(iii) although SPs do induce social costs, these very rarely lead to CHEs. Nevertheless situations approaching the severity of a limited humanitarian emergency can develop when a stabilization programme is introduced in a country where many adverse factors already exist prior to adjustment. These include high income inequality, decreasing GDP/capita in the long term, low public social expenditures for poor households, a substantial income gap between regions or regions with very low income levels. Stabilization programmes applied in these circumstances without a complementary safety network will further erode the already existing dismal living conditions. Increasing poverty, malnutrition, infant and child mortality rates, and a deterioration of primary education and health services are commonplace occurrences and the term 'limited humanitarian emergency' can be applied to the poorest regions, despite the fact that the term may seem to be an exaggeration in comparison to the average indicators of the country.

Having completed the overview of the studies by OECD, UNICEF, and the World Bank, this chapter's conclusions are also examined against other literature on the social effects of stabilization programmes. This additional survey focused on Latin America and Africa, where the risk of heavy social costs is most significant.

The most recent assessment of poverty and adjustment in Latin America is by Morley (1995). To analyse changes in poverty during the 1980s, Morley relied on the poverty estimates by Psacharopoulos in a 1993 World Bank Report. Poverty in Latin America increased during 1980–89, with the proportion of the poor rising from 26.5 to 31 per cent. But since 1989 with economic recovery, this proportion has decreased. As the adjustments took place before 1989, what is crucial is the 1980–89 period and the circumstances that enabled only four countries—Costa Rica, Colombia, Paraguay, and Uruguay—to avoid the social costs of SPs. In evaluation of social costs, the structure, or pattern, of poverty constitutes an important factor. A majority of the poor have lived until the 1980s in rural areas (as in Africa and Asia). But by 1989, the number of urban poor slightly exceeded the number of rural poor—the former increased by 33 per cent, whereas the latter only rose by 18 per cent. This change in the living environment is important with regard to stabilization programme impacts. Some stabilization measures can benefit poor households in rural areas if they produce tradable goods, but these gains will not reach the unemployed living in towns.

Thus, it can be assumed that the overall social costs of SPs increase as the proportion of rural poor declines. Lack of education and a high dependency ratio (defined as the number of family members per working adult) characterize poor families. This being the case, the main link between stabilization programmes and increasing poverty becomes clear: the fall in employment which added to the dependency ratio. The cost of increasing unemployment in towns largely cancelled the benefits resulting from higher prices for tradable goods drawn by some of the agricultural poor.[9]

Morley's conclusions are more optimistic with regard to social expenditure and social indicators. Net enrolment rate[10] for children in primary schools increased in all countries except Chile and Costa Rica, where it was very high already in 1980. The efficiency of primary school systems improved and the completion rate for primary school increased everywhere, except in Guatemala. Secondary school enrolment ratios showed the same continuing improvement, with a decline of this ratio in only three countries. In all but four countries, educational spending per capita fell during this period. Nevertheless, despite the reduced budgets, improvements were made by cutting costs for teachers' salaries, investments, and teaching materials.

Health performance also seemed rather satisfactory. Mortality rates for infants and for children under 5 years of age decreased during the period in question and Grosh (1990) found declining percentages of underweight children for many countries, except for Chile which already in 1980 had the lowest index. A paradox exists between health expenditures which remained constant in real terms and the improved availability of health services (the number of inhabitants per physician and per hospital declined).

Morley observed that some governments reacted to increasing urban impoverishment with support measures. A special employment programme was initiated in Chile in 1983 to create 500,000 jobs, which

---

[9] These benefits were enjoyed only in a few countries, such as Costa Rica.

[10] 'Net ratio' takes into account only primary school-aged children, whereas 'gross ratio' also includes older children.

equalled 11 per cent of the labour force. This policy effectively counter-
acted the rise in poverty. Peru and Bolivia experimented with similar programmes, but on a smaller scale; other governments created or expanded
in-kind transfer programmes. Among the most efficient support measures, Morley highlights the Chilean effort for poor mothers and children
and the 1989 Venezuelan programme, also targeted at poor households,
which by 1991 captured 1.8 per cent of the country's GDP.

Based on his detailed analysis of certain countries, Morley concluded
his report with a very interesting hypothesis in which the main factor is
the size and the role of the traded goods sector:

From the point of view of poverty, the most favourable situation is to be a country
where the poor are producers but not consumers of traded goods, because real
devaluation will raise their wages by more than it will raise their cost of living. The
least favourable situation is one in which the poor consume but do not produce
traded goods. Clearly, no country is a perfect example of either polar case, but it
appears that countries like Costa Rica, Paraguay, and Colombia have a relatively
favourable structure compared to Venezuela and Argentina (Morley 1995: 164).

This observation is important because it highlights the fact that the same
stabilization programme can induce either substantial or minimal social
costs depending on the employment sector of the poor.

Frances Stewart (1992) offers evidence confirming many of these points.
According to Stewart:

  (i) the percentage of the poor in Latin America as a whole increased; this
       is confirmed by a large rise in urban poverty, whereas rural poverty
       remained approximately constant;
 (ii) growing urban impoverishment was caused mainly by falling wages
       and rising unemployment rates;
(iii) expenditures for education and health as a share of GDP often
       dropped. This was evident in ten countries while in five others, the
       reverse was true. Primary education was often prioritized. In con-
       trast, health services for the poor were low-priority items. However,
       Stewart found evidence of progress in immunization rates and
       decreasing infant mortality rates;
 (iv) malnutrition decreased in most countries, albeit some cases of wors-
       ening child nutrition were observed.

In their report on the impact of adjustment on health in Mexico, Rivero,
Ascencio and Vinagre (1991) confirmed Stewart's last point. Development
on a global level may be satisfactory, but at the same time, social costs may
be almost unbearably heavy in a particular region. Mexico is one such
country: during adjustment, in spite of a dramatic drop in health expenditures, health services increased,[11] and infant mortality and child mortality

---

[11] In 1987, health expenditures corresponded to only 47 per cent of the 1981 level.

rates decreased, although at a slower rate. Concurrently, however, the share of infant deaths due to malnutrition increased significantly in some regions and in one region in the south, child mortality rate increased by 114 per cent between 1978–84, whereas this rate declined in other regions.

These studies on Latin America highlight the complexity of an analysis—national data constitutes one level of evaluation and regional or local data the second level. Even when data for a country are favourable, as in the Morley report which indicated a constant percentage of poor and improving indicators for health and education, it is possible that in a given region poverty deepens or that malnutrition worsens. Education and health indicators can often improve in a country concurrently as its expenditures decrease.[12] Caution, therefore, should be exercised in explaining the adverse development of poverty or social indicators. Global recession, touching all countries, can have similar deteriorating effects on poverty and social indicators in different countries, regardless of whether or not they have introduced adjustment. Finally, the same SP can cause different social impacts, depending on whether or not the poor of that particular country produce traded goods. In summary, a few countries in Latin America survived stabilization programmes without major social costs; a greater number of countries endured some social costs, affecting either the entire country or some regions only. Very rarely and only in certain places could these social costs be defined as a limited humanitarian emergency.

To review the situation in Africa, the study by Diop, Hill and Sirageldin (1991) was selected. The study on adjustment's consequences with regard to health analysed ten countries with demographic and health surveys that covered some 20 per cent of the births in Sub-Saharan Africa, and was, therefore, fairly representative. The most important finding was that adjustment policies did not increase child mortality at the national level, nor in the short run, as compared to non-adjusting countries. More precisely, SPs may be associated with some increase in child mortality in towns, particularly among the urban poor. But in the rural areas, the same measures may have reduced child mortality among the poor and perhaps even more among the non-poor. It should be remembered that social expenditures, including health, primarily favour urban populations, which means that rural households are less vulnerable to cuts in these services. Furthermore, although SP costs are absorbed by urban households, these programmes often benefited rural households. The improvement in child mortality rates in rural areas should not be surprising: it reflects the general long-term trend of declining child mortality as well as the fact that income or consumption *per capita* increases or remains constant in rural

---

[12] It is possible for quantitative indicators to show an increasing trend concurrently with a decrease in the quality of services. This happens, for instance, when the wages of teachers or doctors have dropped considerably.

areas during adjustment. But at the same time, the health of poor urban households was severally affected by stabilization measures.

The study by Dorosh, Bernier and Sarris (1990) on the impact of adjustment on the poor in Madagascar provides an enlightening example of this polarization. In 1981–83 low-income urban households were hit the hardest by an SP, particularly by the increased consumer prices, falling wages (including minimum wage), and cuts in social expenditures that followed. But rice-selling farmers profited from the price increases[13] and were less concerned with diminishing social expenditures because their access to education and health services was already limited.

This section on the direct impact of stabilization programmes is concluded with a comprehensive study by Kakwani, Makonnen and van der Gaag (1990). The authors analysed the evolution of economic and social indicators from 1960 to 1987 in 86 developing countries, 55 of which were adjustment loans recipients, 31 were not. Comparing the performances of these two country groups, Kakwani, Makonnen and van der Gaag found no evidence of a link between adjustment and trends in infant or child mortality rate. In the early 1980s, the percentage of decline was approximately the same for both groups. Among the adjusting countries, the degree of malnutrition increased between 1980–83, but then dropped between 1983–86. The non-adjusting countries showed improved nutritional levels during 1980–87, a period of positive GDP/capita growth rate, but the situation worsened in countries where this rate was negative. On average, the performance of the two groups showed no great deviation.[14]

It is only for primary school enrolment that the authors found a significant difference. This ratio decreased between 1980 and 1985 in the adjusting countries, whereas in the non-adjusting countries, it increased. So, except for this single deviation, the authors concluded that, 'The review of social indicators does not reveal a discernible difference between adjusting and non-adjusting countries'. Nevertheless, this statement should be interpreted with caution[15] because only average indicators were examined for both adjusting and non-adjusting countries. Kakwani's observation is consistent with the fact that high social costs, such as increasing malnutrition or infant mortality rate, can culminate in a country whether it is adjusting or not. Similarly, a country with these problems may be burdened with limited a humanitarian emergency in one particular region. But as was noted above, these events are never triggered solely by adjust-

---

[13] For the poorest peasants who were forced to purchase rice, the situation was the opposite.

[14] In some respects, this finding was rather surprising because external aid was much more generous for adjusting countries.

[15] In a later study Kakwani (1995) concluded that the rate of progress in living standard improvements was lower in countries which had adopted adjustment programmes than in non/adjusting countries.

ment programmes—they are the result of many concomitant factors, including SPs.

3. The Political Cost of Stabilization Programmes

In some respects, incidents of harsh repression that can almost be defined as limited humanitarian emergencies are well documented, as governments cannot play down confrontations that produce dozens of casualties. These events are given global coverage by the media, whereas growing malnutrition and increasing infant mortality in remote villages remain unrecognized for a long time.

Following the threefold typology of this chapter—no repression, soft repression, and harsh repression defined as a limited humanitarian emergency—the potential danger of a stabilization programme triggering these political crises is examined next. The OECD study, with its database covering 23 African countries from 1980 to 1990 (Haggard, Lafay and Morrisson 1995), was utilized for this examination.

The most interesting example of an LHE is the crisis of 1989 in Venezuela because the country had a democratic regime and the highest per capita income of all the countries analysed in the project. Nevertheless, Venezuela is an excellent example of a limited humanitarian emergency. The stabilization programme and adjustment had been delayed as long as possible by the ruling Social Democratic party in order to win the presidential election. But after the election, it became necessary to introduce drastic stabilization measures, including sharp increases in the prices of petroleum, various public services, and goods produced by public enterprises. The increase in fuel prices pushed up urban public transport fares, which were enforced at the worst possible time, at the end of the month. The result was massive riots and looting, not only by the poor but also by the middle class. The army's efforts to quell the situation resulted in 300 deaths according to the official reports. Unofficial reports list the death toll at about 1,000. Partial blame[16] for the crisis can be placed on the IMF for its insistence in promoting shock therapy instead of a more gradual approach preferred by the Venezuelan government. The IMF acknowledged the violence in some respect as a limited humanitarian crisis, and subsequently approved a revision of the stand-by agreement to include a compensatory programme that in 1990 covered 73 per cent of poor households.

This crisis serves to highlight two obvious facts: (i) harsh repression of political turmoil after a stabilization programme may escalate to a limited humanitarian emergency; and (ii) confrontations of this type could have

---

[16] Responsibility for the mishandling of information and for the poor timing of the measures must be charged to the Venezuelan government.

been easily avoided with more appropriate timing of the stabilization measures and with compensatory transfers to poor households.

There are several other examples of similar, albeit less dramatic crises. In Morocco, agitation in the universities began in 1981 after a reduction in student grants. This was compounded by an ill-conceived stabilization programme. A price increase of over 40 per cent for essential foodstuffs was introduced but following hostile reaction by unions and opposition parties, these were reduced to 20 per cent a week later. A general strike, nevertheless, was staged in Casablanca in June and spread throughout the country. The ensuing riots and harsh repression by the army resulted in tens of fatalities and hundreds injured. The finance minister was dismissed and stabilization programme postponed.

De Janvry's *et al.* study (1994) on Ecuador cites many similar incidents. Between 1982 and 1991, three presidents successively tried to apply stabilization programmes in order to reduce the budget deficit, but each effort caused strikes and, at times, riots. The economy was paralysed by a general strike; the unions halted work in the oil sector and the president was forced to send the army to re-start production. During the turmoil and suppression, hundreds of people were arrested or wounded. Some were killed. These events exceed 'soft' repression and, in some instances, can be considered a limited humanitarian emergency.

Africa has experienced similar incidents, ranging from soft repression to limited humanitarian emergencies. In Côte d'Ivoire, the government undertook a stabilization programme in 1990 and announced a reduction in salaries of 10 per cent for the private sector and of 15 to 40 per cent for civil servants. This triggered numerous demonstrations and strikes in the universities and schools, banks, and in the health sector. In April 1990, a demonstration supporting President Houphouet-Boigny turned into a two-day riot during which a young demonstrator was killed. The wage cuts were postponed but restlessness persisted with transport strikes and demonstrations by soldiers who took over the television station and the airport. A few days later, hundreds of police also went on strike. These events were a threat to the regime itself and the unrest lasted until September. Stability returned only after the re-election of Houphouet-Boigny in October. These troubled incidents do not meet the standard criteria of a CHE, but they did constitute a temporary collapse of the state and of the urban society.

The stabilization programme applied in Gabon in 1989 had similar consequences. The wages of civil servants and of workers in the parastatal sector were cut, and producer prices of cocoa and coffee were reduced by 50 per cent. In January 1990, these measures triggered strikes in the university and schools, and led to riots and looting which focused on Lebanese shops. In spite of a state of emergency being declared, 300 persons were arrested and 50 wounded. In March 1990, new strikes were set off in public utilities, banks, and the manufacturing sector. Turmoil spread all over the country, culminating by June in a rebellion in Port Gentil with barricades in the streets. Two people were killed, many public buildings and shops were burnt, embassies were closed, and some 1,600 individuals, mainly foreigners, were evacuated. Dozens of people were arrested. The government maintained the state of emergency for some weeks in Port Gentil and in one of the provinces. As the Gabon case indicated, the stabilization programme induced a situation that bordered on a limited humanitarian emergency, particularly for the shopkeepers and foreigners whose lives were threatened.

During its history as an independent nation, Nigeria has been characterized by political, ethnic, and religious conflicts and, in some instances, by LHEs. Some of the instability was the result of stabilization measures. In conjunction with a stand-by agreement with the IMF in December 1988, the government applied a rigorous monetary and fiscal policy, and fired a thousand Nigeria Airways employees. The price of gasoline was increased by 43 per cent, prompting strong protest by the unions. In June 1989, several riots shook the main towns and hundreds of demonstrators were killed by the army. The students went on strike and the universities were closed. Certain well-known people were arrested simply because they had protested openly against adjustment. Despite these strong reactions, the stabilization programme was applied. The government, however, introduced compensatory measures, such as price reductions for essential foodstuffs and medicine. Thus the events of June 1989, marked by hundreds of deaths, closed universities and a state of emergency, can be considered as an LHE. Unions continued to protest and to instigate strikes until the end of 1989, but the June crisis was not repeated. A conflict of this magnitude was not surprising in a country like Nigeria, which is permanently unstable.

Senegal is a good example of a reverse situation. In the 1980s, several adjustment programmes were applied which set off many demonstrations and strikes but government reaction was always limited to soft repression, even in its riot control efforts. Obviously, it can be stated that it is not possible to compare Senegal and Nigeria because of the different size of the two countries and of their populations. However, situations similar to those experienced in Nigeria have also been observed in Sierra Leone, a neighbouring country the same size as Senegal. In each country, stabilization programmes prompted unstability: strikes, demonstrations and riots (including looting and burning of shops or public buildings) that were put down with harsh repression, causing tens of deaths.

As these example situations indicate, it is clear that the political consequences of stabilization programmes are mixed. In some countries, reactions were similar to those experienced in European countries, whereas in other African countries, stabilization programmes induced serious conflict, harsh repression and eventually LHEs. To further examine this type of crisis, three other examples are given: Congo (Brazzaville), Kenya, and Zambia.

In 1990, the Congo government signed a stand-by agreement with the IMF. Two weeks later, a three-day general strike was staged, followed by a stoppage in the petroleum sector, an industry essential for Congo as its major source of foreign exchange. Finally, numerous strikes occurred throughout the country, followed by riots, looting and arson in the schools and shops, forcing the government to close all schools and the university. A strike by the bakers caused a general shortage of bread. These confrontations were the result of the people's refusal to submit to stabilization measures that included cuts in wages and in student grants, and of their reluctance to accept privatization. Considered as a threat to the socialist regime, the stand-by agreement was rejected by the masses. The government retaliated with repression, causing injuries to tens of people. Eventually the government cancelled some of the stabilization measures and the prime minister resigned.

In Kenya, reactions were different. First, in 1982, after a stand-by agreement with IMF and a structural adjustment loan from the World Bank, the army attempted a coup with the support of university professors. The government took vigorous counter-measures that resulted in more than 200 killed, 500 wounded and 2,000 arrested. A curfew was imposed for a week. The second episode took place in 1990. Some people were killed when they protested against work in the shanty towns. This escalated into strikes, demonstrations, and riots in Nairobi, which gave rise to harsh repression. Twenty deaths occurred and more than 1,000 people were arrested. The university was closed and students were sent home. While the term 'complex humanitarian emergency' may be an overstatement in the case of Kenya, the situation in the country can definitely be classified as a limited humanitarian emergency.

In Zambia, permanent macroeconomic disequilibria necessitated the introduction of several stabilization programmes. After each introduction, there was a succession of strikes and riots, which evolved into crises in 1986 and 1990. In 1986, the government eliminated subsidies and increased the price of maize by 100 per cent, causing a series of riots and looting during which many shops and houses were destroyed. Government repression ended in 15 people being killed. Ultimately the maize price increase was cancelled. In February 1990, the government announced privatization measures, and again the price of maize doubled. These caused huge riots in Lusaka with demonstrations by 100,000 people, as well as a takeover of the radio and TV stations by mutinous soldiers. The government imposed a curfew, closed the universities, and arrested many students. More than 50 people were killed during efforts to control the riots.

The reactions of Egypt and North Africa to stabilization programmes are more difficult to analyse because the resultant unrest can be linked not only to the unpopular measures introduced by the SPs, but also to the Islamic opposition. The Islamic parties' support was based on religious discontentment and increasing hardships that were, at least partly, caused by the stabilization measures. These two factors together served to ignite confrontation. In Egypt in early 1986, a stand-by agreement with the IMF triggered a mutiny by the troops and more than 100 people were killed during its repression. In retaliation, the public prosecutor demanded that 1,205 mutineers be sentenced to death.

In Algeria, increased prices for foodstuffs gave rise in October 1988 to riots in the capital with looting and fires. More than 500 people were killed as the army took action to subdue the riots. The anger of the population was probably fuelled by the Islamic propaganda (some of Egyptian mutineers were militant Islamists) and it is difficult to separate the influence exerted by the Islamic forces and by the unpopular stabilization measures in triggering the conflict. The situation was more straightforward in Tunisia where the price of bread increased 100 per cent during the last days of 1983 when subsidies were cut. Looting and subsequent riots in towns in the south were harshly repressed with more than 100 casualties. The price increases were cancelled and the minister of the Home Office dismissed. Apparently this rebellion in the south was sparked by adverse stabilization measures.[17] Libyan and Tunisian Islamists, promoting popular dissatisfaction, may have had some influence also in this incident.

It is obvious from these incidents that in Egypt and North Africa the relationship between unstability, harsh repression, and stabilization programmes cannot be clearly defined because other factors, such as Islamic discontentment, play a role.[18] Therefore, events relating to Sub-Saharan Africa alone are more relevant. This chapter has reviewed seven examples of harsh repression. Each has resulted in numerous casualties, injuries, and arrests as well as incidents of looting and burning. Based on our sample, which included 18 Sub-Saharan countries, it can be concluded that roughly in half of the cases a crisis of some sort evolved from the introduction of stabilization measures. But this assertion needs to be qualified. In some countries—as in Côte d'Ivoire—several stabilization programmes have been applied, yet only one triggered a severe crisis. Therefore, it is more accurate to state that the risk of a crisis developing from stabilization measures existed in one out of two countries. However, as can be noted from the examples presented, these crises were relatively short term,

[17] Cf. Haggard, Lafay and Morrisson (1995) for a correlation between this measure and political unrest.

[18] There is, nevertheless, one exception—the crisis in Morocco in 1981. The dissatisfaction of the urban population was fuelled by the unions, as no Islamic group existed in the country at that time.

lasting a few days or, at a maximum, weeks. Thus, a political crisis set off by stabilization measures differs in this respect from the heavy social costs caused by some SPs.

A political crisis results from a combination of circumstances, whereas a social crisis is structural and lasts a long time. Any stabilization programme or measure which diminishes the already very limited purchasing power of the masses of urban poor who live in shanty towns, who are not integrated in the modern sector and who often lack basic services such as primary schooling, water, sewerage, etc., can touch off serious demonstrations or riots. As governments often do not benefit from the legitimacy of universal suffrage, they fear these confrontations and are prone to use harsh repression. This creates on the one hand a vicious circle of strikes, demonstrations, riots, looting, fires, murders by rebels, and, on the other, arrests, on-the-spot executions or trials which pass out death sentences. These situations have escalated far beyond the soft repression experienced in developed countries, and may, in some towns, be approaching the severity of an LHE.

Such crises can be avoided by recognizing two important factors. First, it is obvious that policies which alleviate poverty in towns can limit potential violence. Second, rising consumer prices are the main cause of demonstrations that eventually lead to riots. Thus, if subsidies need to be reduced, steps should be taken by the government to maintain subsidized products for the benefit of the poor. Careful planning is also needed to introduce price increases gradually, to influence public opinion, and to ensure judicious timing.[19] It is essential to avoid the first negative reaction to an unpopular measure. Once the feeling of frustration and exclusion of the masses is vented in demonstrations, it is very difficult to stop and easily leads to riots, to suppressive countermeasures, and to casualties.

4. The Social Impact of Structural Adjustment

While stabilization programmes pursue the sole objective of reducing the external deficit of a country by means of a single set of measures, structural adjustment (SA) involves a larger range of reform measures. Although all structural adjustment programmes adhere to a mutual goal (increasing supply) and to a common philosophy (liberalizing both domestic and foreign trade), each SA is designed to respond to the specific problems of the country concerned. Liberalization, depending on the country, can focus on agriculture, manufactures, finance or utilities. In some cases, in-depth reform or privatization of a part of the public sector

---

[19] Grants for secondary school and university students are politically a very sensitive issue, and efforts should be made to avoid any reduction in student allowances, with the exception of the well-to-do.

is necessary if this is large and inefficient. Nearly all SAs include liberalization of foreign trade, the most common component of structural adjustment.

The social and political impacts created by structural adjustment are very different from those induced by stabilization programmes, which have an immediate—and often very negative—effect for poor households. Structural adjustment takes more time to implement and hence its consequences become apparent only after a certain delay. Moreover, SA rarely has a negative impact on poor households. Usually structural adjustment brings about complex and contradictory consequences, i.e. as in the case of freed interest rates which are an advantage for individuals lending or saving, but a disadvantage for those borrowing money. Likewise, import liberalization may benefit consumers but can also generate resistance among entrepreneurs and those working in the formerly protected sectors. Because of these different distributional consequences, governments are able to build coalitions of winning groups to neutralize or offset political reactions from the losers. A government can readily avoid political trouble and violence with this strategy.

Trade liberalization can induce resistance, but this resistance has nothing to do with the social costs for poor households or a limited humanitarian emergency. For instance, liberalization in Ecuador caused discontentment among certain entrepreneurs and, as a result, President Cordero lost support. President Borja, his successor, also encountered hostility from the private sector and investments fell, as entrepreneurs feared a decline in profits in the protected sectors. The same reaction was also observed in Venezuela's entrepreneurs in sectors benefiting from protection. In Morocco, opposition to liberalization was massive and ranged from entrepreneurs, senior officials, left-wing parties, and academic economists. The communist newspaper was resolutely opposed to import liberalization. But it is evident that these reactions do not pose a serious threat to governments. Entrepreneurs and workers in the protected sectors are unlikely to contest liberalization. Furthermore, as liberalization does not add to the poverty of a country, demonstrations and riots are not likely to develop. On the contrary, these measures may introduce some gains for poor households. The downward pressure on prices of manufactured goods improves the terms of trade between the agricultural and the non-agricultural sectors to the benefit of the farmer. As the majority of the poor are smallholder peasants, this downward pressure increases the purchasing power of this group and lessens impoverishment. Moreover, the growth of exports of agricultural and manufactured goods has a favourable effect on income distribution and poverty reduction.[20]

---

[20] Agricultural exports produced on large plantations are an exception.

Consequently in balancing the losses and gains of liberalization, the over-all social impact is often positive.

Internal liberalization generally has the same effect. Farmers benefit from the liberalization of agricultural prices because price controls are used to appropriate agricultural surplus to finance the non-agricultural sector. In addition, farmers may profit from the cancellation of monopolies granted to state enterprises that had overcharged for their services.

Financial liberalization has the tendency to add to the financial costs of enterprises through increased interest rates, provoking discontent on the part of businesses. But poor households, who are able to save, gain from positive real rates. In the case of Morocco, special foreign accounts with higher rates of interest were set up to help migrant workers. But it must also be remembered that financial liberalization is linked to anti-inflationary policy and that poor households are hit more severely by inflation tax than rich households.

As these diverse examples of structural adjustment show, governments are able to solicit support for various SA measures from wide sectors of the population, thus minimizing risks of political turmoil and the need for eventual harsh repression. As the cases cited also show, these measures never have a large negative social impact and there is no risk of increasing poverty.

But this optimistic conclusion is challenged by the problems in privatization. In countries with a large public sector, privatization (or the reorganization) of state-owned enterprises gives rise to negative social and political effects. If the public sector is extensive, lay-offs can significantly increase unemployment. It takes some time before exporting enterprises begin to hire and when they do, they do not recruit former public sector workers. Consequently, increasing unemployment and poverty become serious social problems. It was against this background that the World Bank financed a compensation programme in Ghana to help the unemployed set up their own businesses or small farms.

Privatization also induces serious political problems by threatening the interests of many people. These may include senior civil servants hoping for well-paid posts in the parastatal sector as well as managers and employees of enterprises that enjoy the security of public employment and wages comparable to the private sector. These potential losers are affected immediately by privatization and, if the parastatal sector is large, they have considerable political weight. In contrast, the advantages of reform become evident only after several years and are very diffuse, making it difficult—if not impossible—for the government to mobilize support for privatization. Privatization can provoke strikes in such strategic sectors as transportation, mining, petroleum, electricity, etc., and violent reactions in the form of demonstrations and riots. If reform coincides with a stabilization programme, the opposition coalition can be very large and the risk of violence very high. These events do not necessarily classify as limited humanitarian emergencies, but the unemployment of thousands of workers is a genuine social cost and the subsequent repression has both a human and political cost.

Nevertheless, in the long term structural adjustment—including privatization—has positive effects. Liberalization of domestic markets and the development of a market economy favours economic integration, which increases the economic costs of political conflicts. In this respect, it may help to avert harsh repression or a limited humanitarian emergency in the future. Some of political conflicts result from rent-seeking strategies. The major benefits of rent-seeking will be eliminated with privatization, which in turn may reduce the possibility of political conflict. An assessment of structural adjustment would not be accurate without acknowledging both the long-term benefits as well as the short-term costs of privatization.

5. Social Costs and Limited or Complex Humanitarian Emergencies without Stabilization Programmes

Stabilization programmes have been characterized at times as being damaging programmes which lead to social costs and soft repression or on occasion, albeit rarely, to a limited humanitarian emergency with high social costs such as a substantial increase in infant mortality rates or harsh repression with numerous casualties. To provide an accurate comparison, it is also necessary to analyse the consequences of non-adjustment and of an autarkic strategy. Indeed, it is impossible to avoid autarkic strategy if a government adopts a nonconforming stand with regard to adjustment[21] (cases of political aid by a friendly country are excluded).[22] Thus, taking into account the costs of adjustment, the main issue is not whether a country should accept or refuse adjustment. Instead, it needs to be determined which alternative—adjustment or an autarkic policy (aiming for national self-sufficiency by means of drastic cuts in imports and zero borrowing from abroad)—is preferred. In order to answer this fairly, the costs of each option must be compared. The experiences of Ghana and Algeria, two countries which chose non-adjustment, are examined in an effort to estimate the costs of this alternative solution.

In Ghana, from 1972 to 1983 when an adjustment programme was finally introduced, successive governments had refused this option despite increasing disequilibria. In 1972, two-thirds of the Busia devaluation was reversed, a strict system of import controls was reinstated, and price controls were intensified. The autarkic policy manifested in a

---

[21] Autarkic strategy implies adjustment by means of a single measure—the exchange rate—without the normal procedure involved in stabilization programmes.

[22] This type of aid is very costly in terms of national independence.

negative growth of GDP, a 50 per cent decline in cocoa revenue (the main cash crop), and external deficits followed by increased import rationing. In 1982, imports amounted to just 18 per cent of the 1968 level, a fact which serves to highlight the effects of an autarkic policy. The decline of GDP as the population increased at a rate of nearly 3 per cent a year resulted in the per capita income dropping over 35 per cent in 11 years. The share of the poor was considerably higher in 1983 than in 1972 and by 1983 the per capita calorie availability in the country had dropped to 65 per cent of the national needs. This figure in 1972 had averaged about 95 per cent. By 1983, the majority of children under five years suffered from malnutrition. Infant mortality rate declined during the period, but remained high. Children under five made up 19 per cent of the population, but accounted for half of all reported deaths. As a consequence of decreasing public receipts, government expenditure on health care had declined by 1983 to about only one-quarter of the 1972 level in per capita terms. Nevertheless, some improvements must be acknowledged: the ratio of people per registered medical practitioner declined significantly during the 1970s. But the great reduction in the availability of drugs and the weakening commitment by medical staff in the face of declining real salaries resulted in a drop in the number of outpatient attendances from 11 million in 1975 to less than 4 million in 1984. Finally, the employment situation also deteriorated. The concept of open unemployment may be of limited relevance in the case of Ghana, but open unemployment rate increases exceeding 100 per cent were observed for the urban centres from 1970 to 1980.

These statistics prove that non-adjustment as a strategy also has high social costs. An increase in the number of the poor and the unemployed, and a drop in health expenditures were clearly social costs that caused suffering to the majority of the population. The drop of per capita calorie availability from 95 to 65 per cent certainly represented a very high social cost. The adjustment policy in effect since 1983 also induced certain social costs but, based on the estimates of Roe and Schneider (1992), these seemed to be much lower.

The case of Algeria is much more complex. The civil war between the Islamists and the army caused tens or hundreds of deaths each week. Other forms of violence such as rape, torture, incarcerations, arson, and censorship as well as the stifling of democracy were common occurrences, and a part of the population lived in circumstances resembling a humanitarian emergency. But as may be emphasized by some scholars, the crisis was linked to the political and religious conflicts of the country and may not have had any bearing on adjustment or non-adjustment. Reality, however, contradicts this theory. The Islamic party was able to recruit numerous young men to its mercenary ranks because the rate of unemployment among this particular group exceeded 50 per cent. Had these young men been working, the Islamic party would have gained very few, if any, supporters. This extreme rate of unemployment stems from the autarkic strategy in effect since Algeria's independence and particularly during Boumediénne's leadership. Socialist strategy, based on collectivization (also for the agricultural sector) and central planning, was promoted during 1967–79. The government, repeating the Stalinist strategy, favoured an inward-growth model and gave priority to capital-intensive sectors as steel production, chemicals, and building materials.[23] Thus, there were huge investments, but these created very few jobs. At the same time, the development of small or middle-sized enterprises in labour-intensive sectors was repressed.

After 1980, and particularly after the fall of the East European communist regimes, successive governments have tried to liberalize the Algerian economy. But the socialist structure has not changed and disequilibria has increased.[24] For example, the debt service-exports ratio rose from 20 per cent in 1980 to 82 per cent in 1993. During the 1980s, the incremental capital/output ratio reached 12, the rate of youth unemployment (16–25 years) exceeded 50 per cent, and households could not spend their cash because there were increased shortages of goods. In 1991, adjustment was undertaken, thanks to a stand-by agreement with the IMF, but in early 1992, with the resignation of the president and the nomination of a 'Haut Comité d'État', the programme was postponed, and protectionism was intensified. In fact, it would have been impossible to apply SPs or structural adjustment measures in Algeria because the coalition of hostile interest groups is sufficiently strong to block the reforms. In this respect, Algeria continues to be a good example of the consequences of non-adjustment.

It is not possible to state categorically that the present Algerian crisis (which in some respect is a complex humanitarian emergency) is a direct manifestation of non-adjustment. But the Islamic opposition would have been weakened, if the government in the early 1980s had decided on adjustment with stabilization measures, privatization, and liberalization similar to what were carried out in Eastern Europe after 1990. Tunisia witnessed similar Islamic movements in the early 1980s. The country went through a socialist period in the 1960s, but in 1969–70, market mechanism was restored. Land, handicraft industry, and all retail as well as wholesale trade were reverted to the private sector. Then in 1987–88, total liberalization[25] of Tunisia's economy, because of adjustment, changed the functioning of the country. By 1990, Tunisia's per capita income was 10 per cent higher than that of Algeria, whereas in 1960 it had been 37 per cent lower. Most importantly:

---

[23] For an overview of this period and of reforms in the 1990s, see Benissad (1994).
[24] Agriculture is an exception; certain progress in decentralization has been made.
[25] This included most prices as well as a liberalization of the financial sector, of imports and by means of privatization, also of some parastatal enterprises.

(i) the rate of unemployment among the young in Tunisia was less than 20 per cent, compared with more than 50 per cent in Algeria; and

(ii) the incidence of poverty was much lower in Tunisia than in Algeria.

Without the devastating rate of unemployment and debilitating poverty, growth of the Islamist opposition in Algeria would have been impossible. But these factors became crucial because the Islamic party in Algeria recruited young jobless men for terrorism and provided social services and aid to poor households through the mosque. Yet, these two factors are also linked to the country's rejection of adjustment. The present crisis evolved from the Islamic movement, which incidentally is present in all Arab countries, and from the adverse circumstances induced by Algeria's stand of non-adjustment.

6. Social Costs of the Recent Crisis in Indonesia (1997–98)

Indonesia, where a dramatic and brutal increase in the number of poor people has been attributed to an economic crisis, offers an opportunity for analysis. Although the financial and economic crisis has been felt in several Southeast and East Asian countries simultaneously, this analysis focuses on Indonesia because the threat of a limited humanitarian emergency, or perhaps even a complex humanitarian emergency is much higher here than in other countries.[26]

There are widely cited figures which indicate that poverty incidence has risen, according to Central Bureau of Statistics, to 39 per cent from a pre-crisis level of 11 per cent, or according to ILO, possibly to even 48 per cent. Obviously, if the number of the poor was quadrupled during the course of only a year, a limited, or even a complex humanitarian emergency may threaten. But these estimates are based on outdated household surveys and the ILO figure results from the highly debatable hypothesis in which ILO assumes an 80 per cent rate of inflation and unchanged nominal incomes. This is impossible because in such circumstances, sellers would have automatically benefited from rising prices. True, poverty indeed increased significantly, but recent data offer a less pessimistic view.[27]

The Indonesian crisis is mainly an urban one: the percentage of the poor in cities and towns rose from 5 per cent in 1996 to more than 9 per cent in 1999, while the relative increase in rural poverty was much less, from 15 per cent to 18 per cent, respectively. Moreover, it was the sharp reduction in the non-agricultural sectors that explains this increase, as nearly 40 per

---

[26] For example, GDP is ten times higher in South Korea than in Indonesia, and two and a half times higher in Thailand.

[27] Data were based on households in the '100 Villages' survey conducted both in July and August 1998, as well as on the 'Indonesian Family Life Survey', which tracked changes during 1997–98.

cent of rural households earned their main income from activities other than farming. Urban unemployment was rising but rather slowly because poor people could not afford to be 'unemployed'. In fact in some cases, they worked longer hours, or shifted increasingly to informal activities where the wages were lower. Real wages for the unskilled fell 20–40 per cent in the towns as well as in some provinces, a fact which attributed to the number of urban poor being doubled. The wage drop also explains the changes in expenditure shares: an increase in the share of staple foods and a decrease in meat as well as in all non-food items. Furthermore, taking into account the drop in the absolute value of incomes, many poor households may have been forced to reduce their food intake. This assumption can be checked against nutritional status indicators. Although the situation for children under 9 years improved during 1997–98,[28] the reverse was true for adults and the percentage of the population with body mass index less than 18 increased. There was also an increase in the percentage of adults reporting that they were ill, while the percentage reporting that their children were ill dropped. On the other hand, there was no significant change in enrolment rates in primary school and it can therefore be concluded that since 1997 the adult population of the poor suffered more severely from the crisis than their children.

It should be mentioned that this estimation of an increase in adult poverty and malnutrition is the average for Indonesia, a country of nearly 200 million inhabitants. The situation may have been worse in certain urban areas where, for instance, the closure of the only source of employment would hit a community hard. Poor rural households also suffered from conditions not related to the economic crisis such as the adverse effects of El Niño, droughts or forest fires.

Local emergencies did occur in Indonesia, but these did not escalate into a CHE. These events, however, did not result from stabilization programmes *per se* but from a financial and economic crisis caused by the massive outflow of short-term capital from the region, which accelerated inflation and the dramatic reduction in formal, non-agricultural employment. The depreciation of the exchange rate increased the prices of drugs and of diagnostic tests two or threefold, while a 50 per cent increase in the price of rice between August 1997 and February 1998 reduced real income by 12 per cent. All of this was disastrous for the poor households.

The stabilization programme which involved massive devaluation, substantial reductions in expenditures, and high interest rates contributed to substantial social costs of the country. To be sure, the adjustment programme supported by the IMF and other international agencies included several measures aimed at poverty alleviation with subsidies on rice, corn, and wheat flour at a value of 0.5 per cent of GDP in 1998–99, subsidies for

[28] The percentage of children with Z score ; < –2 standard deviation for height-weight for age decreased.

petroleum products and electricity (1 per cent of GDP), community-based public works, financing for basic drugs and health centres, and the provision of shelters for the poor. On the other hand, while acknowledging the highly negative impact of the SP on the urban poor, its benefits for the smallholder exporting farmers also need to be recognized.

The financial crisis in Indonesia offers an illustration of the social and human costs of an economic crisis and its ensuing SP. The Indonesian situation, similar to the Russian crisis of 1998, entailed very high devaluation rates and price increases, which soared to 80–100 per cent within a few months. In each country, these increases and the subsequent plummeting of pensions and salaries in real terms caused millions of people to fall into poverty or even extreme poverty.

7. Conclusion

Before presenting a summary of the results, the author would like to point out that a limited or a complex humanitarian emergency can evolve independently of whether an adjustment or a non-adjustment policy was in effect in that particular country prior to the emergency. This is illustrated by Klugman and Stewart (1997) in their study on Uganda: 'The relatively poor macroeconomic performance followed rather than preceded the most horrendous episodes of violence. Amin and then Obote II were largely responsible for instigating violence, which in turn led to economic regress.' When Amin ousted Obote in 1971, the economic situation of Uganda was relatively good, but it was Amin who led his country to chaos by institutionalizing violence and murders. Medical facilities were destroyed, health indicators worsened, primary and secondary enrolment rates fell, and daily calorie supply dropped by 25 per cent.

Table 6.1 above presents a synopsis of the costs of adjustment. It is clear that adjustment without any social costs and without any repression (the two being interrelated) is possible, but is rather rare. Asia is an exception. Even the most critical evaluation shows that the majority of Asian countries have succeeded in introducing adjustment without social costs or conflict. But it is equally clear that adjustment programmes which lead to limited humanitarian emergencies are also rare. An LHE may occur in two different situations. First, it is a hidden, silent disaster that affects locations already afflicted with serious poverty before adjustment, compounded by the high price increases for staple foods of the poor, and the absence of a safety net that could have been incorporated into adjustment measures. It manifests in the form of a substantial increase of malnutrition and infant mortality rates, a drop in the daily calorie intake, etc.

The second type of limited humanitarian emergency develops when certain unpopular measures—price increases for food or public trans-

Table 6.1. Social costs and limited humanitarian emergencies with adjustment or non-adjustment

Level of social costs	Adjustment countries	Non-adjustment countries
No social costs	Malaysia Indonesia (1983–86)	
Social costs only	Indonesia (1997–98) Morocco (urban areas only) Côte d'Ivoire[c] Ecuador Chile Several African and Latin American countries[d]	Similar costs in 86 countries[a] 32 countries[b]
Social costs with an LHE	Few examples from the UNICEF study for the early 1980s[e]	Ghana Algeria
No repression	Malaysia Indonesia (1983–86)	
Soft repression	Senegal Several African countries	
Repression without an LHE	Indonesia (1997–98) Ecuador Côte d'Ivoire (1990) Several African countries	
Harsh repression with an LHE	Venezuela (1989) Tunisia (1983) Gabon (1990) Nigeria (1989) Morocco (1981)	Algeria

[a] Data from Kakwani, Makonnen and van der Gaag (1990).
[b] Jaayarajah, Branson and Sen (1996).
[c] Social costs were apparent in urban areas only during 1980–85, but expanded to entire country during 1985–90.
[d] For Latin America, social costs were more frequent and more debilitating during the early 1980s than during 1988–93.
[e] Social costs evolved only in certain locations, and on a temporary basis.

portation—trigger demonstrations, strikes and riots. These are repressed so severely that tens or hundreds of persons are killed and daily lives are temporarily disrupted. This type of LHE generally lasts for only a few days, and its human costs, although dramatic, are less than those of the hidden, silent 'limited humanitarian emergency'.

In conclusion, it can be summarized that the most frequent results of SPs consist of social and human costs with a certain degree of confrontation which may entail repression, but almost never a limited humanitarian emergency. Nevertheless, the risk of an LHE exists and this factor must be taken into account in the formulation and design of stabilization programmes. It must also be added that the risk of an LHE seems to increase if stabilization is attempted without the approval of IMF and subsequent IMF credits. Nafziger and Auvinen (Chapter 3) indicate that IMF adjustment programmes are econometrically inversely associated with a complex humanitarian emergency. The authors explain this result by the adverse impact of slow (or negative) growth as a determinant of a CHE. Presumably, a similar correlation exists between negative growth and limited humanitarian emergencies. Therefore, any government that meets IMF conditions will benefit from loans granted by the World Bank, other international agencies, bilateral contributors, and commercial banks as well as from debt reductions that it would not have been granted otherwise. Usually, these inflows of capital reverse negative growth and thus eliminate the risk of a limited or a complex humanitarian emergency.

Table 6.1 also indicates the costs of non-adjustment. Social costs are as frequent in non-adjusting countries as in adjusting countries and both types of limited humanitarian emergencies may occur in non-adjusting countries. Consequently, there is no reason to advocate non-adjustment in order to avoid social costs and limited humanitarian emergencies. The adjustment programmes of the Asian countries could provide useful lessons in this respect. It is more rational to recognize the risks involved in adjustment measures and to improve stabilization programmes so that reformed adjustment policy is more gradual, more sensitive of its impact on poor households, and more growth-oriented. These policies could minimize the heavy social and human costs of adjustment, and thus avoid conflict and eventual limited humanitarian emergencies.

References

Benissad, H. (1994). 'Algérie: Restructurations et Réformes Économiques 1979–1993'. Alger: Office de Publications Universitaires.

Bourguignon, F., J. De Melo, and C. Morrisson (1991). 'Adjustment with Growth and Equity: A Symposium'. *World Development*.

Bourguignon, F., and C. Morrisson (1992). 'Adjustment and Equity in Developing Countries, a New Approach'. Paris: OECD Development Centre.

Cornia A., R. Jolly, and F. Stewart (1987). *Adjustment with a Human Face*. New York: UNICEF.

de Janvry, A., E. Graham, E. Sadoulet, R. Espinel, W. Spurrier, H. Nissen, and F. Welsch (1994). *The Political Feasibility of Adjustment in Ecuador and Venezuela*. Paris: OECD Development Centre.

Diop F., K. Hill, and I. Sirageldin (1991). *Economic Crisis, Structural Adjustment and Health in Africa*. Washington, DC: Population and Human Resources Department. World Bank.

Dorosh P., R. Bernier, and A. Sarris (1990). 'Macroeconomic Adjustment and the Poor, the Case of Madagascar'. Cornell Food and Nutrition Policy Program.

Glewwe, P. and D. de Tray (1988). 'The Poor during Adjustment: A Case Study of the Côte d'Ivoire'. LSMS Working Paper No. 47. Washington, DC: World Bank.

Grootaert, C. (1992). *The Evolution of Welfare and Poverty during Structural Change and Economic Recession, the Case of Côte d'Ivoire, 1985–88*. Washington, DC: Poverty and Social Policy Division, World Bank.

Grosh, M. (1990). *Social Spending in Latin America: the Story of the 1980s*. Washington, DC: World Bank.

Haggard S., J-D. Lafay, and C. Morrisson (1995). *The Political Feasibility of Adjustment in Developing Countries*. Paris: OECD Development Centre.

Jayarajah, C., W. Branson, and B. Sen (1996). *Social Dimensions of Adjustment. World Bank Experience, 1980–93*. Washington, DC: World Bank.

Kakwani, N., E. Makonnen, and J. van der Gaag (1990). *Structural Adjustment and Living Conditions in Developing Countries*. Washington, DC: Population and Human Resources Department, World Bank.

Kakwani, N. (1995). 'Structural Adjustment and Performances in Living Standards in Developing Countries'. *Development and Change*.

Klugman, J., and F. Stewart (1997). 'Socio-economic Causes of Conflict: A Comparative Study of Kenya and Uganda'. Paris: OECD Development Centre. Mimeo.

Morley, S. (1995). *Poverty and Inequality in Latin America, The Impact of Adjustment and Recovery in the 1990s*. Baltimore: The Johns Hopkins University Press.

Ravallion, M., and M. Huppi (1989). *Poverty and Undernutrition in Indonesia during the 1980s*. Washington, DC: Agriculture and Rural Development Department, World Bank.

Rivero, C., R. Ascencio, and J. Vinagre (1991). 'The Impact of Economic Crisis and Adjustment on Health Care in Mexico'. Innocenti Occasional Papers, No. 13. Florence: UNICEF.

Roe, A., and H. Schneider (1992). *Adjustment and Equity in Ghana*. Paris: OECD Development Centre.

Schneider, H. (1991). *Adjustment and Equity in Côte d'Ivoire*. Paris: OECD Development Centre.

Stewart, F. (1992). 'Protecting the Poor during Adjustment in Latin America and the Caribbean in the 1980s. How Adequate Was the World Bank Response?' Oxford: International Development Centre, University of Oxford. Mimeo.

7

Political Causes of Humanitarian Emergencies

KALEVI J. HOLSTI

1. Introduction

This is a diagnostic exercise to locate political sources of contemporary humanitarian emergencies. Several assumptions guide the inquiry. First, although the aetiology of each humanitarian emergency has distinct features, I reflect the bias of social scientists in holding that a comparative methodology can uncover both patterns and significant anomalies. Second, the task is to identify political sources of the dependent variable. This is a disciplinary convention that substantially simplifies the analysis, but it necessarily omits economic, demographic, geographic, cultural, and historical conditions, all of which may play relevant roles. I will abstract out of those very complex situations those political factors that seem particularly relevant. By political, I refer to structures, actions, practices, and norms that relate to access to, or allocations of, formal positions of authority within the society. Finally, a comparative study must be alert to non-events. It is important to know what conditions correlate with the incidence of humanitarian emergencies; it is equally important to acknowledge that humanitarian emergencies are not inevitable where certain conditions prevail. We need to ask, also, given that a number of conditions predisposing toward humanitarian emergencies exist in society or country X, why did not such an emergency occur? The entire discussion below is thus set in probabilistic terms. If, as I suggest in the body of the text, there are certain conditions and/or processes that increase the likelihood of a humanitarian emergency, there is no certainty that such an emergency will in fact ensue.

2. Locating the Political: The Problem of the Modern State

A diagnostic exercise begins by hunting for clues among the numerous past cases of humanitarian emergencies. The common denominator in humanitarian emergencies is armed conflict and population displacement.

Disease and hunger often accompany violence and forced population movements, but they are rarely sufficient conditions by themselves for a humanitarian emergency. Occasional natural disasters do play a role, and while the politics of relief efforts are ubiquitous and sometimes even prolong human suffering, the analysis will examine only those cases where violence and war are present.

Humanitarian emergencies do not occur randomly through time or location. For example, Gurr's study (1996) shows a clear and dramatic increase of the level of threat to endangered minorities through the 1980s and a slow decline beginning about the middle of the 1990s. More significantly, numerous data sources indicate that almost all such emergencies have taken place within relatively new states in the third world or in the post-Soviet republics. For the period 1993–95, for example, Raimo Väyrynen's study of humanitarian emergencies (Chapter 2) indicates that all of the cases have taken place either in what is known as the third world or in post-socialist states. Second, 79 per cent of the emergencies in Väyrynen's list of 24 incidents occurred in new states. Only five states in the list (Afghanistan, Colombia, Haiti, Ethiopia, and Liberia) have a history of statehood that precedes World War II. From these figures we can see the profile of societies that have some risk of enduring humanitarian emergencies. They are relatively new states located in the third world, Central Asia, or the Balkans.[1]

A further characteristic of the states in Väyrynen's list is that they contain more than one significant ethnic group in the national population. Most of them, in fact, contain two or more ethnic groups, distinct cultural traditions, religions, and languages. Haiti and Colombia are the only exceptions. Both are relatively homogenous, although divided deeply by class and colour distinctions. There is substantial empirical support for the proposition that states with several distinct communities based on religion, language and/or ethnicity (fragmentation) have a higher risk of political violence, including civil wars, than more homogenous societies (cf. Ellingsen 1996).

But ethnic heterogeneity does not correlate strongly with complex humanitarian emergencies. Rather, it is the access to political office and other political goods, as well as economic opportunities among identity groups, that is crucial. Ethnicity may be used as a tool for political mobilization, and it is often connected to political leaders' attempts to gain or maintain power and privileges. Significant economic inequality among groups in society is also significant. Perhaps the most dangerous situation

---

[1] In a more recent compilation of 46 state crises and communal wars between 1980 and 1996, however, Harff and Gurr (1998: 554–5) report that 19 (41 per cent) occurred in pre–1945 states, including Russia (Chechnya), China, Iraq, Iran, Turkey, Guatemala, and Nicaragua. However, not all the cases led to humanitarian emergencies as defined by Väyrynen.

is where a minority rules through patronage and plundering, often at the expense of a majority (cf. Ahmed 1996: 25; Klugman 1999: 8–9).

Standard income figures do not show similar commonalties. They range from per capita incomes of more than US$ 3,000 in the case of Croatia and Bosnia, to less than US$ 300 annually in Ethiopia and Haiti. While most of the locales of humanitarian emergencies are poor by Western standards, the great disparities in the sample suggest that degrees of poverty or wealth averaged out in per capita figures do not correlate strongly with violence and refugee movements. We must also consider the large number of countries with low per capita incomes where war and resulting refugee flows have not occurred. Income divisions within the societies might be more significant, however.

In the event that the years 1993–96 may not be typical, it may be useful to extend the time horizon. I do not have a list of humanitarian emergencies that go beyond those available in the Melkas study (1996), but figures on wars involving over 1,000 deaths are available (Holsti 1996; Chapter 2). Not including de-colonizing wars of national liberation, there have been 164 armed conflicts between 1945 and 1995, of which 126 (77 per cent) were internal. The remaining 23 per cent were wars or armed interventions between states, but a high percentage of these (for example, Afghanistan, Vietnam) began as domestic wars. Virtually all of these wars resulted in very high casualty rates, as well as displaced populations and refugees. And when we look at the locales where these wars took place, the pattern in Väyrynen's data is reinforced. Countries with the highest risk of being the locales of wars and, therefore, of humanitarian disasters are overwhelmingly (i) new states with (ii) weak political legitimacy and (iii) significant discrimination against one or more identity groups.

What political characteristics are commonly found in these states? The literature on state-making is extensive, and often comparative. A number of observers have, for example, compared the state-making process after 1945 to the pattern of developments in early modern Europe (Tilly 1990; Ayoob 1995). While we must remain sensitive to significant historical and cultural differences, there are suggestive points of comparison. The state-making process in Europe, as in the post-1945 world, involved attempts to centralize authority, to extract resources from the population, and to constrain or destroy local rule-making individuals and bodies (cf. Migdal 1988; Bereciartu 1994; Chapter 1; Young 1994: 39–41). This process often undermined or destroyed local authority structures and incumbents, homogenized cultures, imposed national laws to replace local customs, diluted local languages, and not infrequently, as in Sudan, led to the expropriation of lands and resources of indigenous and other peoples, usually designated a 'minority' so that they can be dealt with more efficiently. Harff and Gurr (1998: 558) similarly report that a history and actual loss of autonomy by identity groups within states dramatically increases the risks of violence.

Numerous civil wars, rebellions, armed resistance, and massacres punctuated the state-making process in Europe. Hobbes, whose views of political life were particularly austere, was one observer of them. Given that Western imperialism had no intention of creating states, it is little wonder that the state-making project in the post-colonial territories really began only after independence and that political life in many of these states should resemble in some respects a Hobbesian state of nature. Colonial legacies vary between locations, but some of them are common and continue to have major impact on the character of political life and on the daunting tasks that 'state-building' demands. The legacies include, among many others, the following:

- artificial borders that do not coincide with demographic, cultural, or commercial characteristics;
- the creation of multi-cultural societies through the slave trade and settlers, where reasonably homogenous societies had existed prior to colonization;
- a tradition of 'politics from the top', with colonial authorities commanding and with limited, if any, local participation;
- exacerbation of class, ethnic, language, and other divisions, frequently anointing some groups with a preferred 'right to rule' while systematically excluding others;
- prohibition of indigenous political activities, particularly at the 'national' level.

From this list we immediately see major differences between Europe and many of the post-1945 states. In Europe, the shift of sovereignty from the dynastic figure to the 'people' took many centuries and, in many places, through violent revolutions. The processes of democratization did not even approach universality within Europe until the 1970s with the passing of military/authoritarian regimes in Greece, Spain, and Portugal. In contrast, the post-1945 states mostly began with democratic constitutions, and with an international set of norms that promoted and sustained self-determination, self-government, and democratic processes. Many of these paraphernalia of popular sovereignty were 'delivered' as part of the de-colonization process. But the problem was that many of the colonies-turned-states were in fact fictions. They had the appurtenances of states—flags, armies, capital cities, legislatures, and ambassadors—but they did not have the other requisites that make states cohere. Most had only weak civil societies (cf. Harbenson, Rothchild and Chazan 1994). Few populations had deeply-ingrained senses of national identity; most, in fact, remained primordial, fixed around clans, tribes, religious groups, or geographic regions. The fiat of the 'national' government often extended no further than the suburbs of the capital city, after which local leaders, based on a variety of claims to legitimacy, ruled. The modern symbol of sovereignty, a monopoly over the legitimate use of force, plus the effective disarmament of society, existed more in rhetoric than in fact.

These and other characteristics of new states constitute a syndrome which Buzan (1983) has called the *weak state* and others (cf. Jackson 1990) have termed *quasi-states*. The terms may differ, but the phenomena to which they direct attention are similar. Weak states have all the attributes of sovereignty for external purposes—they are full members of the international community and have exactly the same legal standing as the oldest or most powerful states in the system—but they severely lack the internal attributes of sovereignty, including those mentioned above.

Weakness is a variable, not a teleological destination or origin. Throughout their history, states move back and forth along a continuum of weakness and strength. The comparative politics literature alludes to the various components of state strength, including capacity to extract resources, degree of social control, the extent to which the public is effectively disarmed, the provision of government services in exchange for tax extractions, and the degree to which national legislation is effectively applied throughout the designated territory. These are all material bases of state strength or weakness. However, the critical dimension of state strength is *legitimacy*, which is an idea or feeling. It is a measure of citizens' attitudes toward the state, whether they withhold or grant the 'right to rule' to those who act in the name of the state. Rebels and armed insurgents of various kinds often grant no legitimacy to the incumbent government. They challenge its 'right to rule', and take actions to replace incumbents with those who can make a superior claim. Others withdraw legitimacy from the state itself. Either they wish to change the entire constitutional order (not just incumbents), or they wish to secede. Radical Muslim elements in Algeria are an example of the former; contemporary separatists in Quebec or in Kosovo are examples of the latter. Their purposes differ, but they fundamentally make the same claim: the leaders of the state in which they reside do not have the right to rule, and so they want to rearrange matters either by changing the fundamental contours of the state or by creating a new state.

3. Born to Weakness: Legitimacy and the Colonial Legacy

To locate the sources of weak or declining legitimacy, we have to explore colonial legacies, the overhang of the past that has contemporary consequences. The new states were not created as mature political entities. They began with certain fundamental weaknesses that have constrained and even prevented the development of strong legitimacy ties.

Whatever the motives for colonization—and there were many—the colonizers never intended to convert their territories into states. Even as late as the 1950s, colonial officials in most territories denied that their native populations were ready for self-government. Although some of them had legislatures, courts, and police forces, colonial authorities on the whole proscribed or prohibited native political organizations, particularly those that spoke of independence as a goal. Colonial rule was based on a system of command, not participation. Moreover, in order to carry out administration, colonial officials usually had to co-opt or work through indigenous political structures and individuals. In this way, local chiefs, caudillos, effendis, mullahs, khans, and others were strengthened against the claims of authority and jurisdiction of post-independence governments.

The leaders of colonial independence movements never seriously considered alternatives to the Western state format. They rejected their own historical political forms and simply assumed that the *colony*—which was an imperialist-created fiction—should become the state. Few colonies made sense from a political point of view. They were administrative units created for imperialists' reasons and conveniences. Borders were usually artificial, and incorporated numerous groups of tribes, cultures, and religions whose members had never previously lived within a single political jurisdiction. Contrariwise, in Central Asia in particular, Russian colonial frontiers divided previously organic groups, interrupted ancient trade routes and demarcated zones of exclusivity that had never existed previously. In many mono-cultural islands, the importation of slaves and indentured labour from other regions of the world created multi-cultural communities,[2] and in Central Asia Stalin forcibly removed populations precisely so that they would *not* constitute coherent societies.

Many colonies, then, were political fictions in the sense that they incorporated populations that had never existed previously as distinct historical communities. Sudan, for example, had been a geographical expression designating that vast region that divides the headwaters of Muslim and Arabic cultures from black Africa. But a region may be a poor candidate for a state. Today, Sudan contains a Muslim majority that is badly divided among itself, and a large Christian and animist minority comprised of 597 tribes speaking 115 different languages, and nomadic groups that move back and forth between the official Sudan and its African neighbours. If there is a Sudanese identity, it certainly does not extend to the large numbers of its so-called citizens. Sudan's situation may be extreme, but it is not

---

[2] One African intellectual has commented: 'Are we really right to put faith in the Berlin Charter (1884), which established our present boundaries, and take for an African Bible a document whose stipulations were a mere arrangement of convenience between foreign powers?' (Uwechue 1972: 12). Uwechue might have added that no African was invited to attend the Berlin Conference.

unique. Like Sudan, the populations of most colonies at independence did not constitute nationalities. There was no reason why a Muslim Hausa in Northern Nigeria should feel any affinity to, or identity with, a southern Christian or animist Ongoni except that they in common had been colonial subjects of the British crown. Such diversity makes poor foundation for post-independence legitimate authority. There is nothing in the colonial history of Nigeria, Sudan, Cameroon, Burma, Central Asia or dozens of other territories that parallels the growth and evolution of national identities and affinities in Europe.

Yet, if the post-independence states were not to collapse (aborted state) upon the departure of the colonial authorities, there had to be some basis of legitimacy. Who claimed the right to rule, and on what basis? In some cases, claims to legitimacy were based on achievement or merit through colonial administrative or political institutions. Sometimes these claims were validated through elections or referenda. The constitutional order, the fundamental rules of the new states, were also validated through the wholesale importation of Western political 'rules of the game', assumed to be of universal validity and therefore acceptable to the post-colonial state. In many other cases, however, post-colonial legitimacy was based on warrior accomplishments, the oldest of the claims of 'right to rule'. The majority of colonies attained independence through peaceful means, but there were at least nineteen 'wars of national liberation' whose leaders, upon achieving victory, claimed the right to rule the post-independent state by virtue of their military victories. Many then turned themselves into presidents-for-life and instituted one-party states to make certain that those who had different views of the requirements of presidency and leadership would not establish rival claims of a right to rule.

Whether through peaceful or violent means, the leaders of the new states claimed the right to rule on behalf of the 'people'. The people were the colonial populations, no matter how culturally diverse or socially incompatible. The 'people' claimed the inherent right of self-determination, a doctrine again imported from the West and thus one that could not be denied by the West. The 'people' were unified in their struggles for independence, but as the numerous instances of humanitarian emergencies since independence attest, once independence had been achieved, it was not at all clear that the 'people' of anti-colonialism would remain a 'people' for the purposes of governing the post-colonial state. Indeed, quite a few national liberation movements were divided by ethnic, religious, and/or language lines even during the height of the anti-colonial struggle. The division between Muslims and Hindus which led to the bloody partition of India is the best known, but less dramatically, similar movements in, for example, Angola, Mozambique, Zambia, and Burma had already been divided years before formal independence. There were many who wanted a Western-state format, but not automatically one defined in colonial terms. Many groups feared—often correctly, as it turned out—that there can be internal as well as external forms of colonialism.

Anti-colonialism settled the question of who should rule the post-colonial territories. The crude answer was 'indigenous' rulers. But it did not settle the question of over whom rule should be exercised. The question of *community*—who is a citizen, and what are to be the relations between citizens of different communities—was not settled. The failure to resolve this issue has been at the heart of erosions of legitimacy and the collapse of states since independence. Diverse peoples could come together to oust the foreigners, but once that was accomplished, how could these peoples, divided by religion, ethnicity, language, and culture, live in harmony in the post-independence state? A political diagnosis of weak states has to focus on the question of community and the relationship of community to rule. Many colonial practices, such as indirect rule by divisive strategies, helped to create or exacerbate social divisions within the colony. The range of these practices is wide and diverse, beyond the scope of this essay, but it is a prominent theme in post-colonial literature. The general rubric, however, is that the colonial 'state' was created in London, Paris, Brussels, Moscow, and other European capitals with scant attention to indigenous modes of rule, or to the mechanisms that had sustained in some places reasonable harmony among and between communities.[3]

4. Weak States: Types

Weak and failed states have become the object of considerable attention during the 1990s. With the end of the cold war, analysts began to acknowledge that rebellions, civil wars, and massacres taking place in the third world and elsewhere were not just the manifestations of great power competition or ideological incompatibilities. Suddenly, observers discovered the phenomenon of 'ethnic wars', quite overlooking the fact that wars within states having nothing to do with cold war competition had been a part of the third world landscape for many years. Civil wars and wars of secession in Burma, Sudan, Eritrea, Nigeria, and elsewhere long preceded the collapse of the Berlin Wall (Holsti 1997). The list of humanitarian emergencies also goes back long before 1989 or 1991. What makes all the cases comparable is that in addition to being new multi-communal states, most shared the characteristic of state weakness defined in terms of the erosion

---

[3] One should not romanticize pre-colonial societies. Slavery, oppression, and genocides were not European inventions. The Europeans did not create the Hindu caste system, nor were relations between Hindus and Muslims in that area always characterized by harmony and tolerance. However, as in the case of Rwanda, colonialism often buttressed the position of ruling groups and thereby helped sustain social divisions (cf. De Swan 1997).

or absence of legitimacy. There are, however, different kinds of weak states. While many of them have been the sites of humanitarian emergencies, not all have been 'failed' states in the sense of collapsing totally, and not all entailed mass violence.

Gros (1996) distinguishes between (i) anarchic states, (ii) phantom or mirage states, (iii) anaemic states, (iv) captured states, and (v) aborted states. While this is formally a typology, in fact, except for type (v), it is actually a continuum.

4.1. Anarchic states

Anarchic states represent one end of the continuum. Here, there is no central authority. There are no government services and no laws, and commands of the ostensible central authorities, if they exist, are widely ignored and ineffective. In the anarchic state, according to Gros (1996: 457), there is an 'overall breakdown of the corpus of formal and informal rules governing society, accompanied by the disappearance of formal authority or its emanations'. Examples include Somalia by 1991, and contemporary Liberia and Sierra Leone.

4.2. Phantom states

In the latter years of rule under Mobutu Sese Seko, Zaire was an example of the phantom state. There is a semblance of authority, with constitutions, incumbents, armed forces, police, national currency and the like. In fact, rule does not extend beyond the chief and his immediate entourage, and authority within society has devolved largely to local centres. The armed forces symbolize the vacuity of rule. They are often undisciplined and unpaid, thus resorting to widespread graft, extortion, and pillaging in order to survive. They are under no central control and in the event of fighting, could not be counted upon to save the regime.[4] A former American assistant secretary of state for Africa (Cohen 1993, quoted in Weiss 1995: 157) describes the essential attributes of the phantom state—in this case, again, Zaire:

To say that Zaire has a government . . . would be a gross exaggeration. A small group of military and civilian associates of President Mobutu, all from the same ethnic group, control the city of Kinshasa by virtue of the loyalty of the 5,000-man Presidential Guard . . . This same group also controls the Central Bank which provides both the foreign and local currency to keep the Guard loyal. While the ruling

---

[4] The Zaire army in the last months of Mobutu's reign became primarily a marauding force. The few troops who actually engaged in armed combat against the Kabila rebel army admitted that they operated under no central authority and had not been paid for months. Mobutu had to use mercenaries to fly his few aircraft. Overall, the official Zaïre army was as much a phantom as was the Mobutu state.

group has intelligence information about what is going on in the rest of Zaire, there is no real government authority outside the capital city.

4.3. *Anaemic states*

Anaemic states, according to Gros, are characterized by the inability to deliver government services due to lack of infrastructure or the expenditure of a high proportion of government resources on fighting insurgencies. There is a semblance of state authority, but capacity does not meet demand. Gros makes the following symbolic distinction between the phantom state and the anaemic states: in the former, garbage never gets collected; individuals have to rely on themselves or move elsewhere as the garbage piles up. In the anaemic state, garbage is *eventually* collected. The *captured state* is not, in fact, a different kind. Zaire is a captured state; indeed, most weak states are captured states, as we will see below.

4.4. *Aborted states*

An aborted state, according to Gros, is a type of political entity which never gets off the ground upon achieving independence. Its authority structures are never put into place initially, or the peaceful succession of power from colonial status is not achieved with independence. In 1918–19, the new ethnically-based states of Eastern Europe made a reasonably peaceful transition from their status as units in the Russian, Ottoman, and Austro-Hungarian empires, partly because the great powers insisted that they adhere to constitutional rule and respect the rights of minorities. Since 1945, the international community has been much less involved in setting stringent conditions for recognition of independence. States such as the Congo, which were patently unprepared for independence, were granted it solely on the grounds of colonial status. Upon reaching independence, several began to break apart into secessionist and civil wars. Examples in addition to the Congo include Mozambique, Angola, Tajikistan, and Georgia, the latter with the violent secession attempt of Abkhazia. There is a high risk of humanitarian emergencies resulting from aborted states.

Most post-1945 states began their independent life as relatively weak polities because of the legacies of colonialism. There was little or no sense of national identity, the bases of government legitimacy—anti-colonialism—were inherently of limited duration, and the foundations of strong economic performance were seldom laid or solid. But some states were able to overcome these conditions and to move along the trajectory of strength. Others remained weak, but managed to survive without major conflagrations. And finally, some moved along the trajectory toward greater weakness and, for a few, toward ultimate collapse. Some of the scenes of humanitarian emergencies have taken place within weakening or collapsed states.

4.5. Collapsed states

In 1991, Somalia became the symbol of the collapsed state, ostensibly a new phenomenon in international politics. But state collapse long predated the event of 1991. Lebanon in 1976, Angola and Mozambique, perhaps more aborted than collapsed states (Gros 1996: 461), and Chad between 1980 and 1982 all had the symptoms of the state moving toward collapse: the bankruptcy of the government, often caused by spending on the military to control insurgencies and rebellions; absence of central authority throughout much of the territorial configuration of the state; proliferation of states within states; lack of personal security except within the context of sub-national units, including gangs; and cessation or paralysis of government services, including essential police, education, sanitation, health, and welfare functions (cf. Kaplan 1996). These services do not necessarily cease, but it is no longer the state that supplies them. Zartman (1995: 1) offers the following definition of the collapsed state:

State collapse is a deeper phenomenon than mere rebellion, coup, or riot. It refers to a situation where the structure, authority (legitimate power), law and political order have fallen apart . . . On the other hand, it is not necessarily anarchy. . . [W]hen the state collapses, order and power (but not always legitimacy) falls down to local groups or are up for grabs. These ups and downs of power then vie with central attempts to reconstitute authority. For a period, the state itself, as a legitimate, functioning order, is gone.

The exact details may differ from case to case, but the symptoms are remarkably similar. Central government withers away or suffers from paralysis; laws are not made, nor are existing ones enforced; the provision of security devolves to armed groups, whether ethnic, clan, religious, quasi-military, or just gangs. There may be *governance* within the collapsed state—local, contrived, often ineffective, and often also based on terror—but there is no government in the sense required by the concept of sovereignty. In Lebanon after 1976, authority devolved to numerous sectarian armed groups who themselves provided some semblance of governance. The central Lebanese government continued to exist on paper and in a few offices, but its fiat rarely extended beyond a few kilometres in Beirut. Elsewhere, local groups ruled. In the absence of central authority, social groups or individuals may settle old scores, particularly if mobilized by local leaders and gangsters. We witnessed this phenomenon in Indonesia following the 30 September 1965 counter-coup, and during the Bosnian war, particularly within the Bosnian Serb community. From the point of view of humanitarian emergencies, the problem is that spontaneous local 'authorities' may be more murderous than the predatory state whose power they inherited or grabbed. As one example, the infamous Serbian 'Arkan' (aka Zeljko Raznjatovic) controlled an 800-man paramilitary unit ('Tigers') who 'raped and tortured their way through Eastern Slavonia' in the Croatian war of 1991 (Ignatieff 1993: 29). Despite being indicted by the International War Crimes Tribunal in the Hague, Arkan re-emerged as a military figure in the humanitarian emergency in Kosovo in 1999. The civilian and military leaders of the Republika Srpska have been indicted for war crimes. The Aidid clan in Somalia ruled through localized terror, extortion, and systematic looting of international aid. Similar patterns have been observed in the collapse of state authority in Sierra Leone and Liberia.

We now have profiles of several high-risk types of states. All share the characteristic of weak legitimacy. Gros' concept of the 'phantom' state is difficult to deal with because while it suffers from all the symptoms of weakness, particularly predatory behaviour, it persists somehow. It is therefore a residual category that crosses the other types; since it is not mutually exclusive of the others, we cannot use it further. A state is classified as weak when its rulers govern without an articulated basis of legitimacy or when two or more major communities within the state deny each others' legitimacy within the political community (Holsti 1996; Chapter 6).

We must think in terms of risks and probabilities. There may be cases where states with high risk profiles, including predation or social cleavages, do not lead to humanitarian emergencies. Why, for example, was there widespread bloodshed in 1965 Indonesia, or in Burma since 1962, but not in Malaysia or Singapore at the same time? Given similar profiles of state weakness, what transpires between high risk conditions in many states and actual war or other forms of domestic armed turmoil in only a few? Why do some weak, collapsing, or anarchical states lead to humanitarian emergencies, while others do not? At the level of the individual, how do we account for the transformation of ordinary citizens and neighbours into killers and agents of 'ethnic cleansing' or genocide?

5. Squandering Legitimacy: Post-colonial Predation

Many weak states lack legitimacy because their governments are predatory. Rulers use the state to enrich themselves and to purchase the loyalty of groups that can help ensure their status and hold on power. Gros calls these 'captured' states, but this does not mean that they are necessarily phantom or anarchic states. Most, in fact, have well-articulated bureaucratic structures, domestic intelligence units, and a variety of police and armed forces that can root out resistance and opposition. Yet, they are weak primarily because they have forfeited the loyalty, trust, and affection of significant groups and individuals in the country. Under certain conditions, particularly with the removal from office of the predatory incumbents, the state may move toward anarchy. This was the case, for example, in Sierra Leone in 1992 when a military coup ousted a highly corrupt regime and then lost control of the troops who went on a 3-year rampage of looting, terror, and extortion throughout the countryside. The erosion of legitimacy through years of widespread corruption and government predation was the condition that led to the *coup d'état* which, in turn, led to the development of the anarchic state.

In some post-colonial states, reigning regimes have become predatory. Predators 'capture' the state apparatus and practise two kinds of activities that seriously compromise their legitimacy. First, they systematically exclude specific groups in the society from access to policy-making positions and from equal access to government services. Supporters of the regime, in contrast, hold privileged positions in complex systems of patronage and clientelism. Second, the incumbents of the captured state use their positions and access to resources to plunder the national economy through graft, corruption, and extortion, and to participate in private business activities. Jackson and Rosberg (1982) have termed these states 'kleptocracies'. In Africa, estimates of government-plundered wealth stashed in European banks up to 1986 amounted to US$ 150 billion. The former president of Zaire, Mobutu Sese Seko, was reputed to have transformed more than US$ 10 billion of his country's wealth into personal assets, all sent abroad (Ergas 1987: 299, 320). When the funds transferred abroad by Mobutu's clients and entourage are added, one can only conclude that governance in Zaire was primarily a system of national looting (cf. Callaghy 1984). During the height of his tenure as permanent president of the Philippines, Ferdinand Marcos looted the wealth of his country to the tune of about US$ 12 billion.

The problems of 'capturing' a state and plundering are, of course, connected. Presidents-for-life, self-proclaimed emperors, and the founders of family dynasties and their one-party supporting apparatuses have to be paid for. Client loyalty carries huge costs. The post-colonial state in a poor economy is the main vehicle for status, prestige, jobs, and wealth. In cultures where there is no fundamental norm separating personal profit from public service, the latter becomes the means to the former. Long after the myths of anti-colonial struggle have worn thin, predatory regimes must rely increasingly upon clientelism and patronage as the sole basis of their 'right to rule'.

By definition, clientelism and patronage involve only small portions of a state's population. Those who are victims of graft and corruption, and those who do not have privileged access to centres of authority, are likely to form oppositions. A particularly high risk situation develops when a minority group captures the government and then systematically excludes a majority group from power and allocations (cf. Ahmed 1996: 25). This was the situation in Rwanda in the 1960s; it remains the case today in Syria, Iraq, Kashmir, and Burundi. Samuel Doe's regime in Liberia replaced the Afro-American elite with its own marginalized minority ethnic group, which in turn was overthrown by a warlord. A more primitive variant is where a small social segment, in many cases a single family, uses the state to build a virtual dynasty. The Duvalier family in Haiti systematically looted the country's wealth to ensure its perpetual power, a pattern observed in Somoza's Nicaragua and among the ruling families of El Salvador.

The regime of a predatory state, while squandering or lacking legitimacy, nevertheless controls the means of survival. These include intelligence agencies, the national police, and the military. The military itself may be the prime engine of plunder, as in Burma during the 1960s and 1970s. Whatever the case, rule ultimately is based on a combination of purchased loyalty of a few, formal or informal exclusion of all who are deemed to be the opposition, and persecution of those who protest or resist. The policies used to maintain power and to silence the opposition range from informal means of exclusion, such as fraudulent elections, to formal means such as outlawing opposition political parties or *apartheid*, and coercive means such as expulsion of select groups from the country (New Win's expulsion of Indians from Burma in 1962–63, Idi Amin's expulsion of Asians from Uganda in the 1970s). Extra-legal policies include assassination and killing of dissidents and resistance leaders (death squads in El Salvador, Guatemala, and Argentina during the 1970s and 1980s), and organized massacres of identifiable social and political groups (the Hutu extermination of Tutsis in Rwanda in the 1960s, the Tutsi massacres of Hutus in Burundi in 1965, Macias Nguema's liquidation of 'disloyal' social elements in Equatorial Guinea during the 1970s, and Pol Pot's massacre of approximately 1.5 million 'class enemies' in Kampuchea in 1976–78). In the predatory state, there are likely to be mass exoduses of potential victims and their families (Haiti under Cedras, Liberia under Taylor, Rwanda throughout much of its history) as the state usually has a significant advantage of coercive power. In all these cases, most of which resulted in humanitarian emergencies, the state becomes the main threat to the security of individuals and often to entire social groups.

Predatory regimes sometimes set communities against each other as a means of mobilizing a modicum of popular support. This is 'playing the ethnic card'. In 1993, for example, Mobutu Sese Seko deliberately set communities in Shaba (Katanga) against each other, though they had lived harmoniously for generations. Half a million refugees fled the carnage (Lee 1997). In 1965, the military-dominated government that had crushed a coup attempt in Indonesia mostly stood by while at the local level individuals and groups slaughtered suspected communists and distinct identity groups, particularly the Chinese minority. The killing went on for about 6 months, encouraged and tolerated, if not always organized, by government officials. These actions have the consequence of destroying the ties of empathy, tolerance, and even common identification that bind multi-communal societies together.

Exclusion and discrimination are found extensively in most states, but their pervasiveness is notable in third world and former socialist states. These practices strengthen group identities, foster violent responses, and help begin a cycle of resistance and further oppression. Gurr's (1993: 6) empirical work sustains this observation. In the period 1945–89, for example, 233 ethnic groups around the world experienced economic and/or political discrimination, and of these, 200 organized politically to defend their interests against the government or other communities. Eighty cases escalated to civil war. Extra-legal and extreme measures of discrimination and exclusion have been equally frequent, resulting in extraordinarily high numbers of casualties, usually much higher than those sustained through civil and secessionist wars. Since 1945, there have been nearly 50 episodes of genocide and politicide directed against more than 70 different ethnic and religious communities, resulting in at least 9 million and perhaps as many as 20 million civilian fatalities (Gurr 1996: 65).

The policies of exclusion, corruption, and playing the ethnic card, often organically related, destroy the foundations of legitimate rule within states. State agents become the main threats to the security and welfare of individuals and groups. As legitimacy is squandered, rule has to be based increasingly on exclusion, coercion, and theft. The post-colonial state, which was weak in many dimensions at birth, enjoyed a euphoric period of solidarity and hope. But states cannot be put along the trajectory of strength merely by getting rid of a colonial master or mouthing slogans of socialism and equality. Ultimately, the post-colonial states had to find new bases for legitimacy. Some succeeded—often on the basis of adequate or strong economic performance and/or deliberate policies designed to establish social harmony between groups (Malaysia, Singapore)—but many failed and resorted to policies of exclusion, plunder, and social division.

There is an inverse relation between legitimacy and the security of government incumbents. The rulers of predatory states tend to isolate themselves physically and socially from the societies over which they rule. They surround themselves with cronies and family members whose loyalty is often purchased. In this setting, the phenomenon of 'group-think' (Janis 1972) is likely to appear. Rulers see the external world as constituting threats; information is not processed to suggest a variety of policy options; emphasis is on group solidarity and defense rather than analysis; and those who raise questions about policy directions are expelled (or worse) from the group. The extreme insecurity of some tyrants helps to explain their brutal repression of even mild forms of dissent within the society.

There is little in the history of Western political thought that adequately analyses the origins and character of predatory practices. The nature of tyranny and the limits of political obligation are old themes in political philosophy, but most modern thinkers starting with Hobbes fail to describe states that parallel those found frequently in the twentieth century. Hobbes's Leviathan was a stern keeper of public order. But it was also a relatively disinterested mediator and judge of private conflicts. Subjects or citizens could stand in 'awe' (to use Hobbes's term) of the state, but awe is not terror. The state had the means to punish, but it employed them primarily to maintain law and order so that people could go about their daily lives in reasonable security and peace. Similarly, nineteenth century liberals' concepts of the 'night-watchman' state bear no relationship whatsoever to the predatory Nazi, Soviet, Kampuchean and other murderous states of this century. Even Marx' bourgeois state, the executive committee of the capitalist class, was only a supporter of an exploitative economic system, not an instrument of mass murder. Marx' imagined 'dictatorship of the proletariat' could never have remotely resembled Stalin's state that, according to even conservative enumerations, killed more than 50 million Soviet citizens (Rummel 1994: 7). Most post-1945 predatory states, with some significant exceptions such as Kampuchea, Vietnam, and Pakistan, have not reached such heights of human destruction. But many have gone far beyond the brutalities of state-making in seventeenth century Europe. When we examine individual cases of humanitarian emergencies, the evidence suggests that few of them are caused by primordial ethnic hatreds or spontaneous communal violence.[5] Contrary to many Western media characterizations of recent humanitarian emergencies, they are not always 'ethnic conflicts' representing some sort of primordial hatreds between social groups (cf. Schoeberlein-Engel 1994; Woodward 1995). Predatory states, often as a matter of policy, undermine the sources of their legitimacy by undermining the autonomy of, plundering, threatening, and killing distinct communities of their own citizens. This results in extreme political insecurity that feeds further repression, and often-massive retaliation against dissenters (cf. Krain 1997).

---

[5] One of the few spontaneous acts of massive inter-communal violence followed the assassination of Indira Gandhi in 1984. Hindus in Delhi and elsewhere hunted down and killed thousands of Sikhs, purportedly to punish the Sikh community, two of whose members—the prime minister's personal bodyguards—assassinated her.

6. Tipping Events

Hardin (1995) has argued that 'tipping events' are critical in explaining the transformation of weakness to violence. These events are, speaking metaphorically, lit matches thrown into a pool of gasoline. There is a common structural dynamic here. It is the situation where individuals, often as 'representatives' of identity or attribute groups, confront the situational logic of 'kill or be killed'. Contrary to many recent analysts of 'ethnic war', primordial ethnic hatred is seldom a sufficient explanation for violence. Nationalism is a means of group mobilization, not an inherent cause of conflict, as we can readily observe from the countries in which distinct groups coexist, work together, and intermarry for long periods of time. It takes a particular situation, usually driven by fear and insecurity, for leaders and followers to become killers. It is when violence becomes anticipated, when the risks increase, and when self-defence becomes a compelling necessity, that violence breaks out. Hardin (1995: 143) describes the situation:

Self-defense against possible (not even actual) attack suffices to motivate murderous conflict. Risk aversion is enough. And the risk, unfortunately, of not preemptively attacking may be heightened by the fact that the other side . . . cannot commit to not attacking, and therefore cannot be trusted beyond what can be inferred from their interests. An ethnic group that depends on relatively spontaneous organizations . . . cannot make credible guarantees about what it might do. Indeed . . . internal competition for leadership might make any commitment automatically the target of some faction among those supposedly making a commitment.

Events recently in ex-Yugoslavia, Lebanon, Tajikistan, Rwanda, and Burundi, among others, illustrate this logic. It is often but not inevitably associated with collapsing state authority, where increasingly there is a structural compulsion to attack pre-emptively, where the logic of 'kill or be killed' takes over. It was particularly the case in several domains of the secession wars of Yugoslavia, as well as in Somalia. Ignatieff (1993: 16) argues that in these circumstances, 'there is one type of fear more devastating in its impact than any other: the systemic fear which arises when a state begins to collapse. Ethnic hatred is the result of the terror which arises when legitimate authority disintegrates'. This is exactly the condition of anarchical and aborted states, and not infrequently in predatory states. It is a Hobbesian world where no disinterested Leviathan can provide security. Describing the situation in ex-Yugoslavia in 1990, Ignatieff writes:

No one in these (Yugoslav) villages could be sure who would protect them. If they were Serbs and someone attacked them and they went to the Croatian police, would the Croats protect them? If they were Croats, in a Serbian village, could they be protected against a nighttime attack from a Serbian paramilitary team, usually led by a former policeman? This is how ethnic cleansing began to acquire its logic. If you can't trust your neighbours, drive them out. If you can't live among them, live only among your own. This alone appeared to offer people security. This alone gave respite from the fear which leaped like a brush-fire from house to house.

But tipping events leading to humanitarian emergencies may occur also in states in which there *is* effective, if not always legitimate, authority. The massacres in Rwanda in 1994, in Kampuchea after 1976, in Kosovo in 1998–99, or several times in Burundi, did not take place in a condition of collapsing or disintegrated state authority. Quite the contrary, *it was the state itself that launched the massacres, ethnic cleansing, or genocides.* The state used its superior coercive capacities, intelligence, and organizational capabilities to hunt down opponents and resisters, or it sat idly by after encouraging public pogroms against designated populations. Yet, 'tipping events', sudden and usually unexpected events or provocations, were usually used to justify government-sponsored mass killings. In April 1994, it was the downing of the aircraft that was bringing home the president of Rwanda from a peace conference in neighbouring Tanzania. In 1988, it was an armed incursion of Somali refugees from Ethiopia that led to Siad Barre's massive razing of two Somali cities, Hargeiso and Barao, resulting in 60,000 predominantly civilian deaths. Kosovar terrorist attacks against Serbian officials in 1996 began the long spiral of violence that resulted in the 1999 humanitarian crisis.[6] Such 'tipping events' preceded a high proportion of government-caused humanitarian emergencies since the early 1960s.[7]

7. The Political Processes leading to Humanitarian Emergencies

There may be patterned *processes* that precede humanitarian emergencies. The model appears in Table 7.1.

Risks increase as we move from column to column toward the right. We can predict with little accuracy any direct connection between background attributes and the incidence of humanitarian emergencies. The reason is evident. Numerous states—probably a significant majority—that share these background characteristics or attributes have not experienced humanitarian emergencies. States with these background conditions,

---

[6] The revocation of Kosovo autonomy by the Yugoslav government in 1989 was perhaps the more important tipping event that resulted in the ethnic cleansing of 1998–99.

[7] The role of propaganda and incitement in fomenting humanitarian emergencies is explored in Snyder and Ballantine (1996). They argue that in democratizing countries with weak civil societies, and where often the media are controlled in oligopolistic or monopolistic fashion, free speech can actually exacerbate relations between communities.

Table 7.1. A probability/process model of humanitarian emergencies

Background conditions	Exclusion policies	Tipping event(s)	Outcomes	Humanitarian emergencies
New state	Informal (e.g., election fraud)	Death/assassination of leader	Politicides	Violent (war casualties, refugees, displaced persons)
Multi-community state, particularly with group imbalance	Formal (constitutional distinction among communities)	Armed resistance Sudden political change(s), post-revolution or post-independence	Civil war Ethnic cleansing	Complex (casualties, refugees, disease, hunger)
Colonial legacy	Expulsion	Riots	Armed secession	
Weak legitimacy	Segregation Expropriation Death squads	Coup attempts Elections State collapse	Genocide	

however, are more likely to have a high incidence of informal and formal exclusionist policies, military government, and kleptocratic and dynastic practices that seriously erode the legitimacy of governments. Lacking legitimacy, and therefore politically insecure, governments are more likely to use coercive methods to maintain authority, thereby further eroding their legitimacy. They may also create or exacerbate social divisions as a means of gaining political support among certain groups. These are not, however, sufficient conditions. They do increase risks, but again because we have many instances where such policies did not result in humanitarian emergencies (for example, Fiji 1988), there is no direct cause-effect relationship. Finally, if dramatic tipping events take place, then the probabilities of violent outcome increase dramatically. Do recent cases of humanitarian emergencies conform to this model?

8. Humanitarian Emergencies in Weak States

We do not yet have a comprehensive list of post-1945 humanitarian emergencies. The studies by Melkas (1996) and Väyrynen (Chapter 2) launch important work in this domain, but their data cover the period only from the late 1980s to the mid-1990s. This was an era of increased incidence of emergencies and more international *responses* to them, but the critical variables are not incidence or responses. Humanitarian emergencies not related to international war or to wars of national liberation began in the early 1960s, shortly after the independence of most new states.[8]

I have selected 18 cases. This is not a random sample because the total population is not known. The choice was determined partly by the documented and accessible facts and figures, and reasonable literatures that narrate the contexts in which the emergencies took place. The cases also come from several regions. They cover the period since the early 1960s so that the artefact of a single historical event, the end of the cold war and the collapse of the Soviet Union, does not skew them. This single and signal event has led directly to a significant increase in the number of complex humanitarian emergencies in the 1990s, such as those of Tajikistan, Azerbaijan, Georgia, Chechnya, Yugoslavia and, indirectly, Sierra Leone.

---

[8] The concept of humanitarian emergency is a social construct designed to deal with only a limited range of phenomena. The numbers killed or at risk do not seem to be the prime criterion for qualification as a humanitarian emergency. Massive killings and refugee flows have usually been dubbed a humanitarian emergency only when there is some prospect that the international community can do something about them. There was substantial if not entirely accurate knowledge about the massive starvation in China that resulted from Mao Tse-tung's 'Great Leap Forward' in the late 1950s and the Great Cultural Revolution of the late 1960s, but no one called them humanitarian emergencies. Similar comments would apply to the 1965–66 events in Indonesia, Idi Amin's killings in Uganda in the 1970s, and the like.

However, cases from the 1990s alone would significantly distort any patterns or anomalies that might emerge from a longer purview. A longer period also helps reverse the common misconception that 'ethnic wars' and their resulting humanitarian emergencies have been mainly a consequence of the destruction of cold war 'controls' over developments in the third world.

The profiles of the 18 cases in Table 7.2 conform well to the model. All the states, with the exception of Lebanon and Ethiopia (of which Eritrea was part of a United Nations-sponsored federation), are 'new', either as post-colonial states, or as successor states of the Soviet Union or Yugoslavia. All contain numerous and often imbalanced language, religious, and ethnic groups. With the possible exception of Indonesia in 1965, and Sierra Leone in 1992, in all the other cases a specific and identifiable social group or community was formally discriminated against or excluded from national political participation and/or from government allocations.

In many instances, the forms of exclusion included physical threats to members of the community or to their institutions. A tipping event is a matter of judgement, perhaps easier to make *post-facto* than at the time of the event. But the events in these cases were so distinct and such marked deviations from the patterns of ordinary life in the communities, that they have a special political significance. In *all* cases, they preceded massive bloodletting that resulted in many thousands of deaths and large refugee flows. Consistent with the Harff and Gurr findings (1998: 553–6) major political upheavals (revolutions, secessions, and the like) preceded the humanitarian emergencies in 13 of the 18 cases.

The argument that insecure and weakly legitimate governments rather than primordial hatreds or spontaneous communal strife are a main source of humanitarian emergencies is partly borne out by the data. In six of the cases, governments clearly initiated the killing. In the case of Pakistan in 1971 and Rwanda in 1994, the mass murders had been planned and organized by governments long before the bloodletting. In seven other cases, including Kosovo, relatively minor armed incidents organized by rebels or insurgents led to massive government-sponsored and/or organized reprisals against designated groups within society. In these instances, the government clearly used minor provocations as justifications to unleash 'politicides' or ethnic cleansing against its own citizens. In the remaining five cases, armed secessionist movements began the killing (Nigeria, Sri Lanka, Eritrea, Croatia, Bosnia), but this had usually been preceded by government-sponsored or tolerated pogroms against the resisting or seceding communities. We conclude, then, that it is usually the policies of governments, often lacking legitimacy and therefore highly insecure, rather than random or spontaneous violence between communities that precede most humanitarian emergencies.

Table 7.2. Structure and outcomes: political sources of humanitarian emergencies

State, year/type	Power holders	Excluded groups	Means of exclusion	Tipping event(s)	Outcomes	Victims
Ethiopia, 1961–91 (weak)	Ethiopian monarchy	Eritreans and Eritrean autonomous status as part of Ethiopia–Eritrea federation	Steps to erase Eritrean autonomy, including dissolving legislature, banning trade unions, replacing president, removing flag, 1953–62	Formal dissolution of federation; attempts to impose Amharic as sole national language; first ELF military attacks September 1961	War of secession, 1961–91	60,000 military casualties; 40,000 civilian casualties; 750,000–1 million refugees
Burma, 1962 (weak/predatory)	Burman military élites	Shan, Chin, Indians, Mons, etc.	Rescind constitutional autonomy arrangements; expulsion	Military overthrow of civilian, constitutional regime	Armed resistance; wars of secession by minorities	85,000 war casualties; 250,000 refugees
Rwanda, 1962 (weak)	Hutu	Tutsi, moderate Hutu	Mass killings, executions, forced exile, imprisonment; total exclusion from power	Electoral victory of virulently anti-Tutsi Hutus in 1961; Tutsi refugees attempt military return, small incursions from Burundi and Uganda	Politicide: mass killing of Tutsi civilians	Up to 30,000 killed; more than 100,000 Tutsi flee to neighbouring countries
Indonesia, 1965–66 (weak)	Sukarno	Most organized opposition groups, particularly PKI (communists)	'Guided Democracy', with only informal consultations at national level	Sept. 30 military coup, with PKI complicity, followed by military counter-coup	Politicide: military and civilian slaughter of PKI members and a few minorities; gov't stands aside	250,000 to 500,000 killed; thousands displaced but few refugees

Case						
Burundi, 1972 (weak)	Tutsi (military)	Hutu	Tutsi-dominated military takeover and cancellation of elections; subsequent Tutsi-dominated kinship alliances	Hutu small armed raid from Zaire on coastal settlements, with Tutsis targeted	Politicide: purge and slaughter of educated Hutus by military and youth-wing militia while thousands of private scores are settled, October 1965–March 1966	100,000–200,000 Hutu deaths, about 750,000 refugees to Rwanda, Zaire, Tanzania
Nigeria, 1966 (weak)	Majority of posts held by northern Nigerians	Ibos felt discriminated against, excluded from political participation	Informal means, help to create Ibos as 'outgroup' par excellence	Military coup July 1966; rule by northerners; Mob riots directed against Ibos in northern Nigeria, September 1966	'Thousands' killed in mob riots, more than 1 million Ibo refugees flee northern Nigeria; war of secession	1 million killed
Pakistan, 1970–71 (weak)	Power sharing, but inequitable access to positions + allocations to Bengalis. Severe economic discrimination against Bengalis, failure to provide aid after 1970 hurricanes with many thousand casualties	Bengalis of East Pakistan	Cancel election results in maldistribution of gov't positions and allocations	Dec. 1970 constituent assembly elections; subsequent meetings cancelled. Gov't moves 70,000 troops into E. Pakistan with order to murder politicians, intellectuals, and Hindus	Politicide: arrest of East Pakistan leaders; massacres of Hindus and Bengalis; formation of 'Mukhti Bahini' secession movement. Reprisals against East Pakistani troops and sympathizers; Bengali murder of Bihari Muslims	1 million to 3 million murdered; 6 million to 8 million refugees go to India for safety

Table 7.2. *cont.*

State, year/type	Power holders	Excluded groups	Means of exclusion	Tipping event(s)	Outcomes	Victims
Sri Lanka, 1978– (strong)	Sinhalese	Tamils	Constitutional revisions reducing Tamil access to power and social services	Ambush of army troops by LTTE, with 13 casualties, 23/7/83, followed by anti-Tamil pogroms	War of secession (continuing)	Initial pogroms lead to 200–600 deaths, several thousand homeless; about 60,000 casualties since war began
Uganda, 1976 (weak)	Idi Amin (Nubians/Kakwa)	Acholi, Langi, East Asians	Rule by terror, no legal basis for exclusions and killings	Assassination attempt on Amin, June 1976	Politicide and partial ethnocide: slaughter of actual and potential opponents	50,000–300,000 killed
Lebanon, 1976 (weak)	Political system dominated by Christian groups constituting a minority of population	Muslim groups, constituting a majority of Lebanese population	Refusal to alter 1942 constitution to better reflect population distributions		Civil/sectarian war	25,000 killed
Sudan, 1983 (weak/predatory)	Muslim domination of government	Southern animists, Christians, Africans, tribals	Renege on 1972 decentralization agreements; undermine self-rule in south; impose Islamic criminal law on non-Muslim populations	Boor mutiny, by southern troops in Sudan army, violently repressed, 1983; 1988: gov't withdraws all constitutional proposals	SPLM-led insurrection to create a 'democratic, united, socialist Sudan'	70,000 combat casualties; 260,000 deaths through starvation/disease; 400,000 refugees, 3.5 million displaced persons
Somaliland, 1988 (weak/anarchical)	Somali clan (Siad Barre)	Isaaq clan	Formal/informal exclusion from power and gov't allocations	Small armed incursion by Somali refugees in Ethiopia, into Somaliland	Reprisal, politicide: violent razing of Hargeiso and Barao by Barre (Somali) forces; followed by full secession war	60,000 civilians killed 400,000–500,000 refugees flee to Ethiopia

Croatia, 1991 (medium)	Croatians	Serbs	Constitutional revision, dismissal of Serbs from official positions	Armed resistance, Serbian armed intervention	Territorial war and armed resistance	10,000 war casualties; 200,000 refugees
Bosnia, 1992 (weak/aborted)	Power-sharing among social groups	Serbs (potential only)	(Potential only)	April 1992 plebiscite producing Muslim-dominated independent Bosnia	Armed secession/Serbian intervention	10,000–30,000 war casualties; ethnic cleansing; 906,000 refugees
Tajikistan, 1992 (aborted)	Communist party	Clan-based leaders, Muslim organizations, democratic opposition	Party monopoly on participation, fraudulent elections	Collapse of USSR, opposition demonstrations, Feb. 1990 riots	Civil war	20,000–50,000 war casualties; 174,000 refugees
Sierra Leone, 1992 (weak/anarchical)	None	None	Massive corruption	April 1992 coup	Breakdown of civil authority; widespread army looting/killing	Unknown civilian casualties; 280,000 refugees to Guinea, 100,000 to Liberia
Rwanda, 1994 (medium)	Hutu	Tutsi, moderate Hutu	Killing, forced exile, formal exclusion of all Tutsis from office and gov't allocations	Tutsi invasion from Uganda, shootdown of plane/death of Hutu president, April 1994. Government radicals order militias to begin killing Tutsis and their sympathizers	Politicide/ethnocide	250,000 to 500,000 killed, 1.5 million refugees
Kosovo, 1999 (medium)	Serbs	Kosovars	Withdrawal of autonomous status (1989); repression of Kosovar institutions	KLA attacks on Serb police beginning in 1996; NATO bombing, March 1999	Ethnic cleansing; local massacres, rapes, disappearances of Kosovar men	At least 750,000 refugees abroad, hundreds of thousands displaced; some starvation

Correlations and observation of common processes do not meet ordinary standards of causal analysis. Each of the cases in this account ended with a humanitarian emergency. Causal explanations, in these circumstances, would be self-fulfilling tautologies. For this reason I have avoided causal terminology and emphasized correlates, risks, and probabilities. To provide more than suggestive portraits of high-risk situations, we would have to include a number of states that share the characteristics of the sample, and yet which did *not* end with a humanitarian emergency. We would have to ask questions about non-events and entertain counter-factuals. For example, why did not Malaysia in the early 1960s break down into communal warfare or government repression? How did Singapore secede peacefully from Malaysia? Why was there no communal war or government-sponsored exclusion in Fiji in the late 1980s? Why has Guyana avoided major bloodshed, even though in the 1970s the government practised various forms of exclusion against the non-Indian population? Why was the secession of Slovenia relatively peaceful compared to the secessions of Croatia and Bosnia? Why has Cameroon, with about 130 major ethnic groups and two official languages, managed to avoid humanitarian emergencies, while neighbouring Nigeria suffered a major war of secession and until 1999 continued to practise systematic violation of human rights? In brief, to make statements endowed with a reasonable degree of causal certainty, a study of the political sources of humanitarian emergencies would have to include both states that were the scenes of disasters and states that somehow avoided them even in the presence of high risk characteristics.

Table 7.3 summarizes the facts in Table 7.2. If not certain causes, there are significant correlates of humanitarian emergencies. First, high proportions of the cases take place in new states which were or are socially diverse and often fragmented. Second, all but three of the cases occurred in states that were weak in terms of legitimacy and one of these, Rwanda, was certainly not a strong state (designated medium). Significant proportions of the national community did not extend loyalty to the state, usually because they were the objects of systematic discrimination and exclusion. Not infrequently, they were also targets of organized violence. Sri Lanka is the possible exception. Here, discrimination and communal violence organized by segments of radical nationalist Sinhalese against Tamils were not sponsored by the government. The government in the 1970s was in fact a functioning parliamentary democracy, but was under severe pressure from radicals who wanted to create a state Buddhist religion, a single official state language (Sinhalese) and formal discrimination against Tamils in the field of education. Government leaders who resisted these pressures were often the targets of assassination attempts. I classify Sri Lanka as the only strong state, but it is a matter of degree. By the early 1980s, the state no longer commanded the loyalty of either the extreme Sinhalese nationalists or a significant proportion of Tamil separatists.

Table 7.3. Political correlates of humanitarian emergencies

State	New	Weak	Exclusion	Tipping	Gov't org. killing	Group org. killing	External involvement	Type of emergency
Ethiopia	X	X	X	X		X		C
Burma	X	X	X	X	X			V
Rwanda	X		X	X	X			V
Indonesia	X	X	X	X	X		?	V
Burundi	X	X	X	X	X			V
Nigeria	X	X	X	X		X		V
Pakistan	X	X	X	X	X			V
Sri Lanka	X		X	X		X		V
Uganda	X	X	X		X			V
Lebanon		X	X			X	X	V
Sudan	X	X	X	X		X		C
Somaliland	X	X	X	X		X		V
Croatia	X		X	X	X	X	X	V
Bosnia	X	X		X		X	X	V
Tajikistan	X	X	X	X	X			V
Sierra Leone	X	X		X	X		X	C
Rwanda (1994)	X		X	X	X		X	C
Serbia/Kosovo		X	X	X	X	X	X	V

Note: V = violent humanitarian emergency; C = complex humanitarian emergency.

Formalized systems of discrimination and exclusion were in place in 16 of the 18 cases, a finding that is consistent with Gurr's conclusions (1996: 65) based on a much larger universe of cases. Since 1992, Sierra Leone had a predatory and corrupt government but apparently did not select distinct groups for formal exclusion. Prior to the armed secession of the Republika Srpska in 1992, Bosnia had a functioning parliamentary system. There were undoubtedly unofficial forms of discrimination against Serbs, but the Muslim majority institutionalized no systematic exclusionist policies.

Tipping events were prominent in a large majority of the cases. Here it is important to point out that in some cases it was *elections* that led to the carnage. In Rwanda, 1961, the electoral victory of radical anti-Tutsi Hutus paved the way for subsequent mass executions of Tutsis and moderate Hutus. The 1970 Pakistan elections, in which the Awami League based in East Pakistan won a massive victory, led the federal government under Yahya Khan to organize a plan to crush the Bengali separatists and to maintain the unity of the country through murder and violence. In 1992, the referendum validating a Bosnian declaration of independence from Yugoslavia turned the Bosnian Serbs from a majority in Yugoslavia into a minority in Bosnia. This was the signal to begin the armed secession of the Serbs, the creation of the Republika Srpska, and the subsequent ethnic cleansing of territories under its control.

There are circumstances, then, when elections and referenda may help lead to humanitarian emergencies. This is particularly the case where social cleavages are deep and thus where elections amount to little more than a census. In fact, they may have the consequence of formalizing and perpetuating these cleavages by destroying cross-cutting loyalties that may have existed prior to the elections. Elections in weak, multi-communal states may also have a very different meaning than they do in liberal democracies, for they signify not the victory of a shifting coalition that can be unseated later, depending upon performance, but the virtual or real *perpetual* rule of one group over other(s). De Tocqueville worried about the 'tyranny of the majority' in early nineteenth century America, but in the United States there were checks and balances and a lively civil society. In contrast, in many of the scenes of humanitarian emergencies there are no checks and balances and the civil society, if it exists at all, has few means to deflect authorities who are bent on curbing the rights and opportunities of minorities and other groups (cf. Young 1994). Whether justified or not, following the 1992 plebiscite validating independence from Yugoslavia, a number of Serbs in Bosnia suddenly perceived themselves to be a beleaguered minority within a Muslim-dominated independent Bosnia. In other words, their security as a community was threatened, if not undermined, by the ostensibly democratic device of a plebiscite. Elections in these circumstances are not instruments of conflict resolution, but tipping events that help transform social tensions into pogroms, armed combat, riots, and 'ethnic cleansing' (Holsti 1996; Chapter 9).

In the other cases, tipping events provided justifications for taking up arms or implementing previously planned government programmes of mass executions. Rwanda in 1994 is the most infamous recent case, but Pakistan in 1970–71 shows the same pattern, as does Indonesia in 1965. Attempts at secession, however weak, also often gave rise to massive government retaliation. Localized guerrilla operations in Eritrea starting in 1961 brought forth major armed reprisals from Ethiopia. Minor rebel incursions into Burundi in 1972 provided the justification for a government-organized slaughter of up to 200,000 Hutus. Siad Barre's response to an armed incursion of Somali refugees from Ethiopia into Somalia led to the razing of two cities with about 60,000 civilian casualties. Once Croatia seceded from Yugoslavia, its Serb population, primarily in Krajina, rose to secede from the new Croat state, ultimately to be physically removed by invading Croatian forces in 1995. NATO bombing of Serbia in March–April 1999 altered Serbian policy from fighting the secessionist KLA to forcibly expelling the entire Albanian population of Kosovo to neighbouring countries.

9. The International Factors

To this point, the diagnosis has isolated states from the international environment in which they exist and interact. States are frequently the targets of actions by others. Some are designed to sustain and strengthen them; others may have the reverse effect. Let us examine some of these external sources of strength and weakness. The literature is robust with hunches, speculations, and generalizations. It is less impressive from an empirical point of view. The statements below offer only a checklist of *possible* or *potential* influences rather than firm causal connections.

9.1. *The international system as a sustainer of state strength*

European powers, as well as the United States, did not abandon their great colonial projects easily. All of them expended lives and considerable fortunes after World War II in efforts to maintain the integrity of their respective empires. The French paid the highest costs, the Belgians the lowest. However, under prodding from the United States, from such newly-independent countries as India, and the non-aligned such as Yugoslavia, the imperial powers ultimately ceased to resist the principle of self-determination which was, after all, of their own making. Once the principle of independence was granted, the former imperial powers, supported by a number of smaller countries with no imperial history (Canada, the Scandinavian countries), joined with the increasing majority in the United Nations in the great 'nation-building' (sic) project.

This was fundamentally an enterprise to sustain and help develop the 'peoples' and territories that had been emancipated from colonialism into something akin to modern Western states. Like the anti-colonial leaders, the former imperial powers never considered alternatives to the state. The colonies, no matter how fictional, were simply to be transformed into carbon copies of France, Denmark, or the United States. In short order, developed United Nations members quickly helped to transform colonial institutions into state institutions. Hordes of Western and socialist advisors, including missionaries and private experts, descended upon the new states to help develop their bureaucracies, to write constitutions, to organize elections, to train police, and above all, to help create modern military forces. In the economic realm, technical assistance, loans, grants, and educational exchanges (usually only in one direction) were all designed to assist in the process of 'modernization' and economic 'takeoff'.

The new states were welcomed to the rapidly growing network of international institutions, often without requiring any credentials for membership such as effective sovereignty. Where former colonies, upon achieving independence, began to disintegrate—as in the Congo—the United Nations intervened militarily to prevent successful armed secessions. The United Nations also passed resolutions underlining the view that the act of de-colonization was an expression of self-determination and that any subsequent attempts 'aimed at the partial or total disruption of the national [sic] unity and territorial integrity of a country is incompatible with the purposes and principles of the United Nations Charter (UN Document A/4684, 1960). The colonial populations, in brief, constituted a 'people' for purposes of self-determination, and any groups within the new territorial states that might seek independence on the basis of ethnicity, language, or religion, would not have a valid claim.

The former imperial powers' commitment to the success of the 'nation-building' exercise is measured in part by the money they were willing to spend to strengthen the new states. A very rough figure of US$ 60 billion annually (not including aid from socialist countries) in foreign aid is one indicator. Another is the grant (not sale) of weapons and the provision of training facilities. In some new countries, as much as fifty per cent of the government budget came from external sources. And for the militaries, frequently 100 per cent of their arms came from abroad. No doubt a large part of these massive expenditures can be explained in terms of the strategic interests of cold war participants. Others would claim that the funds were spent primarily to maintain the coherence of the world capitalist system, and were thus just features of neo-colonialism (cf. Galtung 1971). The great powers certainly intervened to support indigenous regimes (France in West Africa, the United States in Central America), or to topple them if too radical (the British and Americans in Iran, 1951, the United States crusades against Guatemala, Cuba and Nicaragua, the Soviet Union in Afghanistan), but their purpose was to support or sustain government personnel, not to weaken the state. The consequences of these armed interventions might very well have been to prolong civil wars and, ultimately, to weaken the state, as in Afghanistan, but that was not the original intention.

On balance, then, the actions, policies, and norms, such as the entitlement of the poor to receive from the rich and the prohibition against granting recognition to sub-national self-determination movements, were designed to support, sustain, and strengthen states.

9.2. *External forces that weaken states*

But there is a case to be made that sometimes the support did in fact weaken the state, whatever original intentions. The charge that the Western powers were overly sympathetic to, and supporting of, odious regimes so long as they paraded strong anti-communist credentials, has foundations. The same charge can be levelled against socialist governments that spent considerable fortunes supporting the Mengistu regime in Ethiopia, Siad Barre in Somalia, Fidel Castro in Cuba, and Pol Pot in Kampuchea. Many of these regimes had terrible human rights records and in their predatory and exclusionist practices, they undermined their fragile legitimacy. When they had run the gamut of policies to kill their opponents, and when foreign assistance dried up or was switched elsewhere, the states broke down into civil war and some, such as Kampuchea and Somalia, collapsed. The values of 'stability', anti-communism, and 'socialist solidarity' appeared to override more democratic values, or values that promoted harmony rather than strife between communities in weak states. Finally, great power armed intervention to support or topple regimes frequently prolonged rather than shortened the agonies of weak states. It was not by chance alone that with the end of the cold war, peace was made swiftly in Angola, Mozambique, Ethiopia, and the Middle East, all areas of great power rivalry and occasional armed intervention.

These are all cases of overt state-weakening actions. There are also more subtle international forces that may work to weaken states and, hence, to increase the risks of humanitarian emergencies. The international arms trade certainly has to be considered. Today, unlike the 1960s, even though major weapons producers do not actively promote arms sales, the availability of weapons on international markets is unlimited and unregulated. Predatory regimes no longer need foreign military aid to exclude and threaten their populations. It is the case, nevertheless, that a large portion of the official grants and sales of arms to weak states were made in the full knowledge that those arms would probably be used against civilians and domestic insurgents rather than against external enemies—if there were any. It would be stretching credulity, for example, to believe that Indonesia or Burma, which purchased arms from a variety of external sources, would use them against some external threat in the 1960s.

But arms are symptoms, seldom causes. It is the fundamental nature of the international system and the values, practices, and structures that were implanted in the non-western areas of the world through imperialism and colonialism that fundamentally created the dilemmas of many weak states. The colonial legacy has already been mentioned, particularly in relation to the construction and destruction of communities. The imperial system also deeply affected the nature of statehood. Dependency theorists have noted, for example, that the structural relationship between local and metropolitan economic and political élites led to 'disarticulated' economies and weak states that were cut off from the masses (Wendt and Barnett 1993: 331–2). These élites were integrated into the world system and ultimately came to depend on foreigners for developing coercive capacities with which to rule over their restive populations. Rather than make compromises with those populations, they resorted to coercion, usually backed by external parties. This is a plausible account for the development of weak states, but it is not a universal one. It would not, for example, cover the numerous cases where nationalist/populists such as Nehru, Sukarno, Nkrumah, and Nasser set their own terms for collaboration with the West. If their states were weak, it was not because of their very thin integration into the world capitalist system.

Finally, recent critiques of the World Bank and International Monetary Fund suggest that some of their policies fundamentally diminish the legitimacy of loan and credit recipients. The imposition of severe austerity measures within states that already suffer from a legitimacy deficit may help provide conditions for armed resistance. Some, for example, have noted a correlation between the successes of the Sendero Luminoso in Peru and the imposition of severe economic retrenchment policies in that Andean country. Woodward (1995) has noted the role of the IMF in helping to weaken the federal state in Yugoslavia when it was faced with increased fragmenting pressures from the constituent republics in 1989–90. There was no intention on the part of the IMF to bring about the weakening of the federation—actually quite the reverse was intended—but the orthodox formulas for transition from a socialist to free market economy helped undermine the legitimacy of the federal authorities and provided increased leverage among republic political leaders for demanding the dilution of federal powers.

It is difficult to offer any generalizations about how the international system and external actors impinge upon the problems of weak states. There is much evidence that can be marshalled on either side of the argument. We can suggest, however, that the international community in general has provided strong support for the juridical status of states; that is, it supports their sovereignty in law, and the practice for the most part has been to withhold support from secessionist groups. Even the Soviet Union, a champion of 'national liberation' of colonies, scrupulously avoided providing material support for secessionist movements in post-colonial states. Heraclides (1990) found on the basis of seven in-depth case studies that on balance the forces favouring state integrity have prevailed.

On the other hand, foreign powers and arms merchants have frequently intervened in weak states to help undermine the legitimacy of regimes. It is a generalization, perhaps, but the United States with considerable consistency favoured Pinochet-type regimes, those committed to economic orthodoxy and anti-communism at the cost of political pluralism and social experimentation. The Soviet Union's record of support for murderous regimes, such as in Ethiopia during the 1970s and 1980s, is well chronicled. The French have frequently intervened in the internal affairs of francophone African regimes to protect their interests. Questions of democracy, human rights, political pluralism, often promoted by weak but budding indigenous civil societies, have seldom been encouraged when they might oppose regime interests. But these are general observations that await empirical validation. For further clues to the role of the external environment in individual cases, we need to examine the selection of cases used in this study.

9.3. *External influences on humanitarian emergencies: evidence from the cases*

External actors, both governmental and non-governmental, become involved in the domestic politics of almost all weak states. The act of diplomatic recognition, for example, provides a regime with international and domestic legitimacy that an unrecognized entity (for example, the Turkish Republic of Cyprus) does not enjoy. If external agents become involved only *after* a war of secession, civil war, or politicide begins, it is not part of the analysis. Such post-event interventions may help explain why a crisis ends or is prolonged, but it does not help locate its aetiology.

9.3.1. Eritrea After the formal federation of Eritrea with Ethiopia, thanks to a UN General Assembly decision in 1949, the Ethiopian monarchy received considerable outside assistance, both economic and military. There is no evidence, however, that it received encouragement from abroad to abrogate the federation and forcibly to incorporate Eritrea into the unitary empire. It should be noted, however, that many of Haile Selassie's foreign patrons did not oppose his project of imperial consolidation (Iyob 1995). Some Arab countries provided assistance for the Eritreans, but it came only after the start of the armed campaign of secession. It can be argued that had the great powers and a few others formally embargoed all arms sales to Haile Selassie, he might not have had the physical means to destroy the federation. This is at best speculation.

9.3.2. *Rwanda* Belgian help in strengthening distinctions between Hutus and Tutsis has been chronicled and documented. The Belgians favoured the minority Tutsis, but they did not create the social division. The Tutsis had ruled over the Hutus long before the Belgians governed it as a League of Nations Mandate. Perhaps the Belgians could be faulted not so much for what they did as for what they did not do, namely promote a more inclusive political system and take active measures to reduce the social distance and discrimination between Tutsi and Hutu.

9.3.3. *Indonesia* There is no evidence of a direct foreign complicity in the massacres of 1965–66. Nevertheless, the PKI (communists) had close relations with China and a load of weapons from China, ostensibly sent to PKI cadres, was on its way to Indonesia when the attempted 30 September coup took place. This attempt, however, was a tipping event that brought forth massive reprisals against Indonesia communists. The PKI-Chinese connection was a factor, but hardly a sufficient condition for the killing.

9.3.4. *Burundi* Some of the comments about Rwanda, above, would apply to Burundi as well. Belgian colonial policy that strongly favoured maintaining the Tutsi domination of Burundi politics was an overhang that significantly increased the risks of humanitarian emergency, in this case massacres of Hutus. We should keep in mind, however, that similar French policies in West Africa did not lead to similar outcomes.

9.3.5. *Nigeria* There is no evidence of direct and instigating external forces in the very complicated politics of Nigerian federalism in the 1960s. There were constant social and political tensions between the different peoples and regions of the country. These were certainly among the legacies of the British decision to create a Nigerian federation instead of a collection of separate ethnic/religious/language states. Given the extreme social diversity of the Nigerian federation, conflict was highly predictable. However, without the tipping events of the July 1966 coup and the massacres of Ibos in Northern Nigeria in the autumn, the probabilities of armed secession by Biafra would have been much lower. Oil politics and French influence over the Ibos may have played a role in this tragedy, but there is little to indicate that they were either necessary or sufficient conditions for armed violence.

9.3.6. *Sudan* There is no evidence of external forces instigating the war between the Muslims and Africans of Sudan. As in most of the cases, however, the colonial overhang of creating a state out of the social maelstrom that constituted Sudan's society at independence is a factor. The colonial legacy certainly increased the risks of humanitarian disaster. The partition of the colony prior to independence might have helped avoid the prolonged civil war that continues.

9.3.7. Sri Lanka The war between the Tamil LTTE and the national government forces was essentially an indigenous affair. India's peacekeeping force ultimately ended up fighting on behalf of the territorial integrity of Sri Lanka. There was some clandestine support for the LTTE from Tamils in India that may have helped sustain the military campaign to this day, but that would help explain only why the war continues, not why it started.

9.3.8. Uganda Colonial overhang again is relevant in the sense that the politics of Uganda prior to Idi Amin were strongly influenced by ethnicity, but there is no direct connection between Amin's atrocities and external forces. To the extent that there was any effort to influence domestic politics in Uganda, it was on the side of reining in Amin rather than assisting him. The United States applied economic sanctions against Uganda, OAU members expressed their displeasure at his behaviour, and ultimately Tanzania intervened militarily to depose him. Amin's unique style of tyranny and atrocity reflects individual psychopathology more than systemic sources.

9.3.9. Lebanon Syria, France, and the United States, among others, played direct roles in Lebanese politics. Israel played an indirect role, although after the beginning of the civil war, it became directly involved through military and other means. The Lebanese civil war was played out against the backdrop of the larger Middle East problem. However, despite impressive arguments to the contrary (Rasler 1992), most of the evidence points predominantly to local sources in the origins of the armed conflict. The basic issue was the predominance of Christian sects, established through the 1942 constitution, in a society in which Muslims had become a majority and were frequently excluded from official positions. External influences, mostly Syrian, certainly complicated issues and might have helped propel the situation toward war, but it is difficult to make a convincing case that they were necessary or sufficient causes of the conflict. Nevertheless, I have categorized the Lebanese war as having been in part instigated by external sources.

9.3.10. Somaliland Ethiopia played a minor role in the first attempted secession of Somaliland from Somalia in 1988. It provided haven for Somaliland refugees, but it strictly desisted from providing more than sanctuary and some humanitarian assistance. The record is largely incomplete, and one could suspect greater complicity given the traditional animosity between Somalia and Ethiopia (the Ogaden War), but at this point the evidence is stronger toward Ethiopian neutrality (Pegg 1998).

9.3.11. Croatia   The Croatian declaration of independence and the subsequent YPA (Yugoslav People's Army) invasion to maintain the integrity of Yugoslavia and to protect and aid the Serbian minority was a sufficient condition for the war. Domestic policies of excluding Serbs from government positions were equally important, perhaps more so. Premature recognition of Croatia by Germany, the EU and the United States also helped to promote armed activity (cf. Woodward 1995; Chapter 6). Even more than Lebanon, the foreign factor in this case is very strong and helped convert a high-risk situation (new state, unbalanced multi-community) into a humanitarian emergency.

9.3.12. Bosnia   European presumption of the break-up of Yugoslavia, the premature and unconditional recognition of Croatia by Germany, and encouragement for holding the plebiscite in April 1992 helped to trigger the war (Woodward 1995; Chapter 6). Serbian military assistance and political encouragement were also vital in transforming the multi-ethnic Bosnian republic in Yugoslavia into an arena of mass murder, rape, and ethnic cleansing.

9.3.13. Tajikistan   Russia was no doubt a background factor, but external forces did not occasion the collapse of post-communist authority. This is largely a homegrown civil war typical of aborted states. Russian military involvement, though low-keyed, has played a role in the war, but was not a major source of the war.

9.3.14. Sierra Leone   There is no evidence of direct external promotion, organization, or funding of the insurgency. However, several Liberian 'armies', themselves refugees of their own collapsed state, had fled to Sierra Leone and were using its territory for actions into Liberia. There may have been some collaboration between Sierra Leone insurgents and the Liberian factions, but the sources of the crisis were predominantly local. Withdrawals of Western aid to Sierra Leone after 1991 helped precipitate an economic crisis that was instrumental in motivating the military coup of 1992.

9.3.15. Rwanda   Uganda had offered sanctuary for Tutsi exiles from Rwanda and helped arm the Rwanda Patriotic Front (Tutsi). Most external actors, however, were working to create peace in Rwanda. The 1993 Arusha accord was brokered by United Nations, and was specifically designed to promote ethnic reconciliation. The United Nations also sent a small force (UNAMIR I) to monitor the fragile cease-fire and accompanying process of demilitarization. The outside community, in other words, sought to help bring peace and ethnic harmony to the country.

9.3.16. Kosovo As in the case of Rwanda, the international community initially sought to create some sort of reconciliation between Serbs and Kosovars. In 1998, the American ambassador in Macedonia attempted to promote discussions between Belgrade and the fractured political leadership of the Kosovars. Neither party to the conflict responded in a fashion to bring any sort of reconciliation. The Kosovars were demanding secession and independence, and the government in Belgrade refused to enter into formal discussions with 'terrorists'. At the same time, the 'Contact Group' unilaterally drafted a settlement agreement that was presented to the two protagonists at Rambouillet in the late autumn and early winter of 1998–99. In effect, they sought to impose peace as they had in Bosnia in 1995. The Rambouillet formula sought to use a referendum as a conflict resolution device. It called for a vote in Kosovo three years after the restoration of peace. Since ninety per cent of the population in Kosovo consisted of Albanians, this was a virtual guarantee of the eventual partition of Yugoslavia. When the Milosovic government rejected the Rambouillet agreement, NATO took the decision to compel it to accept through bombing. In this case, external intervention attempted unsuccessfully to mitigate the conflict through diplomacy, and later through bombing brought on the massive ethnic cleansing that resulted in the humanitarian emergency.[9]

The cases in the study reveal no consistent pattern of external promotion, organization, direction, or high-level funding of conflicts that led to humanitarian emergencies. There is not a single case in which either a great power or lesser neighbouring states' activities were necessary or sufficient conditions for armed conflicts, although Woodward (1995) has made a strong case that European policies in Yugoslavia in 1990–92 weighed heavily on the ultimate outcome of war, and the NATO bombing of Serbia/Kosovo in March 1999 may have caused the ethnic cleansing. There were some instances where a more aggressive stance by external powers or the United Nations might have helped *avert* armed conflict— Eritrea and Rwanda might be examples—but this is usually a view based on hindsight. In any case, the sovereignty norm precludes overt intervention in the absence of a direct request from ruling authorities. Only in the

---

[9] There is some evidence that prior to the bombing, Milosovic's policy in Kosovo was to decimate the KLA, not to remove the Kosovar population from the province. NATO bombing instigated the change in policy in Belgrade to one of ethnic cleansing. However, some have claimed that the ethnic cleansing campaign was planned and organized long before the bombing began.

Lebanese, Sierra Leone, and Yugoslav cases is there reasonable evidence that the actions of foreign powers significantly helped to exacerbate local conflicts to the point of armed violence. But, given the local dynamics, it is unlikely that these actions (for example, premature German recognition of Croatian independence) were sufficient to propel the rivals to war.

10. Weak State Types and Types of Humanitarian Emergencies

A final question is whether the different types of state weakness, ranging from weak, 'phantom' and collapsed states, produce different types of humanitarian emergencies. Väyrynen (Chapter 2) distinguishes violent from complex humanitarian crises. The former involves primarily war casualties and refugee flows (displacement). Complex crises include, as well, large-scale disease and hunger.

Of the 18 cases, I have classified four as complex. In Sudan, drought was associated with the on-going civil war, but it was not drought that caused the conflict. The war, however, seriously disrupted humanitarian assistance, thereby increasing casualties. The same situation prevailed during part of the 30-year secession war in Eritrea. In Sierra Leone, disease and malnutrition followed upon the rampage of looting and expropriation of the leaderless military. In Rwanda, disease and hunger were primarily the legacies and not the causes of the genocide and the resulting flow of refugees into neighbouring countries. No particular conclusions flow from the figures.

Absolute numbers of victims follow no particular pattern either because of the great variation in the conflicts that gave rise to humanitarian emergencies. The Eritrean secession war claimed at least 100,000 lives, but the armed conflict lasted for thirty years. In contrast, about half a million perished as a result of the Rwandan genocide that took place within several weeks; in Somaliland, 60,000 perished in several days.

The only safe generalization is that by and large, government-sponsored and/or organized politicides and ethnic cleansings have the greatest human costs. On average, the number of victims of politicides has been significantly higher than those resulting from civil and secession wars.[10] The most infamous post-1945 politicide was Pol Pot's decimation of Cambodia's population in 1976–78. Following not far behind was the organized murder of Bengalis by Pakistani troops in 1970, the 1994 Rwandan genocide, the 250,000 to half a million victims of the post-coup carnage in Indonesia in 1965–66, and the targeted destruction of 100,000 to 200,000 Hutus in

[10] Using Gurr's (1996: 65) figures based on 50 episodes of genocide and politicide, a minimum of 9 million and a maximum of 20 million civilians perished. If we take the median of 14.5 million casualties for 50 events, the average casualty rate is 290,000 victims per politicide, a figure substantially above the casualty rate for civil and secessionist wars.

Burundi. Idi Amin's victims in Uganda numbered up to 300,000. There are many other cases where either the absolute number of deaths neared or exceeded one million (the Great Cultural Revolution in China, another politicide) or where the number of victims—either murdered or sent flee-ing—exceeded ten per cent of the country's population (for example, Macias Nguema's victims in Equatorial Guinea, where hundreds were killed and one-third of the country's population fled, and Kosovo in 1999).

The number of casualties resulting from secessionist wars, civil wars, and state collapse are in general substantially lower than those resulting from politicides. The average number killed in the six cases of politicide is 588,000. The average number of combat and civilian casualties from inter-nal wars, including wars of secession and state collapse, is 266,000, or a ratio of 2.2:1. Politicides result, in brief, in more than twice as many casu-alties as internal wars.[11]

Even allowing for the great uncertainties and unevenness of casualty statistics, differences of this magnitude cannot be due to chance or to imprecise data. There seems to be a very distinct profile of victims—par-ticularly those killed. In politicides, specific groups made up mostly of citi-zens are targeted for extermination. The purpose is not to destroy a military force or various types of armed resistance to the state, but to elim-inate an entire segment of the civilian population. In many cases, it is the higher educated, politically active élites of social and ethnic groups. Wars, in contrast, have the specific purpose of (i) defeating an armed adversary; (ii) capturing state power; and/or (iii) seceding from the state. Civilians become trapped in war zones, or they may be coerced to provide haven, sanctuary, and sustenance to armies. In wars for territory, populations may be forcefully expelled, as in Bosnia, Croatia, and Kosovo. Any type of resistance may bring death, but the normal purpose of wars is not to destroy distinct elements of the society but to capture or maintain power. Citizens in these wars are usually innocent victims. In politicides, they are deliberately targeted. The collapse of states may lead to high civilian deaths if no local sources of security can develop, but usually as in Somalia, civilian deaths, hunger, and disease are consequences rather than the purposes of military actions.

11. Evaluation of Findings

All humanitarian emergencies have their individual and unique charac-teristics. However, when we compare across several cases, there seem to

---

[11] In making these calculations, numbers are partly skewed by several outliers or extreme events. If we eliminate them (the Pakistan politicide of 1970–71 and the Eritrean and Biafran wars), the ratio of average victims of politicides to victims of wars increases from 2.2:1 to 3.7:1. The generalization holds.

be common patterns, or a morphology of crisis. To use Suganami's (1996) work on the methodology of war causation, there may be 'families' of causes that share many features, but where individual details are not identical. In the cases reviewed here, we can identify few necessary or sufficient conditions, but many of the background attributes of states, combined with exclusionist policies and tipping events, seem to predict increasingly high risks of humanitarian emergencies. I have chosen to characterize the problem as a process, where attributes combine with actions to create increasingly dangerous risks of political and social violence. New and weak states, often bearing structural colonial legacies such as arbitrary borders, provide the background attributes. Governments, however, make choices, and frequently these undermine their legitimacy. The choices frequently include discrimination and exclusion, and sometimes great peril and threat to specific communities within the state. Often these measures are designed to strengthen the government. In fact, they have the reverse effect: they diminish both vertical and horizontal legitimacy. Playing the ethnic or community card is a dangerous strategy. It may bring short-term political gains for incumbents, but in the long run it destroys the affective foundation of the state. Elsewhere, I have termed this the state-strength dilemma (Holsti 1996; Chapter 6).

Tipping events transform the weakening structure of legitimacy between communities and between communities and the state, into violence. Either governments go after real or imagined opponents or, more frequently, they target entire communities for 'extreme measures'. Communities at risk take up arms in self-defence or attempt to secede from the state that has become a threat to their autonomy, culture, economy, or existence. The resulting battles and massacres lead to hundreds of thousands of deaths and millions of refugees.

The political sources of humanitarian emergencies are complex, but this diagnostic exercise has sought to demonstrate that there are conditions, policies, and paths that significantly increase the risks. Frequently those can be identified prior to the disasters, but the international community seems to have little political will to intervene in a preventive sense. The warning signals of war in Yugoslavia or Eritrea, of politicides in Uganda, Rwanda, and Burundi, and of state collapse in Somalia were highly visible, in some cases months before the tipping events that sparked the catastrophes took place. But despite pleas by successive secretaries-general of the United Nations, and sometimes by individual governments, there is no sure path to political prevention. To the extent that diagnostic exercises can help uncover patterns and paths, we might at least begin to develop the informational base upon which political action must be based.

References

Ahmed, Ishtiaq (1996). *State, Nation and Ethnicity in Contemporary South Asia.* London and New York: Pinter.

Ayoob, Mohammed (1995). *The Third World Security Predicament: State Making, Regional Conflict, and the International System.* Boulder, CO: Lynne Reinner.

Bereciartu, Gurutz J. (1994). *Decline of the Nation-State.* Trans. William A. Douglass. Reno and Las Vegas: University of Nevada Press.

Buzan, Barry (1983). *States, States and Fear: The National Security Problem in International Relations.* Chapel Hill, NC: University of North Carolina Press.

Callaghy, Thomas M. (1984). *The State-Society Struggle. Zaire in Comparative Perspective.* New York: Columbia University Press.

De Swan, Abram (1997). 'Widening Circle of Disidentification: on the Psycho- and Sociogenesis of the Hatred of Distinct Strangers: Reflections on Rwanda'. *Theory, Society and Culture*, 14 (2): 105–22.

Ellingsen, Tanja (1996). 'Colorful Community or Ethnic Witches Brew? Political Regime and Armed Conflict During and After the Cold War'. Paper prepared for the 37th Annual Meetings of the International Studies Association, San Diego, April 16–20.

Ergas, Zaki (ed.) (1987). *The African State in Transition.* London: Macmillan.

Galtung, Johann (1971). 'A Structural Theory of Imperialism'. *Journal of Conflict Resolution*, 8: 387–417.

Gros, Jean-Germain (1996). 'Towards a Taxonomy of Failed States in the New World Order: Decaying Somalia, Liberia, Rwanda, and Haiti'. *Third World Quarterly*, (17) (3) (September): 455–71.

Gurr, Ted Robert (1993). *Minorities at Risk: A Global View of Ethnopolitical Conflict.* Washington, DC: United States Institute for Peace Press.

Gurr, Ted Robert (1996). 'Minorities, Nationalists, and Ethnopolitical Conflict', in Chester A. Crocker and Fen Osler Hampson (eds.), *Managing Global Chaos: Sources and Responses to International Conflict.* Washington, DC: United States Institute for Peace Press.

Harbenson, John W., Donald Rothchild, and Naomi Chazan (eds.) (1994). *Civil Society and the State in Africa.* Boulder and London: Lynne Rienner Publishers.

Hardin, Russell (1995). *One for All: The Logic of Group Conflict.* Princeton: Princeton University Press.

Harff, Barbara, and Ted Robert Gurr (1998). 'Systematic Early Warning of Humanitarian Emergencies'. *Journal of Peace Research*, 35 (5): 551–79.

Heraclides, Alexis (1990). 'Secessionist Minorities and External Involvement'. *International Organization*, 44 (3): 341–78.

Holsti, Kalevi J. (1996). *The State, War, and the State of War.* Cambridge: Cambridge University Press.

Holsti, Kalevi J. (1997). 'International Theory and Wars within States: The Limits of Relevance', in Stephanie Neuman (ed.), *International Theory and War in the Third World.* New York: St. Martin's Press.

Ignatieff, Michael (1993). *Blood and Belonging: Journeys into the New Nationalism.* Toronto: Penguin Books.

Iyob, Ruth (1995). *The Eritrean Struggle for Independence: Domination, Resistance, Nationalism, 1941–1993*. Cambridge: Cambridge University Press.

Jackson, Robert (1990). *Quasi States: Sovereignty, International Relations and the Third World*. Cambridge: Cambridge University Press.

Jackson, Robert, and Carl G. Rosberg (1982). *Personal Rule in Black Africa: Prince, Autocrat, Prophet, Tyrant*. Berkeley: University of California Press.

Janis, Irving L. (1972). *Victims of Groupthink: a Psychological Study of Foreign-Policy Decisions and Fiascoes*. Boston: Houghton Mifflin.

Kaplan, Robert D. (1996). *The Ends of the Earth: A Journey at the Dawn of the 21st Century*. New York: Random House.

Klugman, Jeni (1999). 'Social and Economic Policies to Prevent Complex Humanitarian Emergencies: Lessons from Experience'. UNU/WIDER Policy Brief No. 2. Helsinki: World Institute for Development Economics Research (UNU/WIDER).

Krain, Matthew (1997). 'State-Sponsored Mass Murder'. *Journal of Conflict Resolution*, 41 (3): 311–60.

Lee, Shin-wha (1997). 'Not a One-Time Event: Environmental Change, Ethnic Rivalry, and Violent Conflict in the Third World'. *Journal of Environment and Development*, 6 (4): 365–96.

Melkas, Helinä (1996). 'Humanitarian Emergencies: Indicators, Measurements, and Data Considerations'. RIP 5 (Research in Progress). Helsinki: World Institute for Development Economics Research (UNU/WIDER).

Migdal, Joel (1988). *Strong States and Weak Societies: State-Society Relations and State Capabilities in the Third World*. Princeton: Princeton University Press.

Pegg, Scott (1998). *International Society and the De Facto State*. Aldershot, Hants.: Ashgate.

Rasler, Karen A. (1992).' International Influences on the Origins and Outcomes of Internal War: A Comparative Analysis of the 1958 and 1975–6 Lebanese Civil Wars', in Manus Midlarsky (ed.), *The Internationalization of Communal Strife*. London and New York: Routledge, 93–117.

Rummel, Rudolph J. (1994). *Death by Government*. New Brunswick, NJ and London: Transaction Books.

Schoeberlein-Engel, Eric (1994). 'Conflict in Tajikistan and Central Asia: The Myth of Ethnic Animosity'. *Harvard Middle Eastern and Islamic Review*, 1: 1–55.

Snyder, Jack, and Karen Ballantine (1996). 'Nationalism and the Marketplace of Ideas'. *International Security*, 21 (2): 5–40.

Suganami, Hidemi (1996). *On the Causes of War*. Oxford: Clarendon Press.

Tilly, Charles (1990). *Coercion, Capital, and European States, A.D. 990–1990*. Cambridge, MA: Basil Blackwell.

Uwechue, Ralph (1972). 'From Tribe to Nation'. *Africa*, 7: 9–12.

Weiss, Herbert (1995). 'Zaire: Collapsed Society, Surviving State, Future Policy', in I. William Zartman (ed.), *Collapsed States*. Boulder, CO. and London: Lynn Rienner, 157–70.

Wendt, Alexander and Richard Barnett (1993). 'Dependent State Formation and Third World Militarization'. *Review of International Studies*, 19 (4): 321–40.

Woodward, Susan (1995). *Balkan Tragedy: Chaos and Dissolution After the Cold War*. Washington, DC: The Brookings Institution.

Young, Crawford (1994). 'In Search of Civil Society', in J. W. Harbeson, D. Rothchild and N. Chazan (eds.), *Civil Society and the State in Africa*. Boulder and London: Lynne Rienner, 33–50.

Zartman, I. William (ed.) (1995). *Collapsed States: The Disintegration and Restoration of Legitimate Authority*. Boulder, CO, and London: Lynn Rienner.

8

War, Crime, and Access to Resources

DAVID KEEN

1. Introduction

One very common view—particularly in the media and in aid agency discourses—is that violence is irrational and dysfunctional. But such discussions typically suggest few practical remedies. It is important to recognize that negative phenomena may have functions as well as causes and symptoms. Infectious disease has functions for the germ, and recognizing this was a major step on the road to more successful interventions. We need, similarly, to take seriously the functions of violence and, more broadly, of humanitarian crises.

Insofar as the functions of violence *are* taken seriously, discussion typically centres on political and military goals. Thus, war has often been seen as a contest between two 'sides', with civilians 'caught in the crossfire'. In most discussions of civil war, the focus is on the state and the system of laws and administrative procedures originating from the capital. However, the goals of those involved in both insurgency and counter-insurgency may be more complex, and more local, than such discussions imply (Keen 1994; 1998). Often, the aim is not so much to overthrow or maintain a particular system of law as to circumnavigate the law—to 'take the law into one's own hands'—in order to realize some immediate material gain. In other words, 'war' may dovetail into 'crime',[1] and we need to rethink the relationship between the two.

Some of the local and immediate functions of violence may be economic. Some may be psychological. And some may centre, paradoxically, on enhancing an individual's security. Existing approaches to the study of crimes-during-war have often been inadequate, and the shortcomings of three of these approaches are discussed below.

One approach has been to focus on the relatively narrow category of crimes known as 'war crimes'. Where civilians have been deliberately

---

[1] Even so, it is important to remember that rebellions (including anti-colonial rebellions) have habitually been dismissed by governments as 'criminal' (Furedi 1994). The fact that crime becomes commonplace in a war does not mean that political grievances can be ignored or disparaged.

targeted for violence, many observers speak of 'war crimes' and the need for international or national tribunals to try the alleged perpetrators. In this conception, a 'war crime' is a particularly evil act that contravenes the international laws of war, and particularly laws designed to protect civilians.[2] Usually the focus is on a few key individuals, who are seen as particularly 'evil' or at least particularly responsible. However, to prevent or minimize the suffering that arises from war, we need to think not only about such matters as the 'root causes' of war and negotiations between rival leaders; we need to start looking more systematically at the circumstances in which crimes-during-war become likely, to examine their rationality and their functions—both for 'leaders' and for quite large groups of people who participate in them. These crimes, considered together, should not be seen simply as aberrations. Rather, they increasingly constitute part of the *essence* of war.

A second approach, perhaps most famously manifest in Robert Kaplan's article 'The Coming Anarchy', has been to label crime as a threatening and essentially uncontrollable 'other' which threatens to engulf the civilized world, which by implication should seal itself off from the gathering chaos. While not without analytical insights, Kaplan's work is highly emotive and has little to suggest on the issue of how crime-during-war might be made less likely.

A third unsatisfactory approach has been to adopt analytical frameworks which implicitly or explicitly exclude crime (and violence more generally) from their purview. This has been the practice of a great many economists. Even though economists frequently claim to be studying the forces that determine the production and distribution resources in society, as a group they have generally failed to consider that rational action to maximize one's access to resources may involve using violence—whether in 'peacetime' or 'wartime' (Keen 1995; 1997).[3] It is difficult to disagree with Garfinkel and Skaperdas (1996: 1) when they portray the rational 'economic men' in economic textbooks as intriguingly schizophrenic figures:

While completely rational and self-interested when it comes to truck, barter and trade, they are also saints of sorts, obeying a stronger version of the ten commandments: they simply will not take what does not belong to them, even when it is in their interest to do so.

Such saintly figures may be convenient for many economists but are not necessarily very helpful for those analysing conflict, particularly when this takes the form of outright civil war.

---

[2] It is implicit in the idea of a war crime that war itself is acceptable—as long as it is not taken 'too far'.

[3] Peacetime may see the use of violence in protection rackets, for example; and violence (embodied in the law) plays a key role in shoring up systems of ownership even in peaceful democracies.

A rather specific economic/philosophical framework that explicitly excludes consideration of crime is Amartya Sen's 'entitlement framework'. Since this has probably been the single most influential tool for the understanding of humanitarian disasters, it is worth considering in some detail its significant silence on the subject of crime (and violence more generally). This 'noiseless noise' in Sen's work is discussed in the following section.

2. The Entitlement Framework—Some Limitations

Though this is a major contribution to our understanding of famine, Amartya Sen's entitlement may also have helped deflect attention from the close connection between violence and crime on the one hand and contemporary complex emergencies, on the other. The entitlement framework explicitly excludes illegal acts and takes a rather static and rigid view of the law. It concentrates on how particular systems of ownership can translate into famine in the context of an external shock like the Second World War (Bengal famine in 1943), drought (Sahelian famine in the early 1970s, Ethiopian famine in 1972–74) or flooding (Bangladeshi famine in 1974). Such shocks may translate into famine through the mechanism of market prices. The focus is on the ability of individuals to stake a claim to resources within a particular system of laws. As Sen notes (1981: 45):

The entitlement approach . . . concentrates on those means of commanding food that are legitimized by the legal system in that society. While it is an approach *of some generality*, it makes no attempt to include all possible influences that can *in principle* cause starvation, for example illegal transfers (e.g. looting) . . . (my emphases).

If this statement plays down the likelihood of illegal transfers causing famine, Drèze and Sen go further in their subsequent elaboration of Sen's original thesis (1989: 22):

It would be, particularly, a mistake to relate the *causation* of famines to violations of legality . . . the millions that die in a famine typically die in an astonishingly 'legal' and 'orderly' way.

Sen's framework is certainly helpful in understanding the Bengal famine of 1943 and the three peacetime famines considered in the rest of his book, *Poverty and Famines*. But a rounded understanding of contemporary civil wars and associated famines demands a more subtle and realistic view of the law and its purview. It is simply not the case that those who die in contemporary famines do so in 'an astonishingly "legal" and "orderly" way'. Indeed, it is precisely because of *illegality*—and the 'grey area' between what is legal and illegal—that the great majority of recent famines have occurred.[4]

Understanding why crimes occur—and why they are tolerated and even sometimes encouraged by the relevant authorities—offers an important insight not only into the famine process but also, more generally, into civil wars (with which recent famines have almost always been associated). To come to grips with contemporary complex emergencies, we should not regard crime as an aberration, as something that lies outside our analytical framework, but as a phenomenon of extreme importance which we need to acknowledge and explain.[5]

In addition to explicitly excluding illegal acts, the entitlement framework tends to take property rights as *fixed rights* that translate into famine in the context of external shocks. Yet such rights may in practice be quickly undermined by political and military processes, as when the property rights of a particular ethnic group are removed.[6] The entitlement framework gives little consideration to the fact that *rival systems of law and entitlements may clash with each other*.[7] And it gives little attention to *whether the state attempts to, or is able to, implement laws that exist*.

A rounded understanding of people's vulnerability to both violence and famine will involve, firstly, consideration of actions that lie outside the entitlements framework because they are unambiguously illegal. Second, it will involve examining actions that are *on the margins* of the entitlement framework (or insufficiently considered within this framework). The latter category of actions includes:

- Actions that are legal at the national level but illegal in terms of international law. The two legal systems do not necessarily coincide, and this is one difficulty with dividing actions neatly into those that are legal and those that are illegal. (At the Nuremberg trials after the Second World War, Göring famously argued that the accused were innocent under German law which had legitimized their actions.)
- Changes in the law that are in some sense imposed by unconstitutional means.
- Actions that are illegal within one system of entitlements (for example, those systems adopted by indigenous populations in Australia and the Americas) but nevertheless legal within a rival system of entitlements (the 'paper systems' instituted by settlers, for example).

---

[4] See also de Waal (1997).

[5] The need to place violence at the centre of the analysis is ably brought out in a critique of Sen (and, incidentally, the 'complex emergency theorists', including myself, who have challenged him) by Jenny Edkins.

[6] I am particularly indebted to discussions with Valpy FitzGerald on static and dynamic conceptions of the law. As FitzGerald notes, while entitlements may be eroded, they can also be created, notably in a revolution or social reform.

[7] Even within a particular system of laws, one law may be in tension with another.

- Actions that are illegal at the national level but in practice considered to be, or treated as, legal at the local level. This might be called 'sanctioned illegality'. Formally illegal acts may nevertheless be sanctioned at the local level by actors such as warlords, militias, or rebels. They may also be sanctioned, in some sense, by the state—as when human rights abuses by militias are tolerated, or encouraged, by a government. This category of actions is considered further in the section below.

3. Sanctioned Illegality

How do crimes-during-war arise? It is not possible to give a comprehensive answer here. Part of the responsibility clearly lies with those who reject or ignore the authority of the state.[8] But part of the responsibility lies, paradoxically, with the state itself. Weak and undemocratic states have repeatedly encouraged various kinds of crime—for military, political, and economic reasons. Counter-insurgency in a weak state brings together, powerfully and destructively, a politically repressive violence and a range of more local and immediate agendas that are served by non-élite groups resorting to violence.[9] The coming together of these two sets of agendas is part of what gives contemporary 'complex emergencies' their complexity. It stands in contrast to the pattern of violence in civil wars during the cold war era, where confrontations along ideological lines were more evident (even though, as Tim Allen points out, there were frequently powerful local agendas that were disguised behind a shrewd appeal to international backers). Rebel groups, too, have encouraged and tolerated crime—particularly in circumstances where they lack the finance, external support, and coherent ideology that might allow them to impose discipline on their followers (see, for example, Outram 1997; Keen 1998). While civil wars that dovetail into crime represent only one end of the spectrum (with countries like Sierra Leone, Liberia and Somalia perhaps manifesting this trend most strongly), such wars, nevertheless, appear to be becoming more common.[10] The end of the cold war has probably encouraged the blurring of war and crime: we have seen a diminishing role for political ideology; there has been diminishing external support for governments and rebel groups (encouraging them to wage war 'on the cheap'); and with processes of democratization having been encouraged by the fall of communist regimes in the eastern bloc, élites in a number of

---

[8] This may, of course, be part of a progressive political movement.

[9] See Keen (1998).

[10] Not that they are without historical precedent. In certain respects, wars that dovetail into crime are reminiscent of conflicts during the medieval era, when the absence of a strong state encouraged a proliferation of factions who supported themselves through robbing the civilian population.

countries (former Yugoslavia, Rwanda, Sierra Leone) have repeatedly responded to this 'threat' by inciting ethnic and factional violence.

Rather than simply analysing a civil war in terms of 'background causes' and then 'tactics', or in terms of 'insurgency' and 'counter-insurgency', it may sometimes be more helpful to adopt the kind of framework that one might use in understanding (or indeed investigating) crime. That is, one can look at the opportunities for crime, at the motives for crime and, finally, at the degree of impunity which those carrying out crimes enjoy (and expect to enjoy). This analysis can be applied to those orchestrating, funding, and actually carrying out acts of violence. Correspondingly, when designing (or evaluating) external interventions, it may be helpful to consider the likely (or actual) impact of interventions on the opportunities for crime, on the motives for crime, and on the degree of impunity enjoyed by those perpetrating crimes.

This approach demands a subtle but important reformulation of the type of questions we ask about civil wars. Some military historians and strategists, adopting a more sophisticated model of conflict than that of a contest between two sides, have asked how warring parties have (or have not) been able to garner civilian 'support'. The importance of civilian support was emphasized by Mao (with his famous belief that sympathetic civilians were the 'sea' in which guerrilla 'fishes' could flourish). It also informed the (patchy) US attempts to win over 'hearts and minds' in Vietnam and Central America. However, the most revealing question may not be which groups *'support'* a rebellion or counter-insurgency campaign but which groups (whether politicians, traders, or ordinary civilians) *seek to take advantage* of a rebellion or a counter-insurgency campaign for what kinds of purposes.

Paradoxically, coalitions of counter-insurgency forces, ostensibly seeking to uphold the law in the face of rebel attempts to subvert it, have habitually carried out a variety of illegal acts in the course of their operations. Such illegal acts have often been tolerated and even actively encouraged by higher governmental authorities, contributing to a climate of impunity. Even where the forcible appropriation of assets by groups associated with the government has been legal, this legality has sometimes stemmed only from recent changes in the law (for example, changes in laws governing access to Somali land and Sudanese oil, or changes in laws governing the military's right to raid private houses in Sierra Leone). Sometimes, 'legality' has been improvised and coercive, as when Bosnian Muslims were forced to sign contracts saying they had 'voluntarily' given away their homes and possessions in return for transport out of areas that were being 'ethnically cleansed'.

3.1. War on the cheap

Where governments and/or rebel leaders have lacked the resources to fund disciplined armies, the economic exploitation of civilians has tended to play a critical role in funding warfare and sustaining the fighters. As noted, loss of external funding (notably as a result of the end of the cold war) has often encouraged this pattern of warfare.

Civilians (despite their traditional portrayal in the media as 'innocent victims' who are 'caught in the crossfire' of warfare or abused by powerful war criminals) have increasingly been *implicated* in war-time atrocities, notably as members of unpaid or underpaid militias. The active role of many women, local aid workers, doctors, and church workers in the Rwandan genocide has been particularly shocking (*African Rights* 1995b), underlining limitations in the media's propensity for venerating particular groups as 'good' whilst dismissing others as 'evil'. The use of militias (especially ethnic militias) has offered considerable opportunities for fighting war on the cheap, for exploiting existing ethnic tensions and, critically, for confusing the international community and 'buying time' for abusive governments.

In large part because they are unpaid or underpaid, militias (including those associated with rebel groups) have frequently 'broken away' into patterns of violence that reflect individual and local agendas—often economic or centring on some notion of 'revenge'—more than military or national ones (Keen 1998).

3.2. Economic functions of violence: some types and conducive conditions

To understand the reasons for crimes-during-war, we need to understand the possible economic functions of such crimes. Economic gains during civil war can be made not only from control of the state but also, more locally and immediately, from pillage, from charging 'protection money', and from control of land, labour, aid, and trade. While Sen stressed the role of market forces in propelling famine, contemporary famines have often been propelled by what I call 'forced markets' (Keen 1994), in other words by the workings of markets that are profoundly shaped by various kinds of force. Where force is widespread, its economic benefits may lie not just in those assets that are directly appropriated but also in the way that markets are distorted. For example, labour prices in a particular geographical area may be artificially depressed by an influx of migrants whose assets have been stolen and by threats of violence against labourers.

Economic violence appears to be particularly likely when the principal areas of military operations have a large, or increasing, resource potential in relation to the resources commanded 'at the centre' by rebel or govern-ment leadership. In these circumstances, groups associated with the gov-ernment or the rebels may be given, in effect, a licence to use violence to accumulate wealth at the local level.

3.3. *Militarily counter-productive actions*

There is more to war than winning. Many acts of violence are militarily counter-productive but at the same time serve a range of local and imme-diate agendas.[11] 'Winning the war' may not be the only, or even the most important, aim of the diverse groups involved in funding, orchestrating, and carrying out acts of violence. War has habitually legitimated all man-ner of crimes. And the desire to make money through exploiting civilians may be actively counter-productive from a purely military point of view, driving civilians into the arms of the opposing side. A number of other actions—such as selling arms and ammunition to one's opponents—make sense from an economic, rather than a strategic, perspective. Militarily counter-productive actions tend to prolong and widen a conflict, thereby often legitimizing economic exploitation. Correspondingly, militarily effective action may pose a significant threat to the economic beneficiaries of conflict.

The use of violence for economic ends may sometimes precede—and precipitate—outright conflict; in any case, it is likely to contribute to the strength of armed opposition, perhaps turning a small guerrilla move-ment into a large one as more and more people, realizing that the state is not providing them with protection, turn elsewhere for their physical and economic security. In the 1980s, such a process of radicalization was observable among the Isaak of Somalia and the Nuba and Dinka of Sudan, to give two examples.

Warfare in Somalia in the late 1970s and the 1980s was usually discussed as a political conflict between the government of Siad Barre and rebel groups like the Somali National Movement, which began armed resistance in northern Somalia in 1981. However, conflict was also fuelled and shaped by prosaic local struggles—over trade, land, household property, and jobs. For example, the SNM revolt served as an excuse for widespread (and profitable) abuses against the Isaak clan that was seen as providing most of its support. One resident of Buroa town in northern Somalia said:

The government deliberately put all the power in the hands of non-Isaaks. By 1984 there was no Isaak in any position of authority in Buroa . . . If an Isaak had a busi-ness coveted by a non-Isaak or which was regarded as a competitive threat, he or she would be labelled a 'trouble maker' and harassed till they got fed up and closed the business—better still, left town (*Africa Watch* 1990: 117).

---

[11] For a fuller discussion of this issue, see Keen (1998).

In Sudan, from 1983, Arab militias carried out attacks on civilians from several sections of the Dinka that had had, until that point, no connection with the Sudan People's Liberation Army (SPLA) rebellion. This helped to radicalize the Dinka and increase support for the SPLA. The SPLA in turn alienated possible supporters through encouraging the raiding of southern Sudanese groups associated with pro-government militias. Exploitation of particular ethnic groups may help to generate its own legitimacy, by stimulating the growth of armed opposition and by encouraging a perception that rebel-linked groups are 'fair game' and undeserving of the protection of the law.

For both rebels and forces associated with the government, picking on unarmed civilians may be a more attractive prospect than confronting armed opponents. And with some groups trying to take advantage of civil war, others may be compelled to join the fighting out of self-defence. Where armed gangs are engaged in the violent exploitation of civilians, it may be safer (as well as more profitable) to be in an armed gang than to remain as an unarmed civilian, particularly since those remaining unarmed may risk being accused of collaboration with rebel (or government) groups. Sierra Leone and Burma would appear to be good examples of this dynamic.

We are confronted with a deep paradox: rebellion may be functional for governments and government forces. Part of the reason is the cover rebellion may provide for various kinds of crime (notably by government forces). In Sierra Leone, Peru, and Guatemala, rebels have been blamed for a range of government soldier activities, including looting, illegal mining and drug-running (Keen 1998; Simpson 1994).

For an undemocratic regime, economic violence may be advantageous not just in rewarding supporters but also in prolonging a conflict that legitimizes authoritarian or military rule and serves as justification for attempts to stifle political opposition. Undemocratic or 'exclusive' regimes have often sought to protect the economic interests of their supporters by portraying certain kinds of political opposition (including trades unions) as manifestations of 'rebel activity'. This can provide cover for moves against the opposition, and the concept of a 'rebel' may be kept conveniently fluid.

This would appear to be a particularly important phenomenon in parts of Latin America. In Colombia, civil war has served as a cover for all manner of repression. As Ramon Emilio Arcila, leader of the civic movement[12] of Eastern Antioquia, said shortly before he himself was assassinated in 1989:

... leaders from all the regions of Colombia have been assassinated. They are indiscriminately linked with the armed movements to justify the repression. The state

---

[12] Unaffiliated to political parties, the movement established a reputation for committed opposition to price rises and peasant expulsions.

has issued a series of repressive measures in which any expression or demonstration practically constitutes a terrorist act, and leads to searches and arrests (Pearce 1990: 157).

In Cambodia, opponents of government corruption have been tarred with the brush of 'rebel sympathizer': those who voice dissent have often been attacked by the government as supporting the Khmer Rouge (Shawcross 1996). In Sierra Leone, journalists questioning the complicity of government soldiers in the violent exploitation of civilians have repeatedly been labelled as 'rebels' or 'rebel sympathizers'.

A continuation of conflict may serve to stifle political opposition through the preservation of a military regime, the declaration and prolongation of 'states of emergency' that accord special powers to repressive governments or the military, and through restrictions on freedom of speech that are justified as part of a 'war effort'. Prolonging conflict may also offer the significant advantage that it may be very difficult, from a practical point of view, to hold elections. Preventing elections may be particularly tempting for those whose previous violence and exploitation might lay them open to prosecution under a more democratic regime.

The 'uses' of violent rebellion for elements of the government seem to be underlined by events in Algeria. The Algerian government has repeatedly blamed massacres there on Islamic extremists, notably the GIA, or Armed Islamic Group. For a long time, the Western media was content to echo the condemnation of Islamic 'fundamentalists'. However, through 1997 it became increasingly clear that elements of the Western-backed government of General Liamin Zeroual—which seized power after elections had given a victory to the Islamic FIS party—were actively encouraging the climate of insecurity in Algeria, apparently in an attempt to perpetuate military rule in the face of the 'Islamic threat'. The GIA is thought by Western intelligence services to have been infiltrated by the security forces, who are believed to be deeply implicated in the cycle of killings (Fox 1997). Violence seemed to intensify whenever progress towards peace becomes manifest, reinforcing suspicions that extremists in the government shared an interest in violence with extremists in the Islamic groups they claimed to be opposing (Hirst 1997). Massacres have repeatedly taken place right under the noses of government security forces, who seemed to be not just unable to prevent the massacres but also, in many instances, unwilling (see, for example, *Guardian* 1997; Sweeney 1997). Suspicion of government forces was further fuelled by the government's opposition to an international commission of enquiry into the massacres.

3.4. Falling 'below the law'

Insofar as war can be depicted as an accumulation of crimes (both in terms of local and international laws), it will be important to understand the way that some groups come to be effectively 'above the law' (that is, immune from prosecution and punishment, according to national or international law) whilst others come to be effectively 'below the law' (that is, unprotected, in practice, by national or international law). In terms of national laws, groups that are 'below the law' have very often been groups deemed to be associated with a rebel movement. This label has rendered such groups vulnerable to extreme violence and exploitation—abuse that has habitually been deemed legitimate in the context of war. Those resisting (or simply seen as resisting) a key geo-strategic ally of the major world powers may face particular difficulties in securing in practice the protection which international law accords them in theory.

Whether through coercive contracts, through changes in the law, or through a diminishing willingness to enforce the law, communities may perceive themselves being deprived of legal protection (as with the Serbs in Croatia in 1990–91, or the Nuba and Dinka in Sudan in the 1980s and 1990s). One of the advantages of the government side in a civil war is that it can define what is legal—both *de jure* and *de facto*—and what is not. Rebel groups—and warlords—may also sometimes possess the ability to decide on what is legal *de facto* in areas they control.

Some groups (and these are often ethnic groups) may come to feel that they have been placed below the protection of the law even before outright conflict breaks out, and this may be precisely why significant numbers resort to outright violence (see, for example, *African Rights* 1995a, on the Nuba in Sudan). Perhaps because of the nature of the law or the way that law is implemented, such groups may feel that the state is no longer ensuring their physical protection and/or their access to critical economic resources. Thus, it is not simply conflict that removes the protection of the law. Rather, the removal of the law's protection may generate conflict. The political economy of war emerges from the political economy of peace, and vice versa. This highlights the importance of examining the role of violence in peacetime, of avoiding a Manichean view that equates war with all things bad and peace with all things good.

In a 'weak state' (where salaries are low and bureaucratic lines of command are weak), ruling in peacetime is likely to mean tolerating a degree of exploitation of civilians and material resources by local élites: since insufficient resources are available at the centre to 'buy' the loyalty of these groups, their loyalty must be bought, at least in part, with toleration of processes of exploitation at the local level (cf. Reno 1995). Whether in peace or war, exercising power in a weak state demands some kind of collaboration with powerful local figures (as Robinson and Gallagher [1961] famously argued in the context of imperial rule). This means that priorities cannot simply be set 'at the top', and that patterns of violence may reflect local (as well as leadership) agendas. The licensing of violence—which may accompany, precede, or even precipitate an outright civil war—can offer opportunities to build political support among influential groups such as merchants, landowners, and traditional leaders.

In the course of Sudan's second civil war (from 1983), northern traders and landowners have in effect been granted the right violently to appropriate fertile land in the Nuba Mountains region, something that has consolidated support for regimes in Khartoum.

In Somalia, the forcible appropriation of land was encouraged and legitimized by the Barre government in the fertile Juba and Shebelle River zones. Meanwhile, in many parts of the country the stigmatization of a variety of ethnic groups as guerrilla supporters offered a range of prosaic opportunities—from improved employment prospects and improved access to grazing land to outright theft—for those from other, more favoured ethnic groups.

In Zaire and Iraq, undemocratic regimes have similarly sought to build political support among particular families, clans, and ethnic groups by granting them economic privileges that include the right to inflict violence without redress. This has sometimes taken the form of ethnic cleansing, and sometimes of intra-ethnic disputes (notably among the Kurds in Iraq). In Zaire, the pattern of aid and development encouraged soldiers to follow their own economic agendas and to promote forms of ethnic cleansing (cf. Emizet, Chapter 9, Volume 2).

Having supported impunity for a long time with some combination of aid and silence (as with Barre in Somali, Doe in Liberia, Mobutu in Zaire), it may be very difficult—practically and morally—for 'the international community' to turn around in a war and demand 'an end to impunity'.[13]

3.5. *Immediate power for the powerless*

Local agendas in civil wars may include not only economic gain and 'revenge' but also a desire for an immediate, on-the-spot restoration of status and power. Violence is not simply a means to power (or wealth) but involves the *immediate* assertion and establishment of power over the victim. In Sierra Leone, civil war has seen repeated attempts to humiliate traditional chiefs and local 'big men' by teenage fighters lacking status or adequate employment within their own communities. Even where violence does not serve economic functions (as in the case of vandalism or revenge killings), it will be important to try to understand how this violence may have been generated by a particular political economy. Addressing the conditions in which (peacetime and wartime) violence

---

[13] Incidentally, wars can be zones of impunity for international as well as local actors: even peacekeepers entering this zone of impunity may carry out their own crimes, witness the looting of ECOMOG troops in Liberia and the brutality of some Belgian, Italian and Canadian UN soldiers in Somalia. This underlines the need for structures of accountability within peacekeeping forces.

becomes likely will almost certainly mean addressing deficiencies in educational and employment opportunities (cf. Richards 1996). Recognizing that 'war' and 'crime' have become somewhat blurred may help those who seek to prevent humanitarian disasters in seeing the relevance of providing improving educational and employment opportunities—measures that have long been advocated by 'the left' as vital in any attempt to tackle the roots of crime.

The way in which wartime impunity can lead to the settling of a variety of grudges—again, an immediate assertion of power—is brought out by Peter Maas's (1996: 52–3) account of a his visit to Omarska prison camp, Bosnia, in 1992:

> The guards even opened the camp gates and allowed their friends to share in the fun. Civilians came from the outside and would spend a night beating or killing or raping. What's extraordinary is the reasons these Serbs entered the gates of hell for a night of twisted pleasure. They wanted to settle old scores. Survivors told me of hiding behind the backs of other prisoners when Serbs they knew suddenly showed up on the camp grounds. A poor Serb might search for the wealthy Muslim who refused to give him a job five years earlier; a farmer might try to find the Croat who, a decade before, refused to lend his tractor for a day; a middle-aged man might look around for the Muslim who, twenty-five years ago, stole away his high-school sweetheart.

Whilst many of the resentments that fuel wartime violence may be petty in nature, many (perhaps most) are related in some way to social and economic inequalities. One neglected aspect of the Bosnian conflict is the resentment of many rural Serbs at what were sometimes seen as privileged middle-class urban Muslims owing their position to 'collaboration' with the Turks. One of the sources of violence under the Khmer Rouge was the widespread resentment at the inhabitants of Phnom Penh, who were often seen as 'leeching' on the countryside and as selling out to the Americans and their devastating campaign of aerial bombing. Although these resentments are often (correctly) portrayed as helping to explain 'support' for the Khmer Rouge, one could also say that the Khmer Rouge provided the opportunity (and the impunity) for expressing these resentments. This is an important distinction: we need to look not only for the 'root causes' of war and genocide but for their immediate and local functions (including economic and psychological functions).

4. Humanitarian Interventions, War, and Crime

The diverse aims of those involved in warfare (and in crimes-during-war) should be taken into account by those who are seeking to intervene in some way, whether such intervention takes the form of emergency aid, of attempts to broker a peace, or of rehabilitation efforts. Rather than simply concentrating on negotiations between the 'two sides' in a war, it may be helpful to try to map the benefits and costs of violence for a variety of parties and to seek to influence the calculations they make. This will include attempts to reduce the economic benefits of violence (for example, through sanctions such as freezing bank accounts), to increase the economic benefits of peaceable activities (for example, through the provision of employment and more geographically-even forms of development), and to reduce the legal (and moral) impunity that may be enjoyed by a variety of groups (for example, by publicizing abuses, initiating international judicial proceedings, and making aid explicitly conditional on human rights observance). We need to investigate what international interventions (aid, diplomacy, publicity, investment, trade) are doing to accelerate or retard the processes by which people fall below the protection of the law. 'Interventions' is not simply something that 'the West' or 'the international community' does to remedy humanitarian disasters once they occur; it is something, more often than not, that occurs prior to the disaster, perhaps helping to precipitate it—witness, for example, the international support for abusive and unrepresentative governments like those of Barre in Somalia, Doe in Liberia and Habyarimana in Rwanda. Aid (including emergency relief) should be designed with an eye on functions and causes of violence, and on the political obstacles to getting aid through to those who need it.

4.1. Getting the aid through

Conventional practice in international relief operations, whether in wartime or peacetime, has been to focus on the 'poorest and neediest' group, to 'target' relief at this group, and then to dispatch a quantity of relief sufficient for its needs, usually with relatively small resources allocated to monitoring the fate of relief. This was the practice in government-held areas of Sudan in the late-1980s (and to a considerable extent thereafter). In Sudan, this approach proved seriously flawed even within the government-held areas, as politically-weaker groups failed to stake a claim to relief, and the small quantities of relief received failed to counterbalance the active creation of famine. In a context where many groups have a vested interest in illegality (including the stealing of relief and the economic benefits from 'forced markets' and depopulation), particular attention needs to be given to how to push relief through to those who need it in the face of predicable opposition. Portraying famine as 'astonishingly "legal" and "orderly"' does not help in assessing the functions of violence or in guarding against the probability that relief will be stolen, diverted, withheld, and manipulated.

4.2. Not supporting the abusers

Development and reconstruction aid offer opportunities for pressure to limit human rights abuses. Conversely, an unquestioning provision of aid and investment can play a key role in shoring up regimes responsible for human rights abuses, particularly where such provision is accompanied by international silence about these abuses.

During the man-made famine in Sudan in the late-1980s, major international donors pressured the government on its macroeconomic policy, but largely turned a blind eye to the abuses of militias that the government was arming and manipulating (Keen 1994). Not entirely dissimilarly, in El Salvador, the US, the World Bank and the IMF have made it clear that continued assistance will be linked to favoured macroeconomic policies, but have not pushed through more politically sensitive initiatives, notably land reforms, with similar vigour. A failure to tackle the root causes of the conflict seems likely to fuel violence in the future (Pastor and Boyce, Chapter 12, Volume 2).

Amnesty International has consistently and rightly condemned the phenomenon of impunity, which lies at the heart of contemporary humanitarian disasters. Urgently needed is a more systematic look at *the conditions that generate* this impunity. There are two parallel processes at work: in the first, national leaders (or rebel leaders) grant impunity to those (often militias or paramilitaries) who carry out violence, frequently along ethnic lines; second, the international community, in effects, grants impunity to these national (or occasionally) rebel leaders. It is important to be aware of the manipulation of militias behind the scenes, rather than simply focusing on the army and formal state administration. The processes by which 'civilians' come to participate in violence need to be examined in detail, a task that is not assisted by media stereotypes of 'innocent civilians' and 'evil warlords'. Civil society, in other words, may not be all that civil—and the common plea among international NGOs that civil society be 'boosted' needs to be looked at critically (cf. Duffield 1998). Which elements of civil society are being considered, for example? What about the ethnic militias?

Particularly important may be the signals that are sent by the international community during the 'early stages' of a humanitarian disaster, since these help to set the parameters of what is 'permissible' and what is not. Thus, for example, as the Sudan government's policy of arming ethnic militias unfolded in the 1980s, it was deeply damaging for the international community to persist in labelling this process as 'tribal violence' or as a legitimate defence against the rebel Sudan People's Liberation Army. Similar signals of indifference to violence were sent by the habitual concentration on the consequences of violence (displacement, hunger, the need for humanitarian aid, etc.) rather than on the causes and instigators of violence.

Despite the periodic massacres of Tutsis in the run-up to the Rwandan genocide of 1994, international donors did not reduce aid with specific reference to human rights violations (although the Belgians threatened to do so). As in Sudan, the donors' emphasis was on encouraging structural adjustment and fiscal reform (as well, in the Rwandan case, as improved accountability for aid given) (Joint Evaluation of Emergency Assistance to Rwanda 1996). The French government gave particularly active support to the Habyarimana government, elements of which were preparing for genocide. This support included military aid, and French military aid to Hutu extremists appears to have continued through June, two months after the start of the genocide. The climate of impunity in Rwanda was further bolstered when the United States refused to call the violence an out-and-out genocide, apparently seeking to avoid commitments (which would follow naturally from the Genocide Convention) that threatened to lead the international community into 'another Somalia'. Intelligence sources and the UN forces on the ground sometimes portrayed the arming of the *interahamwe* militias as a defensive action against the rebel Rwandan Patriotic Front—again, there were echoes of Sudan. And the UN Secretariat denied the proactive role to UNAMIR peacekeepers—notably in searching for arms—that had been requested by UNAMIR commander General Romeo Dallaire. This was despite a detailed report in a now infamous cable from Dallaire to the UN's Secretariat (Department of Peace-keeping Operations) in New York on 11 January 1994, which noted that a 'very important government official' had revealed plans to scare away the UN peacekeepers and for *interahamwe*, who had been training in camps outside the capital Kigali, to kill all the Tutsis in the city (Joint Evaluation of Emergency Assistance to Rwanda 1996). The lack of any vigorous response (particularly in relation to requests to seek out arms caches) seemed, again, to be related to fears of 'another Somalia'. UN Secretary-General Boutros Boutros-Ghali threatened to withdraw the peacekeeping force if the Arusha Peace Agreement (of 1993) was not implemented—a bizarre move that failed to recognize that the now-dominant Hutu extremists would actually be happy at such a withdrawal. On 21 April, in the midst of the genocide in April, the UN withdrew the bulk of the peacekeeping force, sending precisely the wrong signal to those perpetrating the genocide. Authority was portrayed as having 'collapsed', whereas in fact authority was being imposed with ruthless efficiency. During the genocide, UN officials repeatedly called for a cease-fire 'to stop the massacres'; in fact, it was to be the successful advance of the RPF which eventually stopped the genocide and any halt in this advance would have prolonged it (Prunier 1995: 269; *African Rights* 1994).

International attention soon turned to the (predominantly Hutu) refugees in Zaire and Tanzania. As in the former Yugoslavia, provision of large-scale humanitarian aid served to disguise, to some extent, international inaction in relation to the violence that lay at the root of the humanitarian crisis. On top of this, the manipulation of humanitarian aid threatened further to facilitate ethnic violence. Hutu extremists were able to manipulate humanitarian aid to recoup in Zaire. (And in the former Yugoslavia, Serb extremists had been able to use the presence of humanitarian relief operations as a disincentive for military sanctions by the international community.)

Backing the abusers is also a significant risk in conflicts—such as those in Somalia and Liberia—that have become highly factionalized. Those contemplating an intervention such as negotiations with warring factions or warlords will need to consider the possibility that the intervention may strengthen the warlords' ability to command the loyalty of their 'followers', something that appears to have happened in both Somalia and Liberia. Taking warlords' power as an absolute, a given, may run the risk of contributing to the impunity they enjoy. In their enlightening study of Somalia, Menkaus and Prendergast (1995) note that in 1993 and 1994:

The faction leaders—especially Aideed—greatly benefited from rents, security contracts, employment, currency transactions, and a variety of other fringe benefits courtesy of the UNOSOM cash cow. One Somali elder remarked, 'UNOSOM came to save us from the warlords, and ended up aligning with them.'

In addition, the faction leaders benefited from their status as the principal intermediaries with whom the UN chose to deal (*African Rights* 1993). Conversely, the withdrawal of UNOSOM resources and contracts was to undermine the Mogadishu-based faction leaders' patronage systems (Menkaus and Prendergast 1995: 4–5).

The short-sightedness of UN policy did not spring from a historical vacuum, and this brings us back to the role of outsiders in promoting impunity in 'peacetime'. As Menkaus and Prendergast (1995: 16) observe:

The failure of the UN mission in Somalia is to a large degree the extension of a bankrupt donor policy which for decades supported overly centralized, unsustainable government structures in Mogadishu whose legitimacy came primarily from the barrel of a gun. The UN and donor governments have spent the last two years obsessing over the re-creation of a centralized authority in Mogadishu. This greatly exacerbated the conflict, as competing militias positioned themselves for the potential spoils of a new aid-dependent state. In the process, the vast majority of Somalis and their local institutions have been ignored and further marginalized.

A somewhat similar process of legitimating violence and exploitation could be observed in Liberia. Kofi Woods II (1996) points out that unarmed political and civil groups in Liberia opposed the direct participation of armed faction leaders on the sovereign Council of State of the Liberian Transitional Government under the Abuja Accord of August 1995. These civilian groups argued that the arrangement legitimated violence and looting by men whose will to disarm was highly doubtful and whose control of their own armies was fragile at best. The importance of such civilian groups is underlined by the violence their leaders have often attracted from the armed factions.

There is likely to be more to securing a peace than encouraging negotiations between 'leaders'. During the Sierra Leonean civil war that began in 1991 and came tentatively to a close in 1996, many argued that local civil defence groups were being damagingly neglected as donors made unsuccessful attempts to contact the rebels whilst aiding a government that was itself encouraging human rights abuses against civilians.

An additional danger is that those abusing human rights may be supported through the allocation of aid to particular geographical areas and the withholding of aid from other areas. During man-made famine in Sudan, the concentration of aid on neighbouring Ethiopia and (to a lesser extent) government garrison towns in the south helped to speed the depopulation of areas of southern Sudan that were coveted (notably for cattle, land, and oil) by a coalition of interests from the north. In Sierra Leone, the concentration of aid on urban areas has also run the risk of assisting depopulation of rural areas and facilitating exploitation in these areas, whilst simultaneously creating a range of benefits for groups (particularly government soldiers) whose violence has prompted such depopulation (Bradbury 1995; Keen 1998).

4.3. 'Reconstruction' and 'rehabilitation'

Even benevolent words can be dangerous; they may be especially dangerous. 'Reconstruction' implies an attempt to rebuild what was there before. Yet the violence and crime that emerge in wartime are likely to spring precisely from the political economy that prevailed in peace: for example, people have repeatedly grabbed in war the resources and power that they could not access in peacetime. Reconstructing the old political economy may mean reconstructing the causes of violence. 'Rehabilitation', similarly, implies that what was there before was 'healthy'. If it was so healthy, one is tempted to ask, why then did civil war occur?

The construction of a lasting peace involves not simply a 'peace agreement' or a restoration of 'law and order'. It also demands the creation of an inclusive political system. This, in turn, implies the existence (and enforcement) of laws that provide physical and economic protection for all sections of a nation state—in other words, a system that creates and protects essential 'entitlements', *in practice as well as in theory*. (I do not reject the concept of entitlements; merely the assumptions that law can be separated from implementation, that laws cannot conflict with one another, and that famines can be understood without reference to illegality). By removing the perceived need to resort to violence in pursuit of such protection, such a system would address some of the root causes of violence.

One way of improving responses to contemporary civil wars may be to proceed on the basis of war as it is, rather than on the basis of war as we would like it to be. Current approaches to the prevention of crime centre, very often, on an extremely patchy system of punishment for selected 'war crimes'. What is needed is a much more serious attempt to foster the conditions in which violence becomes unrewarding. This means giving serious consideration to the functions of violence, and taking these into account in the prevention and mitigation of humanitarian disasters, as well as in attempts to resolve conflict and to assist in post-conflict recovery. Taking seriously the *political* functions of violence means taking seriously both *regressive* and *progressive* forces and recognizing that conflict is not simply irrational (cf. Voutira, forthcoming). It means thinking about the needs and agendas of political élites who may resort to violence (especially ethnic violence) in a bid to combat democracy and/or rebellion. How can the consent of such groups (or at least of elements of such groups) be secured for a transition to democracy? And how can their strategies of stirring up ethnic violence be countered (for example, with counter-propaganda)? What is the economic context in which democratization is being pursued, and is it realistic to pursue (as was done in Rwanda) a programme of structural adjustment at a time when élites are already being threatened by downturns in commodity prices and by a process of democratization? Taking seriously the *progressive* functions of violence means addressing the social and economic grievances of the poor—as, for example, in the sphere of land reform (Weeks and Cramer forthcoming; Pastor and Boyce, Chapter 12, Volume 2).

Taking seriously the *local* and *immediate* functions of violence means considering these functions in relation to élite and non-élite groups. Can the process of conflict-resolution be assisted by offering a stake in the peacetime political economy to some of those (whether élites or non-élites) who are in some sense benefiting from a war economy? Would not a more equitable development process (between regions, between ethnic groups, between social classes) help to erode the functionality of violence for a ranger of *losers* in this process of development (cf. Keen 1994; Kibreab forthcoming). Would not an increased emphasis on the provision of education encourage youths in particular to perceive a stake in society, and to eschew the kind of crime-come-war that has been associated with both rebel and government forces in a country like Sierra Leone? Might it not be possible to move towards a type of development that gives a sense of status and fulfilment during peacetime, so that youths in particular do not seek status and fulfilment through war (cf. Uvin forthcoming; Richards 1996; Keen 1998). And might it not be possible to prevent a recourse to self-protective violence by propping up the ability of the state to deliver the (currently largely theoretical) rights to economic and physical security and to the protection of the law (cf. Holsti, Chapter 7). It may be a much simpler matter to declare a right than to enforce it. The legal rights to life and to freedom from hunger are enshrined in the UN Charter of 1945. But many groups have a powerful interest in ignoring international and national laws. Providing practical economic and physical protection on the ground will involve a more variegated and realistic appraisal of which groups can be given *an interest in contributing to the enforcement of theoretical rights*, whether these are articulated at national or international level. This should include serious thinking about how to evolve an international peacekeeping capacity that is not undermined by (for example) the fear of losing American lives. It should also involve serious thinking about how to foster the kind of states that are prepared to make equitable laws and, crucially, prepared and able to enforce them. Crime pays (politically and psychologically, very often, as well as economically). It is an integral part of the new world disorder, and not simply an aberration. This underlines the limitations of a dominant framework—the entitlement framework—which (as currently conceptualized) explicitly excludes illegal activities from consideration.

References

Africa Watch (1990). Somalia: A Government at War with its Own People. New York.

African Rights (1993). Operation Restore Hope: A Preliminary Assessment. London.

African Rights (1994). Death, Despair and Defiance. London.

African Rights (1995a). *Facing Genocide: The Nuba of Sudan*. London.

African Rights (1995b). Rwanda—Not So Innocent: When Women Become Killers. London.

Allen, T. (1996). 'International Interventions in War Zones', in T. Allen, K. Hudson and J. Seaton (eds.), *War, Ethnicity and the Media*. London: South Bank University Press.

Bradbury, M. (1995). *Rebels Without a Cause*. London: CARE.

de Waal, A. (1997). *Famine Crimes: Politics and the Disaster Relief Industry in Africa*. London: James Currey.

Drèze, J., and A. Sen (1989). *Hunger and Public Action*. Oxford: Clarendon Press.

Duffield, M. (1998). 'Post-modern Conflict: Warlords, Post-adjustment States and Private Protection'. *Civil Wars*, 1 (1): Spring.

Emizet, K. N. (forthcoming). 'Congo (Zaire): Corruption, Disintegration, and State Failure' in E. Wayne Nafziger, Frances Stewart and Raimo Väyrynen (eds.), *Weak States and Vulnerable Economies: Humanitarian Emergencies in Developing Countries*, Volume 2 of *War, Hunger, and Displacement: The Origins of Humanitarian Emergencies*. Oxford: Oxford University Press.

Fox, Robert (1997). 'Algeria's trail of blood leads to the armed forces'. *Sunday Telegraph*, 26 October.

Furedi, F. (1994). *The New Ideology of Imperialism*, London and Boulder. Colorado: Pluto.

Garfinkel, Michelle R. and Stergios Skaperdas (1996). 'Introduction: Conflict and Appropriation as Economic Activities', in M. R. Garfinkel and S. Skaperdas (eds.), *The Political Economy of Conflict and Appropriation*. New York: Cambridge University Press.

Guardian (1997). 'The killing suburbs of Algiers'. *Guardian* (Editorial), 21 October.

Hirst, David (1997). 'Escalation of blood'. *Guardian*, 26 September.

Joint Evaluation of Emergency Assistance to Rwanda (1996). 'The International Response to Conflict and Genocide: Lessons from the Rwanda Experience'. Study 2.

Kaplan, R. (1994). 'The Coming Anarchy'. *The Atlantic Monthly*, February.

Keen, D. (1994). *The Benefits of Famine: A Political Economy of Famine and Relief in Southwestern Sudan, 1983–89*. Princeton: Princeton University Press.

Keen, D. (1995). 'When War itself is Privatised'. *Times Literary Supplement*, 29 December.

Keen, D. (1997). 'A Rational Kind of Madness'. *Oxford Development Studies*, 25 (1).

Keen, D. (1998). 'The Economic Functions of Violence in Civil Wars'. Adelphi Paper 320. International Institute for Strategic Studies/Oxford University Press.

Kibreab, G. (forthcoming). 'Protecting Environmental Resources', in E. Wayne Nafziger and Raimo Väyrynen (eds.), *War and Destitution: The Prevention of Humanitarian Emergencies*. London: Macmillan.

Kofi Woods II, Samuel (1996). 'Civic Initiatives in the Peace Process', in Jeremy Armon and Carl (eds.), *Accord—The Liberian Peace Process, 1990–1996*. London: Conciliation Resources.

Maas, P. (1996). *Love Thy Neighbour: A Story of War*. London and Basingstoke: Papermac.

Menkaus, K., and J. Prendergast (1995). 'Political Economy of Post-Intervention Somalia'. Somalia Task Force Issue Paper No. 3. April.

Outram, R. (1997). 'Turn Down that Order'. *Management Today*, October: 112–3.

Pastor, M., and J. Boyce (forthcoming). 'El Salvador: Economic Disparities, External Intervention, and Civil Conflict', in E. Wayne Nafziger, Frances Stewart and Raimo Väyrynen (eds.) *Weak States and Vulnerable Economies: Humanitarian Emergencies in Developing Countries*, Volume 2 of *War, Hunger, and Displacement: the Origins of Humanitarian Emergencies*. Oxford: OUP.

Pearce, J. (1990). *Colombia: Inside the Labyrinth*. London: Latin American Bureau.

Reno, W. (1995). *Corruption and State Politics in Sierra Leone*. Cambridge: Cambridge University Press.

Richards, P. (1996). *Fighting for the Rain Forest: War, Youth and Resources in Sierra Leone*. Oxford: James Currey.

Robinson, R. E., and J. Gallagher (1961). *Africa and the Victorians*. London: Macmillan.

Sen, A. (1981). *Poverty and Famines: An Essay on Entitlement and Deprivation*. Oxford: Clarendon.

Shawcross, W. (1996). 'Tragedy in Cambodia'. *New York Review of Books*, 14 November.

Simpson, J. (1994). *In the Forests of the Night: Encounters in Peru with Terrorism, Drug-running and Military Oppression*. London: Arrow.

Sweeney, John (1997). 'We accuse. 80,000 times'. *Observer*, 16 November.

Uvin, P. (forthcoming). 'Rwanda: The Social Roots of Genocide', in E. Wayne Nafziger, Frances Stewart and Raimo Väyrynen (eds.), *Weak States and Vulnerable Economies: Humanitarian Emergencies in Developing Countries,* Volume 2 of *War, Hunger and Displacement: The Origins of Humanitarian Emergencies.* Oxford: Oxford University Press.

Voutira, E. (forthcoming). 'The Language of Complex Humanitarian Emergencies'. *Oxford Development Studies.*

Weeks, J., and C. Cramer (forthcoming). 'Adjusting Adjustment', in E. Wayne Nafziger and Raimo Väyrynen (eds.), *War and Destitution: The Prevention of Humanitarian Emergencies.* London: Macmillan.

9

Ethnicity and the Politics of Conflict: The Case of Matabeleland

JOCELYN ALEXANDER, JO ANN McGREGOR AND TERENCE RANGER

1. Introduction

It is commonplace for conflict in Africa to be labelled as 'ethnic', and to be explained as the product of disintegrating or 'collapsed' states. This chapter reviews a range of recent academic work on ethnicity and conflict which is critical of these explanations.[1] As many scholars have pointed out, the salience of ethnic antagonism in some recent wars cannot be explained as the inevitable resurgence of ancient tensions—rather, they are the product of a reworking of historical memories in particular political contexts. And if some notorious 'ethnic' conflicts have occurred in the context of (or in contestation over) weak or disintegrating states, others have arisen in states which were relatively strong. The 'collapsed' state explanation cannot by itself explain why notions of identity which were once fluid, inclusive, mutually compatible and weakly ethnicized have at times been replaced by understandings of coherent, mutually exclusive peoples with a history of rivalry, persecution and revenge. These reworked memories themselves exert a powerful and unpredictable influence over subsequent events and notions of identity. We seek to review some of the insights academics have offered into these issues, and aim to explore why ethnicity has held such a powerful appeal for politicians, journalists, and those involved in specific conflicts.

Our discussion is not confined to conflicts classified as complex humanitarian Emergencies (CHEs). The conflicts grouped together as CHEs may share some common features, but they do not have common causes, and they vary widely in terms of the extent to which ethnicity played or plays a salient role. They do not necessarily provide the best examples for an

[1] The case study material presented in this chapter draws on the authors' three year joint research project in Matabeleland North. We are currently writing a book provisionally entitled *Violence and Memory* on the history of Nkayi and Lupane Districts. JoAnn McGregor was funded by ESRC grant R00023 527601; Jocelyn Alexander and Terence Ranger by a grant from the Leverhulme Trust. Many thanks to Mark Leopold for comments on drafts of this chapter.

analysis of how and why conflict may take on an ethnic dimension. Understanding the role of ethnicity in CHEs can thus best be achieved through reference to a broader literature.

In the second half of the chapter, we focus on conflict in the Matabeleland region of Zimbabwe. This conflict is not generally classified as a CHE, though from the perspective of those involved, the scale of the killing was devastating. The conflict provoked significant internal population displacements and refugee flows, and it coincided with a severe drought, the impact of which was heightened by the state's withholding of drought relief and imposition of stringent curfews. The absence of humanitarian intervention in this case was partly a product of the state's power to control access to information about the conflict.

The Matabeleland case is instructive for a number of reasons. As violence was the product of the excesses of a relatively strong state (a characteristic which Zimbabwe shares with Rwanda) it demonstrates the inadequacy of state collapse as a blanket explanation for the ethnicization of Africa's recent conflicts. Second, though those involved came to experience the conflict as tribal, the conflict had directly political causes. As in more well-known wars, notions of generations' old tribal antagonism were used by the military during the conflict, and civilians subjected to state violence came to see the war as both political and ethnic in intent. Though popular understandings of tribal opposition and memories of persecution were not causes of the conflict, they were elaborated and hardened during it, and have been sustained in public and private memory since the conflict's conclusion.

2. Ethnicity and Conflict

There is a tension between the language of much current academic writing on ethnicity and conflict on the one hand, and the interpretations of journalists and popular writers, as well as people involved in conflicts with an ethnic dimension, on the other. For academics, ethnicity is widely understood to be unnatural, to be historically 'invented', 'constructed' or 'imagined' and used 'instrumentally' by politicians. Such language—whether drawing on mechanical metaphors or on the idea of 'imagination'—can give the impression that ethnic identities are not real. For people involved in conflicts where ethnicity has become salient, however, ethnic identifications are often understood as both natural and all too real. As David Turton (1997) has recently discussed, ethnicity has proved devastatingly powerful in its ability to motivate people to commit violent acts in particular historical and political circumstances.

Journalists and popular writers also reach readily for the label 'ethnic', partly to try to make wars comprehensible. They have done so increasingly since the collapse of communism. Recent trends in the geography and nature of wars have seen a new predominance of conflicts within rather than between states, of wars which have operated on a cheap budget rather than with sophisticated weaponry and which have targeted civilians rather than soldiers. Robert Kaplan extended his influential popular analysis of warfare in Yugoslavia to West Africa in an article entitled 'The Coming Anarchy: How Scarcity, Crime, Overpopulation, Tribalism and Disease are Rapidly Destroying the Social Fabric of our Planet' (Kaplan 1994; and see Kaplan 1993). Richards (1996) has dubbed Kaplan's analysis 'new barbarism', and has argued that his arguments are underlain by an essentialized idea of cultural identity as fixed and durable, and by a notion of conflict as natural and apolitical. Kaplan's writing is illustrative of how commonplace it has become to talk of recent conflicts as 'ethnic' wars. This is arguably more than just a form of explanation for wars in far away places which are not well understood in the West, a shorthand for conflicts experienced by 'them' rather than 'us'. As Richard Fardon has noted, 'Over the course of the twentieth century, but most startlingly since the end of Eric Hobsbawm's "short twentieth century", it has become difficult to envisage acts of collective violence that are not able from some or other perspective to be deemed ethnic—ethnicity is so available as an explanation for collective violence, that to be against categorizing such violence as 'ethnic' is to go against collective violence in short' (1996: 172). Fardon's point is that journalists are not only reporting on events as 'ethnic' but are themselves incorporated in, and reflecting through their interpretations, a broader late twentieth century world view and popular understanding of identity.

The notion of an 'ethnic conflict' is, of course, misleading for a number of reasons. First, it implies that ethnicity can be seen as the *cause* of such conflicts, and that ethnic conflicts are apolitical, somehow distinctive from other wars fought over resources or political power. Yet, as participants in a recent conference on ethnicity and war concurred, 'competition for political power and the material resources to which such power gives access would do far better as a general explanation of the phenomena we were discussing' (Turton 1997: 3). Fukui and Markakis' collection on *Ethnicity and Conflict in the Horn* discusses a wide range of propaganda and mobilizational appeals used in recent African conflicts, including the invocation of nationalism, socialism, religion, and ethnicity. Because 'ethnicity proved by far superior as a principle of political solidarity and mobilization, and emerged as the dominant political force from the wreckage of the post-colonial state', the editors argue that 'the "ethnic" label usually attached to conflict at all levels in this region is not altogether inappropriate', but 'ethnicity is the ideological form, not the substance of the conflict' (Fukui and Markakis 1994: 10).

A further problem with popular writing on 'ethnic conflict' is that it tends to draw on metaphor and analogy as a substitute for historical and political understanding: the metaphors most commonly used are of the 'freezing' of generations-old tribal antagonism under communism (in the former Soviet Union or in Tito's Yugoslavia), or, in Africa, under the over-arching structures of colonial rule and subsequently the force of a modernizing nationalism. The collapse of communism, the process of decolonization, or the failure of nationalism are represented as the 'unfreezing' of social relations, the lifting of the lid of a 'boiling saucepan', a resurgence or eruption of something ancient—Kaplan even compares war in West Africa to an outbreak of disease. These metaphors imply that conflict is endemic and spontaneous, that it is natural, predictable, and in need of no further explanation.

In contrast, an important strand of scholarly writing on Africa has sought to historicize ethnicity. As Vail argued in the introduction to his influential collection *The Creation of Tribalism in Southern Africa*, ethnic antagonism has often been taken as a 'given' in discussions of politics in Africa—'useful in explaining political actions but itself not really requiring much explanation' (Vail 1989: xi). Vail sought to replace the 'tautological argument that Africans acted "tribalistically" because they were "tribal" people' with an historically informed, contextual approach to ethnicity (Vail 1989: xi). His and others' work built on a longer history of criticism of the idea of bounded, fixed tribes in anthropological writing which had seen the replacement of the term 'tribe' in scholarly (but not popular or media) discourse with the term 'ethnicity' (for example, see Southall 1970). Some of the earliest users of the term were South African liberal intellectuals of the 1930s and 1940s. They were concerned 'to challenge the meaning of biological conceptions of race and the assumptions they underwrote . . . to downplay the importance of heredity as the constitutive element of human behaviour and to stress instead the agency of culture and the environment' (Dubow 1995: 196, citing Kuper 1943: 107; Gray 1944). 'Ethnicity' as a term has, however, presented its own problems as an analytical concept: it can be used as a euphemism for race, as a means of referring to language or culture, or a way of describing almost any type of social group, from groups defined by class or production to those based on race, to members of certain states or to smaller groups of kin and clan. As Fardon has pointed out, the term ethnicity, like tribe, incorporates a wide range of different classificatory systems 'on the fragile basis of assuming that differences can only be of a single type' (Fardon 1987: 183).

A number of academic writers have offered important pointers regarding the question concerning us here: namely, under what circumstances do ethnic antagonisms commonly become salient? Much attention has focused on the transformations and legacies of the colonial period. Historians have showed that colonialism in Africa was far from a period of containment in which pre-colonial social relations were frozen. Rather, it was a time of dramatic change in which administrators and missionaries created new ethnic categories, defined vernacular languages, and fixed ethnic groups geographically to tribal homelands under the authority of chiefs and customary law.[2] In addition to the reification of tribal categories, the economic changes of the colonial period could (in some cases intentionally and in others unintentionally) create or reinforce distinctions between newly-classified groups with regard to access to resources or political power, enhancing inequality and competition between them for the fruits of modernization. In Rwanda, for example, colonial powers institutionalized the domination of Tutsi over Hutu, whilst in South Africa discriminatory ethnic (and racial) segregation of the labour market and of access to land was established.[3] Economic competition thus became a key focus for ethnic division. Pre-colonial systems were, in contrast, described as incorporative, flexible and often weakly ethnicized (for example, see Colson 1970; Kopytoff 1989).

Some of the historical literature has subsequently been criticized for implying that the architects of tribes were solely colonial, thus producing a false dualism between 'alien' ethnic inventions and 'authentic' African custom. Reflecting on such criticisms of his own earlier work, Terence Ranger noted that essentialism, which the historical constructionist approaches had intended to avoid, 'might slip in the back door' (Ranger 1993: 64). He argued that ethnicity was created not only by colonial officials, but was also 'imagined' and manipulated by African nationalist politicians, church leaders and others. If colonial officials used ethnic labels, they did not choose them at random—history acted as a constraint and the content and meaning of such labels were the result of contestation among a wide range of social actors. Wendy James has conceptualized the continuities in historical reference (not specifically in the re-imagination of ethnicity, though not exclusive of such a context) as a

... 'cultural archive', which 'like an archive, may constitute a lasting base of past reference and future validation. They may at times rest dormant but on occasion be drawn upon for the formation of new discourse. The elements of this cultural archive, revealed as much in the repertoire of habitual ritual action as in language, constitute the foundations of a moral world' (James 1988: 6).

The institutional structures of colonial power shaped nationalist mobilization and its legacies with profound implications for ethnicity in the post-colonial state, as Mahmood Mamdani has recently suggested in his influential and provocative *Citizen and Subject: Contemporary Africa and the Legacy of Late Colonialism*. Mamdani contends that colonial rule 'bifurcated' the state, accentuating difference by separating urban from rural, and one

---

[2] On missionaries and language, see, e.g., Harries (1989); Ranger (1989). On customary law, see Chanock (1985).
[3] On Rwanda, see de Waal (1994). On South Africa, see, e.g., Moodie with Ndatshe (1994); Harries (1994).

ethnicity from another under systems of indirect rule. He opens his book with the thought-provoking question of whether anti-colonial struggle took the form of 'a series of ethnic revolts against so many ethnically organized and centrally reinforced local powers—in other words, a string of ethnic civil wars? In brief, was not ethnicity a dimension of both power and resistance?' (Mamdani 1996: 8). This question must be answered empirically, as nationalist mobilization took different forms in different African countries. As we show in our case study below, nationalist movements can be incorporative and explicitly non-tribalistic—loyal in ideology as in practice to the decision taken by the Organization of African Unity to respect 'unnatural' colonial borders and to imagine nations within them.

Other writers have also looked at the role of the legacies of colonial power and nationalism in the re-emergence of ethnicity after independence. Post-independence competition focused crucially on control of the central state. For John Lonsdale, writing on Kenya, conflict between political élites for state (and hence economic) power led to the emergence of 'political tribalism'. Political tribalism was not, however, the only version of ethnic identity: Lonsdale contrasts it to a local level 'moral ethnicity' in which identities could be multiple, fluid, mutually compatible, and typically offered a critique of corrupt politicians' abuses of power (Lonsdale 1992 and 1994). For Lonsdale, ethnicity (like nationalism) was thus a potentially positive force.

'Post-colonial studies' have offered an additional point of view: they have been preoccupied with trying to understand state power and its abuse in independent African states, particularly as it is manifested in violence against ethnic groups or in the form of the 'genocidal state' (Werbner 1996: 12). Unlike Mamdani's insistence on the importance of colonialism in the formation of ethnic consciousness, this body of writing has often emphasized the need for a *longue durée* approach, for recognition of the importance of the pre-colonial period in understanding the 'retraditionalization' of contemporary African political discourse (Chabal 1994). Such studies have not simply implied that the clock has been turned back. One reading of Jean-Francois Bayart's *Politics of the Belly* (1993) is that the influential traditionalist idiom of contemporary politics is derived from a precolonial historical memory—but, as Grignon (1996) has argued, it is an idiom which has been used to reinvent what were basically colonial governmental practices.

Aside from the general point that ethnic antagonism tends to become salient alongside enhanced economic and political competition among reified ethnic groups—a product of the legacies of colonial rule, of some forms of nationalist mobilization, and of competition over the new opportunities of independence—other studies have focused on the more immediate history of conflicts themselves, showing how ethnicity was used by political and intellectual élites prior to, or in the course of, wars. Such studies are important for revealing the contingency of the move towards warfare with an ethnic dimension and of the variable role ethnicity can play.

Many studies have shown that popular ideas of ethnic antagonism have emerged *during* conflicts rather than themselves *causing* conflict. The experience of violence is itself crucial in the transformation of identities. Wendy James, for example, has explored the creation of Uduk identity in the context of conflict and forced displacement. She describes the increasing 'visibility' of the Uduk in the Sudan civil war, their change from a 'dispersed and loosely knit population' into a 'coherent ethnic entity', and makes the more general point that,

Conflicts . . . generate the images of 'ethnicities' in the plural. To what extent these correspond to kin or language communities or moral networks on the ground is problematic. Political conflict in North East Africa has imposed too many intensely uniform 'ethnic' images, conceptually setting apart whole communities while profoundly dividing the actual people in question.

Such images may themselves subsequently play a role in conflict in unpredictable ways (James 1994: 163; see also James 1988). Johnson (1989) similarly shows the key role of conflict in the genesis of Nubi identity. Several of the contributions to Fukui and Markakis' collection reinforce this point, demonstrating how, in the words of the editors, conflict could 'create and maintain political superstructures, that is "tribes"—the latter emerging from rather than producing conflict' (Fukui and Markakis 1994: 6; also see Turton 1994; Fukui 1994; Lamphear 1994).

The experience of exile, particularly when this involves living in refugee camps, has also been shown to be critically important in the formation of potentially aggressive collective memories. Malkki describes such a process in the case of Burundian refugees living in Tanzanian refugee camps:

The most unusual and prominent social fact about the camp was that its inhabitants were continually engaged in an impassioned construction and reconstruction of their history as a 'people'. The narrative production of this history ranged from descriptions of the 'autochthonous' origins of Burundi as a 'nation' and of the primordial social harmony that prevailed among the original inhabitants (the Twa and the Hutu), to the coming of the pastoral Tutsi 'foreigners from the north', to the Tutsi theft of power from the 'natives' (Hutu and Twa) by ruse and trickery, and, finally, to the culminating mass killings of Hutu by Tutsi in 1972 . . . The camp refugees saw themselves as a nation in exile, and defined exile, in turn, as a moral trajectory of trials and tribulations that would ultimately empower them to reclaim (or create anew) the 'homeland' in Burundi (Malkki 1995: 3).

Though much writing in refugee studies has emphasized the hospitality and incorporative nature of rural African society towards refugee populations, the circumstances of exile commonly bring with them the potential for the reification of difference and conflict. As much writing on self-settled refugees has taken the perspective of the host society, it has had 'an uncritical emphasis on ideologies of benign assimilation' (McGregor 1994: 546). The politics of refugee groups, the process of labelling populations in the course of international humanitarian intervention, the segregation of refugees into camps, all combined with severe resource scarcities, can result in the creation of group identities which themselves feed into subsequent conflict.

Interventions intended to prevent conflicts which have become ethnicized can fix and reinforce the categories they hope to break down. Humanitarian interventions in conflicts in Africa have, as Duffield (1995, cited in Richards 1996) has noted, often been based on a natural disaster model in which all that is required is to re-establish the 'normal' state of social life through the short-term delivery of basic relief commodities. But humanitarian relief can be used by warring parties, and may become integral to the conflict itself, while a 'return to normal' can mean a return to pre-existing structures, or a bolstering of the leaders who themselves provoked the conflict and the spread of dehumanizing ideas of others in the first place.

Lemarchand's study of Burundi's war emphasizes the key role of reworked memories in the transformation of amicable ethnic relations into tribal antagonism. He describes the rapidity of Burundi's transformation from '"a model for all aspiring democracies" into a society gravid with premonitions of genocidal slaughter' (Lemarchand 1997: xi). His analysis 'involves a fundamental questioning of "tribalism" as a conceptual tool' for understanding past or recent conflicts: 'For if Hutu and Tutsi increasingly tend to define each other in terms of mutually antagonistic categories, this is not because of ancestral enmities but because ethnic identities have acquired a moral dimension—whether as a martyred community or a threatened minority—they never had before'. Lemarchand goes on: 'In October 1993, as in August 1988, when Hutu peasants suddenly turned against Tutsi . . . , memories of 1972 came back with an emotional charge made more potent by intimations of an impending massacre of Hutu populations'. The media also played a role in popularizing extremist and dehumanizing views of the other. Lemarchand explores how 'Identities . . . like events, are reconstructed according to the norms of a dehumanizing myth. Mythmaking in this sense is not only a privileged field for the deployment of a racist ideology . . . it equally serves to legitimize violence' (Lemarchand 1997: xii, xiv, xvii).

In a not dissimilar tone, Gallagher (1997) has explored the role of the media and the techniques which political and intellectual élites used in Yugoslavia to foment ethnic hatred: they emphasized 'inalienable historical rights', cultivated a 'persecution complex by reminding citizens of past wrongs done by ethnic opponents', and insisted that 'people carry hereditary and collective guilt for such wrongs even though most were not born when they were committed' (also see Sofos 1996: 48).

These historical and political studies of colonial legacies, of politicians' appeals, and of the experience of conflicts are revealing of how ethnicity can become salient. However, the question of why ethnicity is so appealing remains to be answered. Why is it so often invoked both by journalists and by participants in the conflicts themselves and why has it proved more powerful than other collective identities? Ethnicity, though historically constructed, attains its power precisely because it evokes the notion of being natural and timeless. David Turton has explored the particular 'power of ethnic symbols' (Turton 1997: 18). He explains that 'by representing the past in symbolic terms . . . people are able to maintain a sense of the historical persistence and distinctiveness of their communities and, therefore, of their ethnic identities, even while their personal and social worlds are changing, sometimes radically, in response to new economic and political conditions . . .' (Turton 1997: 20). Thus, 'To stress the importance of symbols in arousing and sustaining ethnic sentiments . . . is not to suppose that they hold people in an overpowering and coercive grip, even though they may be *experienced* as unconditional, inescapable and timeless' (Turton 1997: 22).

Many have argued that the appeal of ethnicity is heightened in a period of rapid change. Hroch, for example, explained: 'Where an old regime disintegrates, where old social relations have become unstable, amid the rise of general insecurity, belonging to a common language and culture may become the only certainty in society, the only value beyond ambiguity and doubt' (Hroch 1985, cited in Marks 1994: 107). But why has ethnicity so often become salient in conflicts, rather than other forms of collective identity—such as totemic identification, or clan or race? John Comaroff, in an essay comparing totemism with ethnicity, assigns totemism a decreasing significance with the rise of capitalism and ethnicity an enhanced role, ethnic consciousness being the product of 'historical processes which structure relations of inequality between discrete social entities' (Comaroff 1997: 75). While ethnic consciousness has become increasingly important, other forms of collective consciousness can, of course, also play an important role in conflicts. Somalia's recent war demonstrated that ethnicity does not have a monopoly on the ability to motivate and mobilize collective violence—here, clan affiliation came to play this role. Others have analysed the appeal of race as well as ethnic and religious difference in the 'new racism' of Britain and the United States (Gilroy 1992: 31–4; Dresch 1995). However, the vagueness of the term ethnicity, as noted above, means that these forms of difference and the conflicts they have provoked can also be interpreted as 'ethnic'.

To answer the question of why ethnicity has become so salient, we can also return to the more general point made at the beginning of this chapter. Richard Fardon suggests the appeal of ethnicity lies in global trends which envelop the thinking of academics, journalists, and others in the west, and not just the participants in wars. Fardon argues that difference itself has been reified as 'pseudo natural speciation' in the late twentieth century:

> Attempts to challenge unitary conceptions of personal and collective identity have employed a vocabulary of terms such as hybridity, creolization, mongrelism and so on. But these words describe a condition that can exist only subsequent to speciation—they too share the presupposition that unitary and exclusive identities have a prior or pristine existence . . . for most readers terms denoting 'mixture' actually reinforce the normative status of the presuppositions they are designed to challenge (Fardon 1996: 172).

Fardon concludes:

> The challenge is not to see *through* the shibboleths of the age: to argue that ethnicity is not universal, or to challenge specific ethnicities by showing them self-interested or historically contrived. Such challenges . . . actually have a normalizing effect; perversely, as a phenomenon anchored to accounts of the past, ethnicity thrives on a history of such challenges. The greater challenge is to explain how the shibboleths of the age are produced, why they convince . . . and how the dynamic of increasing ethnic speciation is accelerated (Fardon 1996: 172).

To conclude this review, let us return to the main points which we hope to illustrate through the subsequent case study: first, we explore how wars which are not ethnic in their causation can come to be experienced as (at least in part) ethnic by those involved, and how this entails the reworking of history. Second, we explore how an understanding of conflict in Africa necessitates a detailed understanding of the workings of colonial power, as well as a careful consideration of the nature of nationalism, and of the immediate politics of the period of conflict itself: invocations of the collapsed state are, in themselves, insufficient.

3. Violence and Ethnicity in Matabeleland, Zimbabwe

The case of Zimbabwe's western Matabeleland provinces[4] in the 1980s illustrates the emergence of ethnic antagonism during conflict, and in the context of a powerful state. Conflict was caused neither by ethnic division nor by state collapse. However, the conflict came to be understood as ethnic by the government soldiers responsible for most of the killings, by the small number of armed insurgents who came to be called 'dissidents', by the civilians who suffered the brunt of the violence, and by many of those

---

[4] The violence of the 1980s affected not only the Matabeleland provinces, but also neighbouring areas, particularly the Midlands. We use 'Matabeleland' simply as a shorthand for affected areas.

whose perceptions of the violence were formed only through access to the government media. During the conflict, the army's use of a particular type of violence, and its invocation of a particular interpretation of history, served to harden ethnic antagonism. But the roots of conflict lay elsewhere, in the ambitions of a ruling party which controlled a state of immense power and considerable legitimacy, and which followed a 'majoritarian' political creed: this was not a conflict aimed primarily at an ethnic minority, but one aimed at a political opposition.

Between 1982 and 1987 the conflict in Matabeleland resulted in the death of thousands of civilians; thousands more were tortured, beaten and starved. Some of these were the victims of armed 'dissidents', but the overwhelming majority were unarmed civilians, killed by government forces in the name of countering the 'dissident' threat.[5] This violence coincided with a succession of severe droughts. Much of the population of Matabeleland was dependent during these years on food relief either from the state or from voluntary agencies. Widespread hunger and immiseration was made worse by the closure of shops, suspension of food aid and withdrawal of bus services under a series of curfews (CCJP/LRF 1997; LCHR 1986). Despite the scale of abuses and immiseration, the relative strength and legitimacy of the newly-elected Zimbabwean government, the biased nature of media coverage of government repression, and the widely publicized official denials of excessive force, meant there was no outside intervention in this conflict.

Explanations for the conflict are diverse. The ruling party's interpretation—as presented in the state-controlled media at the time—was predominantly political. According to Zanu-PF (the Zimbabwe African National Union-Patriotic Front), violence in Matabeleland was the result of attempts by the opposition party Zapu (the Zimbabwe African People's Union) and its former guerrilla army, Zipra (the Zimbabwe People's Revolutionary Front), to mount an insurrection, with some help from South Africa.[6] Joshua Nkomo, leader of the opposition party Zapu, saw the conflict as a pretext to crush his party (Nkomo 1984, and see Spring 1986). Ethnicity was rarely invoked explicitly by the government or national media during the conflict. Only one Zanu-PF minister, Enos Nkala, offered a tribal interpretation. The most prominent Ndebele politician in the ruling party, Nkala referred to armed dissidents as 'Ndebeles

---

[5] The most detailed report on human rights abuses in Matabeleland to date is the report of the Catholic Commission of Justice and Peace/Legal Resources Foundation (1997). The report estimates that the number of people killed in the 1980s is very likely over 6,000—the report lists 2,052 named victims, largely from two case study areas. Of these, the report estimates that a full 98 per cent were the victims of government forces. The report also estimates that over 7,000 people were tortured. Property loss was also extensive. See Part Two of the report for an extremely detailed account of the available sources and their analysis.

[6] See the pro-Zanu-PF account in Martin and Johnson (1986), and the government document, Ministry of Information, Posts and Telecommunications (1984).

who were calling for a second war of liberation . . .', to Zapu leader Joshua
Nkomo as the leader of the armed insurgents (or 'dissidents') and the 'self-
appointed Ndebele king'.[7] However, ethnicity was often implied by
association, or as a subtext to official statements which blurred distinctions between the categories of civilians within areas which supported
Zapu, 'the Ndebele' (as opposed to 'the Shona'), and the 'dissidents'.

Other commentators reached for 'tribal' explanations much more
explicitly. A *Guardian* report spoke of a 'thousand years' of hostility
between 'the Ndebele and the Shona'; *Observer* correspondents deplored
the 'tribal' basis of Zimbabwean politics and added that 'the Shona' had
good reason to hate 'the Ndebele', who in the nineteenth century had spe-
cialized in roasting Shona babies alive (quoted in Ranger 1985: 3). A
Zimbabwean academic, E. P. Makambe, accused the dissidents of representing 'an exclusively Ndebele political outfit' and of murdering both
'Ndebele' sell-outs and Shona opponents. Makambe wrote that in
response 'the reaction of the wider Shona society was both swift and violent' and cites calls for draconian government action to prevent 'all . . .
Shonas being eliminated' (Makambe 1992: 20, 34, 69).

3.1. Ethnicity in Zimbabwe

Our research in Matabeleland shows that 'tribal' interpretations of the
1980s conflict and the ethnic consciousness within Matabeleland to which
the conflict gave rise were the product of post-independence transformations. The history of ethnic consciousness in Matabeleland is exceedingly
complex (see Ranger 1985; 1993; 1994; 1996; Alexander and McGregor
1997; Worby 1994). Briefly, the conclusions of the rich literature on
Ndebele identity are that the Ndebele state in the nineteenth century was
not a proto 'tribe', nor even a 'nationality', but an incorporative polity.
Some of the conquering whites wanted to make 'the Ndebele' into an
entity like 'the Zulu', with a single language, customary law, etc. The dominant administrative attitude, however, was to divide and rule. The
Ndebele monarchy was not revived; chiefdoms were broken up; many
'subject peoples' were encouraged to resume their own 'traditional' identities. Thereafter, Sindebele no longer served as the language of incorporation to an African military and administrative system but as the *lingua
franca* of colonial towns, schools and churches.

Under colonialism there *was* an 'Ndebele' political identity but one very
different from that of the nineteenth century. The early twentieth century
'Ndebele' identity derived from alleged promises made to 'the Ndebele'
by the whites. Cecil Rhodes was claimed to have promised a large area of
land for exclusive 'Ndebele' use during the peace *indabas* of 1896 and 1897;

---

[7] See the Zimbabwean daily newspaper *The Chronicle*, 30 June 1980, 7 July 1980.

two huge if wild and barren reserves were set aside in northern Matabeleland for 'Ndebele' settlement. During the struggle against evictions from 'white' land, a great variety of languages and ethnicities were subsumed under an 'Ndebele' claim to the rights promised by Rhodes. After that struggle had been lost and many thousands of families had been evicted into the northern Shangani and Gwaai reserves, the evictees papered over their own great linguistic and ethnic diversity by claiming a progressive 'Ndebele' identity. And if even these proclaimed 'Ndebele' areas were so ethnically complex, the 'Kalanga' areas to the south and the 'Tonga' areas to the north, while influenced by Ndebele language, struggled to maintain their own cultural identities.

When urban élites took up the ideas of cultural nationalism from the 1950s the results were equally complex. There were 'Kalanga' cultural nationalists as well as 'Ndebele' ones. But while they were sometimes bitterly opposed to each other, the general outcome was commitment to a series of identities. Joshua Nkomo, the key cultural broker of the nationalist process, belonged both to the Kalanga Cultural Society and the Matabele National Home Society. He was also a member and then leader of a series of territorial nationalist parties. Nkomo held that Kalanga identity was appropriate to his home area in southern Matabeleland; Ndebele identity was appropriate to the politics of Bulawayo; but as nationalist leader he laid claim to the title 'Father Zimbabwe'. He expected his 'Shona' associates to make use of a similar hierarchy of identities. A 'Shona' political identity, after all, was an even more recent creation than an 'Ndebele' one, 'Shona' self-consciousness really only expressing itself in the 1950s.[8] So, in assembling a powerful set of 'traditional' symbols for the united nationalist movement, Nkomo drew on the pre-Ndebele institutions of western Zimbabwe—like the High God shrines of the Matopos; on the memorials of the Ndebele monarchy, like Mzilikazi's tomb at Entumbane, but also on 'Shona' heroes, monuments and mediums. And the nationalist platform itself was based on a critique of racial domination and discrimination, demands for better wages and land—grievances which drew support across the nation.

By the 1980s, then, it should have been clear that Nkomo's long-established nationalist party, Zapu, in no way represented an 'exclusively Ndebele outfit'. In its heyday Zapu had been the sole nationalist movement for the whole country; even after the emergence of Zanu in 1963, Zapu had retained majority support in most Shona-speaking areas for many years. The development of the guerrilla war of the 1970s—with Zapu's army operating out of Zambia into western Zimbabwe and Zanu's army operating out of Mozambique into eastern Zimbabwe—began to

---

[8] 'Shona' identity was largely the fruit of the development of so-called Standard Shona texts for use in schools. Prior to that a series of 'dialect' identities had developed out of missionary language classifications—'Manyika', 'Zezuru', 'Karanga' etc. See Ranger (1989).

give the two movements a regional character. Voting patterns in the 1980 elections largely followed these regional divisions, with Zapu winning overwhelmingly in the western provinces, and Zanu winning elsewhere (Cliffe, Mpofu and Munslow 1980)—but this did not mean Zapu simply cornered the 'Ndebele' vote: support came from Kalanga speakers and Tonga speakers as well as Ndebele speakers, and the Zapu hierarchy itself boasted prominent 'Shona' veterans.

If ethnic identity was not particularly salient in the support given the two nationalist parties, there was nonetheless a history of animosity and distrust between both the parties and their armies which had at times resulted in violence. The establishment of Zanu in 1963 had left a turbulent trail of conflict in its wake; attempts to unite the two guerrilla armies in the 1970s had broken down subsequent to a series of armed conflicts in training camps in Tanzania and Mozambique. When the two armies shared operational areas inside Zimbabwe, they often clashed with each other as much as with the Rhodesian forces. Though ethnic considerations were present in some of these conflicts (as well as conflicts within the parties and armies), they were far from being the dominant force.[9]

This history of violence and the increasingly regional basis of the two political parties was crucial to producing the basis for the war of the 1980s. After independence, past and present violence between the two parties would increasingly be (re)interpreted in ethnic terms.

3.2. Dissidents, the Fifth Brigade and civilians

In 1980, the newly elected Zanu-PF government faced daunting challenges in reconstruction, army integration, establishing law and order, and overcoming the legacies of distrust between the three armed groups—Zipra, Zanla (the Zimbabwe African National Liberation Army, Zanu-PF's armed wing) and the Rhodesian forces. This latter was to prove the undoing of Zimbabwe's new peace.[10] There was no predictable working out of ancient ethnic tensions in the growing instability. Rather, the conflict can be understood as the product of a series of contingent events (particularly in the process of army integration), which drew on the reworked memories of antagonism between the two nationalist movements and their guerrilla forces.

There were minor conflicts between guerrillas from the two liberation armies as they gathered in assembly points (APs) after the cease-fire of December 1979, and guerrillas of both armies who left APs, or who refused to come in to them, presented a law and order problem through-

---

[9] Despite the ethnic differences produced by the armies' regional recruitment, there were people of all ethnicities within both parties and armies; both armies operated in Shona-speaking as well as Ndebele-speaking areas.

[10] For a fuller discussion of the events leading to conflict see Alexander (1998).

out the country. But the first serious upsurge of conflict stemmed from the decision to move thousands of guerrillas from rural APs to city suburbs—Chitungwiza in Harare and Entumbane in Bulawayo—in an effort to stop rural banditry and provide guerrillas with better accommodation.[11] Fatefully, the movement brought large numbers of Zipra and Zanla guerrillas into close proximity not only with each other but with their civilian supporters, providing an ideal situation for the exacerbation of the existing distrust between them.

Following sporadic gun battles and other incidents between Zipra and Zanla guerrillas at Chitungwiza in mid-October 1980,[12] conflict exploded at the Entumbane camps. Zipra accounts of this conflict stressed the tensions created by a rally at which Zanu-PF Minister Enos Nkala told the assembled crowds that Zapu had 'declared itself the enemy of ZANU (PF)'; that the time had come to 'form vigilante committees' to 'challenge [Zapu] on its home ground. If it means a few blows we shall deliver them.'[13] Following the rally, party supporters clashed in the streets and guerrillas were drawn into the fray. A two-day battle ensued which was brought to a close through the intervention of senior Zipra and Zanla commanders. The incident convinced many guerrillas of the possibility of further conflict. Distrust and tension spread to other APs and newly integrated units of the ZNA as stories and rumours about what had happened at Entumbane circulated. Zipra guerrillas stressed the daily tensions over fears that food was being poisoned; over who held the keys to the armouries; over the justness of punishments; over the rumoured disappearances of guerrillas supposedly sent for training courses, and bias against Zipra promotions.

In February 1981, a much larger conflagration took place, spreading across the country from integrated ZNA units at Ntabazinduna, Connemara, and Glenville to Entumbane once again. Zipra accounts and press reports of testimonies made to the Dumbutshena Commission of Enquiry, which was established to look into the causes of conflict, indicated that fighting had often been set off by fairly minor incidents—an argument, a fist fight—but had then escalated rapidly, revealing a certain amount of preparedness on both sides, as well as the pervasiveness of fear and tension.[14] Again, fighting was only brought to an end through the concerted efforts of senior military figures of both sides. Some guerrillas

[11] See Zanu-PF Minister Eddison Zvobgo's comments on the move in *The Chronicle*, 11 September 1980.

[12] See *The Chronicle*, 17 October 1980; 3 November 1980.

[13] Reported in *The Chronicle*, 10 November 1980.

[14] In these clashes, the upper hand went to those who managed to gain control of the armouries, or of heavy weapons as in Entumbane. At Ntabazinduna, it was Zanla members of 1:2 Battalion who gained control of the armoury; but in one of the worst clashes, Zipra members of 4:1 Battalion at Connemara got there first and 'hunted down' and killed their Zanla comrades.

fled and did not return to their units and arms were certainly cached by both sides in the aftermath of conflict, adding to previous caches made during the war, the repatriation process, and in the tense months waiting in APs.

After this second period of fighting, political relations between Zanu-PF and Zapu deteriorated as armed violence in Matabeleland grew. The Zanu-PF government announced the discovery of large caches of weapons on Zapu owned properties and near APs in February 1982, and accusations of a plot to overthrow the government culminated in the expulsion of Zapu ministers from office and the arrest of senior Zipra leaders on charges of treason. Zanu-PF now explicitly stated that it could no longer tolerate Zapu as an opposition: the solution from Zanu-PF's point of view was the conversion of Matabeleland to Zanu-PF, a solution which was not justified in ethnic terms, but rather as the expression of the voting majority's view. As Zanu-PF Minister Eddison Zvobgo proclaimed, 'We worship the majority as much as churches worship God'.[15]

The political repercussions of the arms caches incident were certainly important, but the critical factor in creating an armed insurgency lay in the consequences for Zipra guerrillas inside and outside the ZNA. Little attention has been paid to this aspect of the burgeoning conflict, but interviews with Zipra guerrillas consistently indicated that their persecution at this time was key in causing mass desertions. Within the army, 'dissident sympathizers' and 'disloyal elements'—that is, Zipra guerrillas—were purged, arrested or worse with such ferocity in 1982 that senior army officers had to make a tour of ZNA units to assure soldiers that 'they wouldn't be victimized for past affiliations'.[16] Many Zipra guerrillas alleged that Zipras were killed, beaten or otherwise victimized. They stressed their persecution for being Zipra, and for their allegiance to Zapu leader Joshua Nkomo, but language and ethnicity were also issues between the two armies. These conditions forced many Zipra guerrillas to flee or demobilize from the ZNA. The desertion in 1982 of thousands of armed former Zipras and their subsequent persecution at home led to a vast increase in 'dissidentry' in Matabeleland, and concentrated violence in this region for the first time.[17]

But ethnicity was, at this time, still not a central aspect of the conflict. Though there were problems within the ZNA due to language and ethnic divisions, there were many ZNA units which managed integration without incident. The first ZNA units sent to Matabeleland in 1981 to confront

---

[15] *The Chronicle*, 12 September 1983.

[16] See reports in *The Chronicle*, 4, 29 October 1982.

[17] The numbers of deserters is a matter of speculation. Drawing on the *Africa Contemporary Record*, Seegers (1986: 153, fn 75) puts the number at 1,800; Hodder-Williams (1983: 15), estimates 4,000 deserted; the Lawyers' Committee for Human Rights, (1986: 32), put the number at 1,000. For further information on the problems of army integration and Zipra desertions, see Alexander (1998).

the dissident problem were not perceived by civilians to be tribalist, and nor did they primarily target civilians in their operations: they were concerned with tracking down armed dissidents. The introduction of ethnicity to the conflict was most centrally the work of one military unit: the Fifth Brigade.

The motivations behind the Fifth Brigade's formation remain unclear. The decision to form the unit was taken early on, in October 1980, when Prime Minister Mugabe certainly nursed grave doubts about the loyalty of Zipra guerrillas, and hence perhaps also of the then nascent integrated ZNA units. He may have worried that Zipra had held back some of its best forces for an eleventh hour bid for supremacy, or that the Rhodesians or South Africa constituted an ongoing threat. The way in which the Brigade was constituted, trained and commanded certainly marked it out as intended to be supremely loyal and efficient: the Fifth Brigade was unlike any other ZNA unit. The Fifth Brigade answered directly to the Prime Minister, and not to the normal military chain of command. Its soldiers were trained by the North Koreans, not the British; it was issued with different equipment and used a different radio communication system from the rest of the ZNA, and it was described as intended for what were termed 'internal defence purposes'. The Brigade's recruits were dominated by Zanla guerrillas. The few Zipra guerrillas in the Brigade were attacked, demoted and posted to other battalions.[18] Those who remained in the brigade seemed to have been kept on solely for the instrumental purposes of including soldiers familiar with the Matabeleland terrain and who could speak Ndebele. That notwithstanding, certain units had not a single Ndebele speaker among them, and relied on interpreters in the field.

But if the Fifth Brigade had merely been an extremely efficient military unit whose purpose was to track down armed insurgents and guard against South African destabilization, it would not have had anything like the impact which it was to make. In fact, the Brigade was a notoriously poor fighting force—most of the successes against armed dissidents were won by other units, particularly the police Support Unit and the élite paratroopers. The Fifth Brigade's targets lay elsewhere: from its deployment in Matabeleland North in January 1983 until its withdrawal from Matabeleland South in late 1984, the Brigade carried out a grotesquely violent campaign against civilians in general and Zapu chairmen in

---

[18] See ' "Gukurahundi"—Ten Years Later', *Zimbabwe Defense Forces Magazine*, 7 (1): 33–4. The only battalion commander in the Fifth Brigade who was not a former Zanla commander was Eddie Sigoge but his career, like that of other former Zipra officers, was brought to a premature end: he was detained at Chikurubi Prison, and subsequently forced into early retirement. Another former Zipra in the Fifth Brigade was demoted and posted to 4:8 Battalion from which he demobilized in November 1982. He was arrested in Bulawayo in June 1983, and interrogated and tortured on suspicion of being a dissident. Interview, G. N., 1995.

particular; it also attacked civil servants, and even police and other ZNA units on occasion.

Crucially, the Fifth Brigade distinguished itself from all other military forces by its soldiers' and commanders' explicit justification of their repression in tribal and political terms. This discourse was consistent, and seems to have been official policy. Civilian testimonies in Matabeleland detail many instances in which Fifth Brigade commanders and soldiers explained their orders. They told people that they had been ordered to 'wipe out the people in the area', to 'kill anything that was human'.[19] They said they had been told that all Ndebeles were dissidents, making women and children as well as men targets. Many recounted how Fifth Brigade soldiers told them that they had come to take revenge for nineteenth century Ndebele violence against their Shona ancestors: a Zapu district chairman recalled 'they didn't hide their real motive, "You have been killing our forefathers, you Mandebele"'.[20] History was thus invoked and reinterpreted.

The Fifth Brigade's arrival in any area was usually characterized by killings (sometimes on a large scale) in the first few days. Those killed were, at times, Zapu leaders identified at meetings, through interrogations or from lists which the Fifth Brigade carried with it. Other groups such as former guerrillas, former Rhodesian soldiers, migrant labourers, and refugees were also extremely vulnerable to summary execution or 'disappearance' throughout the Fifth Brigade's tenure. But killings were often indiscriminate—victims included people met on patrol who could not speak Shona, mothers who could not account for the whereabouts of a son, individuals who did not answer questions quickly enough.

The pattern of violence was notable not only for its scale but also for its humiliating and dehumanizing nature. Subsequent to initial spates of killing, the Fifth Brigade units tended to turn their energies toward beatings and political 'mobilization'. Though the death toll was highest in the early period of the Brigade's deployment, killings and violence also accompanied these activities. People were beaten with logs, forced to fight each other, to climb trees and jump from them, to dig what they were told would be their own graves. Women were raped. The Fifth Brigade forced attendance at meetings during which people were made to sing Zanu-PF songs and chant Zanu-PF slogans in Shona, to denounce Zapu, and to engage in a kind of forced revelry of dance and music.

Civilians in Matabeleland came to believe that the Fifth Brigade's particular brand of violence was not an aberration but part of a plan orchestrated by Zanu-PF's leaders: this belief changed people's perceptions of

---

[19] Interviews, former Zapu Provincial committee member, St. Paul's, 12 September 1995; Councillor, Lupaka, 8 February 1996.

[20] Interview, Lupanda, 22 December 1994. For a full discussion of civilian perspectives, see Alexander and McGregor (forthcoming).

the goals of the 1980s war. They came to see the conflict not as a war fought against the dissidents but against the Ndebele and Zapu. In local accounts, there is a constant slippage between an emphasis on tribalism and on political repression as the motive force behind the Fifth Brigade's violence.

The ethnic interpretation draws heavily on the indiscriminate nature of Fifth Brigade violence, the Brigade's use of Shona, and its frequent recourse to tribalist justifications. Acts of violence perpetrated by the Fifth Brigade were given specific meanings as a result. For example, while rapes committed by dissidents or ZNA soldiers might be described simply as an abuse of power, rapes committed by the Fifth Brigade were perceived as a systematic attempt to create a generation of Shona babies. Such interpretations extended to the Fifth Brigade's bizarre involvement in building schools: these initiatives were not seen as developmental in intent but as heralding the introduction of Shona students to Matabeleland. Tribalist interpretations were also used to explain the pattern of violence in areas which bordered on Shona speaking regions, or where some people were themselves able to speak Shona. In such areas people claimed that the Fifth Brigade did not attack their cross-border neighbours, despite dissidents operating in those areas, or that they were themselves spared attack because they could speak Shona. Fifth Brigade soldiers, as well as Zanu-PF politicians, sought to enhance and exploit ethnic divisions: they tried to convince 'Kalangas' that they were in fact 'Shona'; they tried to convince 'Tonga' that they should distance themselves from the trouble-making 'Ndebele'.

Rural Zapu leaders stressed most strongly the Fifth Brigade's role in destroying Zapu. They noted that, while the Brigade's violence was at times indiscriminate, many of its actions, as well as those of the Central Intelligence Organization, were directed specifically against Zapu structures. They saw the war as a whole as orchestrated to this end. Most commonly, however, people elided the categories of Ndebele and Zapu—an attack on the Ndebele was an attack on Zapu, an attack on Zapu was an attack on the Ndebele. Such attacks struck at the root of people's most cherished political identity, and transformed ethnic identities: the attack on Zapu members *as* Ndebele created a powerful link between political affiliation and ethnic identity. A Zapu veteran aptly summed up such perceptions when he described the Fifth Brigade songs in which he was forced to denounce Zapu in the alien language of Shona as 'songs of self denial'.

4. Conclusion

Understanding the role of ethnicity in conflict requires a careful assessment of history and politics: ethnic antagonism cannot simply be cast as the product of state decay, or as an inevitable, natural cause of conflict. Rather, the means by which historical memories are manipulated in particular political contexts needs detailed consideration. Zimbabwe clearly illustrates the pitfalls of jumping to too simple an analysis.

Ethnicity did not cause Zimbabwe's post-independence war. But if the conflict did not have an ethnic dimension at its outset, it certainly came to have profound implications for ethnicity, reinforcing the idea of an ancient opposition between the two 'supertribes' of the Ndebele and the Shona (Werbner 1991). This was overwhelmingly due to the deployment of one army brigade. The Fifth Brigade's greatest 'success' was in giving an ethnic content to a political identity. Zapu had been a genuinely nationalist party. It had not limited itself to 'the Ndebele', and nor was there any very clear Ndebele identity which it could have mobilized even if it had sought to. But by the end of the 1980s, the people of Matabeleland believed themselves to be discriminated against on the basis of tribe. They nursed terrible wounds and retained a great fearfulness and suspicion long after the re-establishment of peace.

Nor can the Fifth Brigade's use in Matabeleland be cast as a case of an upsurge in defensive ethnicity in response to 'dissident' violence, or the context of a weak or collapsing state. The Zimbabwean state was powerful and ambitious; the ethnic attacks in Matabeleland were not a popular expression of fears and hatreds outside the region: 'the Shona' were not mobilized against 'the Ndebele'. Rather, the state's military might was used against the geographical base of political opposition—ethnicity was introduced as a justification for repression, and used as a means of limiting, delegitimizing and dividing Zapu's sources of support.

In the ten years since the end of violence in Matabeleland, Zimbabwean society has not remained silent about the legacy of the 1980s. Local human rights organizations are calling for government to accept its responsibility for the state violence of the 1980s, and to make reparation. This demand is made not in the name of 'the Ndebele' but of justice for *citizens*. Within the affected areas of Matabeleland a similar distinction is maintained. Local understandings of the sources and agents of violence are based on a subtly differentiated notion of the state itself, and a clear distinction between party and state. Matabeleland's long political tradition has made sophisticated understandings of the recent conflict possible. The state as a whole, and particularly its local manifestations, are not tarred with one brush: people continue to believe state structures should be accountable to them. Such normative beliefs provide a foundation on which legitimacy and democracy could be rebuilt.

It was to this sort of debate and this sort of atmosphere that a remarkable Matabeleland intellectual looked forward in the last months of the conflict. Edwin Mkwananzi deplored the way in which the violence had promoted ethnic division:

The security situation in Matabeleland is particularly bad for the false impression it gives. Thus to many people outside Matabeleland the situation is seen as a Ndebele bid to power while the people of Matabeleland harbour suspicions that the situation is an undeclared war upon them.

But the so-called tribal problem 'is both our making and unmaking'.[21] Mkwananzi called for a proper understanding of the war as a crisis both of the state and civil society:

Is there no end to this cycle of violence? Killing has become a political language. The people of Matabeleland in particular have lost that sense of human touch, having grown to distrust anyone who happens to be a stranger . . . They no longer know that a stranger can be helped with a glass of water when thirsty . . . Children no longer play in the moonlight. The semi-war situation has carved the rural population into insensitive people.

It was time 'the individual' was no longer 'seen only as a political instrument but should be elevated to full status as a human being'.[22] Such voices offer hope, and also stand as evidence of the complexity of conflict.

Zimbabwe is far from the only case in which the complex causes of conflict have been reduced to simple ethnic antagonism. To return to the general theme of this chapter, and the broader purpose of this volume in illuminating the origins of humanitarian emergencies, it is clear that ethnicity cannot be understood out of context or ahistorically, that it cannot be treated as distinct from conflicts over resources and political power. Our review of recent literature at the outset of this chapter has shown that ethnicity should not be viewed as a discrete 'causal factor' in the origin of conflicts. Ethnicity can mean very different things to different actors; its significance can vary from place to place and over time. Indeed ethnicity is such a vague, catch-all term that its analytical utility is questionable, particularly if the intent is to compare different cases, and to make broad generalizations. Where ethnicity is understood in exclusive and antagonistic terms, and where politicians mobilize along ethnic lines, this must itself be closely investigated.

The recent literature has offered explanations for the salience of ethnic antagonism in post-colonial Africa, and for the ways in which such understandings have reflected, produced or reproduced situations of violent conflict. Many authors have focused on the nature and workings of colonial power and its legacies, suggesting that the colonial era was a period in which an essentialized and antagonistic, bounded and exclusive understanding of ethnicity was popularized and became part of the institutions of the colonial state (Vail 1989). Essentialized understandings of ethnicity drew on pre-existing categories, but gave them new meanings. Pre-colonial tribal antagonisms were not 'frozen' in the colonial period.

---

[21] *The Sunday News*, 15 November 1987.   [22] *The Sunday News*, 26 July 1987.

Rather, this was an era in which ethnic relations and understandings were significantly reshaped. Ethnicity was imagined by colonial authorities and subjects alike; ethnicities took on a new dynamic and force as they were given newly exclusive meanings, new territorial definitions, new hierarchies and rules, and as they were transformed into competing interest groups. Comparable arguments to those about colonialism in Africa have been made about communism in the former Soviet Union and Tito's rule in the former Yugoslavia.

African nationalist mobilization took place in this colonial context, and under the rule of repressive states. Africa's nationalist movements were diverse, and if at times they represented an alliance of local 'ethnic revolts' shaped by the institutions of late colonial power (Mamdani 1996), they by no means always did. At other times, nationalist movements built a broad and unified constituency, explicitly condemning and dismissing colonial 'tribalism'. Of course, this did not mean that such movements were not authoritarian and intolerant at the same time. When nationalist movements assumed power at independence, the context in which they operated changed dramatically. They now had the power of the state at their disposal, and new economic interests were at stake. In independent Africa, élites often mobilized and used tribalist sentiment. Even then, however, élite political practice was not the only definer of ethnicity— there were also counter discourses of ethnicity which were moral and inclusive (Lonsdale 1992 and 1994).

Another influential strand in recent writing has located the roots of the violent post-colonial state not in colonialism, but further back, in the pre-colonial era. Writers in this mould have identified a 'retraditionalization' of political discourse, albeit a retraditionalization which has often been used to reproduce essentially colonial practices of authority (Chabal 1994; Bayart 1993; Grignon 1996).

While historical analyses are important, no study of conflict can ignore the immediate period prior to the descent into violence. How and why were extremists able to grasp political power? How were leaders able to mobilize ethnic sentiment? Why did they see it as necessary to do so? Why did moderate political forces, which sought to bridge ethnic divides or to downplay their salience, lose ground? It is all too apparent that the periods preceding some of the worst 'ethnic conflicts' were characterized by economic crisis and restructuring, by immense political insecurity, and by rapid social change. Fine-grained studies of immediate pre-conflict events demonstrate the contingency of the descent into conflict with an ethnic dimension.[23] They are revealing of the role not only of national political actors, but also of regional and international forces (Duffield 1995). International analysts who have portrayed African conflicts as inevitable,

---

[23] See cases explored in the first section of this chapter.

and inevitably ethnic, may have consciously or unconsciously exonerated their governments and international organizations from responsibility, and from any obligation to intervene in situations which are little understood, and deemed peripheral to economic and strategic interests.

Historical and political forces, as well as the immediate contingencies of conflicts are important, but they do not tell us why ethnicity—rather than some other appeal—has proved such a potent mobilizational tool. Here again, the academic literature has offered explanations: ethnicity is powerful precisely because it can come to be perceived and experienced as an ancient, unchanging, natural source of identification and difference (Turton 1997; Fardon 1996). History can be reimagined through this prism by historians, politicians, and peasant intellectuals; past events are given new meanings and significance as a result. A history of persecution and victimhood, if imagined in ethnic terms, can be particularly powerful in heightening a sense of collective insecurity and in creating the conditions for the use of violence. Here again, though, caution is due in making a specific case for 'ethnicity': the term is flexible enough to include conflicts in which ideas about race, nationality, religion or clan have become significant.

To identify ethnicity as a cause of humanitarian disasters begs far more questions than it answers. Ethnicity may come to be experienced as the cause of conflict by perpetrators and victims alike, and it may be blamed for conflict by commentators in the western media, but academics, journalists and those who intervene in such conflicts have a responsibility to explore the historical myths which have sustained violent conflicts, to look beyond simple and reductive explanations to the political and economic context in which understandings of ethnicity are produced.

References

Alexander, J. (1998). 'Dissident Perspectives on Zimbabwe's Post-Independence War', *Africa*, 68 (2).

Alexander, J., and J. McGregor (1997). 'Modernity and Ethnicity in a Frontier Society: Defining Difference in Northwestern Zimbabwe'. *Journal of Southern African Studies*, 23 (2).

Alexander, J., and J. McGregor (forthcoming). 'Democracy, Development and Political Conflict: Rural Institutions in Matabeleland North after Independence', in N. Bhebe and T. Ranger (eds.), *Historical Perspectives on Democracy and Human Rights*. Oxford: James Currey; Harare: University of Zimbabwe Press, Three Volumes.

Allen, T., K. Hudson, and J. Seaton (eds.) (1996). *War, Ethnicity and the Media*. London: South Bank University.

Bayart, J.-F. (1993). *The State in Africa: The Politics of the Belly*. London: Longman.

CCJP/LRF (Catholic Commission for Justice and Peace/Legal Resources Foundation) (1997). *Breaking the Silence, Building True Peace. A Report on the Disturbances in Matabeleland and the Midlands 1980–1988*. Harare: CCJP/LRF.

Chabal, P. (1994). *Power in Africa*. London: Macmillan.

Chanock, M. (1985). *Law, Custom and Social Order. The Colonial Experience in Malawi and Zambia*. Cambridge: Cambridge University Press.

Cliffe, L., J. Mpofu, and B. Munslow (1980). 'Nationalist Politics in Zimbabwe: The 1980 Elections and Beyond', *Review of African Political Economy*, 18.

Colson, E. (1970) 'The Assimilation of Aliens Among Zambian Tonga', in R. Cohen and J. Middleton (eds.), *From Tribe to Nation in Africa: Studies in Incorporation Processes*. Chandler.

Comaroff, J. (1997). 'Of Totemism and Ethnicity: Consciousness, Practice and the Signs of Inequality', in R. Grinker and C. Steiner (eds.) *Perspectives on Africa: A Reader in Culture, History and Representation*. Oxford: Blackwell, also in J. and J. Comaroff (eds.) (1992) *Ethnography and the Historical Imagination*. Boulder, San Francisco and Oxford.

Dresch, P. (1995). 'Race, Culture and—What? Pluralist Certainties in the United States', in W. James (ed.), *The Pursuit of Certainty. Religious and Cultural Formations*. London: Routledge.

Dubow, S. (1995). *Scientific Racism in Modern South Africa*. Cambridge: Cambridge University Press.

Duffield, M. (1995). 'The Symphony of the Damned: Racial Discourse, Complex Political Emergencies and Humanitarian Aid', manuscript cited in P. Richards (1996) *Fighting for the Rainforest. War, Youth and Resources in Sierra Leone*. London: James Currey.

Fardon, R. (1987). 'African Ethnogenesis: Limits to the Comparability of Ethnic Phenomena', in L. Holy (ed.), *Comparative Anthropology*. Oxford: Blackwell.

Fardon, R. (1996). 'Covering Ethnicity? Or Ethnicity as Coverage?', in T. Allen, K. Hudson and J. Seaton (eds.), *War, Ethnicity and the Media*. London: South Bank University.

Fukui, K. (1994). 'Conflict and Ethnic Interaction: The Mela and their Neighbours', in K. Fukui and J. Markakis (eds.), *Ethnicity and Conflict in the Horn of Africa*. London: James Currey.

Fukui, K., and J. Markakis (1994). 'Introduction', in K. Fukui and J. Markakis (eds.), *Ethnicity and Conflict in the Horn of Africa*. London: James Currey.

Gallagher, T. (1997). 'My Neighbour, My Enemy: The Manipulation of Ethnic Identity and the Origins and Conduct of War in Yugoslavia', in D. Turton (ed.), *War and Ethnicity: Global Connections and Local Violence*. New York: University of Rochester Press.

Gilroy, P. (1992). *There Ain't No Black in the Union Jack: The Cultural Politics of Race and Nation*. London: Routledge.

Gray, J. (1944) 'Medical Sociology and Sociological Medicine', in E. H. Cluver (ed.), *Public Health in South Africa*. Johannesburg.

Grignon, F. (1996). 'Understanding African States' Governmentalities: The Case of Kenya', paper presented at the Institute of Commonwealth Studies, London, December.

"Gukurahundi"—Ten Years Later', *Zimbabwe Defense Forces Magazine*, 7 (1).

Harries, P. (1989). 'Exclusion, Classification and Internal Colonialism: The

Emergence of Ethnicity Among the Tsonga-Speakers of South Africa', in L. Vail (ed.), *The Creation of Tribalism in Southern Africa*. London: James Currey.

Harries, P. (1994). *Work, Culture and Identity: Migrant Labourers in Mozambique and South Africa, c. 1860–1910*. London: James Currey.

Hodder-Williams, R. (1983). 'Conflict in Zimbabwe: The Matabeleland Problem', *Conflict Studies*, 151. London: Institute for the Study of Conflict.

Hroch, M. (1985). *The Social Preconditions of National Revival in Europe*, cited in S. Marks (1994) 'Black and White Nationalism in South Africa: A Comparative Perspective', in P. Kaarsholm and J. Hultin (eds.), *Inventions and Boundaries: Historical and Anthropological Approaches to the Study of Ethnicity and Nationalism*. Occasional Paper No. 11. Roskilde: Institute of Development Studies, University of Roskilde.

James, W. (1988). *The Listening Ebony: Moral Knowledge, Religion and Power among the Uduk of Sudan*. Oxford: Clarendon Press.

James, W. (1994). 'War and "Ethnic Visibility": The Uduk on the Sudan-Ethiopia Border', in K. Fukui and J. Markakis, *Conflict and Ethnicity in the Horn of Africa*. London: James Currey.

Johnson, D. (1989). 'The Structure of a Legacy: Military Slavery in North East Africa', *Ethnohistory*, 36 (1).

Kaplan, R (1993). *Balkan Ghosts: A Journey Through History*. London: Macmillan.

Kaplan, R. (1994). 'The Coming Anarchy: How Scarcity, Crime, Overpopulation, Tribalism and Disease are Rapidly Destroying the Social Fabric of our Planet'. *Atlantic Monthly*, February.

Kopytoff, I. (1989). *The African Frontier: The Reproduction of Traditional African Societies*. Bloomington: Indiana University Press.

Kuper, H. (1943). 'The Uniform of Colour in Swaziland'. *African Studies*, 2.

Lamphear, J. (1994). 'The Evolution of Aketer 'New Model' Armies: Jie and Turkana', in K. Fukui and J. Markakis (eds.), *Ethnicity and Conflict in the Horn of Africa*. London: James Currey.

Lawyers' Committee for Human Rights (1986). *Zimbabwe: Wages of War*. New York: LCHR.

Lemarchand, R. (1997). *Burundi. Ethnic Conflict and Genocide*, third ed. Cambridge: Woodrow Wilson Centre and Cambridge University Press.

Lonsdale, J. (1992). 'The Moral Economy of Mau Mau: Wealth, Poverty and Civic Virtue in Kikuyu Political Thought', in B. Berman and J. Lonsdale, *Unhappy Valley: Violence and Ethnicity*. London: James Currey.

Lonsdale, J. (1994). 'Moral Ethnicity and Political Tribalism', in P. Kaarsholm and J. Hultin (eds.), *Inventions and Boundaries: Historical and Anthropological Approaches to the Study of Ethnicity and Nationalism*. Occasional Paper No. 11. Roskilde: Institute of Development Studies, University of Roskilde.

Makambe, E. P. (1992). *Marginalising the Human Rights Campaign: The Dissident Factor and the Politics of Violence in Zimbabwe, 1980–1987*. Lesotho: ISAS.

Malkki, L. (1995). *Purity and Exile. Violence, Memory and National Cosmology among Hutu Refugees in Tanzania*. Chicago and London: University of Chicago Press.

Mamdani, M. (1996). *Citizen and Subject. Contemporary Africa and the Legacy of Late Colonialism*. London: James Currey.

Marks, S. (1994). 'Black and White Nationalism in South Africa: A Comparative Perspective', in P. Kaarsholm and J. Hultin (eds.), *Inventions and Boundaries:*

Historical and Anthropological Approaches to the Study of Ethnicity and Nationalism. Occasional Paper No. 11. Roskilde: Institute of Development Studies, University of Roskilde.

Martin, D. and P. Johnson (1986). 'Zimbabwe: Apartheid's Dilemma', in D. Martin and P. Johnson (eds.), *Destructive Engagement: Southern Africa at War.* Harare: Zimbabwe Publishing House.

McGregor, J. (1994). '"People Without Fathers". Mozambicans in Swaziland 1888–1993'. *Journal of Southern African Studies,* 20 (4).

Ministry of Information, Posts and Telecommunications (1984). *A Chronicle of Dissidency in Zimbabwe.* Harare: Government Printer.

Moodie, T. Dunbar with V. Ndatshe. (1994). *Going for Gold. Men, Mines and Migration.* Berkeley: University of California Press.

Nkomo, J. (1984). *The Story of My Life.* London: Methuen.

Ranger, T. (1985). *The Invention of Tribalism in Zimbabwe.* Gweru: Mambo Press.

Ranger, T. (1989). 'Missionaries, Migrants and the Manyika: The Invention of Ethnicity in Zimbabwe', in L. Vail (ed.), *The Creation of Tribalism in Southern Africa.* London: James Currey.

Ranger, T (1993). 'The Invention of Tradition Revisited', in T. Ranger and O. Vaughn (eds.), *Legitimacy and the State in Twentieth Century Africa.* Oxford: St. Antony's/Macmillan.

Ranger, T. (1994). 'African Identities: Ethnicity, Nationality and History. The Case of Matabeleland, 1893–1993', in J. Heidrich (ed.), *Changing Identities.* Berlin: Centre for Modern Oriental Studies.

Ranger, T. (1996). 'The Moral Economy of Identity in Northern Matabeleland', in L. de la Gorgeniere *et al.* (eds.), *Ethnicity in Africa.* Edinburgh: Centre of African Studies.

Richards, P. (1996). *Fighting for the Rainforest. War, Youth and Resources in Sierra Leone.* London: James Currey.

Seegers, A. 1986. 'Revolutionary Armies of Africa: Mozambique and Zimbabwe', in S. Baynham (ed.), *Military Power and Politics in Black Africa.* London and Sydney: Croom Helm.

Sofos, S. (1996). 'Nationalism, Mass Communications and Public Rituals in Former Yugoslavia', in T. Allen, K. Hudson and J. Seaton (eds.), *War, Ethnicity and the Media.* London: South Bank University.

Southall, A. (1970). 'The Illusion of Tribe', in P. Gutkind (ed.), *The Passing of Tribal Man.* Leiden and New York: E. J. Brill.

Spring, W. (1986). *The Long Fields: Zimbabwe since Independence.* Basingstoke: Pickering and Inglis.

Turton, D. (1994). 'Mursi Political Identity and Warfare: The Survival of an Idea', in K. Fukui and J. Markakis (eds.), *Ethnicity and Conflict in the Horn of Africa.* London: James Currey.

Turton, D. (1997). 'Introduction: War and Ethnicity', in D. Turton (ed.), *War and Ethnicity. Global Connections and Local Violence.* New York: University of Rochester Press.

Vail, L. (1989). 'Introduction: Ethnicity in Southern African History', in L. Vail (ed.) (1989). *The Creation of Tribalism in Southern Africa.* London: James Currey.

de Waal, A. (1994). 'The Genocidal State: Hutu Extremism and the Origins of the "Final Solution" in Rwanda'. *Times Literary Supplement,* 1 July.

Werbner, R. (1991). *Tears of the Dead: The Social Biography of an African Family.* Edinburgh: Edinburgh University Press.

Werbner, R. (1996). 'Introduction', in R. Werbner and T. Ranger (eds.), *Postcolonial Identities in Africa.* London: Zed Books.

Worby, E. (1994). 'Maps, Names and Ethnic Games: The Epistomology and Iconography of Colonial Power in North-western Zimbabwe'. *Journal of Southern African Studies,* 20 (3).

APPENDIX: LIST OF CONFERENCE PARTICIPANTS

Gamini Abeysekera, UNICEF, Jerusalem

Tony Addison, University of Warwick and UNU/WIDER

Adebayo Adedeji, African Centre for Development and Strategic Studies (ACDESS), Ijebu-Ode, Nigeria

Claude Ake, Yale University, and University of Port Harcourt, Nigeria

Jocelyn Alexander, St. Antony's College, University of Oxford, and University of Bristol, UK

Leila Alieva, Center for Strategic and International Studies, Baku, Azerbaijan Republic

Abbas Alnasrawi, University of Vermont, USA

Juha Auvinen, University of Helsinki (Finland) and The European Commission

Karen Bakker, University of Oxford, UK

Albert Berry, University of Toronto, Canada

James Boyce, University of Massachusetts, USA

Andrew Clapham, Graduate Institute of International Studies, University of Geneva, Switzerland

Nat J. Colletta, World Bank, Washington, DC, USA

Giovanni Andrea Cornia, UNU/WIDER, Helsinki, Finland

Christopher Cramer, School of Oriental and African Studies, University of London, UK

Terry Crawford-Browne, Economists Allied for Arms Reduction, Cape Town, South Africa

Jerry delli Priscolli, Institute for Water Resources, US Corps of Engineers, Ft. Collins, Colorado, USA

William DeMars, American University of Cairo, Egypt

Antonio Donini, Lessons Learned Unit, UN Department of Humanitarian Affairs, New York, USA

Dag Ehrenpreis, Sida, Stockholm, Sweden

Kisangani Emizet, Kansas State University, USA

James Fairhead, Queen Elizabeth House, University of Oxford, and University of Sussex, UK

Valpy FitzGerald, Finance and Trade Policy Research Centre, University of Oxford, UK

Sakiko Fukuda-Parr, Human Development Report Office, UN Development Programme, New York, USA

Patrick D. Gaffney, University of Notre Dame, Indiana, USA

Bo Göransson, Sida, Stockholm, Sweden

Alejandro Grinspun, UN Development Programme, New York, USA

Ted Robert Gurr, University of Maryland, USA

Peter Hansen, UN Relief and Works Agency, Gaza, Palestine

Barbara Harff, US Naval Department, USA

Barbara Harrell-Bond, Refugee Studies Programme, Queen Elizabeth House, University of Oxford, UK

Kalevi J. Holsti, University of British Columbia, Canada

Anders Hjort af Ornäs, Linköping University, Sweden

Helge Hveem, University of Oslo, Norway

Mats Karlsson, State Secretary for International Development Cooperation, Sweden

David Keen, London School of Economics, and International Institute of Strategic Studies, London, UK

Gaim Kibreab, Uppsala University, Sweden

Timo Kivimäki, University of Helsinki, Finland

Axel Klein, Institute for African Alternatives, London, UK

Jeni Klugman, World Bank (Washington, DC) and Australian National University, Australia

Philippe Le Billon, Green College, University of Oxford, UK

Thomas J. Leney, Carnegie Commission on Preventing Deadly Conflict, Washington, DC, USA

Roberto L. Lenton, Sustainable Energy and Environment Division, UN Development Programme, USA

Nguyuru Lipumba, UNU/WIDER, Helsinki, Finland

Mats Lundahl, International Economics and Geography, School of Economics, Stockholm, Sweden

Neil MacFarlane, St. Anne's College, University of Oxford, UK

Jo Ann McGregor, Queen Elizabeth House, University of Oxford, UK

Joanna Macrae, Overseas Development Institute, London, UK

Ajeet N. Mathur, University of Tampere, Finland

Helinä Melkas, UNU/WIDER, Helsinki, Finland

Thandika Mkandawire, UN Research Institute for Social Development, Geneva, Switzerland

Christian Morrisson, University of Paris, Panthéon-Sorbonne, France

E. Wayne Nafziger, UNU/WIDER (Helsinki, Finland) and Kansas State University, USA

Leonce Ndikumana, University of Massachusetts, USA

Joyce Neu, Carter Center, Atlanta, USA

Carin Norberg, Sida, Stockholm, Sweden

David Norman, Kansas State University, USA

Jan Öberg, Transnational Foundation for Peace and Future Studies, Lund, Sweden

Magnus Öberg, Department of Peace and Conflict Research, Uppsala University, Sweden

Meghan O'Sullivan, Queen Elizabeth House, University of Oxford, UK

Manuel Pastor, Latin American and Latino Studies, University of California, Santa Cruz, USA

Ralph Premdas, University of the West Indies, St. Augustine Campus, Trinidad

Terence Ranger, St Antony's College, University of Oxford, UK

William Reno, Northwestern University, Evanston, Illinois, USA

Barnett Rubin, Council on Foreign Relations, New York, USA

Kumar Rupesinghe, International Alert, London, UK

Richard Sandbrook, University of Toronto, Canada

Bengt Säve-Söderbergh, Institute for Democracy and Electoral Assistance, Stockholm, Sweden

Ellen Johnson Sirleaf, UNDP Regional Bureau for Africa

Frances Stewart, Queen Elizabeth House, University of Oxford, UK

Ashok Swain, Department of Peace and Conflict Research, Uppsala University, Sweden

Ramesh Thakur, UNU, Tokyo, Japan

John Toye, Institute of Development Studies, University of Sussex, UK

David Turton, Refugee Studies Programme, Queen Elizabeth House, University of Oxford, UK

Peter Uvin, Thomas J. Watson Jr. Institute for International Studies, Brown University, Providence, Rhode Island, USA

Hans J. A. van Ginkel, UNU, Tokyo, Japan

Raimo Väyrynen, Joan B. Kroc Institute for International Peace Studies, University of Notre Dame (Indiana) and UNU/WIDER, Helsinki, Finland

Effie Voutira, Refugee Studies Programme, Queen Elizabeth House, University of Oxford, UK

Peter Wallensteen, Department of Peace and Conflict Research, Uppsala University, Sweden

John Weeks, School of Oriental and African Studies, University of London, UK

Thomas G. Weiss, Thomas J. Watson Jr. Institute for International Studies, Brown University, Providence, Rhode Island, USA

Susan Woodward, Foreign Policy Studies Program, Brookings Institution, Washington, DC, USA

INDEX